FREDERICK D
The Metropolitan S

Philosophy

Confronting the Unavoidable

THOMSON
WADSWORTH

Australia • Canada • Mexico • Singapore • Spain
United Kingdom • United States

Publisher: Holly J. Allen
Philosophy Editor: Steve Wainwright
Assistant Editor: Lee McCracken
Technology Project Manager: Susan DeVanna
Editorial Assistant: Anna Lustig
Marketing Manager: Worth Hawes
Advertising Project Manager: Bryan Vann
Print/Media Buyer: Doreen Suruki
Composition Buyer: Ben Schroeter

Permissions Editor: Robert Kauser
Production Service: Penmarin Books
Text Designer: Andrew Ogus
Copy Editor: Laura Larson
Cover Designer: Yvo Riezebos
Cover Image: Mary Atchison
Compositor: G & S Typesetters, Inc.
Cover and Text Printer: Transcontinental Printing, Louiseville

COPYRIGHT © 2003 Wadsworth, a division of Thomson Learning, Inc. Thomson Learning™ is a trademark used herein under license.

ALL RIGHTS RESERVED. No part of this work covered by the copyright hereon may be reproduced or used in any form or by any means—graphic, electronic, or mechanical, including but not limited to photocopying, recording, taping, Web distribution, information networks, or information storage and retrieval systems—without the written permission of the publisher.

Printed in Canada
1 2 3 4 5 6 7   07 06 05 04 03

For more information about our products, contact us at:
Thomson Learning Academic Resource Center
1-800-423-0563

For permission to use material from this text, contact us by: **Phone:** 1-800-730-2214
Fax: 1-800-730-2215
Web: http://www.thomsonrights.com

Library of Congress Control Number: 2002112744

ISBN 0-534-53476-7

Wadsworth/Thomson Learning
10 Davis Drive
Belmont, CA 94002-3098
USA

Asia
Thomson Learning
5 Shenton Way #01-01
UIC Building
Singapore 068808

Australia/New Zealand
Nelson Thomson Learning
102 Dodds Street
Southbank, Victoria 3006
Australia

Canada
Nelson Thomson Learning
1120 Birchmount Road
Toronto, Ontario M1K 5G4
Canada

Europe/Middle East/Africa
Thomson Learning
High Holborn House
50/51 Bedford Row
London WC1R 4LR
United Kingdom

Latin America
Thomson Learning
Seneca, 53
Colonia Polanco
11560 Mexico D.F.
Mexico

Spain/Portugal
Paraninfo Thomson Learning
Calle/Magallanes, 25
28015 Madrid, Spain

To my sons, Eric and Drake

CONTENTS

Analytical Contents   xiv
Instructor's Preface   xviii

INTRODUCTION
Philosophy and the Forms of Value   1

An Intellectual Discipline   1
Philosophy and Religion   2
The Quest for Comprehension   3
The Shift to Thought   3
The Personal Nature of Philosophy   4
The Role of Imagination   6
No Necessary Method   6
The Main Areas of Philosophy   7
How Philosophy Is Unavoidable   7
The Concern with Ideals   8
The Allegory of the Cave   9
Conclusion   13
Study Questions   13

PART ONE
LOGIC   14

CHAPTER ONE
Knowledge and Understanding 16

Thoughts 16
The Objectivity of Truth 17
Logical Relations 18
Understanding 19
Thinking 20
Judgment 21
Justification and Explanation 22
Rationality 22
Basic Kinds of Knowledge 22
Knowledge and Belief 23
Justified True Belief 23
Being Justified 25
Judgments, Knowledge, and Belief 25
Fallible Justification 26
The Harm of Certainty 27
The Importance of Justification 27
The Importance of Truth 28
Credulity 28
Avoiding Credulity 30
The Credulous Character 31
The Innocence of Belief 32
Truth for Truth's Sake 33
Conclusion 34
Study Questions 34

CHAPTER TWO
Direct Knowledge 36

Sensation and Introspection 36
Objects of Experience 38
The Extent of Introspection 39
Sensation without Introspection 42
Introspection and Self-Control 42
Introspection and Thinking 43
Introspection and Speech 44
Direct Knowledge 44
The Subjectivity of Experience 46

v

The Intellect 47
Memory 48
Ethical Intuition 49
Religious Experience 49
Conclusion 50
Study Questions 50

CHAPTER THREE
Empirical Knowledge 52

Hume's Account 53
The Causal Principle 54
Knowledge of Causality 55
Typical Causes and Effects 56
Competing Hypotheses 56
Scientific Hypotheses 57
Testing 58
Fallible Inference 58
Greater Comprehension 59
The Inconclusiveness of Testing 59
Pseudohypotheses 60
Empirical Knowledge 60
The Example of Darwin's Theory 61
Theoretical Descriptions 63
Explanations of Explanations 64
Three Examples from Science 64
Conclusion 66
Study Questions 66

Glossary for Part One 68

PART TWO
METAPHYSICS 70

CHAPTER FOUR
Nature and the Transcendent 72

Sensible Reality 72
Introspectible Reality 74

Intelligible Reality 75
The Empirical World 75
Religion and the Supernatural 76
Disappointments with Nature 78
God Is Supernatural 78
The Nature of God 80
Empirical Arguments for God 81
The Immortal Soul Is Supernatural 81
God and the Immortal Soul 82
Freedom May Be Supernatural 83
Values 85
Conclusion 86
Study Questions 86

CHAPTER FIVE
Mind and Matter 87

Immortality 87
The Problem of Personal Identity 88
Locke's Solution 89
The Problem of Possible Duplication 91
Dualism 91
Dualism and Duplication 92
The Problem of Interaction 93
Double Aspect 93
The Mind–Body Problem 95
Idealism 95
Strengths of Idealism 96
Idealism and Immortality 97
Objection to Idealism 97
Materialism 98
Aristotle's Version 99
Strengths of Materialism 99
The Task for Materialism 100
Materialism and Idealism 100
The Problem of Free Will and Determinism 101
Hard Determinism 102
Libertarianism 102
Compatibilism 104

Conclusion   106
Study Questions   107

CHAPTER SIX
Basic Reality   109

The First Cause Argument   109
Theism   111
Male or Female?   111
God and the Creation   112
Pantheism   113
Pantheism's Monism   113
The "Mind of God"   114
Plato's Forms   115
Forms as Basic   116
Idealism   116
Hinduism   117
The Mystical Experience   118
Shankara on Immortality   118
Hegel's Absolute Idealism   119
Atomistic Materialism   119
Taoism   121
Conceptions of the First Cause   122
The Teleological Argument   123
The Ontological Argument   124
The Problem of Evil   126
The Free Will Defense   126
The Greater Goods Defense   128
God as Ideal   129
Metaphorical Theology   130
Conclusion   131
Study Questions   132

Glossary for Part Two   134

PART THREE
ETHICS   136

CHAPTER SEVEN
Happiness 139

The Nature of Happiness 139
Crude Materialsm 141
Objection to Crude Materialism 142
Augustine's Dualism 142
Stoicism 144
Plato on Understanding 146
Hinduism on Detachment 147
Buddhism 148
Taoism 150
Epicurus's Hedonism 151
Naturalized Christianity 154
Conclusion 155
Study Questions 156

CHAPTER EIGHT
Morality 157

The Nature of Morality 158
The Problem of Moral Motivation 158
Psychological Hedonism 159
Human Selfishness 160
Ethical Hedonism 162
Prudence 162
An Argument for Psychological Hedonism 164
Disproving Psychological Hedonism 165
Selfishness Is Self-Defeating 165
The Divine Command Theory 167
Plato's Objection 168
Consequences of Plato's Objection 170
Recognizing God's Word 170
Social Relativism 171
Moral Relativism 172
Morality and the Empirical 173
Objection to Social Relativism 174
External Commands 174
Conclusion 175
Study Questions 176

CHAPTER NINE
Benevolence and Justice 177

Altruism 178
Justice 178
Social Virtues 179
Reason or Sentiment? 179
Morality and Practice 181
Practice and Sentiment 181
Practical Reason 182
Discovering What Is Right 183
Moral Agreement 183
Moral Disagreement 184
Hume on Moral Motivation 184
Hume's Moral Theory 185
Benevolence as Fundamental 185
Explaining Justice 186
Superstition and Misery 186
Utilitarianism 189
Objections to Utilitarianism 190
The Pattern in the Objections 191
Deontology 192
Duties to Oneself 192
The Nature of Freedom 193
The Value of Freedom 194
Kant on Moral Motivation 195
Your Own Right to Freedom 196
Others' Right to Freedom 196
The Formula of Humanity 197
Justice 198
Justified Force 198
Freedom as Fundamental 200
The Priority of Justice 200
The Duty of Self-Development 201
The Duty to Help Others 202
Responsibility 202
Kant and the Stoics 203
Hume's Idealism 204
Conclusion 204
Study Questions 205

Glossary for Part Three 207

CONTENTS xi

PART FOUR
SOCIAL PHILOSOPHY 208

CHAPTER TEN
Good Society 210

The Nature of Society 210
Happiness in Society 211
Moral Behavior in Societies 212
Societies in the Best World 212
The Best World 212
The Danger of Society 214
The Need for Society 215
The Ethics of Confucius 216
Hegel on Society 217
Friendship 219
Aristotle on Friendship 219
Hume on Friendship 221
Kant on Friendship 222
Family 222
The Goal of Independence 223
Patriarchy 224
Schools, Churches, and the Media 226
School Education 227
Churches and Spiritual Education 228
The Media 230
Conclusion 232
Study Questions 232

CHAPTER ELEVEN
Economic Justice and Prosperity 233

The Nature of Economies 233
The Value of Economies 234
The Value of Economic Growth 236
Capitalism and Socialism 237
Distributive Justice 237

Deontological Capitalism   238
Locke's Theory of Property   239
A Deontological Defense of Locke's Theory   240
Locke's Proviso   241
Utilitarian Capitalism   243
Market Socialism   245
Good Markets   246
Corporations   248
Deontological Socialism   250
Utilitarian Socialism   251
Conclusion   253
Study Questions   254

CHAPTER TWELVE

Political Authority and Responsibility   255

The Nature of Polities   255
Political Authority and Responsibility   256
The Justification of Force   257
Visions of the Best Society   257
Theocratic Authority and Responsibility   257
Aristocratic Authority   259
Aristocratic Responsibility   260
Liberal Authority   261
Utilitarian Liberalism   262
The Slide to Tyranny   262
Political Competence and Liberal Education   263
Deontological Liberalism   263
Anarchism   264
Hobbes's Defense of the State   265
World Government   267
Liberal Responsibility   268
Libertarianism   268
Reform Liberalism   269
Economic Justice   270
Communitarianism   271
Conclusion   272
Study Questions   273

Glossary for Part Four   274

EPILOGUE

The Value of Philosophy 276

A Philosophy 279
An Overview 279
The Unity of Philosophy 281
The Good of Philosophy 282
Philosophical Knowledge 282
Philosophical Disagreement 283
The Practicality of Philosophy 284
Plato's Upward Path 285
The Allegory of the Cave 287
Plato on Philosophy 287
Philosophy and Happiness 288
Dignity 288
Philosophy and Dignity 289
Study Questions 289

Biographies 291

ANALYTICAL CONTENTS

INTRODUCTION

Philosophy and the Forms of Value 1

The fact that philosophy is an intellectual discipline corrects some mistaken impressions students get from the classroom experience. Philosophy differs from other disciplines in its concern with basic normative questions. This explains what truth there is in the mistaken impressions and how the basic questions are unavoidable for us all.

PART ONE

LOGIC 14

CHAPTER ONE

Knowledge and Understanding 16

Knowledge is justified true belief (by our sympathetic, reliabilist interpretation). Much of our justification is uncertain or ineffable. Ideally, our thoughts are consistent and coherent. Truth is a value for all of us.

CHAPTER TWO

Direct Knowledge 36

Some knowledge must be direct. Sources of direct knowledge presumably include sensation, introspection, and intellect. There may be others, important for religion or ethics.

CHAPTER THREE

Empirical Knowledge 52

Empirical knowledge includes the direct knowledge of sensation and introspection and what we know by inference from this. The causal principle is used in these inferences. Competing hypotheses are subjected to testing, which is necessary for one to be justified.

PART TWO

METAPHYSICS 70

CHAPTER FOUR

Nature and the Transcendent 72

Sources of knowledge correspond to categories of reality. Matter is sensed, mind is introspected, thoughts are connected by intellect. The major religions have suggested orientations to reality that transcend the empirical world. Our interests in God, freedom, and immortality lead us to the transcendent.

CHAPTER FIVE

Mind and Matter 87

Freedom and immortality seem to depend on how mind is related to matter. Basic theories of this relation include dualism, materialism, idealism, and double-aspect theory. The problems of free will and of personal identity are forms of the mind–body problem.

CHAPTER SIX

Basic Reality 109

The conception of God as creator is contrasted with a variety of other views of basic reality, some of which represent major religions, including ones from India and China. Theism seems supported by the world's order or undermined by the world's evil. Metaphorical interpretations of transcendent claims link metaphysics more closely with ethics.

PART THREE
ETHICS 136

CHAPTER SEVEN
Happiness 139

Happiness (as explained by Aristotle) requires the satisfaction of needs more than desires, which produces contentment with and enthusiasm for one's life. Many views of happiness are based on views of human nature that offer contrasting conceptions of what we need. These in turn correspond to positions about basic reality and the relation of mind and matter studied in Part Two.

CHAPTER EIGHT
Morality 157

Moral theories explain what makes one choice better than another, and what makes the better choice more appealing. Their explanations of moral motivation are based on views of human nature that also correspond to metaphysical positions studied in Part Two. Three moral theories are studied, all popular and influential, but discredited by philosophers today.

CHAPTER NINE
Benevolence and Justice 177

The moral theories of Hume and Kant are especially influential today. Hume's has led to utilitarianism by the conception of morality as benevolence through rationalized sympathy. For Kant, justice must be respected for happiness to be good, and morality is seen by reason alone.

PART FOUR
SOCIAL PHILOSOPHY 208

CHAPTER TEN

Good Society   210

Social organizations may be evaluated by the ethical theories of happiness and morality studied in Part Three. Utilitarianism and Kantian moral theory, although significantly different, agree in their humanism. Together they may be used to evaluate families, friendships, and schools, as well as the kinds of organizations studied in the next two chapters.

CHAPTER ELEVEN

Economic Justice and Prosperity   233

Utilitarian and deontological arguments are given for both capitalism and socialism. Capitalism has been proven to be highly productive. It is supported with Locke's theory of property, but this theory restricts the appropriation of limited natural resources. Smith's argument is for a market economy, not capitalism per se, since market socialism is possible. It is questionable whether continual economic growth is desirable. Socialism and capitalism differ in their conceptions of the best society and of human nature.

CHAPTER TWELVE

Political Authority and Responsibility   255

Theocrats, aristocrats, and liberals have different conceptions of the best society, which entail different views of the origin of political authority and the function of government. Liberalism encompasses anarchism, libertarianism, and reform liberalism. It is opposed to communitarianism, but most of all to fundamentalism and fascism.

EPILOGUE

The Value of Philosophy   276

Philosophy is practical for those who genuinely care about truth, goodness, justice, and the like. It is good for these people because it represents a natural development of liberation through reason.

INSTRUCTOR'S PREFACE

This text offers a coherent treatment of issues in a wide range of areas of philosophy. It begins with logic (in a broad, traditional sense that includes epistemology), since the concepts of this area illuminate metaphysics, covered next in the sequence. (Consider, for example, how material reality is what is known through sensation or how mind is what is known through introspection.) Ethics is covered next, because views on happiness and morality have been deepened by being couched in metaphysical views that yield conceptions of human nature. For similar reasons, the section on ethics comes before that on social philosophy. It is my firm belief that the greatest philosophers achieve the depth for which they are admired by constructing systems in which the various areas of philosophy are integrated. With this inspiration, I have put the discussions in a logical order, in which earlier ones anticipate and illuminate later ones. Something like a story is told.

This approach has certain merits. It creates a sense of excitement and respect for the material. Students share with the instructor a sense of direction, and they have a growing body of discussion that provides depth and clarification for the issues currently discussed. Positions in particular areas, such as ethics, appear less arbitrary and better motivated when a basis in another area, such as metaphysics, has been established. And it is simply much more enjoyable to teach the material when such connections can be gradually revealed throughout the course. Many texts offer a smorgasbord of discussions and readings, from which the instructor must somehow pull together a course. This text is written on the conviction that this "flexibility" is no more a virtue than it would be in a novel.

The text is also made coherent by adhering to a definite conception of philosophy, which derives directly from Kant (but which has roots in Plato, Aristotle, and the Stoics). In keeping with traditional understandings of philosophy, Kant explains philosophy in reference to fundamental normative questions, such as "What should I think is real?" "What should I do?" and "What should I care about?" I derive from this metaphilosophy the guiding theme of the book: that philosophy is mainly about questions that all of us face, even if we never think about them, since we commit ourselves to answers just by living a human life. These questions are thus "unavoidable," and we "confront the unavoidable" by raising to consciousness our own commitments and making them subjects of inquiry.

Giving the material this focus completely eliminates the unfortunate impression that there is "no right or wrong" in philosophy or that it is "not practical." It is explained from the start that philosophy has the peculiar character of dealing with questions on which we simply cannot avoid having opinions, which means that we cannot dismiss them as having "no right or wrong" answers. Our only choice on the basic questions is to leave our opinions unexamined, and so relatively confused and arbitrary, or to develop our understanding and justifications through philosophical reflection.

It then becomes easy to explain exactly how philosophy is "practical." It is useful *for* those who have taken up the challenge of examining their beliefs, actions, and goals, because they care about the quality of their mind and behavior. Logic, for example, offers much help for those who care whether their beliefs are true, as ethics offers guidance for those who want their actions to be right or their goals to be good.

The choice of topics is guided by this practical orientation. I pay only passing attention to skeptical dilemmas in epistemology, for example, because too much absorption in them contributes to the impression that philosophy is a silly subject, which deals only with amusing puzzles. Much more attention is paid to the uncertainty of most of our knowledge and to the prevalence of hypotheses and the importance of testing them, since students immediately recognize the practical value of these lessons. In discussing metaphysics, I give extensive treatment to various conceptions of fundamental reality, because this shows how philosophy contributes to understanding and assessing religions. A whole chapter is devoted to happiness, for the obvious interest that all of us have in this topic. In social philosophy, I cover not only economics and politics but also more personal matters such as family obligations and the value of friendship.

In my twenty years of teaching the introduction to philosophy, I have not only collected topics of obvious importance to students and woven them into a coherent discussion. I have also tested them to see how much discussion is needed to achieve a minimal understanding and which topics are better left for subsequent courses. Many texts endeavor to be so complete as to serve more as a reference book than as an introduction for a subject that requires independent thinking. The task I set myself was to cover a very wide range of topics, to give an accurate view of the whole field, while considering each with enough depth so that students could share the experience of genuine philosophical insight.

I have also been inspired by Bertrand Russell's thought that in the best education, knowledge is seen to be difficult but not impossible to obtain. As Russell explained, this view means steering between the two extremes of dogmatic certainty and skepticism. It is especially attractive in philosophy to play it safe, making sure to reveal all the disagreements ever registered on any issue. A good deal of this approach is necessary both for achieving honesty and for avoiding dogmatism. I believe that this is too often overdone, however, producing a sense of despair and fatigue. Because the difficulty of philosophical knowledge is obvious enough, what is especially challenging is to keep hope alive.

To this end, I pay special attention throughout the text to issues on which a great deal of agreement has been reached in philosophy. Consider, for example, the widespread acceptance today of naturalism and fallibilism, or the rejection of voluntarist ethics or moral relativism. Even if the tides change in future, it cannot be inferred that no progress will have been made. To see and feel the sense of achievement and progress, one must come to see the very real fact that a broad consensus in philosophy is sometimes achieved about important matters, and even when this puts philosophers at odds with most of the population at large.

The book is meant to be a comprehensive text for the introduction to philosophy. It is divided into fourteen chapters, suggesting one chapter per week with some slack for tests. My own experience is that the course must be brisk to complete all chapters, so that for a slower pace or for a quarter system, only the first three of four parts is recommended. The four parts are divided by subject matter. It is recommended (though not, of course, required) that a test be given for each part. Instructors are welcome to contact me through e-mail, especially for philosophical queries. An analytical table of contents is given for instructors, which more fully reveals the content and direction of the discussions.

I wish to acknowledge the help I received over many years in bringing this text to completion. Peter Adams of Wadsworth Publishing Company gave friendly encouragement that carried me through the earlier revisions. Steve Wainwright and Lee McCracken, also of Wadsworth, were congenial colleagues, always available during the final stages. During these many efforts, I received enormous philosophical and pedagogical advice from the following reviewers: John Bickle, East Carolina University; Michael Byron, Kent State University; Kenneth F. T. Cust, Central Missouri State University; Timothy Davis, Essex Community College; Roger P. Ebertz, University of Dubuque; Ronald Glass, University of Wisconsin–LaCrosse; Robert B. Mellert, Brookdale Community College; Lani Roberts, Oregon State University; Edgar A. Velez, Columbus State Community College; and Kerry Walters, Gettysburg College. Laura Larson not only served as an expert copy editor, but also helped me to think straight. Hal Lockwood of Penmarin Books held my hand in the final stages and taught me some English.

My colleagues, Tim Gould and David Sullivan, helped me to clarify the conception of philosophy on which the theme of the book is based. The administration of Metropolitan State College of Denver has been generous in supporting my writing, especially with a sabbatical in China and Nepal, where I was able to test the content of the text with students from very different cultures. I received by far the most help in shaping this content, however, from many students in Denver, over a period of two decades, who cared enough about education to engage passionately with philosophical ideas.

This work could only have been completed in the atmosphere of life and joy created by Bethany Doepke.

INTRODUCTION

Philosophy and the Forms of Value

STRANGE THINGS HAPPEN in the philosophy classroom. The material is sometimes not taught in a straightforward manner. The instructor often seems to bounce around, saying one thing and then denying it. Then students are asked *their* opinion, even though they have never studied the issue at all! To make matters worse, they are not shown the way these questions are supposed to be answered. Moreover, ancient texts are often read as if they had more to say than ones written over 2000 years later. And students hear only of the *opinions* of philosophers, never of any solid *discoveries*. This is no wonder, since philosophers seem no more interested in how the world *actually* is than how we might *imagine* it to be. It is true that genuinely interesting questions about life and the world are raised, but then instead of considering *these*, the discussion turns to how we *talk* about them.

What is going on? It sure looks like no one who studies philosophy knows what they are talking about. It seems to be all a matter of opinion, with no right or wrong. What, then, is the point?

AN INTELLECTUAL DISCIPLINE

These are understandable reactions to real observations of the classroom experience. But something is deeply wrong in them. And unless we correct them, we are likely to be misled about what is really going on and so to miss what good may come from studying philosophy. The first thing to realize about philosophy, then, is that it is an **intellectual discipline,** in the sense that, like physics, mathematics, or psychology (to name a few), philosophers are engaged in a kind of *inquiry*. Every intellectual discipline has unresolved issues, calling for a disciplined effort to find the truth. Once an opinion is called into doubt, the only way to resolve it is to find *reasons* for thinking one way or the other. Mathematicians give "proofs"; scientists cite "evidence" on behalf of their conclusions. In general, inquiries end when reasons are found that end the doubt and persuade the inquirers to believe a certain way.

Because philosophy is an intellectual discipline, philosophers *themselves* cannot say that philosophy is all a matter of opinion or that there is no right or wrong. To take a particularly sensitive example, one thing philosophers discuss is the existence of God. Philosophers want to know whether there is any good reason for thinking that God exists. Suppose, then, that a philosopher believes that God does exist and offers reasons meant to persuade others. This philosopher must believe that anyone who denies the existence of God is *mistaken*; he cannot say that there is "no right or wrong" about the matter, since he is trying to *show* what is right. The philosopher does have an opinion on the matter, but no one who has an opinion on *any* issue can say that on that issue there are "only opinions." Presumably this means that all such opinions are equally true. But suppose you have an opinion about some matter. This means that you really think a certain thing is true. If you admit that there are "only opinions" on the issue at hand, you thereby admit that the opinion of someone who *disagrees* with you is correct also! But then you have *contradicted* yourself: You have said that something is true and then denied the very same thing. And this would mean that you really have no opinion at all. To have an opinion on any matter, you must think that someone who disagrees with you is mistaken. Because philosophy is a kind of inquiry, philosophers must regard the opinions of those who disagree with them as *false*.

PHILOSOPHY AND RELIGION

How, then, is philosophy different from other intellectual disciplines? What kind of questions do philosophers try to answer? We can make a good start on seeing what is unique about philosophy by pondering the claim of the Dutch philosopher Benedict Spinoza, that true philosophy and true religion are the same. Now although it is difficult if not impossible to say what all religions have in common, we expect to find two things in any developed religion. One is a general picture of reality and our place in it. Some religions promise that in addition to the world around us, there is a God who creates it and offers us a life hereafter. Others say that God is a force that permeates the world, so that each of us embodies a bit of God. (We will later examine a variety of such views.) The second thing we expect in a developed religion is a prescription for how to conduct one's life. Some tell us to do whatever God says, others to act always with love and compassion. Notice that each of these — the general picture of the world and the prescription for life — is an *opinion*, something that people of that religion take to be *true*. Spinoza is saying that philosophy is mainly about the sorts of opinions that people get from their religion, but since it is an intellectual discipline, it is the effort to get these matters right by reasoning about them. This is plainly not the way that these opinions are typically presented when one encounters them in religious leaders or institutions. We do not find in churches the existence of God or God's commands offered as "hypotheses" to be critically discussed. They are typically "announced" by "preachers" and the like. This does not, of course, make them false. But if you are in doubt about them and you really want the truth, you need more than naked assertions of opinion. You will engage in inquiry, considering alternative answers and reasons for or against these. If your inquiries are successful and you do get the truth, your true philosophy will at the same time be (as Spinoza said) the true religion.

THE QUEST FOR COMPREHENSION

These two great concerns, to know the whole of reality and how to live in it, are central to two main areas of philosophy, called **metaphysics** and **ethics**. *Metaphysics* is the attempt to discover what there is. *Ethics* inquires into what is good, to see how to make the best choices. There is an ancient tradition of dividing all of philosophy into three main areas, including these two. But before the third is introduced, let us try to understand more clearly what questions are being asked in these two areas of philosophy.

In metaphysics, what is wanted is to comprehend all of reality, to see it as a whole. This is how it is different from the various sciences, which study various parts of reality. Biologists and sociologists, for example, certainly do not claim to be studying the whole of reality. But neither do those, such as astronomers, who study a much greater part of reality. Even if all there is is what astronomers study, to *say* this is not to make a claim in astronomy. Two astronomers could agree to all the same astronomy and still disagree about whether this is all there is. They might disagree, for example, about whether in addition to all these stars and planets, there is an "invisible" world containing God and heaven. A comprehensive view of reality is meant to leave nothing out. But astronomers, like other scientists, are not concerned with whether there is more to reality than the part they study. It is in metaphysics, therefore, that we ask such questions as "What are all the different kinds of things that are real?" "Where did it all come from?" and "How great is reality?"

Similar remarks pertain to ethics. In ethics, we want a comprehensive view of what is good. Nutritionists want to know what is good for health of the body, psychologists what is good for mental health. Neither asks about what all good things have in common or what are all the kinds of things that are good. (If health, fairness, and freedom are all good, there ought to be an answer to what they have in common.) Just as in metaphysics we study reality itself, in ethics we study goodness itself. It is true to say that metaphysics asks, "What is real?" and ethics asks, "What is good?" But these questions must be carefully interpreted. In each case what is wanted is a comprehensive answer, one that leaves nothing out.

THE SHIFT TO THOUGHT

Such large questions seem to pose a daunting task. If our most powerful telescopes cannot tell us when we have seen all of reality, what could? Philosophers have a reply that might be surprising. They say that we may get a comprehensive view of reality by shifting attention to how we should *think* about it. This is why philosophers talk so much about talk itself. This is not, however, an irrelevant diversion. Each has many beliefs about how things really are. Let us call the totality of these one's "map of the world." In metaphysics we think about how these maps should be. Suppose it could be shown that in any good map of the world, the distinction between what is real and what is not will be drawn in a certain way. Then we would have a comprehensive view of reality. Take a simple example: Suppose it can be demonstrated that only things that can be seen, heard, or otherwise sensed should be called real. Then we would have shown that reality as a whole consists of only "sensible" things.

It may seem that this is impossible. How can you know what belongs in a good map of the world without *first* finding out what *is* in the world? Astronomers add to our map of the world when they tell us there are galaxies not visible to the eye. To add this information to our map of the world, however, they had to first study the world itself. But this is not always necessary. An obvious example that makes the point is the existence of spherical cubes. We do not have to study the world to know there are no such things. We know in advance that it would be wrong, in any circumstance, to *think* there are.

Not all examples are so obvious or silly. Consider the case of disembodied personal existence. Many people believe that they can exist without their body, as just a mind. They think that although the mind is normally within a certain body, it is the sort of thing that can go on without it, as a captain may leave a ship. But is this the right way to *think* about how a mind is within a body? Maybe we should think of the mind as the way the body is put together or as a process going on in living tissue. If so, disembodied personal existence, like the existence of spherical cubes, would be impossible. Similar questions are raised in metaphysics about God and heaven. Should we think of God as the creator of the world or as a force within it? Should we think of heaven as a place we go after death or as a state of mind? By discovering how to think about reality, we learn about reality itself.

The same strategy is used in ethics. In ethics, we want the answers to practical questions, such as whether it is wrong to live selfishly or whether the torture of terrorists for vital information is permissible. To answer such questions, we seek a general view of what makes anything wrong or permissible, which we can apply to particular cases. As with metaphysics, we aim for comprehension by shifting attention to how, in general, to think about such matters. If we knew enough about how to *think* about what is good, then we would know about what sorts of things *are* good. We would have a *comprehensive* view of what is good.

THE PERSONAL NATURE OF PHILOSOPHY

With this shift to asking how to think about the matter, a reorientation has taken place. We have replaced an *impersonal* question, such as "What is there?" with a *personal* question, which you, as a student, must put to yourself. For now the question is what is the *right* way to think about reality (or goodness). This is something you must see for yourself. Other disciplines contain much that can be taken on the authority of experts in the field. Most of us have not seen distant galaxies through a telescope; we know of them only through the reports of astronomers. But now suppose that you are told that all philosophers think you ought to keep your promises, even if you can break one without getting caught and without hurting anyone. And let us suppose that you have felt nothing is really wrong in breaking promises when no one knows and no one gets hurt. Would the fact that "experts" think otherwise change your opinion? Or would you have to see for yourself what is wrong with promise breaking in these benign circumstances to change your mind? You might even admit that their reasons are probably better than yours, so that they are probably right. Still, there is an important sense in which you would not yet really think they *are* right.

Consider this analogy: Suppose you hear from respected art critics that a certain statue, which you have not seen, is beautiful. Again, you might think that the experts are probably right, but there is a sense in which *you* would not yet think that it is beautiful, until you see it for yourself and experience the pleasure of contemplating it. Analogously, when you think something is *wrong*, you must have an *aversion* to it. If you really think it is wrong to break your promise, you want to avoid doing so. You may feel conflicted and also want to break it for a selfish reason. But if you have no aversion to doing it, your claim that it is wrong will seem insincere. When, on the other hand, you learn that philosophers who have thought much about when it is wrong to break promises feel an aversion for a certain kind of promise breaking, this does not cause *you* to feel an aversion to them. Philosophical questions by their very nature cannot be answered for you by experts.

This explains how, in a way, there really are no authorities in philosophy. Philosophers cannot simply report that they have made certain discoveries. They can teach only by *showing* students why it is right or wrong to think in certain ways. This is why philosophy teachers seem to bounce around, saying one thing and then denying it. For you to see how to think about something, you need to see different sides of an issue. It is also why students are asked their opinions. For your job as a student is to take seriously your responsibility for acting as a judge, coming to a verdict by yourself. Many students have difficulty taking themselves seriously as someone who can think by themselves on an abstract issue. This attitude *must* be overcome to acquire the understanding that philosophy has to offer.

The fact that philosophy is directed to each of us personally does not mean that we can answer any way we please. Some answers must be wrong, since you are asking what is the *right* way to think. Your job is to really try to see what is the right way to think about what there is or what there ought to be. This is what it is to act as a judge, having to make the decision yourself. It may be possible to slip through your first course in philosophy by memorizing and repeating what you hear or read. But in philosophy, if you fail to engage with the material seriously, you might as well not bother at all.

Because students must see for themselves, they must start from the beginning on every issue. Of course, they have the help of the thoughts of many philosophers of the past. Nonetheless, there is a way in which we all start from the same point. It is, therefore, especially helpful to read works from the earliest philosophers. For here you find keen minds approaching the issue for the first time, just as you are. Newer contributions to philosophy are written by and for people who have already heard these first voices and what others said in response. If you enter a conversation too late, you are likely to be mystified. This is why ancient texts are often used for introducing students to philosophy.

THE ROLE OF IMAGINATION

The shift to thought explains why philosophers use imagination as much as actual observation. Suppose that the United States is attacked by a band of terrorists who hide out in Afghanistan. Does the fact that Afghanistan does not turn them over to the United States give the United States a right to invade that country? This question does not really depend on whether it is actually true that the United States was attacked by such a band or that they are now to be found in Afghanistan. Even if we are perfectly sure this supposition is true, this is not relevant to the *philosophical* question. Notice that this example began by saying merely, "Suppose that. . . ." We could as well ask, "Just *imagine* that this occurred. Would it give the United States a right to invade?" This point does not show that philosophy is a matter of fiction and not truth. It is rather that when the question is the very general one of how to think about what is real or good, hypothetical situations are just as relevant as real ones. In this respect, philosophy may be compared with questions that arise about the law. To *apply* a law, you must know what the actual conditions are. But to know the law itself, you must know what the law *would* say in a variety of imagined conditions. Philosophy itself is in a way about "the law." It is about the rules to follow to think well about how things really are or how they ought to be.

NO NECESSARY METHOD

The shift to thought also explains why there is no official procedure to follow to answer philosophical questions. No one is going to tell you "the way" to resolve issues. There are no **necessary methods of justification,** nothing like methods of proving things in mathematics. Of course, philosophers try to "prove" things in the sense that they give reasons for their opinions. But there is no one way of doing so. If philosophers ever came to agree on such a procedure, it would always be open for a new philosopher to challenge it and follow another. When the issue is the right way to think, it is always legitimate to question whether following any particular procedure is right. Philosophy is not a way of proving things. It is the attempt to answer certain questions. There is no such thing as competing with philosophy in how to find the truth. There is no such thing as a philosophical way of proving things that could be replaced by the way things are proven in some other field, such as a science. Any reasoned attempt to solve the problems of philosophy is philosophy.

THE MAIN AREAS OF PHILOSOPHY

Ethics and metaphysics are but two of three main areas of philosophy. Their difference is one of subject matter. It is the difference between whether the issue is how to think about what is real or how to think about what good. **Logic** is about how to think in general, regardless of subject matter. In logic we want to know how to think well, whether we are thinking about reality or goodness.

Let us look at a couple of obvious rules that belong to logic. We ought to have adequate reasons for our conclusions. This is just as true for thinking about what is good as it is for thinking about what is real. When we arrive at a conclusion in inquiry and have found that our reasons were not enough to show that our conclusion is true, we have failed. Since this is a rule that we ought to follow *whenever* we think something is true, it is a rule of logic. Another example is the rule not to contradict yourself. If you say that there is global warming and later deny it, something has to give. If you are disagreeing with yourself, you have failed to put forth a position at all. You must make up your mind. Again, the demand not to contradict yourself applies whether you are talking about what is real or what is good. If you say that all killing is wrong but killing in self-defense is not, you have contradicted yourself and must make up your mind before you even have a chance of getting the truth.

Together logic, metaphysics, and ethics cover the whole of philosophy. There are many other areas of philosophy and other ways of classifying them. But this division will allow us to see how philosophy relates to our lives.

HOW PHILOSOPHY IS UNAVOIDABLE

In the normal course of life, we usually think about matters that serve some particular purpose of ours. You may think about how to get to the supermarket or how to pay your bills. You may think about what amount of money is really in your checking account or whether someone is really being faithful to you. In such cases, you are not thinking about the very general philosophical question of how to think about what to do or about what is real. Remember, these questions are asking for *comprehensive* views of goodness or reality. The philosophical questions are nonetheless *relevant* to your particular situation. In fact, your decisions in these ordinary situations will *commit* you to answers to the philosophical questions.

Let us look carefully at an example to see clearly this important point. Suppose that someone you know is completely selfish. You notice that there is a pattern in their decisions about what to do. This person always looks to her own advantage and does what is best for her, no matter how it may hurt or cheat other people. We may suppose that this person never takes an interest in the philosophical question of what to do *in general*; she is simply uninterested in how she lives her life. But she *does* live her life a certain general way; we can see what, *in general*, this person thinks is good by the *pattern* in her choices. She shows by the way she acts that she believes her own welfare is all that is important to her. This *is* an answer to the philosophical question "What is good?" So there is a way in which this person "answers" the philosophical question, even if she never consciously thinks about it. Even if she never puts the philosophical question to herself and engages in inquiry to answer it, she *commits* herself to an answer by the way she lives.

The same point applies, of course, to all of us. We always choose what appears (at that moment, at least) to be the *better* choice. This is why you can tell by anyone's choice what they thought (at least at that moment) was more *important*. If you could see *all* of the choices a person makes, you could see what *in general* they think is good. No matter who you are, you must make choices throughout your life. By seeing the patterns in your choices, we see how you have "answered" the philosophical question of what really is important in life, even if you have never thought about the question in this general form. (This is why you cannot excuse yourself from Judgment Day by saying that you "just did not think about" how you lived.) It is in this way that philosophy is "unavoidable" (as the title of our text says), and we "confront the unavoidable" by doing philosophy, which means seriously questioning the general ways we think about what is real and what is good.

Everyone also has a map of the world. We need beliefs about reality to get around in it. Even something as simple as walking to the door involves such beliefs as that there is a door there and that the floor will not fall through. And just as we can tell by what people do what they think is good, we can also tell what they think is real. Even if they never take an interest in the totality of their beliefs about what is real, they still commit themselves to an answer to the philosophical question of how, in general, to think about reality. For as before, there will be patterns in these beliefs that can be seen by observers of their behavior. Someone may be so down-to-earth, for example, that he never takes seriously talk of "another world" or a "future life." Someone else may pray and direct her life for a future reward. Living a human life requires drawing a line between what is real and what is not. And the general way one does this amounts to a philosophical opinion about what there is. So, you cannot live a human life without "answering" in this way the comprehensive, philosophical questions of what is good and what is real. You can avoid philosophical questions the way you can avoid any question—by not putting them to yourself consciously and seeking answers through inquiry. But you cannot avoid them altogether. Your only choice is to think about them or to "answer" them in ways that are bound to be relatively confused and arbitrary.

THE CONCERN WITH IDEALS

We have classified philosophy into three main areas. Each of these can be associated with a very succinct question. Logic asks, "What should I think?" Metaphysics asks, "What should I believe in?" Ethics asks, "What should I do?" So long as we bear in mind the qualifications of this introduction, these questions are useful for remembering what each is about. They also help us to see something important about philosophy itself. Putting the questions in the first person, by asking how *I* should be, reminds us of the personal nature of philosophy. Putting them in terms of how I *should* be reminds us that philosophy is concerned above all with certain *ideals*. "What should I think?"—what is *true*. "What should I believe in?"—what is *real*. "What should I do?"—what is *good*. Our ideas of truth, reality, and goodness represent the *right* ways to answer these questions. There are many other ideas like these that philosophers are concerned to understand. The ideas of beauty, authority, and justice, for example, all have a "positive ring" to them. This is because they represent the right way to answer such questions as, "What to contemplate for pleasure?" or "Who to respect?" or "How to resolve conflicts?" There is no definite end to such questions. The classification of all of philosophy into just three areas, associated with just three of these questions, is based on the conviction that the other questions can be seen as arising within one or another of these areas. The question of how to resolve conflicts, for example, is a question of ethics. Philosophers who ask this question are said to be interested in "understanding justice." This can be confusing, since justice is studied in other disciplines. Political science, for example, studies "institutions of justice," such as legislatures and courts of law. Philosophers study the *idea* of justice, what it is *to be* just. This is because of their primary concern with how to think.

THE ALLEGORY OF THE CAVE

In the following passage, which may be the most famous in all of philosophy, the ancient Greek philosopher Plato describes the discovery of such ideals as being like a religious conversion. Plato's writings take the form of dialogues, in which Socrates, Plato's mentor, expresses Plato's own view. You are not expected to remember every detail of this story; try to read through it with pleasure, just to get the general picture and, above all, the *point* of the story.

> Next, said I, compare our nature in respect of education and its lack to such an experience as this. Picture men dwelling in a sort of subterranean cavern with a long entrance open to the light on its entire width. Conceive them having their legs and necks fettered from childhood, so that they remain in the same spot, able to look forward only, and prevented by the fetters from turning their heads. Picture further the light from a fire burning higher up and at a distance behind them, and between the fire and the prisoners and above them a road along which a low wall has been built, as the exhibitors of puppet shows have partitions before the men themselves, above which they show the puppets.
> All that I see, he said.
> See also, then, men carrying past the wall implements of all kinds that rise above the wall, and human images and shapes of animals as well, wrought in stone and wood and every material, some of these bearers presumably speaking and others silent.
> A strange image you speak of, he said, and strange prisoners.

Like to us, I said. For, to begin with, tell me do you think that these men would have seen anything of themselves or of one another except the shadows cast from the fire on the wall of the cave that fronted them?

How could they, he said, if they were compelled to hold their heads unmoved through life?

And again, would not the same be true of the objects carried past them?

Surely.

If then they were able to talk to one another, do you not think that they would suppose that in naming the things that they saw they were naming the passing objects?

Necessarily.

And if their prison had an echo from the wall opposite them, when one of the passers-by uttered a sound, do you think that they would suppose anything else than the passing shadow to be the speaker?

By Zeus, I do not, he said.

Then in every way such prisoners would deem reality to be nothing else than the shadows of the artificial objects.

Quite inevitably, said he.

Consider then, what would be the manner of the release and healing from these bonds and this folly if in the course of nature something of this sort should happen to them. When one was freed from his fetters and compelled to stand up suddenly and turn his head around and walk and to lift up his eyes to the light, and in doing all this felt pain and, because of the dazzle and glitter of the light, was unable to discern the objects whose shadows he formerly saw, what do you suppose would be his answer if someone told him that what he had seen before was all a cheat and an illusion, but that now, being nearer to reality and turned toward more real things, he saw more truly? And if also one should point out to him each of the passing objects and constrain him by questions to say what it is, do you not think that he would be at a loss and that he would regard what he formerly saw as more real than the things now pointed out to him?

Far more real, he said.

And if he were compelled to look at the light itself, would not that pain his eyes, and would he not turn away and flee to those things which he is able to discern and regard them as in very deed clear and exact than the objects pointed out?

It is so, he said.

And if, said I, someone should drag him thence by force up the ascent which is rough and steep, and not let him go before he had drawn him out into the light of the sun, do you not think that he would find it painful to be so hauled along, and would chafe at it, and when he came out into the light, that his eyes would be filled with its beams so that he would not be able to see even one of the things that we call real?

Why no, not immediately, he said.

Then there would be need of habituation, I take it, to enable him to see the things higher up. And at first he would most easily discern the shadows and, after that, the likenesses or reflections in water of men and other things, and later, the things themselves, and from these he would go on to contemplate the appearances in the heavens and heaven itself, more easily by night, looking at the light of the stars and the moon, than by day the sun and the sun's light.

Of course.

And so, finally, I suppose, he would be able to look upon the sun itself and see its true nature, not by reflections in water and phantasms of it in an alien setting, but in and by itself in its own place.

Necessarily, he said.

And at this point he would infer and conclude that this it is that provides the seasons and the courses of the year and presides over all things in the visible region, and is in some sort the cause of all these things that they had seen.

Obviously, he said, that would be the next step.

Well, then, if he recalled to mind his first habitation and what passed for wisdom there, and his fellow bondsmen, do you not think that he would count himself happy in the change and pity them?

He would indeed.

And if there had been honors and commendations among them which they bestowed on one another and prizes for the man who is quickest to make out shadows as they pass and best able to remember their customary precedences, sequences, and coexistences, and so most successful in guessing at what was to come, do you think he would be very keen about such rewards, and that he would envy and emulate those who were honored by these prisoners and lorded it among them, or that he would feel with Homer and greatly prefer while living on earth to be serf of another, a landless man, and endure anything rather than opine with them and live that life?

Yes, he said, I think that he would choose to endure anything rather than such a life.

And consider this also, said I. If such a one should go down again and take his old place would he not get his eyes full of darkness, thus suddenly coming out of the sunlight?

He would indeed.

Now if he should be required to contend with these perpetual prisoners in "evaluating" these shadows while his vision was still dim and before his eyes were accustomed to dark—and this time required for habituation would not be very short—would he not provoke laughter, and would it not be said of him that he had returned from his journey aloft with his keen eyes ruined and that it as not worth while even to attempt the ascent? And if it were possible to lay hands on and to kill the man who tried to release them and lead them up, would they not kill him?

They certainly would, he said.

This image then, dear Glaucon, we must apply as a whole to all that has been said, likening the region revealed through sight to the habitation of the prison, and the light of the fire in it to the power of the sun. And if you assume that the ascent and the contemplation of the things above is the soul's ascension to the intelligible region, you will not miss my surmise, since that is what you desire to hear. But God knows whether it is true. But, at any rate, my dream as it appears to me is that in the region of the known the last thing to be seen and hardly seen is the idea of the good, and that when seen it must needs point us to the conclusion that this is indeed the cause for all things all that is right and beautiful, giving birth in the visible world to light, and the author of light and itself in the intelligible world being the authentic source of truth and reason, and that anyone who is to act wisely in private or public must have caught sight of this.[1]

The story Plato tells is now standardly called "The Allegory of the Cave." Fortunately, Plato tells us what the story is meant to represent. The shadows in the cave symbolize the things we see around us: trees, rocks, people, and so forth. The "real" things outside the cave represent such things as beauty, truth, and justice — just the sorts of ideals with which philosophy is concerned. The prisoner who is liberated from the cave represents one who has come to understand these ideals, who sees them "in the light of day." This "enlightened" person is not merely one who has opinions about what is beautiful or true or just. We all do. Philosophical enlightenment comes from *understanding* these ideals, knowing, for example, *what it is* for something we want to be *good* or for an action of ours to be *right* or for something we believe in to be *real*. But why depict those who lack this understanding as *prisoners*? How is this understanding supposed to be *liberating*?

We might call Plato's cave dwellers *prisoners of circumstance*. For Plato depicts them as having knowledge only of the world as it presents itself to them, in their particular situation. Prisoners in other caves might well be presented with a different "show," which they, of course, take to be an honest representation of reality. Plato means to represent the original state of each of us, when we have absorbed uncritically the opinions and expectations of those around us. These will be the least visible to us when they concern those most general orientations to life that the philosopher questions. And we originally hold these opinions and comply with these expectations because we just happen to have been born in a particular time and place, surrounded by particular people. We are "prisoners" of our circumstances in life in the sense that we are *dependent* on these very circumstances for our basic opinions about life and reality. The search for philosophical enlightenment begins when it strikes us that it is somewhat *arbitrary,* something of an *accident,* that we were born into these peculiar circumstances. We do not want our basic commitments about how we live to be determined by something *alien* to us, which is how we now begin to regard our original circumstances. We want them to come from within, to be somehow chosen by our*selves*. We *liberate* ourselves from this original "imprisonment," according to Plato's allegory, only by using our power of *reason*. It is only by seeing for ourselves what we *should* believe or want or do that we are genuinely in charge of our lives, genuinely the *creators* of the way we live. The point is not that without philosophical reflection we have no good reason for

---

1. Plato, *Republic,* trans. Paul Shorey, 514a–517d.

the way we live (we may or may not). It is that we are not able to see ourselves as having good reasons. Many benefits, both for the individual and for society, are derived from philosophical knowledge and mutual agreement. I believe, however, that most of all, people are drawn to philosophical reflection out of a sense of *dignity*.

CONCLUSION

Major religions have offered comprehensive views of reality and of how to conduct our lives. Philosophy shares these concerns but subjects them to critical inquiry, as suits an intellectual discipline. To achieve comprehension, philosophy asks primarily how we should *think* about reality and life. This shift to how we should think gives it a personal dimension, for only you can see how you *should* think. Imagination is just as useful as actual observation in deciding how to think. And no particular method is necessary, since any can be questioned.

All of philosophy may be divided into three main areas. Metaphysics and ethics deal, respectively, with how things are and how they ought to be. Logic deals with how we ought to think, regardless of subject matter. Each area can be associated with a main question: how to think truly (logic), what to admit as real (metaphysics), and what to do (ethics). Philosophy is thus concerned mainly with values, such as truth, reality, and goodness. The freedom and nobility of understanding these ideals is symbolized in Plato's Allegory of the Cave. In the following, we explore questions in all the main problem areas of philosophy, to get a broad view of how liberation through philosophical enlightenment has been sought.

STUDY QUESTIONS

1. Explain why, if there are "only opinions" on some matter, you should have no opinions about this topic at all.
2. What concerns does philosophy share with religion?
3. What does it mean to say that philosophy is an "intellectual discipline"? How was this fact used to mark a contrast between philosophy and religion?
4. Why are philosophers preoccupied with how to think?
5. Explain what it means to say that there are "no authorities" in philosophy.
6. Explain what it means to say that philosophy is not "a way of proving things."
7. Identify each of the following areas of philosophy by associating it with a central question: metaphysics; ethics; logic.
6. Explain how, in general, the main questions of philosophy are "unavoidable," even if we never think of them.
7. With what kinds of ideals is philosophy centrally occupied? Give a couple of examples to illustrate the point.
8. What is it to be a "prisoner of circumstance"? How is philosophical knowledge supposed to be liberating?

PART ONE

Logic

Logic is that large part of philosophy concerned with the question of how to think well, regardless of subject matter. Other areas of philosophy also pertain to how to think, but they differ from logic in being concerned with a specific kind of question, such as "What is real?" or "What is good?" In answering questions of either kind, we should respect the (correct) rules of logic. Logic thus provides a framework for thinking about both kinds of questions. We therefore begin with logic before turning to each of the more specific areas of philosophy.

*We inquire in order to know. Knowledge is an ideal of thinking. Philosophy is the attempt to understand such ideals. (**Epistemology** is that area of logic that is the study of knowledge.) In Chapter One, we study this ideal. One large and important kind of knowledge is understanding, or knowing why something is so. In every intellectual discipline, it is not just knowledge that is sought, but understanding as well. Astronomers want not merely to be able to track the stars and planets but to understand what they are and why they move as they do. Psychologists want more than being familiar with human behavior; they want to understand it. Since understanding is something we want in any intellectual discipline, it belongs to logic to study the nature of understanding itself.*

Where do we get the truth? We try to get the truth by getting good reasons. But where do we get these? Another question we ask in logic is how to classify the sources of our knowledge. We will find that different questions sometimes require different sources. You can find out where your keys are by looking, but we do not seem to know of God or what rights people have in this way. Controversies about what are the legitimate sources of knowledge therefore have practical consequences. To deny a source of knowledge is to deny a whole body of knowledge. Suppose, for example, that you could know of God only by having a certain profound experience in which God is revealed to you. For you to deny that that experience is a genuine source of knowledge is to deny all your knowledge of God. No wonder that the question of where we get the truth has been considered a serious one. Chapter Two explains several sources of knowledge that are relatively uncontroversial and that some philosophers think are all there are. It also mentions a couple of others more controversial and explains why they are so.

Chapter Three shows how we combine these relatively uncontroversial sources to know about things that we cannot observe. Many of our everyday beliefs and all of science are known in this way. By understanding the nature of scientific knowledge, we can see what science both can and cannot teach us. We will find in particular that science does not address the questions of philosophy, including the questions of metaphysics and ethics.

CHAPTER ONE

Knowledge and Understanding

HOW TO THINK WELL? What can we say in general about how our thinking ought to be? We want to think what is true, since that is the *point* of all thinking (as we understand the term). Is there any other way our thinking should be? Often we say that we want to *know* the truth. Is there anything more to knowing than getting the truth? And why is it good to have the truth? If it is good to have true thoughts, then this is a way that each individual thought should be. But what of whole bodies of thought, such as our map of the world? Are there good ways for thoughts to be *collectively*? These are the sorts of questions we address in this chapter.

THOUGHTS

Since we want to think well, let us start by clarifying what **thoughts** are before we consider what makes them good. *Thoughts* (as we will understand the word) are *what* we think. If you think that snow is white, *what* you think is *that snow is white*. Notice that to say what you think, all that you do is to take the sentence you used and put *that* in front of it. Although we talk about thoughts only by using sentences, the thoughts are not the sentences themselves, any more than you are your name. This becomes clear when you realize that the same thought can be expressed with different sentences. The thought that snow is white is also expressed, for example, by the German sentence "Der Schnee ist weiss." And the same sentence can be used to express different thoughts. If I say that I am hungry and you say that you are hungry, we have expressed different thoughts, even if we both use the sentence "I am hungry." These are different thoughts because the same thought cannot be both true and false. Since you could be hungry when I am not, the thoughts that we express with the sentence "I am hungry" are not the same.

Thoughts are not the sort of things that can be seen or felt. They are abstract. You can see and feel snow but not the thought that snow is white. Nor do thoughts exist "in the mind." Pains and beliefs, for example, are in the mind in the sense that if you feel a pain or believe something, your pain or your belief cannot exist without your mind. When you die, your pains and beliefs cannot carry on. The *act* of thinking that snow is white also exists in the mind. Your thinking that snow is white is something that you do, and your *doings* exist only if you do. But the thought is something of which you are aware by thinking. The thought exists "outside" the mind the way trees and stones do. This is why other people can think the same thoughts you do, even when you are gone.

If we cannot see or feel thoughts, how do we know about them? The traditional answer is to allow that we have other ways of knowing besides the use of our senses. Many philosophers have said that our **intellect** is a power to be aware of thoughts, a kind of "mind's eye." Whatever you call it, it seems undeniable that we have a power to be aware of thoughts.

Some philosophers object to talking about thoughts as if they were *things* at all, along with chairs and rocks. Maybe when we are "aware of thoughts" we are really in some roundabout way aware of tangible things. If we allow this possibility, it is uncontroversial to say that by our intellect we are aware of thoughts. Philosophers can still disagree about what this view amounts to.

THE OBJECTIVITY OF TRUTH

Many students are suspicious about the idea that some thoughts are *just true*. They want to ask, "True *for whom?*" They say that truth is "subjective," meaning that something may be true for one person and not for another. This is an important issue. For if they are correct, then asking about what is true is like asking what is funny. Nothing is just funny: the same joke can be funny to some and not to others. So, funniness really is subjective. If truth is the same way, we should not talk about whether something is true but should be careful to note *who* is doing the thinking.

This is not a popular idea among philosophers, since it is widely believed among them to be based on confusion. Think of an example in which the idea does seem right: one hundred pounds is difficult to lift. "That may be true for me," one might say, "but not for a weightlifter." Of course, we would understand what the person meant. But what really varies from one person to another is the *difficulty of lifting* one hundred pounds, not truth itself. It is *just true* that lifting this weight is difficult *for* the speaker but *not for* a weightlifter. Another example: Is it true that the Earth is round? "Yes, for us," someone might say, "but not for people who lived centuries ago." What varies in this example is what people *believe* and not truth itself. The Earth was round centuries ago, but many people did not believe this. To say that the Earth was flat "for them" is just a fancy (and possibly misleading) way of saying what they believed.

LOGICAL RELATIONS

There are other ways of describing thoughts besides saying whether they are true or false. Logic is also concerned with *relationships* between them. Let us look at a couple of important kinds. Anytime two people disagree with one another, their thoughts are **inconsistent.** If you say the Earth is round and I say it is flat, both of us cannot be right, and this is what it means for thoughts to be inconsistent. Inconsistent thoughts cannot all be true. It is very useful to be able to tell whether what you think collectively is inconsistent. Suppose you are reflecting on a particular body of your thoughts, such as what you think about someone you know. Since these are all things you think, you regard each of them as true. But now suppose you can discover that your thoughts about this person are inconsistent. Suppose, for example, that you thought this person was honest, but then come to think they did something dishonest. You might not be sure which thought is false, but you know they cannot both be true. The discovery of the inconsistency may prompt you to investigate more to find out which thought to deny. The ability to reflect on your own thoughts and discover inconsistencies is, in fact, a very important ability for improving your thinking. (There is a branch of logic, called *formal* or *symbolic logic*, that investigates specifically how to detect inconsistencies.)

Sometimes we can see that one thought **follows** from another. We can see, just by being aware of the two thoughts, that if one is true, then the other must be true also. If it is true that neither Sally nor Fred will live in the city, it *follows* that Sally will not live in the city. One thought can follow from another even when the other is not in fact true. From the thought that the moon crashed into the ocean yesterday, it follows that something crashed into the ocean yesterday. Sometimes the relationship is not obvious. The thought that there are two people on Earth with the same number of hairs on their heads follows from the thought that there are more people on Earth than there are hairs on anyone's head.

It can be useful to know when one thought follows from another. For if you *do* know the first is true, you see that the second is also true. You actually come to know something new just by thinking about a thought you already know. If you wanted to know whether Sally will live in the city, you could get the information you want by learning that neither Sally nor Fred will live in the city. You can also use such knowledge to see the implications of what someone says. If someone says that killing is wrong, you may see that he is *committed* to saying that even killing in self-defense is wrong. If he then goes on to deny that killing in self-defense is wrong, his thoughts are *inconsistent*. As before, the person has to give up one of his claims to have thoughts that *can* all be true.

UNDERSTANDING

After finding out that a particular thought is true, we often want to know *why* it is true. We want not merely to know *that* it is true but to **understand** it. This is a remarkable fact about us, and it is doubtful that any other animals on this planet have this capacity or interest. Other animals certainly learn about their environment and thus come to know many things, at least in the sense of being familiar with them. But we are often not satisfied with this much. Often, even though we are quite sure of a certain truth, we find it puzzling, mysterious why it should be so. We want to understand it to remove the mystery. You come to your front door and find it unlocked. This surprises you, and you want to know why it is. Further evidence reveals that a burglar was there. Now you understand why your door was unlocked. The thought that a burglar was there **explains** why the door was unlocked. Notice that explaining is not the same as showing that it is true. You already *know* that your door is unlocked; what you want is to know *why* it is. You seek another thought to explain the one you already know.

We have already touched on the question of how our thoughts should be collectively. For any body of our thoughts, small or large, we want them to be consistent. To call the thoughts consistent is to say that they do not *conflict* with one another. When we *understand* why some of these are true, we make the body of them more **coherent**. To call them coherent implies a closer relationship. When many things cohere, they form a single whole. When they do not cohere, they are like a disorganized heap of things. When we come to understand why some thought within a body of thoughts is true, we add a new truth to that body that is *connected* with the thought it explains. In our previous example, we add the thought that a burglar was there. But this is not merely one more thought about the house. It *explains* another thought about the house. Explanations are thoughts *about* thoughts. Now a good explanation, as we will see more fully in Chapter Three, is capable of explaining more facts than the original one it was meant to explain. The fact that a burglar was there can explain a host of other facts about the house, including the fact that it is messed up and that things are missing. This increases the coherence of your thoughts about the house. The thoughts that the door is unlocked, that the house is messy, and that things are missing are three separate thoughts. Without the explanation, they appear to have little in common. But with the explanation, these several thoughts are *comprehended*, which means literally to be grasped together.

We humans seem to have a natural desire to understand the world. As we satisfy that desire in a particular collection of thoughts, we make them more coherent. Besides consistency, the coherence that comes from understanding is another virtue of our thoughts collectively.

THINKING

Thoughts are *what* we think. Now let us turn to the mental act of thinking itself. We are understanding "thinking" in a special sense. Often the word is used to describe any of a variety of mental acts, such as hoping, wondering, or supposing. For us, **thinking** means specifically thinking *that* a certain thought is *true*. We will also understand thinking in a way that requires the intellect. Recall that the intellect is our capacity to be *aware* of thoughts themselves. We often say of other animals that they think—for example, that the dog *thinks* its food bowl is full. But in our special sense of the word, we will not call something thinking unless it is *conscious*. What this means is that to be a thinker, one must be able to have thoughts about thoughts themselves. In our example, the dog is aware of the food bowl. There is nothing to suggest that it can also think about its thought that the food bowl is full. Yet this kind of awareness is very common in us humans.

Even something as simple as *denying* what someone says involves having a thought about a thought. If I say that the Earth is flat and you deny this point, your thought (that the Earth is not flat) is *about* the thought I expressed. This means that whenever you spot inconsistencies in what you think, you are using the intellect. If you realize that the thought that killing is wrong and the thought that killing in self-defense is not wrong are inconsistent, you are thinking *about* these two thoughts. Any time you see that one thought follows from another, you are also using the intellect. And any time you give an explanation, you are thinking about thoughts. If you explain why you are not going to a party by saying that you are tired, you have again thought about thoughts, the thought being explained (that you are not going to the party) and the thought doing the explaining (that you are tired). As these examples illustrate, thinking about thoughts themselves is a very common activity of humans.

It helps to understand what thinking is to see that we do not have evidence of thinking in any other animals. Consider this especially remarkable example. Chimpanzees have shown an ability to solve problems. In one famous experiment, some food was dangled too high for a chimpanzee to reach, but sturdy boxes were scattered on the ground. After a period of frustration, the chimp suddenly went to the boxes, stacked them on top of one another, and climbed them to reach the food. The chimp was clearly not acting instinctively. It had to look over the situation before hitting upon a plan. But remarkable as this is (have you ever seen a dog do such a thing?), it does not show intellect. For this is not only the ability to put thoughts together, as one does in making a plan. It is the ability to *think about* thoughts, including those that compose the plan. For all we know, the chimp puts the thoughts together unconsciously, doing it but not being aware of what it is doing (just as we are not aware of many things going on in our bodies). Our ability to think is shown not so much in *creating* plans but in being able to *improve* on them. We can reflect on how we do things and think of ways to do them better. This can be repeated indefinitely, so that continual progress is possible in how we act in the world. It is the intellect that makes possible the continual development of human culture.

JUDGMENT

When an inquiry of yours has ended, you come to a conclusion, an answer to the original question. You come to think a certain thought is true. Let us call this making a **judgment.** The term is apt, since in making a judgment we act like a judge, making a verdict about what it is right to think. Thoughts themselves do not come into and go out of existence. A judgment, however, is an act of thinking, made by a particular person at a particular time, and takes only a moment. Our own judgments always appear to be well grounded. It always seems to us at the moment of judgment that we have sufficiently good reason for coming to think as we do. This is because we make the judgment *by* seeing (what looks to us as) a good reason for doing so. We must qualify what we say about judgments in general to accommodate the fact that we sometimes make judgments on the basis of inadequate reasons. But it never *looks* that way when we ourselves are actually making the judgment. It appears to be the right thing to think, and it is *just because* it does appear right that we come to think it. This is why, when someone says what they think, it is always appropriate to ask, "*Why* do you think that?" It may be impossible to remember why you thought that, but you will be sure that in making the judgment you did have good reasons for it. If you say that you have no good reason for thinking as you do, you will not be taken seriously. We are aware of our reasons whenever we make judgments.

Let us look at an example. Suppose you judge that your door is unlocked and conclude that a burglar has entered the house. In coming to this conclusion, you are making a second judgment. If asked why you think that, you would say that the door was unlocked. In this example you give a prior thought to back up the new thought. The fact (the true thought) that the door is unlocked *is* your reason for your judgment about the burglar. In this example, the reason for your judgment is another thought. If good, this reason *shows that* the new thought is true.

To be taken seriously as a thinker, you must take *responsibility* for your judgments. Above all, you must accept the two principles of logic to avoid inconsistencies and to have adequate reasons. You show by how you behave whether you really accept this responsibility. If you say different things and realize that they are inconsistent, you must retract one of them. Otherwise you look like two people disagreeing with each other—you do not speak "with one mind." You also take responsibility for the adequacy of your reasons. If you realize that you really do not have good reason for thinking something is true, you retract the judgment. This is not the same as *denying* what you thought was true, for this would be another judgment that would take other reasons. It is rather that "the rug is pulled from under" your judgment. You must take it back and remain neutral on the issue until you get good reasons. You are not "free" to make judgments arbitrarily. This applies even to philosophy, where you must judge for yourself what is right to think. Some people have been trained to suppose that certain beliefs of theirs, such as religious ones, are matters of "faith" in the sense that they are held with no good reason at all. But try expressing anything you really think and then adding that you have no good reason for it. No one will be able to take you seriously, not even yourself. (We should expect, therefore, that what the great religious thinkers have *meant* by "faith" is *not* a belief for which there is no good reason.)

JUSTIFICATION AND EXPLANATION

Giving a reason for a judgment is not the same as giving an explanation. As we have seen, explanations are sought only for something you *already* think is true. And the purpose of them is to remove the puzzlement or mystery of its being true. The reason for a judgment is called a **justification.** This is simply a different kind of reason than the kind we give for explanations. A justifying reason is supposed to show that a particular thought *is* true. It is called "justifying" since it is supposed to give you a *right* to make the judgment. The fact that the door is unlocked is what *justifies* your judgment that a burglar was there. (Notice that in this case, the fact that a burglar was there *explains* why the door was unlocked.)

Although many good reasons for judgments are thoughts, good reasons also come in another form. Suppose that on the basis of how it looks, you judge that there is a lake in the distance. Notice that the basis — how it looks — is neither true nor false and hence is not a thought. (It is an experience, as we will see in the next chapter.) Yet it is what gives you the right to think there is a lake ahead. If asked, "Why do you think there is a lake ahead?" you might say simply, "By the way it looks." This is not another thought about which we could ask the same sort of question.

RATIONALITY

Students of philosophy often hear the term *rational* and are confused by it. This is because the word is used with different meanings. There is one meaning, at least, that is particularly important. The ancient Greek philosophers were convinced that **rationality** is our most important characteristic, making humans very different from other animals. This does not mean that we are or should be unemotional. It simply means that we have the ability to be aware of our reasons. Anytime we give a justification or explanation, we demonstrate our rationality. And as we have seen, rationality is always exercised in judgment, since we are aware of the reasons for our judgments, what makes them look right. Because judgment is what we do when we first think something is true, all thinkers are "rational beings."

BASIC KINDS OF KNOWLEDGE

Ideally, our judgments should be both true and adequately justified. How are such ideal judgments to be compared with knowledge? Inquiry is often described as the search for knowledge. But what is it to *know* something? The word has a positive connotation. Knowledge is some kind of achievement, or at least a good thing to have. To have knowledge, it seems, is to be *empowered* in some way.

To get a clear view of the nature of knowledge in general, we should see its most basic varieties. One kind of knowledge is *knowledge of truths*. This is contrasted with *knowledge of things* (including knowledge of people). To know that snow is white or the moon is full is to know a truth. To know Paris or one's neighbor is not thereby to know a certain truth; it is to know, in the sense of being familiar with, a certain place or person. Another contrast is between knowledge of truths and *knowledge of skills*. To know how to ski or cook is not thereby to know a certain truth. It is to have the ability to make something happen.

KNOWLEDGE AND BELIEF

In logic we are especially concerned with knowledge of truths. This is because all of logic is about how to think well, and it is truths that we wish to think. At the end of a successful inquiry, we make a certain true judgment. But we also come to know what we have judged to be true. To know and to judge are, however, not the same thing. As we have seen, the judgment lasts for only a moment. But the knowledge can be retained indefinitely. To know something you do not have to be thinking of it, as you do in judgment. Knowledge is not necessarily conscious, as judgment is. This is why animals who lack intellect can still *know* things.

Maybe knowledge should be compared more with *belief*. When an animal does genuinely *learn* about its environment, what it gets is knowledge. But they can be mistaken just as we can be, in which case they come to have a false belief. Like knowledge, a belief can be retained indefinitely, and you do not lose them when unconscious. Also like knowledge, a belief can be true (which means simply that we can believe a true thought). Also, both have the same sort of effect on how we behave. If you know that there is a hole in the road, you will walk around it. You will behave the same way if you just believe it (even if the belief is false). Maybe the only difference between knowledge and belief is that beliefs can be false, while knowledge must be true. Whenever we discover that something we thought was known is false, we no longer *call* it knowledge.

Some people are tempted to say that there *can* be false knowledge. After all, people used to think that the Earth was flat, and how could they know differently? They were not being foolish, since it really does look flat. What this shows, however, is that we should have a term of praise for these *people*, such as saying that they were *reasonable*. We do not have to praise the belief itself by counting it an instance of *knowledge*.

JUSTIFIED TRUE BELIEF

Not all beliefs count as knowledge, since some are false. But what of *true* beliefs? Is knowledge the same as true belief? The following passage, also from Plato, explores just this question.

Theatetus: I cannot say, Socrates, that all opinion is knowledge, because there may be a false opinion; but I venture to assert, that knowledge is true opinion . . . and true opinion is surely unerring, and the results which follow from it are all noble and good.

Socrates: He who led the way into the river, Theatetus, said, "The experiment will show"; and perhaps if we go forward in the search, we may stumble upon the thing which we are looking for; but if we stay where we are, nothing will come of light.

Theatetus: Very true; let us go forward and try.

Socrates: The trail soon comes to an end, for a whole profession is against us.

Theatetus: How is that, and what profession do you mean?

Socrates: The profession of the great wise ones who are called orators and lawyers; for these persuade men by their art and make them think whatever they like, but they do not teach them. Do you imagine that there are any teachers in the world so clever as to be able to impart the full truth about past acts of robbery and violence, to men who were not eye-witnesses . . . ?

Theatetus: Certainly not, they can only persuade them.

Socrates: And would you not say that persuading them is making them have an opinion?

Theatetus: To be sure.

Socrates: When, therefore, judges are justly persuaded about matters which you can only know by seeing them, and not in any other way, and when thus judging of them from report they obtain a true opinion about them, they judge without knowledge, and yet are rightly persuaded, if they have judged well.

Theatetus: Certainly.

Socrates: And yet, O my friend, if true opinion in law courts and knowledge are one and the same, the perfect judge could not have judged rightly without knowledge; and therefore I must infer that they are not the same.

Theatetus: There is a distinction, Socrates, which I have heard made by someone else, but I had forgotten it. He said that true opinion, combined with reason, was knowledge, but that the opinion that had no reason was out of the sphere of knowledge; and that things of which there is no rational account are not knowable — such was the singular expression which he used — and that things which have a reason or explanation are knowable.[1]

Once we accept the point that all knowledge is true, this raises the possibility that to know something is just to believe something that is true. Plato shows in the preceding passage, however, that knowledge is not the same as true belief, for one can have true belief with *no good reason*.

1. Plato, *Theatetus*, trans. Benjamin Jowett, 187b–201e.

Here is a clearer example than Plato's. Suppose that you buy a lottery ticket but fall asleep early on the night the lottery results are announced. Suppose further that you do win the lottery and that you have a vivid early-morning dream that you did, waking up believing (if for only a moment) that you have won. Your belief is in fact true, but do you *know* that you have won? Philosophers agree that something is missing in such cases, and they have debated since Plato exactly what this is. They call this missing element "justification," in our sense, of a good reason. The only thing that is clear from Plato is that it is possible to get a true belief by sheer accident, and when this happens, you do not really know it. What matters is not only that your belief is true but that its *source* is good. This source must be *reliable* in yielding true beliefs, and dreams are not. As some philosophers put it, knowledge is *reliably caused* true belief.

BEING JUSTIFIED

Notice that nothing in Plato's account suggests that knowers must be *aware* of their reasons, as we must in making judgments. Recall our previous example of judging that a lake is ahead by the way it looks. Now dogs and the like certainly have eyes. If a dog were looking where you are looking, it would presumably look some way to the dog, perhaps much as it looks to you. If the dog comes to believe as a result of the way it looks that there is a lake ahead, then it has a justified belief. But even so, it does not follow that the dog must be *aware* of the way it looks. It could *have* justification or good reason without *knowing* that it does. Of course, it could not then *give* justification, but why conclude from this that it could not *have* justification nonetheless? Plato's account of knowledge says only that the true belief must come from a source that is in fact reliable. Vision is surely a reliable way to get the truth, in dogs as in us. So, when the dog gets the truth about the lake ahead, its source is reliable, and the dog does know, even though it is not a thinker.

JUDGMENTS, KNOWLEDGE, AND BELIEF

Let us summarize to get a clear picture of how judgment is related to both knowledge and belief. Plato explains for us the relationship between knowledge and belief. To know something is to believe something true with good reason. How, then, should judgment be compared with belief? Remember that judgment is momentary, whereas belief can be retained. Normally, when we judge something to be true, this causes us to believe that same thought (which may in fact be either true or false). The belief is retained for some period of time. As we have seen, the belief affects your behavior. You behave differently when you believe there is a tack on your chair than when you do not. This is true of *all* beliefs, regardless of subject matter; this is why we can tell what someone believes by what they do.

We have seen that other animals can acquire beliefs without making any judgments. Modern psychologists emphasize that we do, too. That is, *some* of our beliefs are acquired unconsciously. You may have come to believe that plastic bags are dangerous from having one over your face as a young child. This could happen without your ever knowing that you do have this belief. The fact that you do believe it, however, would show in your behavior, when you act afraid of plastic bags. Judgment is one way of coming to believe something. But judgment is always conscious. We can also acquire beliefs, as other animals do, unconsciously. When we do, we may never know that we do have these beliefs. This is important to remember when you try to think of what you believe.

FALLIBLE JUSTIFICATION

Plato's account of knowledge does not require that a source of information be **infallible**. It does not require that a true belief be produced in a way that *could never go wrong*. For example, a visual illusion sometimes tricks us into forming false beliefs by the way it looks. This does not mean that vision is never a source of knowledge. It just means that vision is fallible.

Beginning about three centuries ago, many philosophers sought sources of information that were not merely generally reliable but infallible. The history of this effort has been so disappointing that many philosophers today are complete "**fallibilists**," who deny that there are *any* errorproof ways of forming beliefs. Although this is not an issue we need to decide, it is highly important not to overestimate what, if anything, can be known infallibly. Indeed, it was a chief concern of the seventeenth-century English philosopher John Locke to show that we humans cause needless suffering by such overestimations. The basis of his view is expressed in the following (archaic) passage:

> He that would seriously set upon the search of Truth, ought in the first Place to prepare in his Mind the Love of it. For he that Loves it not, will not take much Pains to get it; nor be much concerned when he misses it. There is no Body in the Commonwealth of Learning, who does not profess himself a lover of Truth: and there is not a rational Creature that would not take it amiss to be thought otherwise of. And yet for all this one may truly say, there are very few lovers of Truth for Truths sake, even amongst those, who perswade themselves that they are so. How a Man may know whether he be so in earnest is worth enquiry: And I think there is this one unerring mark of it, *viz*. The not entertaining any Proposition with greater assurance that the Proofs it is built upon will warrant. Whoever goes beyond this measure of Assent, 'tis plain receives not Truth in the love of it; loves not Truth for Truths sake, but for some other bye end.[2]

Locke's main point is that someone who really cares about whether her beliefs are true will hold a belief only to the degree that is permitted by the evidence. And he suggests that many people hold their belief with a degree of conviction that

2. From *An Essay Concerning Human Understanding*, ed. Peter H. Nidditch (Oxford: Clarendon, 1975).

far exceeds what is supported by the evidence because of their desire to hold that particular belief. Someone might, for example, be absolutely sure he does not have cancer because he is too afraid to think otherwise. This is one explanation, at any rate, for why people are certain about matters when the evidence does not support this degree of confidence. We can appreciate why this is a serious human issue if we ask what *practical* difference it makes if someone does or does not regard his source of knowledge as infallible. How will it show in the person's behavior? The answer is clear. If someone believes he cannot be wrong, he will see no point in seriously *investigating* the matter any further. The issue is permanently closed for this person. He may discuss the matter, but only to convince others; and given his complete conviction, his attempts at persuasion will sound like preaching.

We must make decisions about what sources of information to accept. We also make decisions (whether we think about them or not) as to how to *regard* these sources. Do we take them as infallible or only as generally reliable? We show in our behavior what choice we make. For if we regard a source of information only as generally reliable, we hold the beliefs formed from it only *tentatively*, always being open to the possibility that new information will show them to be false. In Locke's words, we regard our beliefs as only "**probable**" and not "**certain**." But why did Locke think it so damaging to humanity that we tend to claim certainty when we are entitled to only probability?

THE HARM OF CERTAINTY

What we do depends in large part on what we believe. This is why many conflicts in life are based on differences of belief. The disagreement about whether God wants Palestine in the hands of the Jews or the Arabs, for example, has been a cause of war. If both sides in such disputes claim certainty for their belief, they have foreclosed all possibility of resolving the disagreement peacefully, by reasoning. For neither side has the humility to admit they could be wrong, and thus neither is willing to engage in an inquiry that might show that they are. (Even compromise is impossible, for this requires some alteration in one's original position.) This shows the very great importance of reasoning in human affairs. Reason is often the only peaceful and humane alternative to the use of force and violence in resolving conflicts. So, claiming certainty when one is entitled (at best) to probability can indeed do damage to humanity by inviting brutality.

THE IMPORTANCE OF JUSTIFICATION

Our judgments should be not only true but justified. When they are, the beliefs they cause in us count as knowledge. Shortly we will consider why truth is important. But first, let us consider why justification is important as well. We have seen that one can have true belief without justification. These have all the benefits of being true, whatever these are. So, why is it important that these beliefs be not just true but justified? The importance of justification is seen from the perspective of the inquirer. Unfortunately, thoughts do not come tagged as true or false, so that we can just see which ones are true. To find the true ones, we look for justifying reasons. It is possible to get the truth by sheer accident, but what this means is that the way you got the belief is not reliable (as in the lottery dream example). If you really want the truth, you will try to get it in a reliable way. This means that you look for justification.

THE IMPORTANCE OF TRUTH

Having seen that we must seek justification to seek the truth, let us ask why *truth* is important. Should we *care* if our beliefs are true? I do not mean to ask whether having true beliefs is good for us, that it will somehow add to our happiness. We will take up this question much later, in the epilogue. The question now is simply whether truth is good, whether it is a good thing to have true beliefs. Maybe the truth is important to some people and not others. Is having true beliefs important only to people who are curious, so that if you are not curious, it is not important to you?

A case can be made that the truth is important to *everyone*. Notice, first, that by "everyone" I mean every *thinker*. Truth is the *point* of all thinking. Whenever we think or say what we think, it is *assumed* that we want the thought we think to be true. To see this point for yourself, imagine making a statement, any statement, and then adding that you do not care about whether your statements are true. You will not be taken seriously, and this means that you will fail to make a statement at all. Since statements are just public expressions of thinking, the same absurdity results if you imagine thinking something to yourself and adding the thought that you do not care about whether anything you think is true. You would not be able to take yourself seriously as thinking at all. Analogously, it is assumed that players in chess are trying to win. If someone is not really trying to win, then they are not really playing. To appear as a thinker in the first place, even to yourself, you must be regarded as caring about the truth.

CREDULITY

In light of the fact that the truth is so clearly important to everyone, we may wonder whether it is practically important to point it out. Does not everyone, in fact, care about the truth? After all, humans are all frequently involved in *inquiry* of some kind or another. Even something as trivial as trying to find where to get good coffee is trying to find out some *truth*. So, do not all of us show, whenever we are investigating, a concern for the truth? To understand clearly how this is not so, consider the following passage by the nineteenth-century mathematician William K. Clifford:

> A ship owner was about to send to sea an emigrant ship. He knew that she was old, and not over-well built at first; that she had seen many seas and

climes, and often had needed repairs. Doubts had been suggested to him that possibly she was not seaworthy. These doubts preyed upon his mind and made him unhappy; he thought that perhaps he ought to have her thoroughly overhauled and refitted, even though this should put him to great expense. Before the ship sailed, however, he succeeded in overcoming these melancholy reflections. He said to himself that she had safely gone through so many voyages and weathered so many storms that it was idle to suppose that she would not come safely home from this trip also. He would put his trust in Providence, which could hardly fail to protect all these unhappy families that were leaving their fatherland to seek for better times elsewhere. He would dismiss from his mind all ungenerous suspicions about the honesty of builders and contractors. In such ways he acquired a sincere and comfortable conviction that his vessel was thoroughly safe and seaworthy; he watched her departure with a light heart, and benevolent wishes for the success of the exiles in their strange new home that was to be; and he got his insurance money when she went down in mid ocean and told no tales.

What shall we say of him? Surely this, that he was verily guilty of the death of those men. It is admitted that he did sincerely believe in the soundness of his ship; but the sincerity of his conviction can in no wise help him, because *he had no right to believe on the evidence as was before him.* He had acquired his belief not by honestly earning it in patient investigation, but by stifling his doubts. And although in the end he may have felt so sure about it that he could not think otherwise, yet inasmuch as had knowingly and willingly worked himself into that frame of mind, he must be held responsible for it.[3]

Clifford is *blaming* the ship owner, but not for the fact that he falsely believed that his ship was seaworthy. He condemns him, rather, for the careless way in which he *investigated* the matter. Notice that someone can come to have a false belief by investigating carefully (the evidence available could point in the wrong direction), in which they do their best and should not be blamed. This is why the ship owner is *not* faulted for the fact that his belief is false. And it would be no excuse if the ship owner had been right in thinking that the ship was seaworthy, since then he would have been merely lucky, having done nothing *himself* to ensure that his belief is true. The problem is not even that the ship owner is lazy, not collecting enough data; there is no suggestion of this in the actual story. It is rather that he allows himself to be more influenced by the data that support what he *wants* to be true. This can happen even if the ship owner himself really believes that he is doing an honest job of trying to get the truth and so really is conducting an inquiry (and not merely pretending that he is).

Let us suppose (as we may) that the ship owner really did investigate the matter of whether the ship is seaworthy and thus that he *believed* that he wanted the truth. And let us follow Clifford in giving the name of **credulity** to the way in which

---

3. From *Lectures and Essays* (London: Macmillan, 1897).

he investigated. Credulity is possible whenever the investigator cares about the outcome, wanting it to be a certain way. For then the desire to believe a certain way makes the data supporting that belief pleasant to contemplate and the data supporting the claim that that belief is false to be unpleasant. We like hearing what we want to be true and dislike hearing what we want to be false. Let us call the first kind of data "pro" data and the second kind "con" data. When we allow the pro data to have more effect on us, by paying more attention to it, then we eventually come out believing what we *want* to be true *because* we want it to be true. Now, it is not necessarily wrong to believe what you want to be true; sometimes an honest investigation shows that things are as you wished. What is wrong is letting your desire to believe a certain way bias how you look at the data. Credulous people turn away from unpleasant facts as if from a bad smell and luxuriate in what they want to hear.

AVOIDING CREDULITY

Once we understand what *causes* people to be credulous, we should expect it to be a very common phenomenon. After all, in being credulous people are just doing what they *feel* like doing. We can also see when credulity is more likely to exist. Since what causes people to be credulous is their desire to believe a certain way, the danger of being credulous grows with the strength of that desire. We are most likely to credulous, that is, about precisely those matters that we most *care* about!

But no matter how much we care about the outcome, we do not *have* to be credulous; if we did not have a choice, we could not be blamed for credulity (as Clifford blames the ship owner). The desire to believe a certain way only makes it difficult for us to investigate honestly, requiring the *will* to face unpleasant facts. If we have a reason for performing this unpleasant task, it is, of course, that we want the *truth*. If we care about the outcome, it will take *self-discipline* to avoid credulity. But whether we do discipline ourselves to confront the unpleasant data *is* in our control. This is why it is appropriate to blame people for being credulous.

It is an insidious fact about credulity that it is impossible to be aware of your own credulity while you are investigating credulously. Credulity must, in other words, involve *self-deception*. Remember that credulity is a way of investigating and that people who investigate always *think* they care about the truth, because making a discovery is their consciously adopted purpose. But they *show* us by the way they investigate that they do not *really* want the truth; if they did, they would confront the con data, even though it is unpleasant, just as earnestly as they contemplated the pro data. For only then, by allowing all the facts to have an equal influence, can one hope to have one's belief formed by the way the *world* is and not by the way one *wants* it to be.

Even though you cannot be aware of being credulous *while* you are being credulous, it does not follow that you cannot avoid credulity in the first place. Credulity is a case of *negligence*. It is appropriate to blame people for stepping on your feet, for example, even if they "did not mean it." They should have paid attention to what they were doing. It is the same with credulity. You *should* pay attention to the data even when it is unpleasant. The fact that you are negligent in attending to the data is no excuse.

It is possible to become aware of one's own credulity *after the fact.* There is a pattern in the choices that a credulous person makes in conducting an inquiry, which the person can discover, by reflecting on his own behavior, perhaps with the help of other observers. (But, of course, the only reason one would want to reflect on such matters is if one wants to know the truth.) Once one discovers that one has been credulous, however, the belief formed by the investigation is *lost:* the person is thrown back into the state of doubt. This is because what the discovery of credulity *means* is that you believe something because you *want* it to be true, and no one can take seriously that that is a good reason for thinking it *is* true. Credulity, like dreaming, is not a reliable way of getting the truth. This explains why anyone engaged in a credulous investigation must be self-deceived.

To appreciate fully the difficulty of overcoming credulity, we must realize that we prefer belief over doubt. The nineteenth-century American philosopher Charles Sanders Peirce (pronounced "purse") spoke of the *irritation* of doubt as the stimulus to inquiry. Belief, by contrast, was the state in which the irritation is removed. There is a sense of *mastery* that we have when contemplating our own beliefs. This comes from the fact that we regard our own beliefs as knowledge and thus as a form of *empowerment.* To realize that your belief is unfounded, as you do when you admit your own credulity, is to incur the irritation of doubt and suffer the humiliation, and perhaps the fear, of losing the sense of mastery. These problems are especially acute when the beliefs are those, such as philosophy considers, on which many of your plans are based. It takes courage to face these problems and confidence in one's own ability to find the truth through honest and diligent inquiry.

THE CREDULOUS CHARACTER

I have spoken of the "credulous person" so far only as a way of referring to someone who has been credulous in a certain investigation. In this sense of the term, all of us, unfortunately, are credulous people, for all of us, no doubt, have from time to time investigated some matter credulously. No doubt all of us sometimes engage in "wishful thinking." I have emphasized that it is possible to overcome credulity. The practical value of understanding credulity is that it prepares one mentally. If you know you want the outcome to be a certain way, force yourself to confront the con data patiently and attentively. If you find that you believe what you want to be true, consider the possibility that you got the belief credulously. This is what people do who genuinely care about the truth.

We may speak of a person as credulous, however, who is *characteristically* so. A person who shows repeatedly in the way she investigates that she cares little for the truth may be called a "credulous person" in this sense. It is important to realize that this indicates a weakness of character and is, as such, connected to other such weaknesses. We call people weak who lack the will to do what they know to be right. Everyone will say that they care about the truth, but those who are weak while inquiring do not. And the chances are good that if you allow yourself to be weak in one area of life, this will weaken you in other areas, resulting even in a tendency to credulity.

THE INNOCENCE OF BELIEF

Clifford blamed the ship owner just for the way he investigated and not for what he believed. I want to support Clifford further in this by making the case that we are *never* blameworthy for what we believe. This point is not obvious and is contradicted, for example, by those who believe that God punishes those who do not believe in him. But God is fair, and so he will not punish us for things that are not within our control. It is certainly not obvious that we can believe something just by choosing to do so.

To see the point I wish to make, consider the difference between raising your arm and raising a glass in your hand. You raise your arm just by deciding to do so; you cannot raise your glass in this direct way but must raise your arm while holding the glass. Whether the glass rises is something in your control, but you do not have *direct* control over it, as you do have direct control of your arm and hand. Now in the same way, you can turn your head directly, just by deciding to do so; but you cannot control how it will look after your head is turned in a certain direction. If it looks like there is a door in front of you, you cannot make it look like a swarm of butterflies just by deciding to make it look that way. You simply do not have the ability just to decide how things look, although you can influence indirectly how they will look by deciding in which direction to look.

My claim is that coming to believe something is analogous to having it look a certain way. You can decide whether to investigate some matter, and you can decide (or fail to decide) to avoid credulity in your investigation. But once the evidence stacks up sufficiently high on one side, you simply find yourself believing that way and have no choice over the matter. Now, how do I know this about *you*? My argument is remarkably simple: I have found in my experience that this is one of the many things over which I have no (direct) control. This being so, I am not responsible for what I believe. And I assume that in this respect you are like me.

It seems, however, that we often blame people for what they believe. If I believe the road is clear ahead while driving and it is not, I am said to be irresponsible. But this is because I should have *looked,* and if I had made *that* choice, then I would have believed that the road was not clear. So, what I am really responsible for is what I have direct control over, and my false belief is proof that I did not choose to look ahead. This is entirely in keeping with Clifford's point. It may seem superficially that we blame the ship owner for believing that his ship was seaworthy, but we really hold him at fault for the way he investigated the matter. His false belief *resulted* from his bad choice.

Suppose that I am mistaken and that I really can directly control what I believe, even though I have not yet discovered this power. And now suppose that I discover this new power, say, after an unusually sound sleep. Now that I am able to make myself believe something, would I not be responsible for what I believe? Consider what would happen if I exercised this power to believe. Suppose that I were offered a hundred dollars to believe for five minutes, with all sincerity, that I am Napoleon. I exercise my newfound power and really do believe this. Now suppose that I ask myself *why* I believe I am Napoleon. The answer is that I *wanted* to and that I *choose* to do so. Is this a *good reason for believing that to be true?* Plainly not. The moment after choosing to believe, we would find that our own reason was not good, and the belief would be *lost*. So, even if God gave us the power to believe in him just by deciding to do so, he would not hold us responsible for such beliefs, since in a moment's reflection they would be lost.

When you become convinced that we are responsible not for *what* we believe but for the way we *investigate*, it has a profound effect on how you look at people. When you discover that someone agrees with you, you may be glad that they have found the truth, but you will not admire them for that. When someone disagrees with you, though you think he is mistaken, you may still admire him for the way he investigated the issue. The truth is important, but it is not by whether someone has the truth that his *character* is measured. We admire and condemn people for only what is in their control, only for the *choices* that they make. Those who choose the difficult path of exercising will to avoid credulity show us that they really care about the truth.

TRUTH FOR TRUTH'S SAKE

There is, however, an important difference between caring about obtaining a *particular* truth in investigation and caring about whether your beliefs *in general* are true. People who really want to know how to make money in the stock market will investigate this particular issue without credulity. But even if they genuinely want the truth about this particular matter, they may fall far short of being the sort of people who care about whether their beliefs in general are true. When Locke said that "there are very few lovers of Truth for Truths sake," he meant not only that credulity is widespread but that very few people are concerned with the truth of *all* their beliefs. Suppose, for example, that someone really wants her beliefs about the stock market to be true. She will show that she does by questioning her own beliefs and being properly suspicious about what she wants to be true. She might know, for example, that she is tempted to believe a certain stock will rise rapidly, since if this is true, she will make a good deal of easy money. But knowing that she wants this to be true, she will examine the evidence closely and resist buying until she is sure she has investigated the matter thoroughly. Now this same person, though caring about the truth of her financial beliefs, may be entirely unconcerned about whether her religious or political beliefs are true. She may know quite well that other intelligent people disagree with her on these matters without this knowledge occasioning any doubt nor prompting any investigation. Why? Because she really does not care whether these beliefs are true, even though she herself would never admit this fact.

This example shows how one can care about some truths and not care about whether one's beliefs *in general* are true. Logic is concerned with our beliefs in general, and it will be found useful only to those "very few lovers of Truth for Truths sake." It is only those who want all of their beliefs to be true who will take a genuine interest in the question of how in general we get true beliefs. Do *you* care whether your beliefs are true? If you are honest, you may realize that you do not, if only because you have never had experience in thinking about your beliefs in general, as we do in logic.

CONCLUSION

Since logic is the study of how to think truly, we began by examining thoughts, the things that *are* true (or false). Truth is an objective matter: "subjective truth" is merely belief. Humans have a remarkable ability to be aware of thoughts, which we named the intellect. We use this ability to see relationships between the thoughts themselves, such as inconsistency or the fact that one follows from another. We are also rational, in having an ability to make judgments in light of reasons. These justifying reasons are to be distinguished from explanatory ones. The latter are sought for understanding and make our beliefs coherent. Rationality is not required for knowledge, since true beliefs can be justified without the knower being able to give justification. Much, if not all, of our knowledge is fallible; failure to admit this prevents the peaceful resolution of conflict through reasoning. Truth is important to everyone because truth is the point of all thinking. Despite the value of truth, many people show their lack of commitment to it by credulously avoiding unpleasant facts.

This chapter has given you reason for becoming a "lover of truth for truth's sake," if you are not one already. On the assumption that you have made this difficult step, we begin our look at reliable sources of truth in the next chapter by examining some uncontroversial examples.

STUDY QUESTIONS

1. What are thoughts? How are they different from sentences used to make statements?
2. What does it mean to say that a thought is true "for you"?
3. What does it mean for two thoughts to be *inconsistent*? Give an original example.
4. What does it mean for one thought to *follow* from another? Give an original example.
5. Give an original example in which one thought *explains* another.

6. What is *thinking* (in our sense of the word)? How can other animals *know* things and not *think* them?
7. Why do our judgments always seem right to us?
8. What does it mean to say that we are "rational beings"? Why must thinkers be rational beings?
9. In what way is all knowledge (of truths) justified?
10. What is a *fallibilist*, and how does such a person characteristically behave?
11. Why is it bad for humanity that we tend to overestimate the extent of knowledge which is certain?
12. What good is it to have true beliefs?
13. How is the credulous person self-deceived?
14. How can credulity be avoided?
15. Are we responsible for what we believe? What arguments were given for the conclusion that we are not?
16. How can one be noncredulous in some investigations and not really care whether one's beliefs in general are true? Give an original example that illustrates this possibility.

CHAPTER TWO

Direct Knowledge

WHERE DO WE GET THE TRUTH? To get the truth, we want good reasons, reasons that are adequate to justify our belief. One of the basic principles of logic is to have adequate reasons for the judgments we make. But where do we get these? Knowledge is not just true opinion. The source of knowledge must be reliable. This does not mean it must be infallible, yet it must still be generally reliable in yielding true beliefs.

There are any number of different sources of belief. If your neighbor shares some gossip with you, it is your neighbor who is the source of the beliefs you acquire. But where did your neighbor learn these facts? If we pursue this question, eventually we get back to an *original* source of knowledge. In this chapter, we survey views about the original sources of knowledge. Ideally, we want a comprehensive view of where we all originally get good, justifying reasons for our knowledge. For simplicity, when I speak of "sources" of knowledge, I will mean only original sources.

SENSATION AND INTROSPECTION

The most obvious and uncontroversial source of knowledge is that of the **senses.** In humans, as in many other higher animals on this planet, these consist of seeing, hearing, tasting, smelling, and feeling. But unlike at least many other animals, we humans also have what John Locke called "reflection," or what is now more often called **introspection.** This is like another sense, in that it is the ability to "look within" our own minds and tell what we are sensing, thinking, wanting, imagining, and so forth. To see the nature of these, it is useful to compare and contrast them. We will not in this text try to give justification for the claim that these are, as we normally think, good sources of information (although this is a perfectly legitimate area of philosophical investigation). We will, instead, assume (as we all in fact do) that they are genuine sources of knowledge and try to see what can, and cannot, be known by them. The reason for taking this direction has a good deal to do with the fact that this will help us to understand the nature of *scientific* knowledge (a main topic of the next chapter). For as we will see, although we learn an enormous amount with the help of these, including all of science, the main questions of philosophy transcend the reach of science and cannot, in general, be solved by any appeal to experience.

These two sources of knowledge were compared and contrasted by Locke, in the following passage, in which he defines "**experience**":

> Let us suppose the mind to be, as we say, white paper, void of all characters, without any ideas: — How comes it to be furnished? Whence comes it by that vast store which the busy and boundless fancy of man has painted on it with an almost endless variety? Whence has it all the *materials* of reason and knowledge? To this I answer, in one word, from EXPERIENCE. In that all our knowledge is founded; and from that it ultimately derives itself. Our observation employed either, about external sensible objects, or about the internal operations of our minds perceived and reflected on by ourselves, is that which supplies our understandings with all the *materials* of thinking. These two are the foundations of knowledge, from whence all the ideas we have, or can naturally have, do spring.
>
> First, our senses, conversant about particular sensible objects, do convey into the mind several distinct perceptions of things, according to those various ways wherein those objects do affect them. And thus we come by those *ideas* we have of *yellow, white, heat, cold, soft, hard, bitter, sweet*, and all those which we call sensible qualities; which when I say the senses convey into the mind, I mean, they from external objects convey into the mind what produces there those perceptions. This great source of most of the ideas we have, depending wholly upon our senses, and derived by them to the understanding, I call SENSATION.
>
> Secondly, the other fountain from which experience furnisheth the understanding with ideas is, — the perception of the operations of our own mind within us, as it is employed about the ideas it has got; — which operations, when the soul comes to reflect on and consider, do furnish the understanding with another set of ideas, which could not be had from things without. And such are *perception, thinking, doubting, believing, reasoning, knowing, willing,* and all the different acts of our minds; — which we being conscious of, and observing in ourselves, do from these receive into our understandings as distinct ideas as we do from bodies affecting our senses. This source of ideas every man has wholly in himself; and though it be not sense, as having nothing to do with external objects, yet it is very like it, and

might properly enough be called *internal sense*. But as I call the other Sensation, so I call this REFLECTION, the ideas it affords being such only as the mind gets by reflecting on its own operations within itself. By reflection, then, in the following part of this discourse, I would be understood to mean, that notice which the mind takes of its own operations, and the manner of them, by reason whereof there come to be ideas of these operations in the understanding. These two, I say, viz. external material things, as the objects of SENSATION, and the operations of our own minds within, as the objects of REFLECTION, are to me the only originals from whence all our ideas take their beginnings. The term *operations* here I use in a large sense, as comprehending not barely the actions of the mind about its ideas, but some sort of passions arising sometimes from them, such as is the satisfaction or uneasiness arising from any thought.[1]

OBJECTS OF EXPERIENCE

Locke calls sensation and reflection (introspection) "operations of the mind," and when they do operate normally, they make us aware and thus yield knowledge. Sensation is thus the operation of the senses, including seeing, hearing, and so forth. When a sense is operating, something happens in the mind, a state of awareness is created, such as looking a certain way or sounding a certain way. These are not themselves beliefs, but they immediately create beliefs, about objects seen or heard. Locke calls these *objects* of sensation "**external**," meaning by this that they exist outside, or independently of, the mind. When I turn my head and it looks like my dog is there, the occurrence of this "visual sensation" triggers the belief in me that my dog is there. The dog is the "object" of my awareness, and it exists independently of my mind. (The dog does not cease to exist when I stop seeing it.) In this case, the object of awareness is literally "external" to my body, but this is not in general necessary. If I feel my stomach ache, I am feeling a part of myself, but my stomach is still "external" in the technical sense that Locke means: my stomach does not disappear when I stop feeling it.

The objects of introspection, by contrast, are **internal**. This means that when we introspect, what we learn about is *just* within our own mind. Locke calls this "reflection" because, when we introspect, we look back on what has been going on in our mind. To be clear about this difference between sensation and introspection, it helps to see how the two often combine. Suppose that I know that there is water ahead by seeing it. This is a case of sensation and hence of an operation of the mind that I may know about by introspection. It may be tempting to say that what I know by introspection is that I see that there is water ahead. But this is not quite right, since in saying this I mention something "external," the water ahead. What I know by introspection is just what is going on in my mind, and that is how it *looks*. If I say

---

1. From *An Essay Concerning Human Understanding* (1689), Book 2, Chapter 1.

that it looks like there is water ahead then I do describe just my own mind, for this could be true even if there was no water there (as when "seeing" a mirage). So, the simple-sounding thought that *I see water ahead* is something I know only by combining the knowledge I get from sensation with that which I get from introspection.

In the fashion of his day, Locke marks the distinction between these two sources of knowledge by the "ideas" we get from them. Sensation gives us ideas of colors, shapes, feelings of warmth and cold, hardness, and so forth. Introspection gives us ideas of mental operations such as perceiving, thinking, doubting, and so on. We can understand this better by realizing that to have an idea is to be able to make *discriminations*. To have the idea of red is to be able to compare red things, to see how they are similar, and to distinguish them from things of other colors. One great advantage of thinking of ideas in this way is that it reminds us of the important fact that having ideas is something that makes a difference in how we *behave*. An animal that has the idea of red can *do* something: it can tell the difference between red and (say) blue things and use this information in getting around. Thinking of ideas as capacities for discrimination also reminds us that we possess one idea only by possessing contrasting ones: You cannot have the idea of red without ideas of other colors to contrast with red.

Locke is, therefore, contrasting these two sources of knowledge by the sorts of things we are able to compare and contrast or discriminate among. In sensation, a creature is aware of things external to its own mind, being able to recognize similarities and differences in color, shape, temperature, texture, and so on. But in introspection, what is discriminated are operations, or states, of the mind itself. And Locke makes clear that it is only one's *own* mind that one knows this way. (We do not, for example, really *feel* another's pain; whenever we know there is a pain by feeling it, we automatically know it is our own.) In introspection, you discriminate your feelings from your visual sensations, your sensations in general from your desires, and these from your beliefs. Just as in sensation we can contemplate a single thing, such as a flower, and distinguish its shape from its color, we can contemplate ourselves in introspection and distinguish states of mind.

THE EXTENT OF INTROSPECTION

Many students have difficulty seeing what introspection encompasses. There is a famous discussion in modern philosophy that will help. In the following, the seventeenth-century French philosopher and mathematician René Descartes presents a possibility that will help us to understand more clearly what introspection covers:

> Several years have now elapsed since I first became aware that I had accepted, even from my youth, many false opinions for true, and that consequently what I afterward based on such principles was highly doubtful . . . [but] reason convinces me that I ought not the less carefully to withhold

belief from what is not entirely certain and indubitable, than from what is manifestly false, it will be sufficient to justify the rejection of the whole if I shall find in each some ground for doubt. Nor for this purpose will it be necessary even to deal with each belief individually, which would be truly an endless labor; but, as the removal from below of the foundation necessarily involves the downfall of the whole edifice, I will at once approach the criticism of the principles on which all my former beliefs rested. . . . All that I have, up to this moment, accepted as possessed of the highest truth and certainty, I received either from or through the senses. I observed, however, that these sometimes misled us; and it is the part of prudence not to place absolute confidence in that by which we have even once been deceived. . . . But it may be said, perhaps, that, although the senses occasionally mislead us respecting minute objects, and such as are so far removed from us as to be beyond the reach of close observation, there are yet many other of their informations (presentations), of the truth of which it is manifestly impossible to doubt; as for example, that I am in this place, seated by the fire, clothed in a winter dressing gown, that I hold in my hands this piece of paper, with other intimations of the same nature. . . . Though this be true, I must nevertheless here consider that I am a man, and that, consequently, I am in the habit of sleeping, and representing to myself in dreams those same things, or even sometimes others less probable, which the insane think are presented to them in their waking moments. How often have I dreamt that I was in these familiar circumstances, that I was dressed, and occupied this place by the fire, when I was lying undressed in bed? . . . I perceive so clearly that there exist no certain marks by which the state of waking can ever be distinguished from sleep, that I feel greatly astonished; and in amazement I almost persuade myself that I am now dreaming. . . . I suppose, accordingly, that all the things which I see are false (fictitious); I believe that none of those objects which my fallacious memory represents ever existed; I suppose that I possess no senses; I believe that body, figure, extension, motion, and place are merely fictions of my mind. What is there, then, that can be esteemed true? Perhaps this only, that there is absolutely nothing certain. . . . But how do I know that there is not something different altogether from the objects I have now enumerated, of which it is impossible to entertain the slightest doubt? Is there not a God, or some being, by whatever name I may designate him, who causes these thoughts to arise in my mind? But why suppose such a being, for it may be I myself am capable of producing them? Am I, then, at least not something? . . . But I before denied that I possessed senses or a body; I hesitate, however, for what follows from that? Am I so dependent on the body and the senses that without these I cannot exist? But I had the persuasion that there was absolutely nothing in the world, that there was no sky and no earth, neither minds nor bodies; was I not, therefore, at the same time, persuaded that I did not exist? Far from it; I assuredly existed, since I was persuaded. But there is I know not what being, who is possessed at once of the highest power and the deepest cunning, who is constantly employing all his ingenuity in deceiving me.

CHAPTER TWO: DIRECT KNOWLEDGE   41

> Doubtless, then, I exist, since I am deceived; and, let him deceive me as he may, he can never bring it about that I am nothing, so long as I shall be conscious that I am something. So that it must, in fine, be maintained, all things being maturely and carefully considered, that this proposition (pronunciatum) *I am, I exist*, is necessarily true each time it is expressed by me, or conceived in my mind.... I am therefore, precisely speaking, only a thinking thing, that is, a mind (*mens sive animus*), understanding, or reason, terms whose signification was before unknown to me. I am, however, a real thing, and really existent; but what thing? The answer was, a thinking thing.[2]

In this passage, Descartes is looking for certain knowledge, something he can believe without possibly being wrong. He argues that all knowledge by sensation is fallible. This itself is not surprising, since everyone knows about sensory illusions such as mirages or ringing in the ears. The dramatic possibility he raises, however, is that we might have no knowledge from sensation at all! Suppose that all of your life you have been in one extended dream, so that you do not really know about any of the external objects that seem so familiar to you. You might think this is absurd, because, after all, what is a dream if there is no waking life with which to contrast it? Well, then, what if all of your sensations have been created by an evil demon, so that there really are no such things as external objects? There only *appear* to be furniture and houses, trees and rocks, and so on. Descartes eventually argues to his own satisfaction that he can be sure of such things after all. (His argument is based on his belief in God, who would not permit such massive deception.) The only positive result reached in the prior passage is that he can be certain at least that *he exists*. Even if he has been dreaming all his life, he cannot take seriously that he himself is only part of the dream. For this would mean that *he* does not really exist. But he finds that he cannot doubt of his own existence. For even if he is merely filled with doubt, it follows still that he *exists*.

Now I said that the possibility raised by Descartes will help us to understand *introspection*. Here is how. Suppose that you are in Descartes's initial position, of wondering whether it is all a dream. If this were so, you would have *no* knowledge by sensation. Remember that sensation tells us only about external things, and it is our own knowledge of *any* of these that is called into question by Descartes. While in this state of doubt, for all you know, there *are no* external things. Suppose that this is so. Is there anything you would still be aware of? You might be tempted to say no, since all seems illusion. But this is not right. You would still know about what is going on in your mind. You would still be awake, knowing how it looks, how it feels, what you are thinking, what you want, and so on. You would still have knowledge by introspection. What the dream hypothesis does for us is to show us more clearly what we know by introspection, by peeling away in imagination all knowledge by sensation. If you want to see what you know *just by* introspection,

---

2. From *Meditations on First Philosophy*, 1 and 2, trans. John Veitch.

imagine that there is no external world, and examine what kind of awareness would be left.

SENSATION WITHOUT INTROSPECTION

We have seen that introspection is an entirely distinct operation from sensation, giving rise to an entirely different kind of knowledge. Moreover, introspection is a "second-order level" of awareness, in being awareness *of* awareness. In seeing my dog, I am aware of my dog by having a visual sensation, the way it looks. My visual sensation is a state of awareness, the sort of state any animal is in when its sense of vision is working. If I *think* of the way it looks to me, then I have a *second* state of awareness, a *thought* about the visual sensation. It is thus clearly possible that an animal could have sensation without introspection. And this, I suggest, is the way it is with at least most animals around us. I believe my dog, for example, sees his food bowl and thereby knows about an external object, but he has no capacity to know about how it looks to him. Of course, in seeing the food bowl, it *does* look a certain way to him, but this does not mean that he actually knows how it looks. In Locke's terms, my dog has the sorts of "ideas" that enable him to recognize external objects. We know this, because he shows through his behavior that he distinguishes shapes, smells, locations, and so forth, of the objects around him. But as Locke points out, he would have the ideas by which we describe minds — ideas of perception, of beliefs, of thoughts, of wants, and so on — only if he can introspect. Of course, an animal could have ideas of external objects without *also* having ideas of how it is aware of these objects.

INTROSPECTION AND SELF-CONTROL

Introspection gives us a certain control over our beliefs and actions. This point is explained in the following passage by the contemporary American philosopher Christine Korsgaard:

> A lower animal's attention is fixed on the world. Its perceptions are its beliefs and its desires are its will. It is engaged in conscious activities, but it is not conscious *of* them. That is, they are not the objects of its attention. But we human animals turn our attention on to our perceptions and desires themselves, and we are conscious *of* them. That is why we can think *about* them.
>
> And this sets us a problem that no other animal has. It is the problem of the normative. For our capacity to turn our attention onto our own mental activities is also a capacity to distance ourselves from them and to call them into question. I perceive, and I find myself with a powerful impulse to believe. But I back up and bring that impulse into view and then I have a certain distance. Now the impulse doesn't dominate me and now I have a problem. Shall I believe? Is this perception really a *reason* to believe?

I desire and I find myself with a powerful impulse to act. But I back up and bring that impulse into view and then I have a certain distance. Now the impulse doesn't dominate me and now I have a problem. Shall I act? Is this desire really a *reason* to act? The reflective mind cannot settle for perception and desire, not just as such. It needs a *reason*. Otherwise, as long as it reflects, it cannot commit itself or go forward.[3]

The "reflective" mind is the mind that "brings into view" impulses to believe or to act. Korsgaard is making the point that without introspection we would have no choice but to believe what we are inclined to believe and to do what we feel most like doing. This is the state of "lower" animals, so called simply because they lack this awareness of their own minds. We who can bring our impulses into view, however, can decide whether or not to be influenced by them. What good is it to have this power? Is it simply a nuisance that interferes with the joy of spontaneity? The senses are good for informing an animal of its immediate environment, showing it things it needs to approach or avoid. But if I know my dog is here by the way it looks, what good does it do to know also how it looks? The answer is that looks can deceive. Sensations naturally create in us the *tendency* to believe that things are as they appear. But by introspecting we can pay attention to how things appear and question whether they really are that way. A mirage inclines us to believe that there is water ahead; but we can think of how it looks, and why this appearance might be deceiving. We can distinguish between "appearance and reality," deciding whether to trust our senses and say, "This is *real*," or deny them and say, "This is only *apparent*." So also we can question our beliefs, distinguishing between ones that are *true* and those that are *false*; we can question the objects of our desires, distinguishing between those that are *good* and those that are *bad*; and we can sense what we are inclined to do and determine whether doing that would be *right* or *wrong*. Introspection is valuable because it is only by being *aware* of the operations of the mind that we can see when they go wrong and have the opportunity to correct them.

INTROSPECTION AND THINKING

In the last chapter, we contrasted ourselves with animals that could not think. Because all of philosophy is about how to think, let us ask whether a thinker will need to introspect. We have both abilities. But can we make sense of the idea of creatures that think but that do not introspect? Recall that judgment is the act of first coming to think something is true, and when we make a judgment, we do so in light of reasons for thinking one way instead of the other. When you judge that there is water ahead, it is like answering the question of whether there is water ahead. You realize that you *could* have *denied* that there is water ahead, but if you had, you would have been *mistaken*.

---

3. From *The Tanner Lectures on Human Values*, vol. 15 (Salt Lake City: University of Utah Press, 1980).

In making a judgment, we are conscious of having made a decision on the issue at hand, and since we think our decision is right, the alternative decision must appear mistaken. Now, often we *are* mistaken in our judgments, and sometimes we find out that we have been. If you judge that there is water ahead and it turns out to be a mirage, you will not continue to think that there is water ahead. You will retract this judgment by thinking that you *thought* there was water ahead. This is where introspection comes in. If you had simply thought first that there is water ahead and then that there is not, your two thoughts would be *inconsistent*. But you avoid having inconsistent beliefs by describing yourself as having only *thought* one was true. Introspection allows you to see yourself as having had a false belief. By using this ability when you change your mind, you are able to avoid inconsistency and see yourself as doing so.

INTROSPECTION AND SPEECH

Introspection gives a special quality to human speech. Many other animals *communicate* with others of their kind by doing things that in fact inform the others of something that they know. A bird may see an incoming predator and give out a cry that signals this information to the other birds of its flock. Humans not only communicate information, however; they know that they do. When we give a cry of alarm, we not only mean something by it; we know what we mean. This requires introspection. Knowing what you mean when you speak is knowing what you want and are trying to say. The capacity to understand our own talk enables us to construct *conversations*, in which later remarks are made as deliberate additions to earlier ones. It is possible for us accordingly to tell stories or engage in debate. Because we can talk about our talk, we can expand on what has been said or question it. Not only can we say things that are in fact true or false, complete or incomplete, appropriate or inappropriate; we can talk about things said and question whether they can be *assessed* in such ways. This not only allows the continual development of human culture but also enables humans to achieve a higher level of cooperation. Animals that cooperate only instinctively, such as ants and termites, and even those that can become habituated to new surroundings, such as dogs and deer, easily find themselves at a loss in new situations. Their instincts and habits in such situations are not likely to lead them into coordinated action that is mutually beneficial. Humans, on the other hand, can achieve through language a shared understanding of the new situation and create a new plan of coordinated action. This has enabled them to live around the planet in environments to which their ancestors were not adapted.

DIRECT KNOWLEDGE

Now that we have seen how sensation and introspection are different, let us see how they are alike. They are both sources of knowledge, but Locke means to imply more than this when he suggests that we may consider introspection an "inner sense."

There is something importantly correct about this comparison that calls for thorough explanation. Let us *contrast* the knowledge that is obtained by both kinds of experience with knowledge that is obtained by **inference.** We saw in the last chapter that the ancient Greeks called us the rational animals, since we could give justification for what we believe. When we give justification, we appeal to something we already know and use this to show that our belief is true. We might justify our belief that deer have passed through during the night, for example, by citing our knowledge of tracks in the snow. When we establish the truth of our belief this way, we do so by making an inference *from* what we already knew *to* what we believe.

It is not difficult to see that if there is any knowledge at all, some of it *must* be obtained *without* inference. The reason is that we must already have knowledge before we can make any inferences at all. This "prior" knowledge is called "**direct,**" because knowledge by inference is always obtained indirectly, through something already known. Now, this could itself be derived from a prior inference, but there could not be an infinite series of them, since we must know something to begin with before we can make the first inference. The important comparison that Locke wishes to make between sensation and introspection is that both are sources of *direct* knowledge.

When we give justification for something we know by inference, we give some other truth that we already know. Since all knowledge is justified, it must be possible to give justification for this former knowledge too. We need to know some truths directly, however, before we can know anything by inference. How, then, can we give justification for what we know directly? Suppose that you know that deer passed by in the night by inference from the fact that there are recognizable tracks in the snow. How do you know that there are tracks in the snow? You would probably say that you see them. This does not mean, however, that you first knew that you see the tracks and then you infer from this that there are tracks in the snow. To know by sensation of external things, such as tracks in the snow, you do not actually have to be thinking about how you are aware of them.

As we have seen, sensation does not require introspection. It is true that in making a *judgment* you are aware of your reasons, and often your judgment results in direct knowledge. So we may ask, "Of what reason are you aware when you judge directly that there are tracks there?" Since this example involves knowledge by sensation (specifically, vision), your reason will be the sensory experiences themselves. When you see the tracks, it looks a certain way, and *the way it looks* is the experience that is the reason for your direct judgment. This is why you can answer the question "How do you know there are tracks there?" by saying, "By the way it looks." If you judge that there are tracks there by the way it looks, it is the visual experience itself that makes your judgment appear *right*. How do you know of this visual experience? Notice that it makes no sense to ask, "How do you know the visual experience is true?" Only thoughts are true. Recall, however, that knowledge of truths is contrasted with knowledge of things. You would know, in the sense of being *familiar with*, your visual experience. This kind of knowledge does not have to be expressed with a thought. Giving justification for something you know by inference involves turning from one thought to another thought. Since this other thought must also be known, either you repeat the process by turning to another thought, or you give the experience itself that justifies a thought known directly.

To give justification for a direct judgment, you cite the relevant experience. This is our solution to the problem of how to give justification for direct knowledge. This means that for any form of direct knowledge, there must be a kind of experience on which such knowledge is based. Because introspection is a source of direct knowledge, there must be "introspective experiences." This is a harmless assumption, provided that not much is read into it. To introspect is to become aware of yourself in a certain way. Other ways of being aware of yourself are possible, including looking in the mirror. We can describe the different ways of being aware of yourself as different "experiences" of yourself. When we use our power of introspection, we become aware of ourselves by an "introspective experience."

THE SUBJECTIVITY OF EXPERIENCE

Sensation and introspection are alike in a way other than the fact that both are sources of direct knowledge. What you know directly by them provides you with a certain *perspective*, that only you have. Let us consider sensation first. There is something in common to the external things you know by sensation. They have *locations*. You can distinguish one from another by the fact that they are in different places, even when they appear exactly alike. Two coins of the same denomination, made in the same year, at the same mint, can look and feel exactly the same. Yet we think of them as different coins when we see them in different places. Moreover, the places where things are can all be identified in relation to where you are now. Each is a certain distance from you, in a certain direction. And no other person shares the same place where you are at the same time. So, at any time in which we are using sensation, each of us has a different view of the world.

"Lower" animals, which lack introspection, also have a unique perspective. But they have no way of knowing that they do. We who can introspect can reflect on our sensations and the direct knowledge they produce. When you do, you see that you are unique. You see that you have a unique place at the present point in time. We also realize that the present is but one moment in time, poised between the past and the future. (There is no evidence that any other animals, including chimpanzees, have this sense of time.) We need a sense of time to correct inconsistencies in what we think. You see a balloon filled with water, and then you see it break. You think first that the balloon is full and then that the balloon is empty. But are these not inconsistent thoughts? How can the same balloon be both full and empty? We resolve the apparent inconsistency by distinguishing two different times in which the balloon is full or empty. There is no inconsistency in the thoughts that the balloon is empty *now* but *before* it was full. At any time, we can distinguish the present moment from the past and the future. We can distinguish other places from where we are at that time. Simply put, we can distinguish now from then and here from there.

THE INTELLECT

The next chapter explores the knowledge that we get by inference from sensation and introspection: how we know about the "then and there." In this chapter, we are canvassing original sources of knowledge, and so far, it is only these two sources of direct knowledge that we have examined. These are uncontroversial sources of knowledge, if any are (though expect almost anything to be questioned at some time in philosophy!). What other sources of direct knowledge are there? Shortly we will look at a couple of sources of belief that are very controversial. Before then, let us reexamine the intellect.

The intellect is the power to be aware of thoughts. We "thinkers" are capable not only of believing thoughts but of knowing what we believe. We show this especially clearly when we discuss a particular thought, giving reasons for it or denying it, giving an explanation for it, using it to build a story, and so on. Very often we cannot tell that a particular thought is true or false unless we have extraneous information about it. To know that there is a tree in front of you, it is not enough to contemplate the thought with your eyes closed. You must also have sensory information, such as how it looks, before you can know whether it is true. But there are some thoughts that appear to be **self-evident.** Consider this obvious example: either you are married or you are not. Do not be distracted by the fact that it is obviously true. The point is simply to see that it is possible to know that a thought is true without having any information other than that of the thought itself. Here is another example: If neither Sally nor Fred will live in the city, then Sally will not live in the city. Once again, all you need to tell whether it is true is to understand the thought itself.

Let us understand by the intellect not only the ability to be aware of thoughts, singly or in combination with others, but also the ability to grasp self-evident truths. The intellect, then, appears to be a third source of direct knowledge. Some philosophers would not allow this. One worry of theirs is that the whole category of the self-evident seems to invite misuse. There have been people in the past who were quite sure that what they believed is self-evident and so did not bother to give justification. Controversial religious or ethical beliefs were simply asserted by them. To help avoid this problem, one thing to notice is that saying of a thought that it is self-evident is not the same as saying that it is *certain.* You can be mistaken in judging that some thought is self-evident. A good rule to follow is that a thought may be considered self-evident only if it is uncontroversial. If it is self-evident to you, it ought to be to others. So, if they do not accept it, they obviously do not find it self-evident. It has seemed rather plain to many philosophers that there *are* self-evident thoughts, such as the two examples given earlier. We will assume that the intellect is a source of direct knowledge, but we admit that this is not entirely uncontroversial.

Once again we may cite Locke for clearly recognizing (albeit in other words) the fact that the intellect is a distinct source of knowledge:

> [I]f we reflect on our own ways of Thinking, we shall find, that sometimes the Mind perceives the Agreement or Disagreement of two *Ideas* immediately

by themselves, without the intervention of any other: And this, I think, we may call *intuitive Knowledge*. For in this, the Mind is at no pains of proving or examining, but perceives the Truth, as the Eye doth light, only by being directed toward it. Thus the Mind perceives, that *White* is not *Black,* That a *Circle* is not a *Triangle,* That *Three* are more than *Two,* and equal to *One* and *Two.* . . . This part of Knowledge is irresistible, and like the bright Sun-shine, forces it self immediately to be perceived.[4]

The extent to which we use self-evident truths should not be underestimated. Consider this common sort of example. You say the Earth is round, and I say it is flat. Clearly, we disagree with one another, but *how do you know* that our two thoughts are inconsistent? You will probably say that it is obvious, that you "just see" that both cannot be true. Notice that this amounts to saying that a certain thought is self-evident—namely, the thought that *if the Earth is round, it is not flat.* The common phenomenon of recognizing disagreements always involves the use of intellect to grasp self-evident truths. So does the phenomenon of recognizing implications. If all killing is wrong, then killing in self-defense is wrong. Now look at the last sentence and ask yourself how you know that the whole thought it expresses is true. Again, you will probably say that it is obvious or that you just see it. But, of course, you do not literally see it, by using your eyes. As primates, seeing is one of our favorite forms of getting direct knowledge. This is why we use it to describe getting direct knowledge from other sources, including the intellect.

MEMORY

What about *memory?* How do you know that you had breakfast this morning? You will probably say that you *remember* it. Should we, then, add memory as another source of knowledge? There is something to be said for this. Let us suppose that you are asked the name of your kindergarten teacher, and the name "just comes to" you. If asked, "How do you know this is the right name?" you might say simply that it *seems* to be right. Some philosophers would say that your judgment about the name is based on a "memorial" experience and that (if correct) this is what justifies your judgment. Even so, anything you know by memory will still have to come from some other source.

Because we are concerned with *original* sources of knowledge, we will not count memory as a source of knowledge. Some philosophers insist that memory is not a source of knowledge but only the capacity to retain knowledge. This is also in keeping with the idea that it is not an original source.

---

4. From *An Essay Concerning Human Understanding,* ed. Peter H. Nidditch (Oxford: Oxford University Press, 1975), Book IV, Chapter II.

ETHICAL INTUITION

By sensation we are aware of our immediate surroundings. By introspection we are aware of what is going on in our own mind. By intellect we are aware of thoughts, and connections between them.

Are these *all* the original sources of knowledge? Many, but not all, philosophers think so. As we will see when we get to metaphysics, these three sources together enable us to know about a vast amount of reality. But it may be that there are beliefs that can be justified only by other sources. We will complete our survey by looking at two sources that are definitely controversial. The first pertains to our knowledge of ethical truths.

To take what I hope is an uncontroversial example, it is wrong to kill humans for fun. Let us grant that this is true. How do we know it? Some philosophers have been convinced that despite the fact that this is clearly true, we cannot know it given only our three sources of sensation, introspection, and intellect. We do not, for example, see the *wrongness* of killing the way we can see blood and corpses. These philosophers have supposed that there is still another source of knowledge, concerned specifically with ethical truths, about how things *ought* to be. Ethical "intuition" allows us to know directly that certain things are right or wrong. We have the power of just "seeing" the difference between right and wrong. This is not a popular position today. A major problem is that people sometimes disagree about what is right or wrong. They disagree about when it is wrong to wage war, for example, or whether abortions amount to murder. But if such truths are known by "intuition" and we all have this power, why would we disagree? And if one can be mistaken in such judgments, how can they be corrected? Without answers to these questions, the supposed power of "intuiting" ethical truths will not appear *reliable*.

RELIGIOUS EXPERIENCE

Another controversial source of knowledge is religious experience. Many people are, for example, convinced that they have direct knowledge of God. They are sure that God has, at one time or at many times, "appeared" to them. This does not mean that they literally see God, by using their eyes. They are convinced that, perhaps at special moments, they have felt God's presence. Some of these people experience God as being involved in their lives, giving encouragement at difficult times, or simply conveying a sense of unlimited love. It is no objection to this view to say that God cannot be known by the senses. For as we have seen, sensation is but one of several sources of knowledge that we commonly accept.

There are a couple of problems with this view, however, that are worth noting. One is that many people claim to have compelling religious experiences that reveal an ultimate being other than God. People who have what are called "mystical" experiences claim to have an experience of the whole world as a seamless whole in which we "individuals" are absorbed. This is not the experience of a loving being, capable of thought and communication with us. Can we allow that both kinds of religious experience are equally valid? A second problem is that many people do not have such experiences at all. We all share the conviction that there are self-evident thoughts, so the claim that the intellect is a source of knowledge simply codifies this. But because many of us have not had either the mystical experience or the religious experience of the presence of God, the religious experience in general remains controversial.

These remarks about ethical intuition and the religious experience should not be taken as disproofs of their legitimacy. They are meant only to explain why they are controversial. And as we will see in Parts Two and Three, many religious and ethical thinkers have not relied on them. If nothing else, they help to illustrate how important it is to identify what sources of information are genuine sources of knowledge. It is also worth emphasizing that we have seen no reason to suppose that any particular list is complete.

CONCLUSION

Direct knowledge provides a basis from which inferences can be made. In humans, sensation and introspection supply much of this. The intellect also supplies some, pertaining to thoughts themselves. Sensation can exist without introspection and presumably does in many other species of animals. Sensation teaches us and them about external things, from one's own point of view. The extent of introspection is only one's own mind, as may be seen clearly with the dream hypothesis of Descartes. Introspection is what makes possible self-control. It enables thinkers to remain consistent by correcting their judgments. It also lends to human speech a perspective from which improvements in thought and talk can be made.

These three sources of knowledge are relatively uncontroversial. Let us next explore the topic of how we use these to make inferences to the unobserved.

STUDY QUESTIONS

1. What are the two kinds of experience, according to Locke? Explain each in general and give examples.
2. Explain how both count as sources of knowledge by the Platonic account of knowledge given in the last chapter.
3. Suppose it is true now that you know that you feel a pen in your hand. Explain how both kinds of experience are needed for this knowledge.
4. Describe an imaginary example of an animal that has sensation but no introspection. What would its consciousness be like and not be like?
5. What advantage do we have by being able to introspect?
6. What would you honestly say in response to Descartes's question "How do you know you are not dreaming now?" What would he say in reply?

7. Why must there be *direct* knowledge for there to be any knowledge at all?
8. What is knowledge by inference? Give several examples.
9. What does it mean to say that experience gives us knowledge only of a subjective perspective?
10. How does introspection allow you to make your beliefs consistent when you change your mind?
11. Give an original example of a self-evident truth that allows a disagreement to be recognized.
12. What objections are there to the idea that we have ethical or religious "intuition"?

CHAPTER THREE

Empirical Knowledge

HOW DO WE KNOW what we cannot observe? We observe external things by sensation. We observe our present state of mind by introspection. In a way, we also "observe" thoughts themselves by the intellect. Each of these sources of knowledge provides us with *direct* knowledge. Memory allows us to retain and recall knowledge acquired directly in the past. In this way we do have some direct knowledge of events not presently occurring. But even when we allow this, it is clear that a vast amount of what we know has not yet been explained. Through sensation and introspection, you know that you have a certain perspective on the world. But you know that there is much more. Historians tell us of events from long ago, even before any humans lived. We are sure that the sun will rise tomorrow, that there are galaxies other than the Milky Way, that the things around us are composed of atoms, and that other people have minds. Yet we know none of these directly.

In all of these examples, even though our knowledge of the phenomenon in question is not direct, we still need some direct knowledge to have this knowledge at all. This is because (as we saw in the last chapter) knowledge by inference always depends ultimately on direct knowledge. We would not know whether there were dinosaurs without observing bones and footprints. We know that the sun will rise tomorrow only by having observed it rising in the past. Scientists know of distant galaxies only after observing photographs taken from telescopes. And we know what others are thinking and feeling only by observing what they do. In short, we know about all these cases of "the unobserved" only by inference from what we know directly.

Not all inferences from what we know directly are good. It would be wrong to infer from the presence of dinosaur bones that they came from elephants. Juries sometimes convict the wrong person by making a bad inference from the evidence before them. Some people make "premature" judgments about someone else's character after knowing them for only a short time. So, the question arises as to how to make such inferences *well*. Once again the question is one of *how to think*. But now the question is specifically how to think about the unobserved, *given* what we know directly in observation.

HUME'S ACCOUNT

Our understanding of these issues has been greatly advanced by the eighteenth-century Scottish philosopher David Hume; the following passage conveys his main idea:

> It may . . . be a subject worthy of curiosity, to enquire what is the nature of that evidence, which assures us of any real existence and matter of fact, beyond the present testimony of our senses, or the records of our memory. . . .
> All reasonings concerning matters of fact seem to be founded on the relation of *Cause and Effect*. By means of that relation alone we can go beyond the evidence of our memory and senses. If you were to ask a man, why he believes any matter of fact, which is absent; for instance, that his friend is in the country, or in FRANCE: he would give you a reason; and this reason would be some other fact; as a letter received from him, or the knowledge of his former resolutions and promises. A man, finding a watch or any other machine in a desert island, would conclude, that there had once been men in that island. All our reasonings concerning fact are of the same nature. And here it is constantly supposed, that there is a connection between the present fact and that which is inferred from it. Were there nothing to bind them together, the inference would be entirely precarious. The hearing of an articulate voice and rational discourse in the dark assures us of the presence of some person: Why? because these are the effects of the human make and fabric, and closely connected with it. If we anatomize all the other reasonings of this nature, we shall find, that they are founded on the relation of cause and effect, and that this relation is either near or remote, direct or collateral. Heat and light are collateral effects of fire, and the one effect may justly be inferred from the other.[1]

To understand Hume, let us see how the relation of cause and effect would be involved in the first example he gives. The fact that the man's friend is in the country is not something that he knows by observation; it is a fact "which is absent." What the man would know by observation is that he received a letter or that he

---

1. David Hume, *An Enquiry Concerning Human Understanding* (1748).

heard the man say that he was going to the country. From these directly observed facts, he would know by inference the "absent fact" that the man is in the country. To do so, Hume points out, he must suppose that there is some *connection* between the facts he takes as reasons — the facts *from which* he makes the inference — and the fact "absent" — the fact *inferred*. Hume identifies this connection specifically as a *causal* one. Suppose, for example, that he infers that his friend is in the country from the fact that he receives his letter; in this case, he connects the present fact with the absent one by regarding the fact that he receives the letter as the *effect* of his friend writing it from the country. If his reason is instead that he remembers the man saying that he will go to country, a causal connection is still assumed. The man's statement and his ending up in the country are *causally connected*: Both issue as effects from the same cause, his intention to go to the country. To see how this is so and to understand Hume's main point, let us explain it with the notion of a *causal story*. This will be a kind of narrative, which starts with certain facts and leads up to others, showing how the first facts lead to a series of facts, producing them, bringing them about. If the man's evidence is the letter, there is a true causal story starting with the friend writing it in the country and ending with the letter arriving with the man in question. If the evidence is that the man remembers hearing of his friend's plans, there is a causal story starting with the friend deciding to go to the country, then telling the man, then going to the country, and then the man later recalling what his friend said. When we see how the story unfolds, with earlier events giving rise to later events, we see how the later facts are *effects* of the earlier ones and the earlier ones are *causes* of the later ones.

THE CAUSAL PRINCIPLE

Hume's example involves an inference to something *real now* (the friend being in the country while the man thinks of it) but *not observable*. But his point clearly applies to all the other sorts of inferences that we commonly make from what we know directly in experience. We make inferences to the *future* by inferring it as an effect of the past and present. We expect an arrow to spring from a bow, since the bow causes the arrow to fly. Inferences to the *distant past* also clearly fit Hume's model. We infer the existence of dinosaurs by accepting a causal story, beginning with large animals no one ever saw and ending with bones and footprints that we do see. Inferences to *very small*, even unobservable, things, such as those described by the theories of physics, also involve causal stories, beginning with descriptions of electrons, protons, and the like, and ending with observable facts such as needle readings in laboratories and pictures from cloud chambers. And so do inferences to the contents of *other minds*. When, for example, you infer from the fact that I wince after stubbing my toe that I am in pain, you do so on the strength of a causal story, beginning with my pain (the cause) and leading to my wincing (the effect).

Hume has taught us much about how we expand our knowledge by making inferences from what we learn directly. We saw in the last chapter that sensation and introspection provide each of us with a unique perspective, owing to our own place in space and time. But we do not believe that this is all there is. We assume what we will call the **causal principle,** that things that happen have causes and effects. We believe that the small bit of reality revealed to us in experience consists of just a few "links" in endlessly unfolding "chains" of events, causes leading to effects, which in turn become causes of more effects.

KNOWLEDGE OF CAUSALITY

The question therefore arises as to how we *know* about relations of cause and effect. It is tempting to suppose that sensation provides us with a wealth of such knowledge. How do you know that fire will burn? Simply put your hand close to it, and you will *feel* the effect. How do you know that dropping an egg on the floor will break it? Drop one, and you can *see* how the floor breaks the egg on impact. Sensation tells us only about what is immediately before us. This seems enough, however, as we consider such familiar examples. Nonetheless, Hume denies that we can really know of cause and effect by sensation.

> Let an object be presented to a man of ever so strong natural reason and abilities; if that object be entirely new to him, he will not be able, by the most accurate examination of its sensible qualities, to discover any of its causes and effects. Adam, though his rational faculties be supposed, at the very first, entirely perfect, could not have inferred from the fluidity, and transparency of water, that it would suffocate him, or from the light and warmth of fire, that it would consume him. No object ever discovers, by the qualities which appear to the senses, either the causes which produced it, or the effects which will arise from it.[2]

You put our hand toward the fire and feel the heat. The motion of your hand is *succeeded* by the feeling of warmth. But the fact that one event comes after another is not enough to show that the earlier event *caused* the later one. If you sneeze right before someone begins talking, your sneeze does not *cause* them to talk. That one event followed another is a mere *coincidence*. They are not *connected* as cause and effect. But do we really see the connection in the cases in which we believe it is there? It seems not. If you had no previous experience with fire, heat, or anything like them, you could have no reason to expect that the bright and shimmering object before you is the cause of the heat you feel in its vicinity. This, too, might be a mere coincidence. For all you *could* know, the heat is coming from a quite different source. How, then, *do* we tell when the causal relationship is present?

Hume's answer is that we learn of the causal connection only by witnessing *repeatedly* the succession in question. It is only by finding that fire is *regularly*

2. Ibid.

attended by heat that we come to believe that fire is the *cause* of heat. On *no* particular occasion do we ever *directly* recognize the relation of cause and effect. If you cannot see fire causing heat the first time you experience them together, there is no future time in which you will. It is only when we find that heat surrounds fire *whenever* fire is present that we come to think it is the fire that is *responsible* for the heat. Were the fire *not* to cause the heat, the fact that heat always comes with fire would have to be a coincidence. But coincidences are improbable. Therefore, as we see more and more cases in which heat comes with fire, the idea that this association is merely a coincidence seems ever more improbable. To avoid believing this, we suppose that heat must be *connected* to fire. This *explains* why heat always surrounds fire. Heat comes *with* fire because it comes *from* it.

TYPICAL CAUSES AND EFFECTS

Very many inferences that we make in daily life fit the pattern Hume has described. You see footprints in the snow and infer that deer recently walked by. Why? Because footprints of this shape are *typically* caused by deer. You hear a voice in the dark and infer a certain friend is speaking to you because, again, a voice that sounds like this is *typically* caused by that person. In tasting your coffee you find it is sweet and infer that sugar has already been put in it. This is because sugar is what *typically* makes your coffee sweet. The causal principle says that there are causes of facts we know directly even when we cannot directly observe the causes themselves. *Something* must be causing the coffee to be sweet, and so, if sweetness in your coffee is typically caused by sugar, it is the causal principle that allows you to infer that sugar is in the coffee, even though you cannot see it. Moreover, we know the kind of *effect* sugar typically has in coffee. When you put sugar in your coffee, you can *predict* that it will be sweet even before tasting it. So also you can predict what kinds of tracks you will see in the snow by seeing deer walking in the snow from a distance, or you can predict how a person's voice will sound before they begin speaking. In very many cases, what we know directly will be a kind of thing with a typical kind of cause or typical kind of effect. In these cases, we may use this knowledge of what typically causes it or what it typically causes to make inferences to "absent" facts, facts that we cannot know by direct observation.

COMPETING HYPOTHESES

The matter is, however, not always this simple. Sometimes something occurs for which there is no typical cause. We can think of two or more possible causes, each of which seem equally plausible. You find your keys are missing and want to know why. Perhaps you misplaced them yourself, or perhaps your roommate took them. You find your front door unlocked and realize that this could be due either to another family member forgetting to lock it or to a burglar picking the lock. The causal principle tells you that *something* is responsible for the missing keys or the unlocked door, but when there is no typical cause, established repeatedly in past experience, how do you know what was the *real* cause?

Let us introduce some new terminology. When two people disagree about how to explain something or what the true cause of it is, we will say that each has their own **hypothesis.** We might say that each has their own "explanation," but often when we say that someone has an "explanation," we mean that they are *correct.* The word *hypothesis* has no such implication, which is why, when you are disagreeing with someone about why something happened, you can refer to their "hypothesis" (which you think is incorrect). Many students hear the word *hypothesis* and suppose that it must be a guess, something for which there is no good justification. This is *not* the way the word is used in logic and the various sciences, and so it is good to learn what the word means in these disciplines. It is a convenient word to refer to the *opinions* that people have about how to explain something. A similar point applies to the word **theory.** Theories are just hypotheses, so they *can* be very well justified. If you do not understand these points, when you hear about the hypothesis or theory of a scientist, you will mistakenly think that this must not express genuine scientific knowledge.

When two people do disagree about how to explain something, their hypotheses are said to *compete.* **Competing hypotheses** are *inconsistent:* They cannot both be true, or otherwise the two people would not be disagreeing. Now we can reexpress our question as "How do we decide between competing hypotheses (or theories)?" Competing hypotheses are not only inconsistent; they compete in trying to give the correct explanation of a certain given fact. If it is just as likely that your sweet coffee has an artificial sweetener in it as it is that it has sugar in it, there are competing hypotheses for why your coffee is sweet. The causal principle tells you that there must be *some* correct hypothesis that explains why your coffee is sweet. Since you can think of equally plausible hypotheses for the same fact, however, the question remains of how can you discover which is true.

SCIENTIFIC HYPOTHESES

Before answering this question, let me make clear the relevance of this to all of science. Sciences are intellectual disciplines. As we saw in Chapter One, in all intellectual disciplines what is wanted is *understanding* and not merely an amassing of facts. When we have understanding we are able to *explain,* which means we have a correct hypothesis for the fact in question. Every intellectual discipline is a kind of inquiry, which means that the participants have a question and they seek reasons to answer it. Not surprisingly, often they debate what the correct explanation is for some known facts. This is characteristic of all the sciences. An odd result occurs in an astronomical observation, and astronomers debate how to explain it. It is discovered that continents move, and geologists argue about what makes them move. Some people deliberately starve themselves, and psychologists disagree about why they choose to do something so painful. Although sometimes the word *science* is used to describe any intellectual discipline, as the word is used most often today, sciences are all involved in trying to explain facts derived originally from sensation and introspection. As we will see in the following discussion, these same facts provide justification for the correct hypotheses. In this important respect, scientific hypotheses are just like the everyday examples of hypotheses that I have used so far in this chapter. Even though a hypothesis about why your keys are missing would certainly not be called "scientific," it is *justified* in the same general way. Let us now see how.

TESTING

The question of how scientific hypotheses are established is itself a matter of much discussion today. However, one fact is commonly accepted, and that is that scientific hypotheses (or theories) must be **testable**. Understanding how and why scientific hypotheses are tested is most important for understanding scientific knowledge. So let us look carefully at what this means by starting with an everyday sort of example.

Suppose your front door is unlocked, and you have two competing hypotheses: A family member forgot to lock it, or a burglar broke in. To discover which is true, you cannot zoom into the past and directly see another family member walking out the door or a burglar picking the lock. But you can test each hypothesis by *supposing* it is true and asking what *else* you would expect to find. Suppose a family member left it open: What else would be true that you could verify directly? For one thing, you would expect your belongings to be undisturbed and that nothing would be missing. On the other hand, if a burglar broke in, you would expect the house to be messed up and things to be missing. Now suppose that you find the house messed up and some valuables are missing. At this point the two hypotheses no longer seem equally plausible. Let us examine why.

FALLIBLE INFERENCE

Notice that it is still *possibly* true that a family member left the door unlocked. This means that when we infer from the facts given that a burglar picked the lock, our inference is *fallible*. But in spite of the fact that the family member hypothesis *could* be true, it seems *unlikely* that it is. For why, if the reason the door is unlocked is that a family member left it open, would the house be messed up or things missing? The point is that the family member hypothesis does not *explain* these other facts, whereas the burglar hypothesis does. It *could* be that someone in this house messed it up and that someone there also took valuables away. But if so, the fact that the door is unlocked while the house is messed up and things are missing is a sheer *coincidence*. Because coincidences sometimes occur, we cannot say with *certainty* that the family member hypothesis is false.

GREATER COMPREHENSION

The problem with the family member hypothesis is rather that it makes a *mystery* of the other facts that the competing hypothesis explains. The fact that the door is unlocked is the *original* fact to be explained. Since there are equally good competing hypotheses for this fact, we test them to see which is true. Testing requires that we first think of what else we would expect to find if each hypothesis is true. When doing this, we are thinking of possible facts that we could learn directly in experience (such as that the house is messed up or that things are missing). Then we go and try to find out if those are the real facts. What we want is to find facts that will favor one hypothesis and count against the other. The facts that favor a hypothesis are those that we expect to find, which is to say facts that are *also* explained by that hypothesis. The burglar hypothesis, if true, explains not only the original fact, that the door is unlocked, but also the other facts in question. These other facts (about the mess and the missing items) count against the family member hypothesis. This is *not* because they "disprove" it, but because they are not explained by that hypothesis—they are not what we would expect to find if that hypothesis were true. Ideally, all the facts found in testing would count in favor of one and not the other. In real life, it is often not that neat. What makes this ideal, however, is that the *better* hypothesis, the one that wins the competition, is the one that *explains more* of the facts we know directly in experience.

The better hypothesis thus creates more *coherence* in one's beliefs (see Chapter One). The facts about the door, the mess, and the missing items are *connected* to one another by the burglar hypothesis but not by the family member one. The burglar hypothesis "comprehends" them. In our example, we started with one fact known directly in sensation (that the door was unlocked) and (in testing) found two more known the same way. The better hypothesis did a better job in explaining the facts learned directly. It gathered them together as facts to be expected, on the assumption that that hypothesis is the true one. The better hypothesis achieved more coherence in the beliefs acquired individually in experience.

THE INCONCLUSIVENESS OF TESTING

Many students initially think that testing can be conclusively ended by just getting the right facts. Suppose you simply asked your family members whether anyone left the door unlocked, and one admitted it. Now, surely, in real life that would be the end of the matter. Nevertheless, it is important to realize that these inferences are *always* fallible, no matter how much data you get. After all, the family member *could* be lying. "But why would he want to do that?" you might ask. This is a good question, since what we are seeking is the hypothesis that *explains* the most facts. If the burglar hypothesis is true, one thing we would expect to find is that no family member would confess. Yet the fact that someone confessed would not be *inconsistent* with the burglar hypothesis. It is rather that it seems highly improbable.

Now, the claim that the family member is lying is itself something that can be tested. But no matter how many facts you get in favor of any empirical hypothesis, you can always think of some way, perhaps utterly bizarre, that would show how that hypothesis could still be false. The best way to see this is to try it for yourself. The fact that testing is never completely conclusive is important. For it shows how scientific hypotheses are not "proven." No matter how well justified any scientific theory is, it is always *conceivable* that new facts will undermine support for it. But this does *not* show that we never have any good reason for thinking a scientific hypothesis is true. It just means that our reasons are always fallible.

PSEUDOHYPOTHESES

Scientists generally agree that their theories should be testable. Any theory that cannot be tested is rejected as "unscientific." Some theories are not testable. In ancient times, some people tried to explain the motions of stars by supposing they had minds. But the only apparent fact explained by this hypothesis is just the original one, that the stars move as they do. Unless this hypothesis has further predictable consequences, we might as well say that Z rays from another world cause them to move as they do, adding that for Z rays as well, the only fact they explain for us is this observed movement of the stars. Such hypotheses are called "**pseudohypotheses**," not because they are false but because they are not *testable*. With no way to test, there is no reason to choose between them. This shows why a hypothesis must be testable to be known. Because science seeks genuine knowledge, scientific hypotheses must be testable.

EMPIRICAL KNOWLEDGE

In the last chapter, we allowed that for each kind of direct knowledge, there was a kind of "experience" one has in making such a judgment. However, in the passage by Locke (in the last chapter) in which he compares and contrasts sensation with introspection, it is only these two direct sources of knowledge that are called "experience." Locke's usage of the term is very influential, so let us adopt it in the rest of this chapter. This allows us to explain a very important term in philosophy. **Empirical knowledge** is knowledge "based on experience." This is meant to include not only all that we know *directly* in experience but all knowledge that can be legitimately *inferred* from this. The word *empirical* comes from the Greek word for experience, and many students forget about inferential knowledge when thinking about empirical knowledge. This is a serious mistake you must school yourself not to make. The idea of empirical knowledge is well known in academics, and it is important not to misunderstand it. Correct scientific hypotheses or theories express empirical knowledge because they are *inferred* from the direct knowledge of experience. Now that we have discussed testing, we can see how.

Remember that when we test a hypothesis, we look for the one that explains the most known facts. Now the point to see is that it is these same facts that provide the *justification* for the best hypothesis. Recall the example of the unlocked door. We imagined that testing occurred by learning more facts that would be explained by one but not the other hypothesis. The burglar hypothesis explained not only the original fact but the new facts, too. So now suppose we ask, "How do you know that the burglar hypothesis is more likely at this point?" To answer this question *is* to give justification for that hypothesis, and we do this by pointing to the very same facts that are *explained* by that hypothesis. If (as in our example) the facts in question are directly known in experience, then the hypothesis is inferred from these, and this is enough for such hypotheses to express empirical knowledge when true. Scientific hypotheses or theories are like this, in that their justification always requires some knowledge from experience. Without such direct knowledge from experience, they cannot be known. It is in this way that science is ultimately tied to the facts of observation that we learn in experience.

The growth of science is one of the most important phenomena in modern times. Interesting questions, such as whether science conflicts with religion, cannot be answered without understanding the nature of science. Although there is much about science that we have not mentioned, no fact is more important than this: Science consists of empirical knowledge, mainly in the form of hypotheses (or theories) that explain facts of experience. Science seeks the unobserved causes for what we observe.

THE EXAMPLE OF DARWIN'S THEORY

Before examining empirical hypotheses further, let us look at a real scientific theory to see how it is tested. The example is thought by some to be the most important scientific theory ever, yet there are some people today who have doubted whether it is science at all. Charles Darwin, a nineteenth-century biologist, is commonly associated with the idea of the evolution of life forms over a long period of time. And Darwin's theory does indeed mean to explain how such transformations of animal and plant life took place. But the fact that such a process of evolution occurred cannot be the "original fact to be explained," for the simple reason that we do not know this directly from experience. As the story of evolution is now told, it stretches back some 4 billion years on a planet that humans have inhabited for only about 100,000 years.

What fact known in experience, then, is the theory originally designed to explain? It is the fact that all around us we see life forms well suited to their environment. Giraffes have long necks, which suits them well for their environment, in which their food sources are high above the ground. Squirrels live near predators that would eat them, but fortunately they are fast enough usually to escape. Polar bears live in cold water, which would be unbearable were it not for their thick fat and insulating fur. The examples are practically endless and fascinating in their details. Prior to Darwin, many people claimed to see in these happy correspondences evidence of design: the action of a person, acting with conscious purpose in making life forms and their environments match. In fact, the so-called **design hypothesis** was often cited as evidence of the existence of God. Now, it is telling that Darwin's theory is described in terms of "natural" selection, for what occurs naturally is contrasted with what occurs artificially or by design, and this is called **Darwin's theory of natural selection.** Darwin meant his theory to be a competitor of the design hypothesis. Let us see how this is so by considering how the correspondences in question were explained by him without reference to the activity of a powerful and intelligent person.

Darwin was impressed by the fact that all over Earth there tends to be an overproduction of living beings, so that they are thrown into competition with one another for scarce resources, especially food. The question arises, Which ones will survive in such a situation? Suppose that there are chance variations in physical makeup among the competitors—for example, that some giraffes happen to be born with longer necks. The crucial point for our purpose is that this variation "just happens" in the sense that it does not result by anyone's plan. Now suppose that this physical difference gives them a competitive advantage in their environment in obtaining food. Then it can happen that those with this trait will survive in greater numbers and pass on this trait to their offspring. If this situation occurs over generations, the trait for long necks is "naturally selected"—just *as if* someone had actually picked out the long-necked giraffes for breeding. Just as human breeders can change the physical makeup of a breed of animals or plants by deciding which ones get to reproduce themselves, "nature itself" can do this, which means it does not really happen by conscious design at all.

I have actually heard it claimed that Darwin's theory is not science since science deals only with observable facts, and no one has observed the very old past described by Darwin's theory. The previous discussion shows the errors of this reasoning. First, science *standardly* deals with unobservable facts, insofar as it seeks the unobserved causes of what we know in experience. The correct sense in which it "deals with" observable facts is just that it starts with facts known directly in experience and hypothesizes about these. We have seen that Darwin's theory does indeed start with observation, the fact that life forms are well suited to their environments. It attempts to explain this fact, as science typically does, by telling a causal story that has roots in the unobserved. But Darwin's theory is scientific only if it is not a pseudohypothesis. This means that it must make predictions, other than the original fact to be explained, which can also be verified in direct experience. And this it does. For if the correspondences between life forms and their environment have resulted from competition for survival, there must have been many losers. The chances are good that we should find remains of them, such as bones, or other traces, such as footprints. Dinosaurs were not the only extinct species to be so discovered, but they are such dramatic examples that they swayed many minds away from the design hypothesis. To see why this should be so, we must be clear about the nature of an inference to the best hypothesis.

Evidence of extinct species is just what we *expect* to find if Darwin's theory is true, and because of this, Darwin's theory explains not only the original fact (about the correspondences) but *also* the observed fact that there are traces of extinct species. The design hypothesis *could* still be true; after all, maybe the designer wanted some species to be temporary. But to point out this possibility does not show that the design hypothesis is just as likely to be true. For our standard for choosing between hypotheses is that of which *explains the most* of what we know in experience. Darwin's theory also explains other observed facts such as the presence of vestigial organs and the fact that more complicated skeletal structures are consistently found in younger strata of Earth. All of these observed facts are *consistent* with the design hypothesis, but this means only that Darwin's theory is not *certain*. It is still the better scientific hypothesis, because it genuinely explains these facts, whereas the design hypothesis relegates them to mystery.

Perhaps it is worth pointing out that Darwin's theory is consistent with the existence of God. God himself could have made the world so that a process such as Darwin describes takes place. What Darwin's theory denies is what is called the young Earth hypothesis. Supposedly based on the Bible, this claims that the Earth is only about 10,000 years old, not several billion. Ingenious attempts have been made to show that the young Earth hypothesis is a credible scientific theory in light of what we know. In assessing this claim, what is important to remember is that the issue is not whether Darwin's theory has been "proven" but rather how well it *explains* the known facts. It is on this score that the theory is widely held by scientists today. Now that the importance of testing has been driven home, let us return to our general discussion of empirical hypotheses.

THEORETICAL DESCRIPTIONS

It is not necessary that a hypothesis be expressed in the sort of terms that describe observable things. In the Humean sort of case, by contrast, two kinds of observables are seen to go together repeatedly, and from this we infer that they regularly go together. From the fact that all the lemons we have ever tasted were sour, we conclude that all lemons are sour. What we infer in this sort of case is expressed in observational terms. We can see and feel *lemons*, and we can taste things as *sour*. The thought that lemons are sour is close to observation in that it describes a pattern within our experience. When we infer a hypothesis to explain a variety of facts already known, however, there are no restrictions on the sort of terminology we use; what counts is how well that hypothesis explains the known facts. This point is made clearly in the following passage by Carl Hempel, a twentieth-century philosopher of science:

> [S]cientific hypotheses and theories are usually couched in terms that do not occur at all in the description of the empirical findings on which they rest, and which they serve to explain. For example, theories about the atomic and subatomic structure of matter contain terms such as "atom," "electron," "proton," "neutron," "psi-function," etc.; yet they are based on laboratory findings about the spectra of various gases, tracks in cloud and

bubble chambers, quantitative aspects of chemical reactions, and so forth—all of which can be described without the use of "theoretical terms." . . . [T]he transition from data to theory requires creative imagination. Scientific hypotheses and theories are not *derived* from observed facts, but *invented* in order to account for them.[3]

Scientific knowledge often describes things that no one ever has or will observe directly. Since scientific knowledge is empirical, this means that we know empirically of unobservable things. This point is important to remember when saying that science must "stick to the facts." We must indeed "stick to" the directly known facts, for these are the justifying reasons for the scientific hypotheses. They are the facts *from which* the theories are inferred. But the theories themselves may describe things quite unlike anything we ever observe.

EXPLANATIONS OF EXPLANATIONS

Hypotheses themselves sometimes call for explanation. If your keys are missing because your roommate took them, you might want to know *why* she took them. The thought that your roommate took them explains why the keys are missing. Like any other fact, we can wonder why it is true. When we find an answer, we have given a hypothesis for a hypothesis. Suppose that your roommate wanted to use your car without your permission. This thought explains the first hypothesis. There is no apparent end to how far we can find explanations for explanations or causes for causes. This means that no matter how far we can go at any given time in explaining the facts of observation, some facts must remain unexplained—namely, the "highest-level" hypotheses that explain many other facts but for which no explanation is known. Because this will be an important matter when we get to metaphysics, let us look closely at several especially significant examples.

THREE EXAMPLES FROM SCIENCE

Scientists presently believe that about 15 billion years ago, all that we see around us, including all the stars in all the galaxies, was compressed into a tiny ball, which has been expanding ever since. This amazing hypothesis is well supported by directly known facts, pertaining to the results of radiowave readings and telescope observations of distant galaxies. What concerns us now is that the theory says that the universe as we know it started with a "Big Bang" (the name of the theory). Does this mean that science has discovered the ultimate cause of everything else, a cause for which there is no cause? If any event deserves this name, it would be the Big Bang. But can we say that no explanation for the Big Bang itself will ever be found? It seems not. The Big Bang hypothesis is based on a limited amount of information.

---

3. From *Philosophy of Natural Science* (Englewood Cliffs, NJ: Prentice Hall, 1966).

For all we know, new information will provide the basis for a new and more comprehensive explanation, including an explanation of the Big Bang itself. Science and empirical knowledge in general grow continually with fresh information. We are never in a position to claim that our empirical understanding is complete.

Another example that illustrates the same point pertains to what things are made of. Many ancient Greeks thought that everything is ultimately made of four "elements": water, fire, earth, and air. But why, one may ask, is it good to reduce the number of stuffs of which things are made to some short list? We see around us many different kinds of materials, including wood, cotton, silk, butter, flesh, various metals, and so on. Why say that these are each composed of one or another of some "elemental" material, of which there are very few? The Greeks would lump wood, cotton, silk, and all the metals into the category of earth. What is the point? The answer is that they were trying to *explain* them. As we have seen, the best explanations *comprehend* a variety of facts, making more *coherent* our beliefs in them. By seeing all the various dry and solid materials as forms of earth, they hoped to *understand* these various materials with which they were familiar. What is cotton? It is earth in such and such a state. By describing wood, metals, and other materials in the same sort of way, we comprehend them under one category.

Once we have satisfied ourselves with this level of explanation, however, we may wonder what the four elements have in common. Is there one most basic stuff of which the four elements are simply different forms? This question arises from our desire for the most comprehensive understanding. Today scientists describe even what atoms are made of. But at any stage in scientific progress, the most basic things go unexplained. Perhaps new experimental data will show a still more basic level. Because this remains a permanent possibility, at no time can we declare that we have "hit the bottom."

Our third and last example pertains to the regularities that Hume described. These are called laws of nature, or simply **laws.** That sugar is sweet is a law, and so is the fact that lemons are sour. As these examples illustrate, laws of nature are themselves facts, or true thoughts, and so we may seek explanations for them, too. A famous example pertains to such laws as these: Unsupported objects fall toward the ground; planets go around the sun; tides go in and out daily. It is hard to imagine three laws that seem to have less in common than these. Yet a pattern was discerned by the seventeenth-century English scientist Isaac Newton. Now taught to schoolchildren, but astonishing in his time, is his law of universal gravitation. Prior to Newton, gravity was thought of as a force that only the Earth exerted on objects. Newton claimed that *all* objects attract each other with the force of gravity. (The reason it does not look this way on Earth is that the force of gravity increases with weight and the small objects around us have very little of it.) With his higher-level law, Newton was able to explain what planets and tides have to do with objects falling on Earth. Planets would fly off in a straight line but for the force of gravity that keeps deflecting the planets so that they travel around the sun, a massive object exerting much gravitational force. Tides go in and out as they are pulled by the moon from different directions as it travels around the earth. Newton's law allows us to *understand* these several laws themselves, making our beliefs in them more coherent.

There is no limit to how many laws can be comprehended by a higher law. But at any time, the highest laws known will themselves not be explained by a higher law. Nevertheless, it always remains possible that such a law will be found.

CONCLUSION

This is a particularly difficult chapter. Before taking a philosophy course, who would think about such questions as how we make inferences to the unobserved or how we decide between competing hypotheses? As we go on, the questions will become gradually more familiar. I can only assure you at this point that we will make important use of our understanding of empirical knowledge in general and of scientific knowledge specifically. Before we turn to metaphysics, here are some key ideas of this and the last chapter.

By sensation and introspection (now called "experience"), you are immediately aware of things here and now, including things both within and without your mind. Although you retain much of this direct knowledge in memory, the most it can ever reveal is your own unique point of view, reflecting your own positions in space and the period of your life. You believe that there is much more to know about despite the fact that this is all you actually observe. How do you justify these beliefs about the unobserved? Mainly by inferring causes of what you do know directly and using this knowledge of causes to infer effects. Often, and especially in science, this requires testing to find which hypothesis makes what you know more coherent. By inferring causes and effects of what we directly observe, we build up a picture that includes the unobserved. Our knowledge of the unobserved is fallible. And we can never say that it is complete. For all we know, new information will allow us to see ever longer chains of causes and effects. Let us now use this understanding of empirical knowledge to examine the reality it is about.

STUDY QUESTIONS

1. Give an original example that shows, as in Hume's example, how we use the causal principle to infer the unobserved from the observed.
2. Defend Hume's claim that we do not know directly of cause and effect.
3. Are scientific hypotheses or theories merely "educated guesses" and not genuine knowledge?
4. How should we choose between competing hypotheses? How in particular do we use the causal principle in making this choice?
5. Why must a hypothesis be testable to be knowable? Make up an original example of two pseudohypotheses for the same fact that illustrates your answer.

6. Why is scientific knowledge fallible?
7. What is empirical knowledge? Explain how it can involve sensation, introspection, or inference.
8. Explain how hypotheses are inferred from direct knowledge of experience.
9. How does a good hypothesis make your beliefs more coherent?
10. Why is Darwin's theory of natural selection a genuinely scientific hypothesis? What sorts of known fact support it?
11. Explain why science, no matter how well developed, always leaves some things unexplained.

Glossary for Part One

Causal principle The thesis that events have causes and effects
Certain (knowledge) Knowledge derived from an infallible source; see *fallibilism*.
Coherence A body of beliefs is made more coherent by a common explanation for all of them.
Competing hypotheses Inconsistent hypotheses designed to explain the same fact
Credulity That way of investigating in which one's desire to believe a certain way causes one to be more influenced by the data that support that belief
Darwin's theory of natural selection A scientific theory that attempts to explain the suitability of life forms to their environment as the result of a nonconscious selection for reproduction of those individuals that happen to be better suited for certain environmental niches than their competitors
Design hypothesis The hypothesis that competes with Darwin's theory of natural selection by supposing that the selection of individuals for environmental niches results from conscious choice
Direct knowledge Knowledge that is not inferential
Empirical knowledge Knowledge that is based on experience, by being either known in experience or inferred from it
Epistemology The branch of logic that studies knowledge
Ethics The area of philosophy that inquires into what is good, to see how to make the best choices
Experience An operation of sensation or introspection that normally yields direct knowledge
Explanation A reason for why something is true, taking the mystery out of it; contrast with *justification*.
External (object) An object is external if it exists independently of the mind
Fallibilism The thesis that there are no infallible sources of knowledge
Follows One thought follows from another if it cannot be false if this other is true.
Hypothesis A statement that is supposed to explain a certain fact
Inconsistent (thoughts) Statements that cannot all be true
Infallible (source of knowledge) One that is perfectly reliable or errorproof
Infer To infer a statement is to conclude it on the basis of other statements assumed to be true.
Inferential knowledge Knowledge that is obtained only by inference from other knowledge
Intellect (as we use the term) The power to be aware of thoughts themselves
Intellectual discipline A kind of inquiry with its own kind of problem to be solved; the knowledge sought includes understanding.
Internal (object) An object is internal if it cannot exist independently of the mind
Introspection The capacity to know directly of one's own mental states
Judgment The mental act of first coming to think something is true; by nature involves awareness of reasons that seem to justify that thought
Justification A reason that shows that a certain statement is true; contrast with *explanation*.

Laws (of nature) Patterns or regularities discovered empirically

Logic The area of philosophy concerned with how to make good judgments, regardless of subject matter

Metaphysics The area of philosophy that aims to understand reality as a whole or reality as such

Necessary methods of justification Methods of justification that must be followed in order to be recognizable as one who is trying to solve problems within a certain intellectual discipline

Probable (knowledge) Knowledge is probable if its source is fallible

Pseudohypothesis A hypothesis that cannot be tested since it predicts no other facts than the original fact to be explained

Rationality The power to be aware of one's reasons (justificatory or explanatory)

Self-evident A thought is self-evident if it can be seen as true without using any information other than what is contained in the thought itself

Sensation An operation of the mind (or the capacity for such an operation) yielding direct knowledge of things in one's immediate environment by being affected by those things (includes the five senses)

Testing (a hypothesis) Performed by inferring possible observable facts from that hypothesis that would be explained by that hypothesis but not by competing hypotheses, and then making the relevant observations

Theory Same as *hypothesis*

Thinking An act of the mind by which one accepts a thought that itself can be thought about

Thoughts Those things that are either true or false; identified by putting *that* in front of a declarative sentence; do not confuse with mental acts of thinking.

Understanding Knowledge of an explanation

PART
TWO

Metaphysics

Metaphysics is that branch of philosophy that inquires into reality as such. The truths it seeks are about how things are, not (as in ethics) about how things ought to be. We need to have beliefs about reality to get around in the world, but we do not need to inquire about how these go together to form a comprehensive view of reality. So we can avoid metaphysics, but we cannot avoid committing ourselves to an answer to the main question it asks. Even if we never think of it, we all have a view of reality, which consists in the totality of our beliefs about how things really are. By not thinking about these beliefs, they remain separate from one another, like so many individual maps that depict different portions of a single area. We gain understanding about reality as such only when we bring these together somehow into a coherent whole.

Because we are parts of reality, we gain a unique understanding of human nature by understanding the nature of reality as such. What this understanding lacks in detail it gains in depth. By understanding how we belong to reality, we know how we are, regardless of circumstances of place and time. As we will see in Part Three, these very general descriptions of how we really are have been used to explain how things ought to be.

The first chapter in this part begins by correlating kinds of reality with the sources of knowledge covered in Part One. Much of the rest of Part Two will involve seeing how these kinds of reality are related to one another. We find also in Chapter Four that religions have traditionally occupied themselves with a portion of reality not yet accounted for and not scientifically knowable. Chapter Five focuses on us and how we fit into the whole of reality. Chapter Six examines the belief in God, comparing this with similar beliefs, some of which are associated with great religions of the world.

CHAPTER
FOUR

Nature and the Transcendent

WHAT IS THERE? Let us begin to answer this question by asking what we know about reality if sensation, introspection, and intellect are indeed genuine sources of knowledge. It is important to realize that a source of knowledge *could* yield truths only about how things ought to be and not about how things really are. As we saw in Chapter Two, some philosophers have thought we have a special sense for "intuiting" purely ethical truths that are not truths about reality. We will begin by taking each of our three sources of knowledge in turn to see what it tells us about reality. Many philosophers in the last two centuries have thought that these three sources of knowledge tell us all we could ever know about reality, and some of these have been confident enough to say that this is all there is. As we will see, however, their view leaves out just the kind of reality that has been affirmed by religions around the world.

SENSIBLE REALITY

In sensation — seeing, hearing, tasting, smelling, and feeling — we become aware of "external" things (see Chapter Two). These are "external" to the mind in the sense that they exist independently of the mind. The tree you see before you does not go out of existence when you turn your attention to something else, as a tingle ceases to exist when you no longer feel it. To see the tree you must have a visual sensation, a way it looks, but the tree exists even if you close your eyes and the visual sensation vanishes. Let us call the things of which we are aware in sensation "sensible" things.

What more can we say about sensible things than that they are "external" to the mind? There is one thing we find out about very many of them, at least, when we touch them. You can pass your hand through a shadow or beam of light, but not through a tree, a table, another person, or practically anything you see around you. We say of such things that they are **material,** that they are made of stuffs like wood and flesh, which make them resist being moved. Scientists have discovered that a beam of light also turns out to be material, since it exerts a force on impact. This force is so small that we do not feel it, but it is there just the same.

One thing to notice about material things is that there are many of them, perhaps an infinite number. It may be that in reality they somehow all merge into a single whole, as waves of an ocean form a single surface. But they appear, at least, to be individual things, separate from one another. And among these, you (or your body) are but one tiny thing, separate from all the rest.

Material things also move in space. At any time, we see a variety of them spread out, occupying various places, and they move by going to new places. These places, moreover, are not points but have a more or less clearly defined volume. Material things occupy places by being "extended," so that they have width, depth, and height. The stuffs of which they are composed (such as wood or flesh) *fill* these places. Space itself is just the totality of all places. Movement also takes place in time. When a material thing moves, we can assign times to when the movement starts and finishes. Time itself is just the series of moments, including the present and all past and future moments. (Modern science envisages space and time together; it describes portions of "space-time" instead of particular times and places, but this point does not concern us now.) Material things are thus *spatiotemporal* things, existing for some stretch of time in which they occupy a series of places.

These movements and other changes they undergo do not occur haphazardly. There are patterns in these changes that we call *laws* (see Chapter Three). Material things fall again and again at the same rate, fire always produces heat, ice always forms at the same temperature, and so forth. It is the laws that make the changes *predictable*. If we know we are approaching fire, we can predict that we will feel heat; if we drop a stone, we know in advance how fast it will fall. The future of any material object is thus *determined* by how it and its environment have been in the past. (Modern science also claims that there is a degree of unpredictability in the smallest constituents of atoms, but this, too, does not concern us now.) For any of the material objects around us, it seems that if we could know enough about how it is now, we could see *exactly* how it will be the next moment. This is what it means for the future of a thing to be "determined" by its past, which is due to the fact that material things change in accordance with laws. Because material things change in such regular ways, the "material world" (the totality of all material things) is said to have *order*. For all the material things we see around us, this appears to be a deterministic order: The entire state of the material world at any point in time appears to be the only one possible, given the way it was in the past.

Finally, it is a very pervasive fact about the material world that material things are ephemeral: They come into existence at a certain point in time and vanish at a later time. It is not necessary for a thing to be material that it be ephemeral. Some philosophers have thought that the smallest constituents of material things are eternal, having always been in existence and never going out of existence. But even if this is so, it is simply a remarkable fact about the vast majority of material things that they exist for only a short duration in time. As we will see in Part Three, the conviction that "everything perishes" is an important realization in some views of how to live well.

INTROSPECTIBLE REALITY

Locke contrasted introspection with sensation on the basis of the fact that its objects are "internal" (see Chapter Two). Whenever you introspect, the only part of reality of which you are aware is just your own mind. The same is, of course, true of everyone else. So in general, introspection makes us aware only of "mental reality" (the totality of all minds). Your *body* is a material thing. It *may* be that in introspecting your mind you are in fact aware of your body in a special way (from "the inside"). This is an issue that we will discuss in the next chapter. For now we will make no assumptions about how the mind is related to the body. Our present purpose is just to become clear about what kinds of reality are revealed by each of the three sources of knowledge that occupied our attention in Part One.

Minds are like material things by existing in time. We undergo changes in what we think, how things look, what we remember, and what we intend to do. Are our minds eternal or ephemeral? This is another topic we will take up in the next chapter. For now we acknowledge only that our minds have *some* duration in time. Do our minds exist in space? The only thing obvious is that our minds are somehow located where our bodies are. But it is not obvious that our minds are extended, and some philosophers have thought they were not. If they are not extended, they are not material. This is another question about how mind and body are related that we postpone for the next chapter.

Minds (or the creatures who have them) are *aware* of things. It is on this basis that many people say that other animals have minds, despite the fact that they do not think (see Chapter One). To have a mind, it is not necessary to be actually aware of anything. Our minds do not go out of existence in a coma. It is rather to have the *capacity* to be aware of things, a capacity that is "exercised" when we *are* aware. Through awareness a creature learns, coming to know something new. This new information is retained (in "memory") to become available for acting more effectively in the world. (This is why plants seem not be aware, since they never change the way they behave when exposed to new information.)

INTELLIGIBLE REALITY

The *intellect*, as we define the term, is the capacity to be aware of thoughts and how they are related to one another (see Chapter One). The intellect thus belongs to the mind, though, of course, not all creatures with minds have intellects. It seems likely that many animals have sensation as their only form of awareness, lacking both introspection and intellect. But the intellect appears pervasively in human life. We are aware of thoughts whenever we interpret what someone says or whenever we think about what we are thinking. We are aware of thoughts whenever we give explanations or justifications. As with the mind, we are now making no assumptions about the nature of thoughts themselves, other than the fact that they are the things that are true or false. Perhaps when you interpret what someone says by grasping the thought that class is over, you are really aware of just the sounds they make. Now sounds, as waves in air, are material things. So are the bits of ink and chalk that we use to make sentences visible. Again, we are not concerned with such matters in this chapter. We want only to canvass the kinds of reality revealed by three sources of knowledge in order to consider whether this is all there is.

Many philosophers have, however, been convinced that thoughts belong to neither the material nor the mental world. They have held that thoughts are just not the sort of thing that is located in space or changing through time. Where, for example, is the thought that snow is white? We are not asking where is the material stuff, snow. This is the bit of reality that the thought is about, not the thought itself. And how does this thought change? If snow were to become green, the thought that snow is white would not change from being true to being false. It would have been false then and now that snow (all snow) is white. Nor do thoughts belong to the mental world. If you think that it is snowing and then go into a coma, your states of consciousness go out of existence, but not the thought itself. That same thought is still available for others to grasp. It is for these reasons that the nineteenth-century German mathematician and philosopher Gottlob Frege said that thoughts belong to a "third realm."

THE EMPIRICAL WORLD

What kind of reality answers to our empirical knowledge? Empirical knowledge is based on the direct knowledge of sensation and introspection. Together, they acquaint us with only our own unique perspective on things in space during times of our existence. But we know a great deal by inference about material things and minds we ourselves have not observed. We may allow that other animals make inferences of a primitive sort, as when a dog infers that there is food by seeing the bowl. We humans, however, are capable of using intellect when making inferences, in which we are aware of the thoughts themselves. You may think there were deer here last night *because* tracks appear in snow, thus connecting one thought with another. This allows us to think of even more connections. Where did the deer come from? If you get an answer, you are constructing a causal story, in which thoughts are linked one after another. To grasp such a story, one must have intellect. As we saw in the last chapter, it is just such causal stories that allow us to build up our empirical knowledge so that it includes far more than information about our own point of view. Let us call **nature** the totality of what must be real for our empirical knowledge to be genuine. Nature, then, consists of material things, minds, and thoughts.

Is this all there is? Many philosophers, called **naturalists,** would say so. Their view is not easy to refute. After all, nature includes all things in space and time, including the smallest particles of matter and the largest galaxies; it includes minds like ours that are known by introspection and sensation as well as an unlimited number of material things. It even includes the thoughts that we discuss. What else is there? As we will see, what is left out are just the sorts of things that religions have thought especially important.

RELIGION AND THE SUPERNATURAL

We will call anything *supernatural* if it does not belong to nature. This is a technical term that is in fact widely used in discussions of religion, and it is not meant to suggest anything derogatory about beliefs in such reality. Religion's concern with the supernatural is indicated by the nineteenth- and twentieth-century American philosopher William James: "Were one asked to characterize the life of religion in the broadest and most general terms possible, one might say that it consists of the belief that there is an unseen order, and that our supreme good lies in harmoniously adjusting ourselves thereto."[1] By an "unseen order," James means to describe the supernatural. In the last chapter, we saw that science in general frequently describes what is literally "unseen"—the unobservable causes of what we know directly in experience, but these are plainly not the objects of religious devotion. We also saw that hypotheses that are not testable are not empirically knowable, so they do claim to describe an "unseen order" beyond the world of nature. And there is no doubt that many religions have claimed to offer explanations of natural events with such pseudohypotheses. Even today many people still pray to and offer sacrifices to gods for such benefits as rain, good luck, the birth of a child, or a longer life. They have been told by their elders that such natural phenomena are under the influence of certain gods, but there is never any suggestion that these hypotheses can be *tested.* They appear to explain these phenomena, but since no possible justification exists for them, the people who accept them have an utterly unjustified sense of control over nature when they attempt to influence the gods in question. Many scientifically minded philosophers have regarded religion as primarily in the business of offering such worthless pseudohypotheses, and they have witnessed in science a major advance in human development. For as we have seen, scientific hypotheses are testable and thus justifiable. Because they are justified by their ability to predict

1. From *The Varieties of Religious Experience* (New York: Viking, 1982).

the future, they give us a genuine ability to control nature. This ability is now shown to all the world by the extraordinary success in applying science to create advanced technology.

Although many religious beliefs take the form of pseudohypotheses, we have no reason to assume that all such beliefs fall into this discreditable category. For all we know at this point, there may be good reasons for some claims about the supernatural, which do not fit the picture of empirical knowledge outlined in Part One. *If* the only reason for such a belief is that it would explain observable facts of the world if true, but the belief cannot be tested, *then* we can dismiss it as unjustified (which is not to say we know it is false).

Let us compare James's view of religion with another, that of the twentieth-century German philosopher and psychologist Erich Fromm.

> The fact that man has reason and imagination leads not only to the necessity for having a sense of his own identity, but also for orienting himself in the world intellectually. This need can be compared with the process of physical orientation which develops in the first years of life, and which is completed when the child can walk by himself, touch and handle things, knowing what they are. But when the ability to walk and to speak has been acquired, only the first step in the direction of orientation has been taken. Man finds himself surrounded by many puzzling phenomena and, having reason, he has to make sense of them, has to put them in some context which he can understand and which permits him to deal with them in his thoughts. The further his reason develops, the more adequate becomes his system of orientation, that is, the more it approximates reality. But even if man's frame of orientation is purely illusory, it satisfies his need for some picture which is meaningful to him. . . .
>
> If man were only a disembodied intellect, his aim would be achieved by a comprehensive thought system. But since he is an entity endowed with a body as well as a mind, he has to react to the dichotomy of his existence not only in thinking but in the total process of living, in his feelings and actions. Hence any satisfying system of orientation contains not only intellectual elements but elements of feeling and sensing which are expressed in the relationship to an object of devotion.
>
> The answers given to man's need for a system of orientation and an object of devotion differ widely both in content and in form. . . .
>
> But whatever their contents, they all respond to man's need to have not only some thought system, but also an object of devotion which gives meaning to his existence and to his position in the world.[2]

Fromm explains why we *need* a "religion" in the sense of a system of orientation with an object of devotion. But he does not say that the object of devotion to which life is oriented must be *supernatural*. A person who oriented her life toward the maximization of personal power or sensual pleasure would have a "religion" in

---

2. From *The Sane Society* (New York: Holt, 1955).

this broad sense even if she had no belief in the supernatural. This raises the question of why so many people wish not merely for *some* object of devotion but one that is *supernatural*. Why does nature itself disappoint many people in offering such an object of devotion?

DISAPPOINTMENTS WITH NATURE

James remarked that according to an ancient saying, the first thing the gods created was *fear*; but he added that it was common for more developed religions to offer *hope*. We might see how this is so by asking whether nature itself addresses our highest hopes. If we take seriously the claim that nature is all there is, do we have cause to be disturbed? Perhaps the first thing that comes to mind is that *death is real*. The only thing we know about ourselves, insofar as we belong to nature, is that we are animals, with bodies that eventually lose life and disintegrate. If nature is all there is, then this is all there is to *us*, and with the death of the body we cease to exist forever. Many people find this fact disturbing, if for no other reason than that they have many hopes for future experiences that would be dashed by permanent extinction.

Another implication, however, disturbs the morally minded, and that is that *nature is unjust*. Many people do bad things and get away with them; many good people are never adequately rewarded. At least this is so if nature is all there is. Religions around the world have, therefore, imagined a "future life" in which justice is done: People eventually get what they deserve. Nature itself can thus seem harsh, bringing a permanent end to our individual existence and allowing injustices to go uncorrected. A supernatural reality would seem to offer the only hope for immortality and for justice to be complete.

GOD IS SUPERNATURAL

Our notion of the supernatural has a precise meaning, referring to reality not implied by our empirical knowledge. To see what belongs to the supernatural and what accordingly transcends the reach of science, we must bear this in mind. Few people claim to know God, for example, the way they know their neighbors—through direct experience. They may think of themselves as acquainted with God personally, but who would attempt to prove his existence simply by pointing him out? It may be, however, that though he is literally "unseen," his existence can be *inferred* from experience, just as we infer the existence of entities mentioned in scientific theories. If so, God is scientifically knowable, and the scientific world-view may include him. It will prove worthwhile to see clearly why this is not so.

In the last chapter, we studied David Hume's account of how we make good empirical inferences; it is not surprising that he should have much to say about whether such inferences can be made to the existence of God.

That all inferences . . . concerning fact, are founded on experience, and that all experimental reasonings are founded on the supposition, that similar causes prove similar effects, and similar effects similar causes; I shall not, at present, much dispute with you. But observe, I entreat you, with what extreme caution all just reasoners proceed in the transferring of experiments to similar cases. Unless the cases be exactly similar, they repose no perfect confidence in applying their past observation to any particular phenomenon. Every alteration of circumstances occasions a doubt concerning the event; and it requires new experiments to prove certainly that the new circumstances are of no moment or importance. . . . But can you think . . . that your usual phlegm and philosophy have been preserved in so wide a step as you have taken, when you compared to the universe houses, ships, furniture, machines; and from their similarity in some circumstances inferred a similarity in their causes?[3]

Hume is supposing that someone who argues empirically for the existence of God will base his case on the observed fact that the universe displays great internal order, so that it resembles a complicated artifact created by intelligent design. Then, on the sound principle of reasoning, that like effects come from like causes, we can reason by analogy to the existence of an intelligent designer of the universe as a whole. If the whole world looks like a complicated artifact, why not conclude that it comes from an intelligent mind, just as we know from experience that artifacts do? Remember that empirical arguments are not supposed to be certain: the claim is only that it is reasonable to believe that the world as a whole has a cause similar to that of artifacts, based on the fact that it resembles them. But Hume objects even to this fallible inference. We have no reason to suppose that the world as a whole is more similar to an artifact than, say, to a cabbage (Hume's own example). But since we do not see cabbages coming from intelligent design, we have no reason to think the universe does.

Although this particular form of empirical argument is common, we may still wonder whether the point carries over to all possible attempts to argue empirically for the existence of God. The eighteenth-century German philosopher Immanuel Kant claims that the whole issue is essentially nonempirical in the following (typically obscure) passage:

[H]ow can experience ever be adequate to an idea? The peculiar nature of the latter consists just in the fact that no experience can ever be equal to it. The transcendental idea of a necessary and all-sufficient original being is so overwhelmingly great, so high above everything empirical, that latter being always conditioned, that it leaves us at a loss, partly because we can never find in experience material sufficient to satisfy such a concept, and partly because it is always in the sphere of the conditioned that we carry out our

---

3. From *David Hume: Writings on Religion*, ed. Anthony Flew (Chicago: Open Court, 1992).

search, seeking ever vainly for the unconditioned. . . . To advance to absolute totality by the empirical road is utterly impossible.[4]

This is going to take a good deal of explanation. Let us be clear about what it is for the existence of God to be an empirical issue. We are *not*, for example, asking whether we *already know* empirically of God's existence. This is why we do not have to establish whether some dramatic event such as the parting of the Red Sea or the bleeding of a statue actually occurred. What we want to know instead is whether, *if* it occurred, it would show that God exists. Since we want to know whether it is even *possible* to get enough empirical data to show that God exists, we can imagine what it *would* be like to be in the best situation for gathering such data. Nor are we asking whether God could get in touch with us, say, by creating a voice in our minds. We may suppose that he exists and that he can create for us any experience; the question is whether we would thereby *know* that it is he who is causing the experience.

THE NATURE OF GOD

We also need to be clear about what the conclusion of an empirical argument for God would mean: What does it *mean* to say that God exists? A familiar answer is that God has three characteristics (called the three "omnis"): he is **omnipotent** (all-powerful), **omniscient** (all-knowing), and **omnibenevolent** (all-good).

It is worthwhile considering why we *care* whether such a being exists. Many people want God to exist because of their hopes for the afterlife. By being omnipotent, he can create another world beyond nature (if this is possible), but any suggestion that he might lack power would undermine our hope that he will have the power to create such a future world for us. By being omnibenevolent, he will want what is best; if it is possible for him to prevent the evil of death, he will want to do so and will want to make our afterlife as good as possible. Also, it is only by being omniscient that we can be completely sure that the afterlife is as he wants it to be; any lack of knowledge could cause him to make a bad product, even with the best of intentions. There are also many people who want God's help in this life. Many want God's guidance in life; these people want in effect that God answer for them the basic question of ethics: "What should I do (with my life as a whole)?" Some of these people think that only God can answer this question, the correct answer being just to do what God says. But surely, we prefer to be guided by a person who is perfect. We do not want to be given bad advice because he fails to transmit correctly his message from a lack of power, or because he fails to give the correct advice through ignorance, or because he himself wants what is bad to happen.

---

4. From *Immanuel Kant's Critique of Pure Reason*, trans. Norman Kemp Smith (New York: St. Martin's, 1965).

There is another kind of help on Earth that some people want from God, and that is to be truly loved and encouraged in life. We want others to see what is good in us and through their love to make us feel that our whole existence is worthwhile. But to really care for us, they must really know us. Only an omniscient being could know us perfectly, and only the support of an omnibenevolent being would give us perfect encouragement in life. Although such a being would not have to be omnipotent, this Perfect Friend would have to be otherwise just like God. The question now is whether God's perfection makes him empirically unknowable.

EMPIRICAL ARGUMENTS FOR GOD

What would be the best kind of experience possible for inferring the existence of God? Since we would be attempting to know of the existence of something of perfect power, knowledge, and goodness, we would expect at least to have these characteristics demonstrated. Let us take just one of them—say, his power. In the best possible circumstance, we ourselves would witness the power and not have to rely on the (fallible) testimony of others. In the best circumstance, it would be God who is creating our experiences, and we can even suppose that he is willing to respond to our requests. We may suppose, for example, that he creates the most amazing displays of power that we can imagine. What would this show? That the being creating these effects is *very* powerful, sufficiently powerful to create *these* effects. But we do not know that this being is omnipotent until we see that it is *infinitely* powerful. The problem is that no matter how many displays of power are revealed in experience, there is never more than a *finite* amount of power revealed. The problem has to do with the limitations of experience itself. Empirical data are collected in time, and all that we can ever know empirically must be derived from a finite stretch of time. But no matter how long this time is, if it is finite, it can never reveal more than a finite amount of power issuing from some cause. We may say, therefore, that empirical *causes* are finite, meaning that any cause that we know empirically can never reveal more than a finite amount of some quantity, such as power. The same reasoning applies, therefore, to infinite knowledge and goodness.

The moral of this story is not that the existence of God is unknowable but rather that if it is, we must have *another* way of knowing besides the empirical. In the sixth chapter, we will examine some nonempirical arguments for God's existence that are respected by theologians. We are now, in this chapter, exploring the limits of empirical reality and thus the limits of science. The prior argument seems to show that—and why—it is not the business of science to reveal the existence of God.

THE IMMORTAL SOUL IS SUPERNATURAL

The same reasoning that led to the conclusion that God's existence is a nonempirical issue can be readily applied to the immortal soul. Many people want there to be a soul distinct from their body that goes on existing forever after the death of their body. Different religions offer different stories of the afterlife: Some tell of "another world" such as heaven; some tell of cycles of reincarnation. But either way, the belief in such an eternally existing soul seems not to be empirical. Notice that this is not to say that we could not have empirical evidence for the belief that we can exist after our body or apart from our body. Some people claim to have "out-of-body" experiences or "after-death" experiences. As with the supposed miracles that have led to assertions of God's existence, the crucial question is what such experiences would prove. If the soul can exist apart from or after the body, this means that the death of the body does not *ensure* the death of the soul. But this is far from saying that the soul will go on forever. Perhaps the soul can exist apart from the body for a time, after which it perishes, like a parasite cut off from its source of nourishment. How would we know empirically that it is destined to go on forever? At each point in time that it exists, we would know that it has not perished by *this* time; but it seems — once again — that it would take an *infinite* amount of time to know that it will *never* perish. Both God and the immortal souls that many hope are associated with their natural bodies seem, therefore, to belong to the supernatural, if they are real at all.

GOD AND THE IMMORTAL SOUL

Some people think that they can be confident that the soul is immortal if only we know that God exists. As mentioned earlier, they may think that God, if real, would not permit so great an evil as permanent extinction. The eighteenth-century English philosopher Mary Wollstonecraft provides one explanation for why God would not permit the soul to be mortal:

> The stamen of immortality, if I may be allowed the phrase, is the perfectibility of human reason; for, were man created perfect, or did a flood of knowledge break in upon him, when he arrived at maturity, that precluded error, I should doubt whether his existence would be continued after the dissolution of the body. But, in the present state of things, every difficulty in mortals that escapes from human discussion, and equally baffles the investigation of profound thinking, and the lightning glance of genius, is an argument on which I build my belief of the immortality of the soul. Reason is, consequentially, the simple power of improvement; or, more properly speaking, of discerning truth. Every individual is in this respect a world in itself. More or less may be conspicuous in one being than another; but the nature of reason must be the same in all, if it be an emanation of divinity, the tie that connects the creature with the Creator; for, can that soul be stamped with the heavenly image, that is not perfected by the exercise of its own reason?[5]

Humans have the capacity to improve their thinking beyond what is ever witnessed in nature. Would it not be absurd for God to implant this capacity in us

---

5. From *A Vindication of the Rights of Woman*, ed. Carol H. Postman (New York: Norton, 1988).

without the opportunity to develop it fully? There must be, therefore, an afterlife in which we are allowed to become all that we can be. If this argument is correct, it means that if you want justification for thinking the soul is immortal, all you need is justification for belief in God.

FREEDOM MAY BE SUPERNATURAL

Some philosophers have thought that human nature contains a power that does not exist in the empirical world. This power is supposed to be displayed whenever we make *choices*. To understand these claims, let us begin by seeing what choices are.

Not everything we "do" results from choice. If your leg rises from a strike under your kneecap, you "do" something (you lift your leg). But no choice is involved, since you did not do it *for a reason*. You can explain why your leg rose by giving the *cause* (the strike below your kneecap). But you did not *choose* to raise your leg, because if you did, you would be able to explain why it seemed a good idea to do so. Whenever we choose, we are faced with alternative courses of action that are open to us. We are "free" in some way to adopt any one of these. And we make our choice only when one of these appears *better* than the others. This is especially clear when our choice has been preceded by much deliberation, or mulling over the alternatives. But even when we act quickly, we still have our reasons, which seem, at least, to *justify* what we do. Sometimes we regret what we have done when we come to see that our reasons were not in fact good. You may have acted quickly on the sudden conviction that another drink at the party would be a good idea, only to berate yourself later for your foolishness. You realize that having this drink was not a good idea. But if you drank as a result of *choice*, then your action must *appear* as a good one when you make the decision. If it does not appear this way even in retrospect, then it will seem even to yourself that you did not *choose* to do it. Making a decision about what to do involves making a *judgment* (see Chapter One). When you choose to do something, you *judge* that action to be the better one among your alternatives. And judgments, as we have seen, are made with an awareness of reasons. This means that only thinkers, like ourselves, make choices. Other animals certainly do things, given what they believe and what they want. But this does not mean that they choose. Choice requires awareness of alternatives and a selection of one by a judgment that it is best.

It is uncontroversial that we make choices. What is at issue is whether our choices display a supernatural power. Why does choosing seem (to some philosophers) not to issue from the empirical world? The answer lies in the fact that whenever you choose to do anything, you *initiate* the action, all by yourself. At least this is how we commonly describe it. If you push someone else in a state of anger, we say that *you* were the one who "started it." But the very idea that there are beings in nature who "start" things is problematic. We can see why by recalling that events in the empirical world (at least at the level with which we are familiar) are *determined* by prior causes. Given the prior causes, only that event *could* happen. Given the position, weight, and so forth, of the eight ball and the direction, speed, and so forth, of the cue ball, there is only one motion the eight ball *can* take on impact. If this were not so, the fact that the eight ball takes off as it does on impact would be a complete mystery, even to God. Now the actions that we perform in making a choice certainly belong to nature. Squeezing the trigger of a gun, for example, involves one material thing (the finger) moving another (the trigger). If the firing of the gun is not to be a cosmic mystery, there must be prior causes that determine why it happened as it did. And there is, since the squeezing of the trigger causes the gun to fire. But then this squeezing is an event that is determined by something prior. Suppose this results by choice. Then it is the fact that the person made this choice that causes the finger to curl. The crucial question is what caused this *choice* to occur. It would seem to be the fact that the person *wanted* to fire the gun and *saw* that he could do so by squeezing the trigger. But why did the person come into the situation with this desire and belief?

Determinism is the claim that everything that happens in nature has causes in nature that determine it, making it the only event possible. If determinism is true, we could look into the past of the person who shot the gun and see a series of causes that created the desire to pull the trigger. If we look back far enough, the series of causes will come from events that this individual certainly could not have chosen, including his genetic makeup, social situation, and the manner of his upbringing. Many philosophers have concluded on the basis of such reflections that whenever we "choose," we do *not* really "start" anything.

Many other philosophers, however, have recoiled from this conclusion. If we allow that you do not initiate your actions, we allow in an important sense that it is not *you* who does anything! Would this not mean that you are never *responsible* for anything? Take an ordinary example: If it looks like you have pushed someone, but it turns out that you were forced into this by being yourself pushed from behind, then it was not really *you* who initiated the action, and this makes you not *blameworthy*. Those philosophers who deny that we have a genuine power to initiate actions seem to be saying that *everything* we do is like this. Their belief in determinism seems to mean that we are never responsible, never blameworthy or praiseworthy, for anything! No one ever *deserves* punishment or reward. Our very general practice of holding people responsible for what they do *seems* to be undermined by a very plausible thesis in metaphysics.

As we will see in the next chapter, some philosophers deny that determinism undermines moral responsibility. But many philosophers have thought that it does. Among these, those who still insist that we are responsible for our actions have therefore denied that determinism is true. It is precisely this point that involves the idea that choices have a supernatural source. These philosophers believe that whenever you choose, *nothing* in the natural world determines the choice you make. They will allow that there are causes in the natural world that lead up to your *having* the choice in question. They will allow, for example, that there may be causes that produce the *desire* to shoot a gun. But whether you act on that desire is completely *up to you*. It is just this sort of power to choose that would be supernatural.

For how can we *test* for the presence of such a power? This power is supposed to be exercised only when no natural causes for a choice exist. Just because we do not *know* what the natural causes of a choice are, however, we have no reason to suppose that there *are* none. For all we know, we may get new data that allow us to infer a natural cause. The problem is similar to the one of knowing empirically of the existence of God or immortal souls. It would take an infinite amount of data to know that there are in fact no natural causes for a choice. The claim that such a power exists would be a pseudohypothesis, *if* it were made simply to explain why choices occur. But this is not why some philosophers believe in this power. They believe it exists from the two convictions that we are responsible for our choices and that determinism must be false for this to be so. Each of these convictions is denied by other philosophers, as we will see in the next chapter.

VALUES

The issue of whether we are responsible for what we do raises an important fact about all empirical knowledge. We have been asking what the reality is like that corresponds to our empirical knowledge. We have found that we do know empirically very much about how things really are. This raises the question of whether what we know empirically is *only* about how things are and not at all about how things ought to be. Many philosophers have held this view. As Kant put the point neatly, "Experience tells us how things are, not how they ought to be." When we open our eyes, we see how things are before us; whether this is good or the way things should be does not seem to be the business of the senses to reveal. If it were, it ought to be just as evident to other animals that share our senses. But though we grant that they have *desires*, there seems no reason to admit that they are making *evaluations*. It seems the same in introspection. When you look within your own mind, you may discover what you *believe* to be right or wrong, good or bad, but this does not mean that you are correct. Suppose promise breaking is wrong. This is a fact about promise breaking and not a fact about what is in your mind, so it is just not the sort of fact that we *could* know by introspection.

To see the point more clearly, suppose that someone were to disagree with you on a question of value. Suppose, for example, that while you are strict about keeping your promises, this other person feels free to forget hers. If the issue of whether this is wrong were empirical, we would be able to settle it by finding enough sensory or introspective data. But could not this same person agree to all the same facts revealed in experience and still disagree about the wrongness of promise breaking? Nor does it seem to help when we turn to inferred facts about causes and effects. If someone does not see that she is wrong in breaking a promise, how will it help to explain what causes led her to do it? It may seem that we can persuade this person by pointing to the effects of her actions — the distrust she creates, for example. But if she is really clear about her view, she can accept all of these and still claim it is not wrong. At this point, the person reveals that she has different values from yours. As with the existence of God, this does *not* mean that nothing more can be said; it means only that the issue is not *empirical*.

CONCLUSION

In Part One, we discussed in detail three sources of knowledge that are commonly used: sensation, introspection, and intellect. Empirical knowledge is based on the direct knowledge of sensation and introspection. Each of these reveals a certain kind of reality. Material things are known by the senses, minds by introspection. We are sure that there are many more material things and minds beyond those we observe. We learn of these by inference, which requires the intellect to be aware of the thoughts that form chains of reasoning. Nature, the empirical world, is the whole reality consisting of these three kinds of reality.

No assumptions were made about how these three are related; such questions will be addressed in the rest of Part Two. Here we have been concerned more with what nature leaves out. The supernatural was found to contain God, the immortal soul, and possibly the freedom to choose that underlies our responsibility. Religions around the world have prescribed a way of life oriented to such things. Because science seeks only empirical knowledge, it is not by science that we may expect to know about them. Kant held that all of metaphysics was concerned mainly with the three ideas of God, immortality, and freedom. It is these ideas especially that we will examine in the rest of Part Two.

STUDY QUESTIONS

1. What is the basic question of metaphysics, and why is it unavoidable?
2. What are the main characteristics of *material* things?
3. How is it that plants are not *aware* of their environment even though they respond to it?
4. How are *thoughts* different from material things?
5. How is it, according to William James, that religions are concerned with the supernatural?
6. What needs do religions answer, according to Erich Fromm?
7. What do many people find disturbing about the claim that nature is all there is? (Be complete.)
8. Explain the argument that the existence of God is not an empirical issue.
9. Do the same for the immortality of the soul.
10. Why do many people think it important whether God exists?
11. What justification did Mary Wollstonecraft give for the immortality of the soul?
12. What is the problem in saying that something in nature *initiates* changes?

CHAPTER FIVE

Mind and Matter

WHAT ARE WE? When we ask this question in metaphysics, we want a very general answer, one that shows how we fit into the world as a whole. The last chapter explored the implications of the metaphysical view that nature is all there is. Nature consists of material things, minds, and thoughts. If nature is all there is, we are purely natural things, and it should be possible to describe what we are in terms for these three kinds of reality. We might say, for example, that each of us is a combination of a material body and a mind by which we are of the material things, minds, and thoughts themselves. But we have seen no reason to suppose that nature *is* all there is. Rather, we have found that many people, especially through their religious beliefs, affirm as real other things, including God, immortal souls, and freedom. They would say that no view of ourselves is complete that fails to explain how we are related to God, or how we can live beyond our bodies, or how we can be responsible for our choices. Since we will concentrate in the next chapter on issues related specifically to God, in this chapter we focus primarily on the issues of immortality and freedom.

IMMORTALITY

The soul is immortal only if we do live after the death of our bodies. But how is this possible? What must *we* be like? Must we be able to exist with no body at all? Or would we have a new body in the afterlife? Opinion has been divided on this issue. In the following passage, the twentieth-century theologian Maurice Lamm explains why Judaism insists that we do have bodies in the afterlife:

> Judaism has always stressed that the body, as the soul, is a gift of God—indeed, that it belongs to God. . . . To care for the body is a religious command of the Bible. The practice of asceticism for religious purposes was tolerated, but the ascetic had to bring a sacrifice of atonement for his action. Resurrection affirms that the body is of value, because it came from God, and it will be revived by God. Resurrection affirms that man's empirical existence is valuable in God's eyes. His activities in this world are significant in the scheme of eternity. His strivings are not to be deprecated as vain and useless, but are to be brought to fulfillment at the end of days.[1]

The opposite view is argued for in the following excerpt by the nineteenth-century French philosopher Jacques Maritain. (Maritain is explaining what he takes to be the position of the Roman Catholic Church, as developed in the Middle Ages, especially by the great Christian philosopher Saint Thomas Aquinas.)

> The activity of the intellect is immaterial because the . . . object of the intellect is not, like the object of the senses, a particular and limited category of things . . . it is the whole universe and the texture of sense-perceptible reality which can be known by the intellect. . . . Just as the intellect is spiritual, that is to say, intrinsically independent of matter in its operation and in its nature, so also, and for the same reason, the human soul, the substantial root of the intellect, is spiritual, that is, intrinsically independent of matter in its nature and in its existence.[2]

THE PROBLEM OF PERSONAL IDENTITY

This issue is an illustration of a more general problem in philosophy called the **problem of personal identity.** We will discuss this more general problem to see whether we can make headway about immortality of the soul. There are many examples of the problem, but they take the same general form. A situation involving a certain person (perhaps yourself) is imagined, and then another situation, also involving a person, is imagined; the question is whether it is the very same person being described in both situations. This same kind of problem often occurs in daily life. As a jury member, for example, you might wonder whether the person who committed the murder is the same one who now sits before you in this courtroom. In normal life, this kind of question is empirical, since it would be *possible* to answer it by getting enough observational data. If you had watched the person committing the murder and then had followed him at every moment after this occurrence until he sits before you in the courtroom, then you would have extremely good empirical evidence that it is the same person in both situations. The problem in normal life is that we do not have such data and must make an inference from far fewer facts.

---

1. From *The Jewish Way in Death and Mourning* (New York: David, 1969).
2. From *The Range of Reason* (New York: Scribner's, 1952).

Now, the problem of personal identity in philosophy is different in not being empirical. The problem does not even have to involve actual situations, and typically it does not. Usually we are asked to imagine two circumstances, imagining all the empirical data we might like. In those cases it is not enough to have all the relevant data, so we must ask the characteristically philosophical question of how we should think or talk about them. Consider this science fiction example. Suppose that highly advanced extraterrestrials come to Earth with a new technology. They can scan a person's body just before death and keep an extremely detailed three-dimensional record of the body's exact composition and internal structure, including that of the brain. Suppose they use this technology on a person just before a violent accident, such as an explosion in a mine, that utterly destroys his body. The aliens then use the three-dimensional record to re-create a living body *exactly* like that of the person just before the explosion. The technology is so exact that when it is used to reassemble molecules into this living organism, no one can tell the difference between this new person and the original. The question is whether the new person is in fact the *very same person* as the original.

This is a nonempirical problem, because all the relevant observations that we could make about the case have been given. The question is whether we should say that it is the *same* person with a new body or that it is a *different* person who is exactly like the first (and who no longer exists). We cannot answer the question by just looking, since all we will "see" is what has already been described.

The same kind of problem can be raised with respect to things other than us. If a watchmaker takes apart a watch, then puts all the parts into special bins with many other parts of the same kind, and then later just happens to pick out these same original parts and makes a watch from them, will this "new" watch be the same as the original or a different one just like it? Again, the question is plainly nonempirical. In the case of things other than us, it may not matter to us which answer is true. But with ourselves, the answer seems very important. First, we have desires to do things we have not yet done or to have new experiences. With death, our hopes for the future are dashed. Second, questions of responsibility turn on the issue of personal identity. Suppose that the person who stepped on the mine owed you money. Would the new person created by the aliens "inherit" this debt? It would seem that he would, if this new person really is the same person as the one who borrowed the money; and if it is not the same person, could not this person say that *he* never incurred the obligation to you, having just come into existence? These two kinds of issues, our hopes for the future and our past obligations, seem to show why the question of personal identity is important even though it is not empirical.

LOCKE'S SOLUTION

The whole issue of personal identity got started mainly by John Locke, who presents his own solution in the following passage:

> This being premised, to find wherein personal identity consists, we must consider what person stands for; which, I think, is a thinking intelligent being, that has reason and reflection, and can consider itself as itself, the same thinking thing, in different times and places; which it does only by that consciousness which is inseparable from thinking, and, as it seems to me, essential to it: it being impossible for any one to perceive without perceiving that he does perceive. When we see, hear, smell, taste, feel, meditate, or will anything, we know that we do so. Thus it is always as to our present sensations and perceptions: and by this every one is to himself that which he calls self: it not being considered, in this case, whether the same self be continued in the same or divers substances. For, since consciousness always accompanies thinking, and it is that which makes every one to be what he calls self, and thereby distinguishes himself from all other thinking things, in this alone consists personal identity, i.e. the sameness of a rational being: and as far as this consciousness can be extended backwards to any past action or thought, so far reaches the identity of that person; it is the same self now it was then; and it is by the same self with this present one that now reflects on it, that that action was done.[3]

Locke's answer to what makes a person the same individual at a later time is that the later person has conscious recall of the experiences of the earlier person. He would say of our science fiction example that it clearly depicts a case in which the same person continues to exist with the construction of an exact replica of his body.

Another imaginary example may show the plausibility of Locke's view. Suppose that you suffer a brain disease that completely expunges all memory, including all acquired mental characteristics, such as language skills and character. The mental slate is wiped clean. Let us suppose further that your body is taken to another part of the world, where the disease is completely cured. From this point on, there is a whole new process of learning a different language and culture and making new relationships. This "later" person would have your body, but would he or she be *you*? Many people agree with Locke that this person would *not* be you, since he or she would have no possible way of remembering any of your current or past life.

Locke supported his view with a certain observation about us. Recall that one of the facts that appears to be important about personal identity is that one must be the same person to retain obligations. Suppose now that in the "past life" you committed a crime, and the "new" person is being charged for it. Locke's claims that if someone cannot possibly remember a crime, punishment would appear only like a "calamity" (meaning that it would not appear fair). If to be the same person at a later time one must be responsible for the actions of the "original" person at an ear-

---

3. From *An Essay Concerning Human Understanding* (1689), Book 2, Chapter 27.

lier time, *and* if this requires that one be able to remember these actions, then Locke is right. If your mind were "wiped clean," the person who gets your body would not be *you*.

Locke's influential view is very relevant to our original question of what we must be like for immortality of the soul to be possible. For if correct, it shows exactly how it is possible for each of us to be resurrected with a body. If God chooses to create a body exactly like your current one, no matter how far in the future this takes place, this act, according to Locke, would bring you back into existence.

THE PROBLEM OF POSSIBLE DUPLICATION

A certain objection to Locke's view, however, has turned many philosophers today against it. If God could create one body exactly like yours, could he not create others? But which one would be you? It seems arbitrary to choose one of the copies over the others. Even if he chooses to create just one, can we still say that would be you, knowing that if he *had* created others, that very same person would *not* be you? This **problem of possible duplication** has led many philosophers to conclude that merely creating an exact copy of you after the destruction of your body is not enough to bring *you* back to life. In normal life, what guarantees that "two of you" cannot show up in the future is that you have a single, persisting material body that allows us to "track" you through time. But if the persistence of your body is necessary for your continued existence, then even God cannot bring you back into existence by creating an exact copy of it.

DUALISM

Let us consider the alternative view, then, that immortality involves the persistence of the soul without the body. Because the notion of a soul may be fuzzy to you, it should help to note that in modern times, the soul is typically identified with the mind. You may recall from Chapter Two the dream hypothesis described by René Descartes. Suppose that your entire life has been one extended dream and that the entire material world is but an illusion. You would still have introspection and thus would still know of your own mind. Your mind would exist without your body, just as the soul has traditionally been thought of as the source of life that continues after bodily death. We have seen Maritain's argument for the disembodied soul or mind. Now let us look at Descartes's:

> I know that all the things that I clearly and distinctly understand can be made by God such as I understand them. For this reason, my ability clearly and distinctly to understand one thing without another suffices to make me certain that the one thing is different from the other, since they can be separated from each other, at least by God. The question as to the sort of power that might effect such a separation is not relevant to their being thought to

> be different. For this reason, from the fact that I know that I exist, and that at the same time I judge that obviously nothing else belongs to my nature or essence except that I am a thinking thing, I rightly conclude that my essence consists entirely in my being a thinking thing. And although perhaps (or rather, as I shall soon say, assuredly) I have a body that is very closely conjoined to me, nevertheless, because on the one hand I have a clear and distinct idea of myself, insofar as I am merely a thinking thing and not an extended thing, and because on the other hand I have a distinct idea of a body, insofar as it is merely an extended thing and not a thinking thing, it is certain that I am really distinct from my body, and can exist without it.[4]

Remember that with the dream hypothesis Descartes thinks he has shown that it is possible that your mind can exist without your body. If the whole material world were illusion, your mind would exist without your (material) body. What he argues is that if it is *possible* for your mind to be without your body, then it must *in fact* be a different thing. It is not possible, for example, that the first president of the United States could ever have lived separately from George Washington, since the first president *was* George Washington. If it is even possible for things to exist apart, then they are not the same thing. This seems to be the gist of Descartes's argument, and it certainly deserves to be taken seriously.

Put more precisely, Descartes is arguing for a **dualism** of mind and body, which means that each can exist without the other. A table is not the same thing as its surface, yet the table and surface are not two things that can exist without each other. If the mind of a person is like the surface of a table, then even though it is "different" from the body, it cannot exist without it. Dualism holds instead that each person is really a mind, which can exist apart from the body. Even if a mind naturally exists with a body, as a "separate thing" it can be transferred from one body to another, like a captain taking command of a new ship.

DUALISM AND DUPLICATION

It may be objected that the idea of minds existing without bodies is too bizarre to take seriously. How would they communicate, if they had no lips and there was no air to carry their sounds? How good would it be if they could not touch each other or otherwise engage in physical activities? One possibility is that God could create and orchestrate their sensory experiences in what is called a *preestablished harmony*, so that it *appeared* just like they had bodies even though they did not. Another possibility is that God could create real bodies, just as before, but now the duplication problem would be solved by giving the new body the *same mind* as the

---

4. From *Meditations on First Philosophy*, 3d ed., trans. Donald A. Cress (Indianapolis, IN: Hackett, 1993).

person whose body had been destroyed. The problem of duplication arose when we imagined resurrection occurring *just* by creating an exact replica of a person after their death. If dualism is true, however, even if two or more replicas are created of you at a later time, the one that is you is the one that is inhabited by the very same mind that left your body when your body lost life. Dualism supposes that your mind is like your body in being a thing that occupies a single place at each point of time in its travels. It is different from your body in not being a material thing at all. It may be *located* roughly with the body it inhabits, but it is not extended in space and has no weight. But because the mind can be in only one place at any time, if your mind settles into a replica of you in the future, you will exist where that replica is, even if ones just like it are sitting around.

THE PROBLEM OF INTERACTION

What has most bothered philosophers about dualism is that it gives rise to the **problem of interaction.** There is a great deal of causal interaction between a person's mind and his or her body. Stick the body with a pin, and a feeling of pain occurs in the mind; create an intention in the mind to walk, and the body moves. Dualism makes it utterly mysterious how the mind and body *could* interact. For the essence of the position is to assert that minds and bodies are entirely different kinds of things. This creates the mystery of how such things can affect one another.

Consider this analogy: Suppose that the pen on your desk suddenly shifts several inches to the left. How seriously would you take the suggestion that it was pushed by the number 2? Whatever numbers are, they are just not the *sort* of thing that could push anything around. In fact, it looks like nothing *could* push or otherwise act on a material thing except another material thing. How can something with extension and weight be influenced by something that is like a point? Many philosophers have thought that the problem of interaction disproves dualism.

DOUBLE ASPECT

Dualism suffers from the problem of interaction because it says the mind is an immaterial thing that somehow interacts with a material thing (the body). But what if the mind and the body are not really two different things that can exist independently of each other? What if there is in reality only one thing, the person, that is in fact both a mind and body? This position is called **monism** to contrast it neatly with dualism.

We will look at three different forms of monism. The first says that mind and body are two different *aspects* of the same thing. The shape and color of a balloon are two aspects of the balloon. The texture and elasticity of a piece of rubber are two aspects of it. We can describe anything in different ways, and for each of these ways we can talk about the aspect under which the thing appears when so described. Now even though the color and shape of the balloon are "different things," neither can exist independently of the balloon. You cannot pull apart the aspects of a thing the way you can separate its parts. The difference between the aspects is simply the difference between two ways of thinking or speaking about a single thing.

The **double aspect theory** says that mind and body are different aspects of a person. These two aspects are the ways we think of ourselves in introspection or sensation. You can look at yourself the way others do—for example, by looking in a mirror. When you do, all that you see is "your body." But your body *is* you, so called when looked at from the "outside." There are not two things, you and your body; there is just you. We *call* you a body when concerned with your material aspect, the way you exist in space, with weight and shape. So also the mind is not something separate from the body. When you introspect, you are aware of *yourself*—as something that is conscious, thinking, feeling, and so forth. Your mind is just you, thought of under the mental aspect.

Benedict Spinoza, a seventeenth-century Dutch philosopher, defended the view as a deliberate response to Descartes. The following is one of his clearer expressions:

> [S]ubstance thinking and substance extended are one and the same substance, comprehended now through one attribute, now through the other. . . . This truth seems to have been dimly recognized by those Jews who maintained that God, God's intellect, and the things understood by God are identical. For instance, a circle existing in nature, and the idea of a circle existing, which is also in God, are one and the same thing displayed through different attributes. Thus, whether we conceive nature under the attribute of extension, or under the attribute of thought, or under any other attribute, we shall find the same order, or one and the same chain of causes—that is, the same things following in either case.[5]

This theory has the virtue of *explaining* the assumption of Descartes's argument for dualism—that we can conceive of ourselves without our bodies. Your material features (your weight, shape, composition, and so forth) are simply not *known* from the perspective of introspection. But this does not mean that you do not *have* them. A balloon still has a color even when we describe it only as "that round thing." Introspection makes us aware of ourselves, but only insofar as we have mental features (consciousness, thought, desires, and so forth). According to the double aspect theory, this creates the impression that we are immaterial things. But the truth is just that we are material things but do not appear as material when introspecting.

Needless to say, the double aspect theory holds out no hope for immortality. If the mind is merely an aspect of the person, then it can no more exist after the death of the body than the surface of a table can exist after the table is chopped up

---

5. From "The Ethics," Book II, Proposition VI, note, in *The Chief Works of Benedict Spinoza*, trans. R. H. M. Elwes (New York: Dover, [1951]).

and burned. The great advantage of this theory over dualism is that it avoids the problem of interaction. When "the mind" is affecting "the body," there is just one thing, which is both mental and physical, that is bringing about changes in itself. This is no more mysterious than a dog scratching itself or a plant extending its roots.

THE MIND–BODY PROBLEM

The double aspect theory may seem to have all the advantages over dualism. But it has its own problems. It *says* that mind and body are two aspects of a single thing, but it is not obvious that this is even *possible*. It is not difficult to see how shape and color can be two aspects of a single thing. The shape is a matter of exactly how the thing is extended in space, and the color is a quality of the surface that would be formed by this extension. But many philosophers have found puzzling the idea that something that is material could also be like a mind or whether a mind could be a heavy thing extended in space. It does seem odd to say that your body thinks, talks, or looks around. The double aspect theorist will say that this is because we use the idea of your body to refer to you when we want to isolate just your material aspect. But perhaps the oddness is due to the fact that mental and material features *conflict* with one another, so that the same thing *cannot* have both. The mind has a point of view; it does not seem to have parts that could be separated; it responds to reasons; it is aware of itself; it forms plans and is conscious. *Maybe* a material thing can be all of these ways.

The great virtue of dualism is that it does full justice to the very great differences that *seem* to exist between mind and body. The **mind–body problem** is the problem of saying how the mind and body are related. The reason it is a problem is that the fact of mind–body interaction inclines us to equate them, but whether this is possible is not obvious, owing to the very different ways in which we describe them. Until it is *explained* how the same thing can be both mind and matter, dualism will not have been satisfactorily refuted.

IDEALISM

Double aspect theory avoids the problem of interaction by denying dualism in favor of monism. But it does so in such a way as to make immortality of the soul impossible. Is there a way of being a monist while still making room for the soul's immortality? Yes, and it has been held by many philosophers in the last few centuries. According to **idealism**, you are *just* a mind. This seems to mean that you have no body at all, and some idealists (as we will see in the next chapter) have said as much. But some idealists have wished to avoid saying something so apparently absurd. The eighteenth-century Christian bishop George Berkeley (pronounced "Bark-ly") was an idealist who said that material things like our bodies do exist. How can this be? A contemporary of his, Samuel Johnson, claimed to refute Berkeley by kicking a stone, meaning that nothing is more obvious than the existence of material things. But Berkeley allows that there are material things like stones by saying that there is nothing more to them than the various sensory experiences we attribute to them. Kick the stone, and what happens? Your mind contains certain tactual sensations, including perhaps a bit of pain, and other minds have visual sensations that make it look like a stone is rolling. There is simply no way to "go outside" these sensations and be aware of "the stone itself," since the only way we are aware of material objects like stones is just by having sensations. The following is one of many passages in which Berkeley argues the point:

> The table I write on I say exists — that is, I see and feel it; and if I were out of my study I should say it existed — meaning thereby that if I was in my study I might perceive it. There was an odor, that is, it was smelt; there was a sound, that is, it was heard; a color or figure, and it was perceived by sight or touch. This is all that I can understand by these and the like expressions. For as to what is said of the absolute existence of unthinking things without any relation to their being perceived, that seems perfectly unintelligible. Their *esse* is *percipi* [their nature is to be perceived], nor is it possible they should have any existence out of the minds or thinking things which perceive them.[6]

STRENGTHS OF IDEALISM

Idealism avoids the problem of interaction. When the mind and the body "affect one another," what is really going on is not the actions of two separate things on each other. There is just one thing, the mind, undergoing various changes. When you see a pin stuck into your arm and feel the pain, a series of sensations ensue. First are the visual sensations that make it look like there is a pin there, and then there is the sensation of pain. This is not, however, one kind of thing (the punctured arm) bringing about an entirely different kind of thing (the pain). For there is nothing more to the reality of the pin or the arm than the visual sensations and others like them. In particular, you can present your body to yourself only by having sensations, either internal sensations of the way it feels or visual sensations and the like when you "observe" it. According to Berkeley, there is nothing more to the reality of any material object than the sensations by which we say the thing "appears."

Idealism cannot be refuted empirically. For whenever you produce sensations that we normally think would reveal an "external" thing independent of them, Berkeley will say that the material thing simply *consists* of these sensations. Also, you cannot produce the material thing apart from sensations, since it is only by sensations that we know of it in the first place. Berkeley claims that we have no good

---

6. From "A Treatise Concerning the Principles of Human Knowledge," in *The Empiricists* (Garden City, NY: Dolphin, [1961]).

reason to say that in addition to the sensations that we certainly know, there is also a material object that we cannot present by itself.

Finally, idealism, at least as Berkeley presents it, offers its own *explanation* of how mind and body are related. Minds have sensations, and some *groups* of these *are* the material things. Consider this analogy: Suppose you are unfamiliar with colleges, and this is your first time on campus. You are shown various buildings, but none of them is identified as "the college," so you innocently ask for the location of the college. You are then told that the college is *composed* of the various buildings you have seen. Now you *understand* what a college is and how it is related to the buildings on campus. Idealism offers an analogous explanation of the relation of mind and body.

IDEALISM AND IMMORTALITY

Idealism clearly makes room for the soul's immortality. For what is the "death of the body" but a change of sensations? We think we have a body in this life only because it looks like we do by the particular sensations that we have. When we try to "move," we make an effort that normally results in changes in vision and other sensations, including those that seem to outline a body that follows us. The "death of the body" can only mean that these kinds of sensations no longer occur. But nothing stops us from having other experiences, including the blissful ones we expect in the afterlife. Idealism has the advantage of greatly simplifying the story of what happens to the soul when the body perishes. If the body is an independent thing that the soul (or mind) inhabits, then this soul must travel somehow from the corpse to an entirely different place. In ancient times, heaven could be thought of as just beyond the clouds, so that the journey of a soul was no more mysterious than the rising of smoke. But modern science makes it mysterious where heaven is or whether it is a place at all, located "out there." We have seen very far out there, and heaven has not yet appeared. Does the soul somehow travel the enormous distances by itself to a region not seen? Or is heaven on a dimension not available to our senses in this life?

Berkeley has a simpler story. "Going to heaven" is simply a change that occurs within the mind, no more mysterious in principle than the changes we undergo in everyday life.

OBJECTION TO IDEALISM

Although we cannot refute idealism empirically, for example, by kicking a stone, it still has problems. Perhaps the most serious is that it makes a complete mystery of why we have the particular course of sensory experiences that we do. Why, for example, when we say that a stone is there, does it look a certain way? And why can we successfully predict how our visual experiences will change if we change our perspective on it, say, by walking around it or picking it up? The obvious answer seems to be that it looks and feels these ways *because* a stone is there. For this response to be a genuine explanation, we cannot be simply repeating ourselves by talking about the sensory experiences we are trying to explain. The assumption that a stone is there, a material object existing independently of our sensations (an "external thing," in Locke's terminology), *explains* why it looks and feels as it does. If a material stone were not there, then why would our experiences not be like a dream, in which our expectations are regularly unfulfilled? When our experiences do come out as we predict, they have a *coherence*—they go together in a certain way. The course of experience we have when walking around a stone and picking it up has such a coherence.

Our experiences of mirages are quite different. At first we think water is there, but then our predictions are foiled. If there really were water there, then it would continue to look like water there when we approach it, and we would feel it when we reach down to gather some up. In the case of mirages and other illusions, our experiences are like those of dreams, relatively chaotic and unpredictable.

In normal, nonillusory cases, our experiences have a definite coherence to them. Now why is that? Berkeley claims that the difference between observing a material object and having merely illusory experiences is *only* that the experiences of the first are coherent and those of the second are chaotic. But can we not demand an *explanation* for the difference? The assumption that there are material objects is like a hypothesis of science, which (as we saw in Chapter Four) is justified by its ability to explain. Those who assert the reality of material things like our bodies do so on the ground that they can explain why we have the coherent streams of sensory experiences that we do. Even though the philosophical issue is not empirical, it is argued in much the same way that issues of science are.

MATERIALISM

The double aspect theory says that mind and body are two aspects of the same thing. Idealism says that there are only minds, and bodies exist only in the mind. Idealism has the advantage of offering an explanation of how the mind and body are related that makes clear how the same thing (the mind) is a combination of mind and body. They both avoid the problem of interaction because they are monistic. Is there a form of monism that avoids the problems of idealism while still offering a solution to the mind–body problem?

Idealism explains the relation by explaining how the body belongs to the mind. **Materialism** reverses the order of explanation, claiming that the mind can be understood in terms of the body. As idealism says that each of us is just a mind, materialism says that each of us is just a body. And just as idealism may or may not also allow the existence of the body, materialism may or may not also allow the existence of the mind. In both cases, the more popular versions have allowed both mind and body. The difference, then, is which is more *basic*. The more basic one is the one that will be used to explain the other.

Aristotle's Version

A sophisticated form of materialism was developed by Aristotle (Plato's younger colleague, thought by many to be the greatest philosopher of all time). The following contains the kernel of his theory:

> [T]he soul must be a substance in the sense of the form of a natural body having life potentially within it . . . soul is the actuality of a body. . . . Now the word actuality has two senses corresponding respectively to the possession of knowledge and actual exercise of knowledge. It is obvious that soul is actuality in the first sense, viz. that of knowledge possessed, for both sleeping and waking presuppose the existence of the soul, and of these waking corresponds to actual knowing, sleeping to knowledge possessed but not employed . . . we can wholly dismiss as unnecessary the question whether the soul and body are one: it is as meaningless to ask whether the wax and the shape given to it by the stamp are one, or generally the matter of a thing and that of which it is the matter . . . [soul is] "the essential whatness" of a body of the character just assigned.[7]

According to Aristotle, the mind is the "form" of the body, the way the body is organized so as to be alive. If you look at the organs of any living thing, you will see parts that cooperate so that the organism lives a certain kind of life. In humans, this particular organization enables them above all to think and understand the world around them. To be a person is thus to be a living body with a certain internal structure, and this structure *is* the mind. It is, therefore, no more possible for us to live after our bodies than it is possible for the structure of a house to exist after the materials have been taken apart.

Strengths of Materialism

Many philosophers today are materialists. This is due in large part to the enormous success of the natural sciences, such as physics, chemistry, and biology. These intellectual disciplines have proven themselves capable of explaining so much about our bodies that there seems to be no need to suppose that our bodies are activated by separately existing minds. We have seen how materialism, at least as presented by Aristotle, explains the relation of mind to body. The mind is related to the body as the internal structure of a house is related to the house. Materialism also avoids the problem of interaction. When a pin is stuck in your arm, certain nerves are stimulated. Materialists today would say that the pain that "results" is nothing more than the stimulation of these nerves. There is thus no mystery in seeing why, whenever you are stuck with a pin, you feel pain. This is because the pain you feel is the nerve impulse that science has shown to be associated with pain.

---

7. From "De Anima," in *The Basic Works of Aristotle*, ed. Richard McKeon (New York: Random House, 1941).

It is important to see that science itself does not prove materialism. All that science shows is what kind of event occurring in the body is *associated* with mental events such as pain. A dualist could accept all these same findings and say science has shown that *whenever* a pain occurs in the mind, a certain kind of nerve is stimulated. The materialist goes farther and says the pain *just is* the nerve stimulation. Although this is how materialism avoids the problem of interaction, this sort of claim still bothers some philosophers.

The Task for Materialism

Materialism is closely similar to the double aspect theory, but it differs by saying that the body is *basic* in relation to the mind. What this means is the ways in which we describe the body are supposed to be enough for explaining what it is to have a mind. Bodies are material things, and thus we have the full resources of natural science (especially chemistry and biology) to describe them. But can we explain what it is to have a mind in these terms? Many philosophers today are trying to do just that. Nevertheless, some still do not expect success. Above all, they do not see how consciousness, which is most apparent from the perspective of introspection, can be explained by talking about events in the nervous system. When you look at a beautiful sunset, you can introspect and attend just to *how it looks* to you. This visual sensation is an event occurring within you and so, according to materialism, just is an event in your body, of the same sort that biologists describe in terms of chemical reactions. On the one hand, we are inclined to claim that materialism is true in order to avoid the theoretical problem of interaction; but on the other hand, to do so we must assert that things are identical that could hardly seem more different. Until materialism can answer this sort of question, it will not be found satisfactory to all. To answer this question successfully is to solve the mind–body problem.

MATERIALISM AND IDEALISM

I illustrated materialism with Aristotle's theory and idealism with Berkeley's theory. Since each of these is only one version of a more general position, let us try to get clearer about what the difference is between materialism and idealism. Both are reactions to dualism, and both have the advantage of avoiding the problem of interaction. In spite of this problem, however, dualism has the advantage of doing full justice to the fact that we have both bodies and minds. In the hands of Berkeley, the claim that we have bodies, or a material nature at all, can easily seem to be underestimated, to say the least. But we can say of idealism in general that any form of it will emphasize the fact that we have minds, or a mental nature, and everything we want to say about our minds will not be compromised by the fact that we are material as well. By contrast, a materialist will have to take seriously our material nature, even if this prevents us from saying all we might want to say about ourselves in virtue of the fact that we have minds. An obvious example is the fact that materialists cannot allow for the existence of the mind apart from the body. There may be other *restrictions* in the nature of the mind that materialism forces us to admit. As we will see in the next chapter, for example, some philosophers and religious visionaries take seriously the idea that our individual minds are merely aspects of some collective mind. A materialist who is attracted to this idea might have more difficulty in explaining this than an idealist, since it is plain that my living body is simply a distinct entity from yours. In addition, many philosophers want to say that we have motives that are quite different from those of lower animals. It seems that we are, for example, capable of acting for the good of humanity or of understanding and following God. But materialism says that we are just living bodies, like other animals. Is this view consistent with the idea that we can act so differently? Maybe so, but at least materialism will have to explain how this is possible.

In its crudest versions, materialism tends to associate us closely with other animals (which have bodies just as surely as we do). But if we look to the animal world to understand human nature, we will see a struggle for existence, with concern for others extending only to blood relatives. Idealists, by contrast, stress the difference between humans and lower animals, in what we can know and to what we can aspire. Few philosophers today who call themselves materialists would subscribe to crude materialism. As with Aristotle, they see the fact that we are material as not really being in conflict with having a "higher" nature that sets us off from the beasts. But there is a dimension along which philosophers and other thinkers fall, ranging from idealism down to crude materialism, and by thinking about the extremes, we get a deeper sense of what the difference between being a materialist and being an idealist consists of.

THE PROBLEM OF FREE WILL AND DETERMINISM

We now return to the issue about freedom and determinism broached in the last chapter, but with the advantage of seeing it as another illustration of the mind–body problem. This is an unusually tricky issue, so let us be clear about some key terms. Determinism is the view that everything that happens in nature has natural causes that are sufficient to determine it; given those causes, this event *must* happen. For us to have **free will** is for us to be the original source of our choices, for which we are responsible. The **problem of free will and determinism** is the problem of deciding what to say about the claim that we have free will if determinism is true. It has seemed obvious to many people that if determinism is true, we do not have free will. If determinism is true, whichever way you choose has natural causes that determine your choice, making it impossible for anything else to happen. Does this mean that you could not have chosen otherwise? If so, do you really make choices at all? If it is absurd to deny that we make choices, can we say that we originate our choices in such a way as to be responsible for them?

HARD DETERMINISM

There are three main responses to this problem, each of which continues to have adherents today. Two of these agree that determinism, if true, would rule out free will. They are accordingly both called *incompatibilist*. They differ in which side of this opposition they affirm. **Hard determinists** believe in determinism and, being incompatibilists, conclude that we are not really responsible for our choices. On behalf of determinism, they ask us to consider how bizarre it would be if our choices did not have sufficient natural causes. When you choose, you do so for reasons, including the fact that you want something and that you believe that acting this way will get you what you want. But surely, determinists will say, this desire and this belief did not just pop into existence out of nothing. You may have gotten this desire from conditioning or just by being human. You may have gotten the belief by inference or directly in experience. What does not happen, they will say, is that beliefs or desires just spring into existence with no natural causes. If we ask for the causes of these causes and continue to trace the series of causes far enough into the past, we are bound to arrive at causes entirely out of our control. But remember, these causes *determine* what you will choose, so that given certain factors that precede your birth, no other choices could have occurred. The eighteenth- to nineteenth-century philosopher Robert Blatchford explains this point as follows:

> When a man says his will is free, he means that it is free of all control or interference: that it can over-rule heredity and environment.
> We reply that the will is ruled by heredity and environment.
> The cause of all this confusion may be shown in a few words.
> When the free will party say that a man has free will, they mean that he is free to act as he chooses to act.
> There is no need to deny that. *But what causes him to choose?*
> That is the pivot upon which the whole discussion turns.
> The free will party seem to think of the will as something independent of the man, as something outside him. They seem to think that the will decides without control of the man.[8]

LIBERTARIANISM

Determinism appeals especially to naturalists. If nature is all there is, any event must have natural causes or no cause at all. **Libertarianism** rejects determinism in order to maintain our freedom and responsibility. As incompatibilists, **libertarians** agree that *if* determinism is true, we do not have free will. But because they believe above all in free will, they deny determinism. They would say that there is some-

---

8. From *Not Guilty: A Defence of the Bottom Dog* (New York: Boni, 1913).

thing correct in what Blatchford says about free will existing "outside" the man. Free will exists outside the body—a natural, material thing—in the sense that our choices do not have natural causes. When you choose, there is nothing in the natural world (or anywhere, for that matter) that causes you to make that choice. Your choice can still be *explained*, but only by giving your *reasons*. If you choose to steal to get easy money, that is your reason, and it explains your choice. But there are no causes that made that the only choice possible. You could have refrained from stealing, but since you did not, you are genuinely blameworthy. If the determinist asks why you acted with that reason and not another (such as not stealing because it is wrong), the only possible answer is that you made this choice because you are the kind of person you are. Saint Augustine, a north African of the fourth to fifth centuries A.D., was an early defender of this view:

> Let no one, therefore, look for an efficient cause of the evil will; for it is not efficient, but deficient, as the [evil] will is not an effecting of something but a defect. For defection from that which supremely is, to that which has less of being—this is to begin to have an evil will. Now, to seek to discover the causes of these defections—causes, as I have said, not efficient, but deficient—is as if someone sought to see darkness, or hear silence.[9]

It is significant that libertarianism is defended by a stout believer in God. Although it is possible to be a libertarian and not believe in God, there is a reason why determinism does not sit well with this belief. If God created nature, it would seem that he is responsible for the way the past is, especially before any of us were in existence. If our decisions are ultimately due to past causes, and some of these decisions are evil, then God himself would seem to be responsible for the evil. If our genetic makeup and our environment are what ultimately lead us to make bad choices, why did he not redesign things so that we made good ones instead? Libertarians hold that our choices are undetermined by the past. If God is responsible for the past (as many of them believe), then all that he is responsible for is the *kind* of choices with which we are presented; but it is strictly up to us *which* choices we make. Libertarians are thereby committed to something like dualism, since they hold that when the mind makes decisions, although it influences the natural world, it nonetheless somehow stands outside this world when it creates its own decisions by itself. Libertarianism is, therefore, more idealistic in that it accepts a fact about the mind—the freedom of the will—and distances itself from materialism accordingly.

Hard determinists tend to be materialists, because they see the mind firmly embedded in the material world and conclude from this that the mind is not really free, as libertarian dualists like to think. This position is a good example of how

---

9. From *City of God*, Book XII, Chapters 7 and 8, trans. Marcus Dods (Edinburgh: Clark, 1871).

some philosophers are led to restrict the power of the mind in light of their commitment to materialism.

COMPATIBILISM

It can easily seem that one must choose between libertarianism and hard determinism: Is the will free and thus undetermined, or determined and thus not free? Many philosophers today, however, hold a third position that rejects both of these alternatives. These philosophers notice that what these two positions have in common is the assumption that free will and determinism are *incompatible*. By denying this assumption, they call themselves **compatibilists.** To the newcomer, this position seems contradictory. How can the will be free even if determinism is true? The "trick" for compatibilists is to explain just this possibility. Compatibilists must explain how it is possible for us to be free to choose one way or another even if whichever way we choose has already been determined by past causes.

Remember that, above all, compatibilists must explain how we are free *and therefore responsible* for our choices, for it is the claim that we are responsible (and thus blameworthy or praiseworthy) that makes the whole issue of freedom important. Compatibilists therefore examine the kind of circumstance that exists when we do seem clearly to be responsible for what we do. They see that there are some choices for which we are *not* responsible. If a very young child gives a poisonous substance to another as food, the child is not responsible since she is not old enough to know what is wrong with this or even what poison is. Ignorance really is an excuse. We commonly say in reference to traffic violations that "ignorance is no excuse," since we are responsible for knowing the law in the first place. In the case of the child, there is simply no way the child could have known better. We may even say that the child did not choose *to give poison*, since she is not capable of having such thoughts yet. But this does not deny what compatibilists are looking for— namely, a condition in which a choice is made but the person making it is not responsible. The reason compatibilists want to find such conditions is that these allow them to discover *contrasting* conditions in which people *are* responsible. The present example suggests that a person is responsible for a choice only if she is properly informed about the consequences. (In the case of traffic violations, everyone *is* properly informed of the need to know the law before they drive.)

A second kind of example involves force instead of ignorance. Suppose you are made to steal someone else's wallet by the threat of being shot if you do not. Because of the threat of force, your responsibility diminishes. In a sense you still do choose, since you choose stealing over being shot. But no one would blame you for making this choice, because you were forced into making such a terrible choice by someone else. Together with the previous example, this example seems to show that to be fully responsible, one's choice must be *informed* and *unforced*. Many compatibilists would offer this as a *sufficient* condition of responsibility. They would say, that is, that if a person knows what he is doing and is not forced into doing that, he is responsible for it, period. The important point about it being a sufficient condition is that this means the person is responsible *regardless of the past*. So for example, if a person decides to kill a store owner for easy money, knowing full well what he is doing and why, and no one is forcing him to do it, then (according to the compatibilists) that person is responsible for his crime, regardless of what influences in the past led him to want to make such choices.

Compatibilism is affirmed by Kant in this (unusually clear) passage:

> Let us take a voluntary action — for example, a falsehood — by means of which a man has introduced a certain degree of confusion into the social life of humanity, which is judged according to the motives from which it originated, and the blame of which and of the evil consequences arising from it, is imputed to the offender. We at first proceed to examine the empirical character of the offence, and for this purpose we endeavour to penetrate to the sources of that character, such as a defective education, bad company, a shameless and wicked disposition, frivolity, and want of reflection — not forgetting also the occasioning causes which prevailed at the moment of the transgression. In this the procedure is exactly the same as that pursued in the investigation of the series of causes which determine a given physical effect. Now, although we believe the action to have been determined by all these circumstances, we do not the less blame the offender. We do not blame him for his unhappy disposition, nor for the circumstances which influenced him, nay, not even for his former course of life; for we presuppose that all these considerations may be set aside, that the series of preceding conditions may be regarded as having never existed, and that the action may be considered as completely unconditioned in relation to any state preceding, just as if the agent commenced with it an entirely new series of effects. Our blame of the offender is grounded upon a law of reason, which requires us to regard this faculty as a cause, which could have and ought to have otherwise determined the behaviour of the culprit, independently of all empirical conditions. This causality of reason we do not regard as a co-operating agency, but as complete in itself. It matters not whether the sensuous impulses favoured or opposed the action of this causality, the offence is estimated according to its intelligible character — the offender is decidedly worthy of blame, the moment he utters a falsehood. It follows that we regard reason, in spite of the empirical conditions of the act, as completely free, and therefore, as in the present case, culpable.[10]

Like hard determinism, compatibilism is motivated by acceptance of materialism or at least double aspect theory. The compatibilist views the mind as a feature of the body but refuses to draw the conclusion that this makes the mind unfree. It only

---

10. From *Critique of Pure Reason*, trans. J. M. D. Meiklejohn, A554-5/B582-3.

appears that free will is incompatible with determinism because the freedom of the will cannot be grasped from the scientific perspective of the observer of human behavior. But it is still a real fact, which can be grasped from the legitimate perspective of the person making the decision. This is not the perspective of mere illusion. The operations of the mind are just as real as those of the body. In particular, we really are rational beings. The claim that we act with reasons is just as true as that our bodies move by chemical reactions. And this is all that it takes to be responsible for our actions. The fact that a decision has another aspect, in which it is seen to have prior causes, is simply irrelevant. (Whether the compatibilist can have it both ways is, of course, just what incompatibilists deny.)

CONCLUSION

Naturalism, which includes the whole scientific world-view, denies the immortality of the soul and seems to deny our freedom and responsibility. This chapter examines metaphysical views about ourselves that bear on these two issues. All of these views, in their own way, are responses to the mind–body problem — the problem of giving a satisfactory explanation of how the mind and body are related. They seem to be closely related in light of the mutual influence, yet they seem too different to be the same thing.

We looked at several basic responses to the mind–body problem. Dualism takes the apparent differences between the mind and body to show that they are entirely different things; this is what makes the fact of mind–body interaction a problem for it. Monism avoids this problem but still faces the challenge of explaining how the mind and body are one. Double aspect theory says that the mind and body are merely two aspects of the same thing. But we want to see how this is possible, since the conviction that it is not possible is what leads to dualism. Idealism and materialism both try to explain the relation of the mind and body in terms of one or the other. Each has its own problems.

Answers to the problem of personal identity have affinities with these basic positions. The view that we continue as long as our soul, with or without a body, of course embodies dualism or idealism. But even Locke's position has more affinity with idealism than materialism. For Locke held that a purely mental fact, "sameness of consciousness," made a person the same, even with a change of bodies. By severing personal identity entirely from the identity of the body, however, his view incurs the problem of possible duplication. This has led many philosophers today to prefer a more materialistic view of ourselves in which a single, continuing body marks how we persist.

The problem of free will and determinism was also seen as an illustration of the mind–body problem. Libertarianism is like dualism in affirming that the mind has a power to choose that no one would attribute to the body. This position sees in our freedom the work of a supernatural force. Naturalists tend to be sympathetic to determinism, which claims natural causes for all natural events, including what we do. Hard determinists accept determinism and conclude that free will is an illusion. They tend to be materialists, refusing to allow that the mind has a power that would make it different from the body. Compatibilism is a form of double aspect theory, and it will be held by materialists only if they are rather idealistic. For it says that even if we are just bodies, this does not prevent the mind from having a kind of freedom sufficient for our responsibility.

If we stand back and look at all these metaphysical debates, we can see something similar to the debates of science. The main kind of issue in science is how to explain facts known in experience. Positions are accordingly defended by how well they explain, including what problems they avoid. Even though the metaphysical positions of this chapter are not empirical, it is remarkable how much they are defended or criticized in these terms.

Many philosophers today (though not all) are materialists. Many of these are nevertheless compatibilists. But materialism seems to leave no room for the soul's immortality. Some people feel that any discussion leading to this result is best avoided. Suppose, however, that it is true that "this is it" and that we cease to exist permanently with the death of our bodies. Is this not very important to know? Would you want to stake your hope on an afterlife that does not exist? Philosophy itself is valuable mainly for those who want to take responsibility for the way they live. When you decide how to live, what could be more important than to know the hand you are dealt?

Many philosophers today, as we saw in Chapter Two, are also fallibilists. It is safe to say that no human knows the answer to any of these metaphysical issues with certainty. Materialism, for example, is held because of its conformity with science and its avoidance of the problem of interaction. But the scientific world-view of naturalism may be incomplete. And even if the identity of a person with his living body would *explain* why the mind and body interact, it is still *possible* that the mind is a separate thing from the body and interacts with it in a way we do not understand.

As we saw in the last chapter, some people base their hope for an afterlife on the existence of God. They reason that if we die with the body, this is so great an evil that God would not permit it if he is capable of avoiding it. If he *can* make the mind distinct from the body, he will, so that we can enjoy an afterlife. But can we know that God exists? We explore this and related issues in the next chapter.

STUDY QUESTIONS

1. Why does Judaism affirm the resurrection of the body?
2. Explain Locke's solution to the science fiction example of personal identity.
3. How does Locke explain the possibility of resurrection of the body?
4. How does materialism solve the problem of interaction?
5. What is Descartes's argument for dualism?
6. Explain why dualism suffers from the problem of interaction.

7. How is the double aspect theory different from dualism?
8. How can an idealist like Berkeley say that *there are* material things?
9. Explain why idealism cannot be empirically refuted.
10. How do we "go to heaven," according to Berkeley?
11. What does the assumption of (external) material things allow us to explain?
12. On what do libertarians and hard determinists agree? How do they disagree?
13. When are we responsible for our choices, according to compatibilism? How is this answer consistent with determinism?

CHAPTER SIX

Basic Reality

WHERE DOES IT ALL come from? This is a question that can grip us in our deepest thoughts. It seems that there must be *something* that is ultimately responsible for the world we see. Many people are sure this is God. But first, let us ask why we are so sure that the world comes from anything at all.

Consider this simple-sounding possibility: Suppose that everything comes from something else. This is certainly in keeping with the way things look. Trees and birds do not just pop into existence. They come from seeds and eggs, which themselves come from something else. Now suppose everything is this way. Then there is *nothing* it all comes from. More precisely, there is no one thing that is ultimately responsible for everything else. And it is just such a unique thing that we want to know about when we ask where does "it" (the totality of the things we know about) come from. This "**first cause**" would be that from which everything else comes, and so would be the one exception to the rule that everything comes from something else. So, why do we think this rule must have an exception? Why do we think that in all of reality there is something that is *basic*, something that is responsible for the existence of everything else?

THE FIRST CAUSE ARGUMENT

You may recall from Chapter Three that science never finds such an original cause. Or rather, even if it does, it is never justified in saying that it has. Scientific knowledge is always based on a finite amount of empirical data, which support a finite story of how we got here. For all we know, new data will permit a longer story, in which what was previously unexplained is now explained. To declare that you have discovered the first cause is to declare that the existence of this thing, whatever it is, cannot be explained as a result of something else. No finite amount of empirical data ever justifies this sort of claim.

Yet despite the fact that a first cause is not scientifically knowable, many people still feel sure that there must be one. The thirteenth-century Christian philosopher Saint Thomas Aquinas argued for a first cause as follows. (To understand the following passage, note that the phrase "efficient cause" is what we normally mean by "cause," since it implies that causes are "efficient" in producing effects.)

> In the world of sensible things, we find there is an order of efficient causes. There is no case known (neither is it, indeed, possible) in which a thing is found to be the efficient cause of itself, for if so, it would be prior to itself, which is impossible. Now in efficient causes it is not possible to go on to infinity, because in all efficient causes following in order, the first is the cause of the intermediate cause, and the intermediate cause is the cause of the ultimate cause, whether the intermediate cause be several or one only. Now to take away the cause is to take away the effect. Therefore, if there be no first cause among efficient causes, there will be no ultimate, or any intermediate, cause. But if in efficient causes it is possible to go on to infinity, there will be no first efficient cause, neither will there be an ultimate effect, nor any intermediate efficient causes; all of which is plainly false. Therefore, it is necessary to admit a first efficient cause, to which everyone gives the name of God.[1]

The main point of the argument is that without a first cause, we will never be able to *explain* why anything *exists*. If we allow that each thing comes from something else, then all that we can ever say is that one thing exists because another thing exists, thus immediately creating the question why that second thing exists. But we will never be able to get an answer for why that second thing exists, since if we ask why *it* exists, we will be given a third thing, for which the same question will immediately arise. The problem is analogous to that of trying to get rid of a bump in a rug by stepping on it. As soon as you do, another bump immediately pops up next to it, requiring another attempt to stomp it down. It may seem that an infinite series of past causes is good enough, for after all, it will still be possible to explain where each thing in the series comes from in terms of a predecessor. But this only raises the question why this infinite series itself exists, rather than another infinite series or none at all. According to the **first cause argument,** our only hope is to admit that there is something in the order of causes that we can begin with, something that somehow does not need to come from something else in order to exist.

1. From *Basic Writings of St. Thomas Aquinas*, ed. Anton C. Pegis (New York: Random House, 1945).

Given this foundation, we can then build on it by seeing how everything else comes from it.

Many people base their belief in God on the idea that there must be something from which all else comes. But a survey of metaphysics, including especially the metaphysical pictures offered in different major religions, shows that very different conceptions of the first cause are possible. By comparing and contrasting these, we get good experience in the attempt to comprehend reality as a whole. By looking at conceptions of the first cause from some of the greatest religions, we also gain sophistication in seeing how different cultures have gained orientation in life through different ways of understanding reality. We will look a variety of these before we return in the last half of the chapter to a focused discussion of God.

THEISM

We found in the last chapter that metaphysical views of ourselves have been mainly concerned with the relation of mind to matter. In attempting to account for this relation, four main positions were defined: dualism, double aspect theory, idealism, and materialism. We will find in the first half of this chapter that metaphysical views of basic reality are closely linked with these positions. Let us begin with what is perhaps the most familiar view.

Theism is belief in God. Some people use the word *God* to refer to whatever it is that is the first cause. We do not want to ignore their convictions. We will say that they believe in a first cause or basic reality, but we will use the word **God** to refer to someone of infinite intellect, power, and goodness (the "three omnis" of Chapter Four). This is familiar, not only in daily life but in theology as well. To say that God exists, then, is to say that the source of everything we know to be real belongs mainly in the category of *mind.*

MALE OR FEMALE?

This still leaves open the possibility of significant differences in how God is conceived. For the last few thousand years, especially in the West, God has been symbolized in masculine terms. We now know that there was period before this in which the divine was cast more in the figure of a female, especially a mother. Although no theologian worth his or her salt would take seriously the idea that the Creator belongs to a biological category, the issue is not trivial. In the following, the political implications are explained by a contemporary theologian, Rosemary Radford Reuther:

> The problem of the male image of God cannot be treated as trivial or an accidental question of linguistics. It must be understood first of all as an ideological bias that reflects the sociology of patriarchal societies; that is,

those societies dominated by male, property-holding heads of families. Although not all patriarchal societies have male monotheistic religions, in those patriarchal societies which have this view of God, the God-image serves as the central reinforcement of the structure of patriarchal rule. The subordinate status of women in the social and legal order is reflected in the subordinate status of women in the cultus.[2]

Reuther explains how the use of one sex to depict God helps humans of that sex to gain unfair advantage in society. It may also influence what kind of mind we associate with God. God as the Father reflects a view of God as a maker and enforcer of laws. This influences not only how you think of God but how you think of reality as a whole. If God is the Father, we might expect things to be thoroughly planned, in accordance with his orders; we might expect the obedient to be rewarded and the disobedient to be punished. God as the Mother, on the other hand, suggests fertility and love. On this model, there is no particular reason to expect the world to be orderly or to be leading to Judgment Day. It is rather that we expect the world to be good to us and to continue providing for our needs. Of course, God is neither male nor female. But if we use such images in thinking of God, we may be contributing to political evil or making unwarranted assumptions about reality as a whole.

GOD AND THE CREATION

In the most familiar stories, God creates everything else by an act of will. This is most picturesque when depicted as occurring at a certain point in time, so that the creation has a finite duration up to now. It is important that other versions of the creation are possible, since this version is surely problematic. There is an ancient joke: What was God doing in the infinite time before the creation? Creating hell for people like you who ask such questions! Since God is all-powerful and all-knowing, what took him so long? Why did he wait? Such questions seem to have no good answer. But many theists have envisaged creation as something constantly occurring. At each point in time, nature exists because God wants it to. This allows for nature to have an infinite history.

The picture of God, with nature as God's creation, is reminiscent of dualism. God is separate from nature on this account and could have existed without nature altogether. After all, nature exists only because God wants it to. It would seem in such a picture that God falls completely in the category of mind. If we allow that God has a body, it is hard to see how this could be less than the whole material world. We will consider this view next. But in the traditional picture, God stands separate from nature, including the material world. And since God is intelligent and good, this would seem to leave God as pure mind. If we regard God specifically as the maker and enforcer of laws, the picture of God over nature is similar to the

---

2. From "The Female Nature of God," *Concilium* 143 (1981).

dualistic picture of mind over body presented by libertarianism. Since we will deal with the issue of God more fully later, let us canvass a variety of alternative accounts of the first cause.

PANTHEISM

The traditional picture of God is like that of dualism, for God is separate from the matter under his dominion (or her care). Mind–body dualism creates the problem of interaction, which spurs an attraction for monistic theories in which mind and body are somehow one. Some philosophers have been dissatisfied with the traditional picture of God on similar grounds. Just as the dualist has the problem of explaining how an immaterial mind can move a material body, so the traditional theist is said to have the problem of explaining how the material world can spring from pure mind.

In the last chapter, we saw that Spinoza responded to dualism with the double aspect theory. He took a similar view of God. This means that God has a material as well as a mental aspect, as Spinoza argues in the following passage:

> I do not know why it should be considered unworthy of the divine nature, inasmuch as besides God . . . no substance [no basic reality] can be granted, wherefrom it would receive it modifications. All things, I repeat, are in God, and all things which come to pass, come to pass solely through the laws of the infinite nature of God. . . . Wherefore it can in nowise be said, that God is passive in respect to anything other than himself, or that extended substance [matter] is unworthy of the Divine nature.[3]

God is the sole basic reality, and everything else is dependent on God. In Spinoza's view, this means that everything else is merely a "modification" of God, a way that God is. All things are "in God" in the way that waves on the ocean are in the ocean. If God created a material world separate from him, then this world would not be "in" him. For Spinoza, this means that God could not have created it.

PANTHEISM'S MONISM

Spinoza's view of reality is *monistic*. In the last chapter, **monism** was defined as the claim that mind and body are one. The word is also used to describe views of reality as a whole. Now a *monist* is one who says that reality is a single thing. This, of course, conflicts with the way it looks. As we commonly think of the world, it consists of indefinitely many things, including you and other people. Spinoza thinks that just by thinking consistently, we can see that this view is mistaken, that underlying this

---

3. From "Ethics," Book I, Proposition XV, note, in *The Chief Works of Benedict De Spinoza*, trans. R. H. M. Elwes (New York: Dover, 1955).

apparent diversity is a single, unified whole. Because he accepts the reality of matter (the "extended" world), this single thing must be material. Since he also accepts the equal reality of mind, this thing must have a mental nature as well. Spinoza's view is called **pantheism**, after the Greek god Pan, who symbolized nature. Pantheists say that God is nature itself, conceived on the model of a single person, for whom mind and matter are simply different aspects of the same thing.

THE "MIND OF GOD"

Despite the fact that Spinoza called nature God (and did so seriously), he was excommunicated for being an **atheist** (one who denies that God exists). The problem was not simply that he said that God was material but that his view leads to a strange conception of God's mind. Spinoza's God is said to be **immanent,** as opposed to the **transcendent** God of traditional theism. An immanent God is not separate from nature and so does not "transcend" nature. It is difficult to take seriously that nature itself has a mind by which we can communicate with God and take instructions from him. The interpersonal relationship with God is preserved by the traditional theist only by separating God from his creation. According to Spinoza's monism, all such separation is absurd. So, what could be the "mind of God" if God is immanent — indeed, the same as nature itself? For Spinoza, it is the *order* of the natural world. As we have seen (in Chapter Four), a remarkable fact about nature is that it is predictable, owing to the fact that things in nature act in accordance with laws. The order of the world is the totality of these laws.

It turns out, therefore, that the "mind" of Spinoza's "God" consists of *thoughts.* For what are thoughts but whatever is true or false? Laws take the form of statements judged on this basis. The law that *fire heats,* for example, is a clear example of a true thought. So even though Spinoza describes his God as having both a mental and material aspect, it is true to say that his God is the material world, ordered by true thoughts, and Spinoza himself often gives this sort of formulation.

Spinoza's pantheism was accepted by no less a figure than Albert Einstein. This is understandable, since the world's order is just what is studied by science. Spinoza's pantheism casts the scientific world-view in a religious light. When we understand nature, our minds mirror it, and this is the only way possible of "communing" with God. The order of the world, unlike the things that change in accordance with it, is eternal in the sense of being unchanging. Spinoza interprets the "immortality of the soul" as an imaginative picture of the mind's eternality, which it possesses just by mirroring the eternal order of the world.

As we will see in the next chapter, Spinoza's pantheism was anticipated in ancient Greece. Before we turn to our next world-view, however, it is worth pointing out that pantheism can take a less intellectualistic form. The essence of pantheism is to deify and unify nature. God the Father is transcendent, creating the world according to plan, and laying down the law for all to follow. But the fertility and providence of nature may be symbolized with an immanent Goddess.

PLATO'S FORMS

Plato's view of reality as a whole does not correlate neatly with any of the positions taken on the mind–body problem. But it is enormously influential in Western philosophy and serves our purpose of seeing alternative conceptions of basic reality. Pantheism gives a double aspect view of reality as whole. The "mind of God," as we have seen, turns out to be the laws that comprise the natural order. For Plato, it is this order itself that is basic in reality.

Plato envisages this eternal order as consisting of "Forms" (sometimes translated as "Ideas"). He is not a monist, since there are indefinitely many of them. Material things and minds undergo changes and typically last for only a short period in time. Although the Forms never change, they are said to make the changes *intelligible*. Even lower animals know the changing world by the use of their senses. But lacking intellect, they fail to see the eternal background against which these changes are understood. We *understand* the changing things when we know *what they are*. A dog may see a human while being utterly ignorant of the fact this particular thing is *a human*, a representative of *humanity*.

Now humanity is not something you can see or touch, yet we can think and talk about it. This is because, according to Plato, it belongs to a realm of reality that is known only by the intellect. Earlier we defined the intellect as the power by which we are aware of thoughts. This is not much different from Plato's view, since humanity, for example, seems to be a *part* of some thoughts. Just as sentences are composed of words, the thoughts that they express have corresponding parts. The thoughts that Jim is human and Mary is human have something in common, including the fact that humanity itself is somehow involved in both. In each thought, we classify someone as a representative of humanity. Because there are many different humans, who have their humanity in common, a Form is sometimes called "the one over the many." Plato himself presents the Forms in the following passage:

> [T]here is a many beautiful and a many good, and so of other things which we describe and define; to all of them "many" is applied. . . . And there is an absolute beauty and an absolute good, and of other things to which the term "many" is applied there is an absolute; for they may be brought under a single idea, which is called the essence of each. . . . The many, as we say, are seen but not known, and the ideas are known but not seen.[4]

How do the Forms make changes intelligible? Notice that laws (as we saw in Chapter Three) do not apply in just one circumstance. The law that sugar is sweet applies to any bit of sugar and not just the bit of sugar on your spoon now. This is what makes it possible to apply a law to a new situation you have not yet encountered.

---

4. *Republic*, trans. Benjamin Jowett, 507b–d.

If the law that sugar is sweet applied only to the sugar on your spoon now, you would not be able to use it to predict that the next bit of sugar will be sweet. This means that when we apply a law, we must do so on the basis of something it has in common with all the other things to which this law also applies. What is in common with these many things *is* "the one over the many." Sugar itself, like humanity, is a Form. Sugar itself is not the same thing as the bit of sugar on your spoon; it is what all bits of sugar have in common and what allows us to apply to each of these the law that sugar is sweet.

Forms as Basic

Many philosophers have been happy to acknowledge Plato's Forms without taking the next step. Plato held further that it is the realm of the Forms that is basic in reality. As we have seen, when we say what a particular thing is, we immediately turn to the *kind* of thing it is. What is this on your spoon? We say it is *sugar*, thereby acknowledging that above all this is a representative, or sample, of this kind of thing. A clear case can be made that sugar is more basic in reality that this bit of sugar. This bit of sugar depends for its existence on sugar itself, but sugar would exist even if this bit of it did not. It is the realization that the particular things we see around us are manifestations of the kinds of things to which they belong that was symbolized in the Allegory of the Cave, which we read in the introduction. In this story, material things were represented by shadows, and the real things outside the cave stood for the Forms. Philosophical enlightenment, for Plato, comes mainly from appreciating the significance of the fact that the world of change is a manifestation of the eternal world of the Forms.

IDEALISM

Idealism claims that mind is basic in reality. Traditional theism is idealistic in this sense, since everything other than God, including matter, is created by God. There are purer forms of idealism, but the fact that theism claims the first cause is a mind surely has implications about the rest of reality. The theist does not equate the intelligible order with the mind of God, as does pantheism. But we would expect this order to exist throughout God's creation, at least when God is thought of as possessing an infinite intellect. This faith in the thoroughgoing order of nature contributed to the growth of science among people who believed strongly in just such a God.

A purer form of idealism is presented by Bishop Berkeley. In the last chapter, we saw how he explained his view that each of us is just a mind. Berkeley was, of course, a theist, so he regarded our minds as creations of God. We saw that idealism could claim both to avoid the problem of interaction and to give an explanation for the relation of matter and mind. For much the same reason, Berkeley's idealism can claim to avoid the sort of problem Spinoza mentioned about how God's pure mind can create matter. God creates "the material world" just *by* creating the mind with certain sensations, such as the look and feel of a stone. Unlike pantheism, Berkeley's idealism is certainly not monistic, since our minds are things that are distinct from the mind of God, even though he created them.

HINDUISM

A monistic idealism can be found in Hinduism, the religion of India. Hinduism contains so many conflicting theses that some would call it more a cluster of religions than a single one. It is certainly true that some Hindus are theists. But the dominant interpretation among Hindu scholars today is inspired mainly by Shankara, of the eighth century A.D. His view is emphatically monistic. But he also claims that the material world is illusion (because of the transitoriness of material things). Most important for Shankara is the ancient Hindu claim that your true self *is* the first cause, known in Hinduism as *Brahman*. Of course, this point is true for each of us, which has the effect of denying, or at least diminishing, our differences.

Shankara gives analogies to explain his meaning. You are like a clay pot in relation to the clay that is shared by other clay pots. You are like the space within a jar in relation to space itself. The thrust of these analogies is not just to minimize our differences; it is to deify ourselves. Since the true self is identified as Pure Consciousness, and this is the first cause, Shankara's view of reality as a whole is idealistic. This is how he presents it himself:

> Brahman is supreme. He is the reality—the one without a second. He is pure consciousness, free from any taint. He is tranquility itself. He has neither beginning nor end. He does not change. He is joy forever.
>
> He transcends the appearance of the manifold, created by Maya. He is eternal, for ever beyond reach of pain, not to be divided, not to be measured, without form, without name, undifferentiated, immutable. He shines with His own light. He is everything that can be experienced in this universe.
>
> The illumined seers know Him as the uttermost reality, infinite, absolute, without parts—the pure consciousness. In Him they find that knower, knowledge and known have become one.
>
> They know Him as the reality which can neither be cast aside (since He is ever-present within the human soul) nor grasped (since He is beyond the power of mind and speech). They know Him immeasurable, beginningless, endless, supreme in glory. They realize the truth: "I am Brahman."
>
> The scriptures establish the absolute identity of Atman [the true self] and Brahman by declaring repeatedly: "That art Thou." The terms "Brahman" and "Atman," in their true meaning, refer to "That" and "Thou" respectively.
>
> In their literal, superficial meaning, "Brahman" and "Atman" have opposite attributes, like the sun and the glow-worm, the king and his servant, the ocean and the well, or Mount Meru and the atom. Their identity

is established only when they are understood in their true significance, and not in a superficial sense.

"Brahman" may refer to God, the ruler of Maya and creator of the universe. The "Atman" may refer to the individual soul, associated with the five coverings which are effects of Maya. Thus regarded, they possess opposite attributes. But this apparent opposition is caused by Maya and her effects. It is not real, therefore, but superimposed.... "The apparent world is caused by our imagination, in its ignorance. It is not real. It is like seeing the snake in the rope. It is like a passing dream"—that is how a man should practice spiritual discrimination, and free himself from his consciousness of this objective world. Then let him meditate upon the identity of Brahman and Atman, and so realize the truth.[5]

The Mystical Experience

One of the main sources of support for this view is the **mystical experience.** It is a frequently documented fact that many people, in a variety of circumstances, suddenly experience the world as entirely unified. It appears in these moments that all the division of the world into distinct things is merely illusory. If you combine this conviction with self-awareness, the distinction between yourself and "otherness" evaporates, and you are struck by a sense of the "oneness" of yourself and everything else. In India and surrounding regions today, many people attempt to cultivate these experiences through meditation, a form of mental concentration. Many who have engaged in these practices are convinced that the mystical experience is the most authoritative source of knowledge of the first cause. Since the mystical experience is direct, it is like sensation and introspection, in not being based on reasoning. Of course, we can ask for reasons why we should accept this experience as authoritative. The twentieth-century English philosopher Bertrand Russell suggested that the mystical experience was the way things looked when you achieve complete peace of mind. In the state of peace there is no opposition, and different things appear in harmony, as though not really distinct. At any rate, many today really believe the idealistic monism of Shankara, and it offers an interesting alternative conception of the first cause and of reality as a whole.

Shankara on Immortality

Shankara's view of reality furnishes a distinctive conception of the afterlife. Pure Consciousness is the only thing that is real, and it is eternal, never being created or destroyed. But each of us *is* Pure Consciousness; therefore, each of us is eternally real. We appear to die, but this is just the death of our body, and the body is part of the material world, which is one great illusion. Our minds, however, are not really separate. When I die, what really happens is that a certain series of experiences ends in Pure Consciousness, but only to be followed by other experiences in other

---

5. From *Shankara's Crest-Jewel of Discrimination*, trans. Swami Prabhavananda and Christopher Insherwood (New York: New York Library, 1970).

minds or, rather, in Pure Consciousness itself. Simply put, I live on in people who live after me, since we are not really distinct minds after all. In the most famous piece of Hindu literature, *The Bhagavad Gita*, the main message is that there is an Infinite Spirit in which all of our minds participate and that it is by realizing this point that our anxiety about death is dispelled.

Notice how this view contradicts that of Locke on personal identity. In the last chapter, we saw that for Locke a person lives on as the same person only if she retains memories of earlier times. But no such preservation of memory is guaranteed or even suggested by Shankara. Those who sympathize with Locke will find this promise of eternal existence disappointing.

HEGEL'S ABSOLUTE IDEALISM

There is in the West a position remarkably like Shankara's, the metaphysics of the nineteenth-century German philosopher Georg Hegel. Although Hegel does not deny the reality of the material world, he nevertheless calls his view "absolute idealism," since he emphasizes the extent to which the material world is understood in mental terms. The so-called laws of nature that science describes, for example, he holds to be dictated by the way the mind works. But more to the point, he takes seriously the idea that the distinction between different minds is somewhat illusory, so that together they form a kind of single mind. Since Hegel's language is extraordinarily obscure, let us look at how a sympathetic English philosopher, T. H. Green, describes Hegel's view:

> That there is one spiritual being, of which all that is real is the activity or expression; that we are related to this spiritual being, not merely as parts of the world which is its expression, but as partakers in some inchoate measure of the self-consciousness through which it at once constitutes and distinguishes itself from the world; that this participation is the source of morality and religion; this we take to be the vital truth which Hegel had to teach.[6]

As we will see in Part Four, this metaphysical commitment to an all-encompassing mind has implications for the best society. In fact, Hegel himself draws out just such conclusions.

ATOMISTIC MATERIALISM

In the last chapter, we met materialism as the thesis that the mind can be explained in terms of the body. As a position about the first cause, materialism says that reality is basically material. For a vivid and historically important example of this, let us consider the **atomism** of the ancient Greek philosopher and scientist Democritus.

---

6. *The Works of T. H. Green*, 3 vols. (London: Longmans, Green, 1894).

Democritus noticed that we can explain how things can be cut apart if we suppose they are made of smaller parts that separate. He concluded that there must be very small things that cannot be further cut. Our word *atom* has a Greek root meaning "uncuttable." Since his "atoms" would need something to move around in, he contrasted them with "the void"; today we would think of this as space itself. His total picture of reality was that everything other than atoms and the void is simply *composed* of atoms. Rocks, trees, and people are nothing more than complexes of these atoms. Notice that Democritus can *explain* how these larger things are "created" and "destroyed." Certain atoms come to be arranged in appropriate ways when the larger things are created, and these atoms disperse when they are destroyed.

Democritus's view of the atoms can appear comical today. He supposed, for example, that the atoms of solids must have hooks on them, so that they hold together; in liquids, these hooks are absent, which explains why things made of them do not hold their shape. Historians of science, however, recognize that Democritus's atoms represent the basic idea, still used in physics today, of explaining facts about larger objects in terms of smaller constituents. The important thing for us to notice is that his atoms and the void together represent a kind of first cause. Granted, there are many atoms in his picture, but still the totality of them, in combination with the void, is "that from which everything else comes." The atoms do not, of course, create other things as God is supposed to create them, by an act of will. But because everything else is *composed* of atoms within the void, atomism does provide an alternative conception of a first cause.

Atomism is a form of materialism, since the atoms are material things, extended in space, and they collectively form the basic reality. Because everything else is composed of atoms, whatever is true of the larger complexes must ultimately be simply a result of how the atoms are. Atoms are not, of course, conscious or intelligent, but because we are merely complexes of them, the way in which they combine in us must be enough to explain the existence of our minds. This is the kind of promise that is made by materialism when understood as a thesis about the relation of mind to body. Now there is nothing objectionable in the general idea that complexes of things can be quite unlike the individual things that compose them. No individual part of a house provides shelter, yet the fact that the house itself does is hardly mysterious. But just as some philosophers today doubt whether facts about the body can explain facts about the mind, so the claim that the first cause is material used to be thought by many to make impossible understanding how mind exists in reality at all. John Locke expresses this conviction in the following excerpt:

> If it be said, there was a time when no Being had any Knowledge, when that eternal Being was void of all Understanding. I reply, that then it was impossible there should ever have been any Knowledge. It being impossible, that Things wholly void of knowledge, and operating blindly, and without any Perception, should produce a knowing Being, as it is impossible, that a Tri-

angle should make itself three Angles bigger than two right ones. For it is as repugnant to the *Idea* of senseless Matter, that it should put into itself Sense, Perception, and Knowledge, as it is repugnant to the Idea of a Triangle, that it should put into itself greater Angles than two right ones.[7]

If it is true that understanding could only come from something with understanding, the first cause would then *have* to be intelligent, as theism asserts. One thing in particular that has challenged this conviction is Darwin's theory of natural selection, which we discussed in Chapter Three. By providing a compelling picture of how living organisms have actually *evolved* from smaller, nonliving chemicals, the idea of the emergence of mind from matter seems now firmly established to many philosophers. Of course, this view does not refute theism. It only means that theism cannot rely on the impossibility of the materialists' idea that mind emerges from the actions of smaller parts of matter.

TAOISM

Another form of materialism is **Taoism,** one of the two major religions indigenous to China. (The other main Chinese religion comes from Confucius, whom we will not consider in this chapter, as his main concerns were with social rather than metaphysical matters.) Unlike atomism, Taoism is monistic. Atomists claim that there are many atoms and the void and do not claim that these somehow merge into a single whole. Taoists liken reality to an uncarved block, stressing that reality (called the *Tao*) is really a continuous whole.

What is being denied in this description is the fundamental reality of *distinctions*. When we think or speak about reality, we must make distinctions to be understood. To think, for example, that this rose is red, one must first distinguish this rose from all other things, including other roses, and then one describes this bit of reality by making a distinction between color and other aspects of it, such as its shape or fragrance, and also one makes a distinction between red and other colors. It is the essence of thinking and speaking to make such distinctions, to "carve up the block" (of reality). For the Taoists to say that reality is like an *uncarved* block is therefore to take a dim view of making distinctions at all. This denigration of thinking and speaking, which the Greeks saw as our main source of dignity, is reflected in the opening lines of the *Tao Te Chi,* the most famous of the Taoist literature, believed to have been written sometime in the fifth to third centuries B.C.:

> The Tao that can be told of is not the eternal Tao. . . .
> The Nameless is the origin of Heaven and Earth. . . .
> Tao is empty (like a bowl).
> It may be used, but its capacity is never exhausted.

---

7. From *An Essay Concerning Human Understanding,* Book IV, Chapter X, ed. Peter H. Nidditch (Oxford: Clarendon, 1975).

It is bottomless, perhaps the ancestor of all things. . . .
The gate of the subtle and profound female
Is the root of Heaven and Earth.
It is continuous, and seems to be always existing.
Use it and it will never wear out.
The best man is like water.
Water is good; it benefits all things and does not compete with them.
It dwells in lowly places that all disdain.
This is why it is so near the Tao . . .
infinite and boundless, it cannot be given any name;
It reverts to nothingness.
This is called shape without shape,
Form without objects.
It is The Vague and Elusive.[8]

It is difficult to find a metaphysical outlook more opposed to theism. The Taoists do indeed recognize a first cause, the Tao itself. As in Spinoza's pantheism, this is a single thing, and it is certainly material. The reason for saying that Taoism is materialist is that matter is what we know through sensation, and since the Taoists deny that we access fundamental reality through language and thought, this leaves sensation as the main source of knowledge of the first cause. This does not mean that when we know directly, for example, that there is a tree in front of one, it is this sort of knowledge that is preferred. For in saying or thinking that the tree is in front of one, distinctions are being made. The "block" is left "uncarved" only by pure sensation itself, which cannot be put into words without distortion.

This favoring of sensation over thought greatly influenced the Zen Buddhists of Japan, who find the highest sort of religious experience in an unspoken attention to what is given in immediate sensation. Because the God of theism is nothing else if not a person, and persons are above all those who can think and express these thoughts in speech, the supreme knowledge of God must be expressible in words. This means that reality itself is not a continuous whole, an uncarved block, but has a structure best reflected in the mind of God. Taoists must deny that this structure, the distinctions of thought and speech, are fundamental to reality. They are at most ways in which reality *appears* to us persons, reflecting arbitrary prejudices on our part. As we will see in Part Four, this disdain for what we create, the *artificial*, shaped their view of the value of society.

CONCEPTIONS OF THE FIRST CAUSE

The first cause is whatever is basic in reality, that which is responsible for everything else. We should expect in any metaphysical view that declares a first cause the nature of this origin to be reflected in the nature of reality as a whole. In this chap-

---

8. From *A Source Book of Chinese Philosophy*, trans. Wing-tsit Chan (Princeton, NJ: Princeton University Press, 1963).

ter so far, we have seen a variety of some of the most important examples. And we found that many of these are closely related to positions taken on the mind–body problem.

Traditional theism counts as a form of idealism on this score, since the God who creates nature by an act of will is above all a mind. The world-view of God presiding over nature, however, is reminiscent of dualism. Purer forms of idealism demote matter to a lesser status than God's creation. Berkeley and Shankara provide examples of this. Pantheism denies the supernatural and describes nature in terms of the double aspect theory. Atomism and Taoism represent two forms of materialism.

An exception to this pattern was found in Plato's theory of Forms, which amounted to promoting thought over both mind and matter. In all these metaphysical views, one of the three categories of reality described in Chapter Four was "promoted" to the status of first cause. Since these three correspond to the three sources of knowledge discussed extensively in Part One, we find that the metaphysical views we have surveyed in effect give priority to a particular way of gaining knowledge.

THE TELEOLOGICAL ARGUMENT

Now that we have taken a survey of some of the main views on the nature of the first cause, let us return specifically to theism. The theist believes in God, which means that a perfect person exists—omnipotent, omniscient, and omnibenevolent. Now that we have before us an array of different conceptions of the first cause, we can appreciate the difficulty of defending theism as such. We certainly cannot defend theism with only the first cause argument, since this argument does not favor theism over other views of the first cause. Is there another argument for the conclusion that the first cause is God, or even a person at all?

The **teleological argument** comes in various versions, but the leading idea is that nature appears to embody divine purpose. When, for example, we see the beautiful harmony in the interactions of the natural world, we are led to the idea that a great intelligence, a person, must have *planned* it. The stars in the heaven move with the precision of clockwork, and how do clocks come into existence except by a knowing mind putting the parts together with a purpose? The cycles of life visible throughout the ecosystems of Earth occur with such regularity that they seem to be *orchestrated*. It is difficult, in fact, to describe the parts of the simplest insect except by saying how the parts are "put together," thus using the language of purpose and design. A *telos* in Greek is a purpose. The teleological argument points to facts about nature that we can see for ourselves and that seem to suggest that nature is created with purpose and thus issues from a supremely intelligent and powerful being. The argument is presented by Saint Thomas Aquinas as follows:

> We see that things which lack knowledge, such as natural bodies, act for an end, and this is evident from their acting always, or nearly always, in the

same way, so as to obtain the best result. Hence it is plain that they achieve their end, not fortuitously, but designedly. Now whatever lacks knowledge cannot move towards an end, unless it be directed by some being endowed with knowledge and intelligence; as the arrow is directed by the archer. Therefore some intelligent being exists by whom all natural things are directed to their end; and this being we call God.[9]

The teleological argument is aimed mainly at materialism. It questions the materialist's claim that the order of nature is just the way that matter happens to be. It is not obvious why matter should display the incredibly vast and intricate order that it does, or any order at all. After all, the Taoists conceive of matter as basically without order. (The Taoists would therefore reject the very fact to be explained of the teleological argument.) But assuming, as most would, that the order of the world is real, should there not be an adequate reason *why*? Now, if nature is created by an infinite intellect, as theism asserts, then the fact that it is thoroughly ordered is just what we should *expect*.

The materialist will have to say that theism is not really on better footing. The mind of God must have some kind of order, so should there not be a Supergod imposing this order on the mind of God? Philosophers have disagreed about whether such retorts are sufficient to defend materialism. Kant, for one, did not find the teleological argument persuasive, but he insisted nevertheless that it "should always be mentioned with respect."

THE ONTOLOGICAL ARGUMENT

The first cause and teleological arguments are both ancient. They appeal to a sense of wonder that is easily created in many people. Where did it all come from? And why is there order and not chaos? They have accordingly been thought of independently by many people, including even some inquisitive children. They are two of three arguments that are regarded by many theologians as the chief arguments for theism. The third is the **ontological argument.** It is not ancient and does not appeal to any natural sense of wonder. And it originated with just one person, a Christian monk, Saint Anselm, of the eleventh century A.D. In spite of these differences, the ontological argument has become the favorite of many theists since Anselm wrote. Among the many versions he gave is this:

> This so truly is that it is impossible to think of as not existing.
> It can be conceived to be something such that we cannot conceive of it as not existing.
> This is greater than something which we can conceive of as not existing.

---

9. From *Basic Writings of St. Thomas Aquinas*, ed. Anton C. Pegis (New York: Random House, 1945).

Therefore, if that than which a greater cannot be conceived could be conceived not to be, we would have an impossible contradiction: that than which a greater cannot be conceived would not be that than which a greater cannot be conceived.

Therefore, something than which a greater cannot be conceived so truly is that it is impossible even to conceive of it as not existing.

This is you, O Lord our God.[10]

There are two main assumptions: (1) God is the greatest thing conceivable, and (2) it is greater to be real than not to exist at all. From the second it follows that a nonexistent God would not be as great as an existing one. Therefore, if we think of God, as the atheist does, as nonexistent, we can always imagine a being just like this, but greater still by being real. Given the first assumption, the only being who could *count* as the greatest being conceivable must therefore be real.

The ontological argument is extremely ambitious. For it claims that atheism is not merely false but *absurd*, just as absurd as talking about triangles without three sides. Atheists are not merely wrong; they do not even understand the implications of their own position. *Ontos* is the Greek word for "being," in the sense of "the nature of something." The ontological argument is so called because it claims that all it takes to see that God exists is to reflect on the nature of God, what it is to *be* God. When we really understand what is unique about God, we can see that such a being must exist.

This is a highly controversial argument, with great philosophers weighing in on both sides, and technical versions of it have even been advanced recently. Dissent has focused on the second assumption, that it is greater to be real than not to exist at all. How can something that is real be compared in any way, including greatness, with "something" that is not? Would this not be "comparing" something with nothing? Be that as it may, we may wonder whether even at its best it proves enough. Why must the greatest thing conceivable be a person, capable of thought? Unless this can be shown, even a materialist could claim that matter is the greatest thing conceivable. And what does it mean to say something is a great *thing*? We know what a great piano or a great football team is like, but without saying what kind of thing we are talking about, greatness by itself may seem meaningless.

In medieval times, however, such a notion would not be found strange among scholars. A thing is great, as a thing, to the degree that it displays *power*. Now, being able to think is certainly a form of power. Do we not have a power to gain knowledge that beings without intellect do not possess? If so, the greatest thing conceivable would have this power and thus be a person, as theism says. Materialists would challenge this as they did before, by saying that matter can give rise to thought. Matter does "possess" this power by organizing itself into human bodies that do the actual thinking. If this response fails, materialists must turn to the second assumption.

10. From "The Proslogion," in *The Many-Faced Argument*, ed. Arthur C. McGill and John Hick (New York: Macmillan, 1967).

To say that being real is a form of greatness (as the second assumption does) is therefore to say that one form of power is the ability to be entirely responsible for one's own existence. If so, then the greatest thing conceivable would have to display this power by being real. But is it even possible for anything to be created by itself? Doubt on this point led the seventeenth-century German philosopher Gottfried Leibniz to say that the crucial assumption of the argument is that self-creation is possible. Given this view, it does indeed follow that the greatest thing conceivable exists.

THE PROBLEM OF EVIL

Having looked at theism from the perspective of the theist, let us now see why some philosophers have been atheists. If all they can say is that none of the arguments for the existence of God is successful, then they ought to be **agnostics,** who only deny that the answer is *known*. Like theists, atheists have a definite position, for which justification can be asked.

The most popular argument for atheism is the **argument from evil.** This argument also makes two main assumptions. First, God is omnipotent, omniscient, and omnibenevolent. As omnibenevolent, God wants only the best, and as omnipotent and omniscient, God has the power and knowledge to make the world as good as it can be. Second, evil exists, understood to mean that the world could be better. The evil in the world is said to prove that no being characterized by the "three omnis" oversees it.

This argument is also ancient (a clear expression of it is attributed to the Greek philosopher Epicurus, in the fourth century B.C.). It is also thought of by many people on their own. It is uncontroversial that there is a *problem* for theism. Indeed, there is a whole area of theology, *theodicy*, which deals exclusively with it. We will review several attempts to solve it.

One way to deal with the problem of evil is to change how you think of God. It is true that we have defined the word with the three omnis, but one could sincerely claim to be a theist and not demand that God be perfect in all three respects. Some, for example, are willing to allow that "God" is not all-powerful, so that evil exists because he cannot prevent it. Although it is possible to escape from the argument from evil in such ways, it is understandable that many theists have not found this attractive. After all, if God is not powerful enough to prevent evil, he might lack the power to create an afterlife. If evil exists because he does not know about it, perhaps he fails to hear your prayers. And if evil exists because he is not all-good, is he deserving of our obedience or unqualified love?

THE FREE WILL DEFENSE

The argument from evil was opposed most forcefully by Saint Augustine, whom we met in the last chapter as a defender of libertarianism. This response to the problem of free will and determinism denies that the past determines what we choose.

Even if God is responsible for the past, he is responsible only for the fact that we face certain choices. *Which* choices we make is entirely up to us. This makes us and not God wholly responsible for the evil that men do. The **free will defense** holds *us* partly responsible for making the world as good as it can be. God can only "lead us to the water"; it is up to us "to drink."

Now, the atheist is bound to say that this only raises the question of why God allows us to make such bad choices in the first place. Augustine's answer is that although he could, as omnipotent, force us to make only good choices, to do so would be to take away our free will. But this would make the world worse, since the world is better by having creatures like us, with free will. The background for this view is presented in the following passage:

> If it is said: It would not have been difficult or laborious for Almighty God to have seen to it that all His creatures should have observed their proper order so that none of them should have come to misery. If He is omnipotent that would not have been beyond His power; and if He is good He would not have grudged it; this is my answer. The order of creatures proceeds from top to bottom by just grades, so that it is the remark of envy to say: That creature should not exist, and equally so to say: *That* one should be different. It is wrong to wish that anything should be like another thing higher in the scale, for it has its being, perfect in its degree, and nothing ought to be added to it. He who says that a thing ought to be different from what it is, either wants to add something to a higher creature already perfect, in which case he lacks moderation and justice; or he wants to destroy the lower creature, and is thereby wicked and grudging. Whoever says that any creature ought not to be is no less wicked and grudging, for he wants an inferior creature not to exist, which he really ought to praise. For example, the moon is certainly far inferior to the sun in the brightness of its light, but in its own way it is beautiful, adorns earthly darkness, and is suited to nocturnal uses. For all these things he should admit that it is worthy of all praise in its own order. If he denies that, he is foolish and contentious. Anyone who said that there should be no light would feel that he deserved to be laughed at. How then will he dare to say there should not be a moon? If instead of saying that the moon should not exist he said that the moon ought to be like the sun, what he is really saying without knowing it is, not that there should be no moon, but that there should be two suns. In this there is a double error. He wants to add something to the perfection of the universe, seeing he desires another sun. But he also wants to take something from that perfection, seeing he wants to do away with the moon.[11]

Augustine describes what has been called the **"chain of being,"** which asserts that there is a hierarchy in reality, starting with God, the greatest being, then going to angels and the like, then we humans, then animals, then plants, and finally

---

11. *City of God*, trans. Marcus Dods, Book XII, Chapters 7 and 8.

inanimate things like rocks and water. The underlying assumption is that God will create the greatest creation possible and thus will not leave out human beings. But to put us into reality, we who have free but imperfect wills, he has to allow a certain amount of evil. In being omnibenevolent, he does not condone this, but in allowing us to exist, he allows for the evil we do.

THE GREATER GOODS DEFENSE

The free will defense fails to convince many philosophers, since it relies on a controversial position on the problem of free will. Another problem was pointed out by Saint Thomas Aquinas. Even if libertarianism excuses God from the evil that *we* do, it does not excuse God from *natural* evil, such as earthquakes and diseases. To account for this kind of evil, Augustine has another response, the **greater goods defense.** How do we know that such natural occurrences, which seem to us to make the world worse than it ought to be, are not needed to serve long-term good purposes of God, that only he, with his infinite vision, can see? Augustine puts the point as follows:

> To thee, there is no such thing as evil, and even in Thy creation taken as a whole, there is not; because there is nothing from beyond it that can burst in and destroy the order which Thou hast appointed for it. But in the parts of creation, some things, because they do not harmonize with others, are considered evil. Yet those same things harmonize with others and are good, and in themselves are good.[12]

In relation to your own life, the earthquake that destroys your home or the disease by which a loved one suffers appears to be bad. But this does not mean, according to Augustine, that it makes the whole world worse. If we could see how such events fit into the whole scheme of things, how they "harmonize" with other parts of God's creation, we might see that they are really for the overall good of the whole. Evil in such a view would be only an appearance, something of an illusion, due to our imperfect vision of reality.

The greater goods defense attempts to solve the problem of evil by denying that we know that there really is evil in the world. For all we know, what appears to be bad may not really be bad, because it may be a necessary means for making the whole world better. The free will defense does not actually assert that our bad choices make the whole worse; it says only that if this happens it would not be God's fault and so would not disprove his existence. The two defenses are therefore consistent. The theist can maintain that even if there is evil in the world due to our bad choices, this does not disprove God's existence; and we do not know for sure

---

12. From "Confessions," Book VII, Chapter 13, in *Augustine: Confessions and Enchiridion,* trans. A. C. Outler, Library of Christian Classics, Vol. VI (Philadelphia: Westminster, 1953).

whether the apparent evil, man-made or natural, is really bad, since it could be required for some long-range goods.

The greater goods defense depends on a certain view of evil that is controversial. Is it true that all wrong actions *can* be justified by some future good that they help to create? If an innocent child is treated with cruelty, is there *anything* that can happen in the future that justifies this action? As we will see when we turn to ethics, some philosophers deny that certain sorts of wrong actions can be justified by future good consequences.

GOD AS IDEAL

If you are a theist, you may find these defenses satisfactory, and you may be persuaded by some of the arguments for the existence of God. But just suppose that you think atheism has been proven. What should you say about theism? Was it all just based on wishful thinking and faulty reasoning? Some atheists still have a deep respect for theism. They think that even though it is not literally true, it embodies some important message that should not be lost. What must be retained and respected is the *idea* of God. Our idea of God is not the idea of an actually existing thing, like stars and people and cities. It is about an *ideal*, like fairness, kindness, or truthfulness. The major voice for this position is that of the nineteenth-century German philosopher Ludwig Feuerbach:

> [H]e alone is the true atheist to whom the predicates of the Divine Being,— for example, love, wisdom, justice,—are nothing; not he for whom merely the subject of these predicates is nothing. And in no wise is the negation of the subject necessarily also a negation of the predicates considered in themselves. These have an intrinsic, independent reality; they force their recognition upon man by their very nature; they are self-evident truths to him; they prove, they attest themselves. It does not follow that goodness, justice, wisdom, are chimeras because the existence of God is a chimera.... The idea of God is dependent on the idea of justice, of benevolence; a God who is not benevolent, not wise, not just, is no God; but the converse does not hold. The fact is not that a quality is divine because God has it, but that God has it because it is divine.[13]

Two points in this passage deserve emphasis. The first is that Feuerbach is attacking all of the conceptions of the first cause that deny the *personhood* of God. We may be led through our own experiences or through philosophical argumentation to admit that the first cause is not the way the theist describes God, and we have seen several of these in this chapter. But all such attempts are *pernicious*, according to Feuerbach, because of the importance of the idea of a personal God. Second, the idea of God is not important, as the traditional theist thinks, to describe what is

---

13. From *The Essence of Christianity*, trans. George Eliot (Gloucester, MA: Smith, 1854).

basically real. The idea of God is a focal point for those qualities in persons that command our ultimate respect and allegiance. As Feuerbach says, qualities such as love, wisdom, and justice "force their recognition" on us. It is really such *qualities* that are divine—we cannot help but acknowledge them *as ideals*.

METAPHORICAL THEOLOGY

Feuerbach said that theism represented a natural stage in the development of human religion. Our ancestors had a dim recognition of the divine qualities, but their lack of philosophical sophistication led them to "project" these qualities into the heavens, supposing that there is a being perfect enough to have them. This is a psychological explanation of why they believed in theism, not, of course, a justification.

After Feuerbach, the psychology of religion was recognized as an important branch of religious studies. One development it has encouraged is that of **metaphorical theology,** which advocates that in place of a *literal* interpretation of the existence of God and other supernatural phenomena, we give a *metaphorical* interpretation that conveys a *moral message*. Metaphorical theologians recommend that we treat as *suggestive fables* such stories as that of God's creation and governance over the world, our trial at Judgment Day, and our future life in heaven or hell. Just as Aesop's fables are meant to suggest lessons of life and not to expand our knowledge of history, religious talk of the supernatural does not expand our metaphysical view of reality but rather provides *guidance* in *this* world.

The religious texts of the world offer many possibilities for such interpretations. Here are a few illustrations. We think of God as being omniscient and omnibenevolent, and many accordingly look to God as being the perfect guide throughout life. The picture of God presiding over nature can be interpreted metaphorically as the ethical truth that we ought to act in life as we would *if* God were real and telling us how we should live. We picture God, moreover, as presiding over all people, of all societies, and this can symbolize the ethical truth that common standards of right and wrong apply to us all. How about the picture of Judgment Day? Should we take this as a prediction of what will actually happen sometime in the future? Or is it better understood as a picture of how the most virtuous people live their lives? The most responsible people are those who regularly examine how they are living their lives, *as if* each day were Judgment Day. The picture of Judgment Day serves as a reminder that that we *ought* to examine our lives, as God would, truthfully and thoroughly.

Finally, let us ask what to make of talk of the afterlife, whether in the Western form of heaven and hell, or the Hindu (and Buddhist) form of reincarnation. Jesus himself said that the kingdom of God is within you and around you; perhaps even *he* meant to give a metaphorical interpretation of talk of the "afterlife." Many metaphorical theologians would say that heaven and hell are really states of the soul.

This goes well with a metaphorical interpretation of God as one's conscience. Talk of God damning you to hell is thus to be interpreted as your own conscience bringing you into a state of grief. The serious point of the message is that even if we escape punishment by other people for our wrong actions, we punish ourselves through our sense of guilt and remorse. Heaven is thus the bliss that comes from doing what is right.

These are just a few suggestions for how supernatural talk can be interpreted, and other interpretations are certainly possible, just as different people can have different reactions to great works of art. There is much to be said for metaphorical theology. Since one is not taking claims about supernatural reality to be *true*, there is no need to *argue* for their truth. It does not matter to metaphorical theologians, therefore, that there are objections to the main arguments for the existence of God. Metaphorical theologians say this is just what we should expect, since these arguments are based on the profoundly mistaken idea that supernatural claims should be interpreted literally. There is, for the same reason, no reason for them to be bothered by the problem of evil. Talk of God and the like are not, for them, descriptions of the *real* world but are rather descriptions of the *ideal* world, which the metaphors are meant to depict. Since they do not take holy texts to be offering scientific theories of creation or histories of the beginnings of human life, no amount of current scientific and historical knowledge inconsistent with these causes them to be embarrassed. In particular, the pseudohypotheses that abound in religious myths are not to compete unsuccessfully with scientific theories, since they are best interpreted as giving moral guidance and not as attempting to explain why natural phenomena occur. And, importantly, religious texts are no longer seen as *contradicting* each other. Because of this, holy texts can no longer create *divisions*, such as those that have led different peoples to go to war against each other. Metaphorical theology allows the prisoner of Plato's cave to become a "cosmopolitan," a citizen of the world.

CONCLUSION

Belief in a first cause, most basic in reality, seems to be necessary to make the existence of anything explainable. Many views of the first cause are counterparts of positions taken on the mind–body problem. In all the views we examined, mind, matter, or thought was said to be basic. Many major religions, Eastern and Western, differ in what category of reality is thought to be basic. Another difference is their stand on whether reality is one or many things. Traditional theism is idealistic in seeing the mind of God as the creator of nature. It is more dualistic than some other forms of idealism in admitting the reality of material world. It also views God as transcendent. The best defense of traditional theism would show why the first cause has these special characteristics. That mind is at the root of reality, as theism claims, has been argued from the order of nature. Atheism is argued from the evil in the world. Atheists sympathetic to theism have offered metaphorical interpretations of religion's descriptions of supernatural reality.

Although metaphorical theology does not take talk of the supernatural literally, the interpretations themselves still make some commitment to *truth*. One can disagree and argue about the truth of the moral messages themselves. When we come to question *these* truths, we have entered the realm of ethics, one of the main areas of philosophy and the subject matter of Part Three.

STUDY QUESTIONS

1. State the first cause argument in your own words. Make clear that the main point is that if you do not accept the conclusion, you will not be able to *explain* why anything exists. (Do not confuse explanation with justification. See the glossary of Part One for clarification on this distinction.)
2. What is objectionable about thinking of God as male?
3. Why is it problematic to think of God's creation as happening a finite time ago?
4. How is traditional theism reminiscent of dualism? How does it have a problem analogous to the problem of interaction?
5. How is pantheism associated with the double aspect theory?
6. How does traditional theism preserve the possibility of having a personal relationship with God?
7. How did Spinoza describe the mind of God? How, according to him, can we "commune" with God?
8. According to Plato, what is basic in reality, and how do we know about it?
9. How are Forms supposed to make the world intelligible?
10. How did traditional theism contribute to the growth of science?
11. What is your relation to basic reality, according to Shankara's Hinduism? How is his view supported by the mystical experience? How is it supposed to dispel anxiety about death? How does it conflict with Locke's view of personal identity?
12. How has Darwin's theory of natural selection been used in support of materialism?
13. How is Taoism's view of basic reality different from that of the atomists? How is it extremely opposed to theism?
14. What is the teleological argument? Why does this perspective support theism specifically and not merely the existence of a first cause?
15. How does the ontological argument rest on the assumption that self-creation is possible?
16. State the argument from evil in your own words. Why is it only theism that this argument is directed against, and not other conceptions of the first cause?
17. What is the free will defense, and what position does it assume on the problem of free will and determinism? Explain your answer.

18. What is the greater goods defense? What ethical view does it assume?
19. According to Feuerbach, how is our idea of God originally a "projection" of human nature? How has his view contributed to the development of metaphorical theology?

Glossary for Part Two

Agnostic One who neither believes nor disbelieves that God exists

Argument from evil An argument that God does not exist, which defines God by the three "omnis" and claims that such a being would not permit the evil that we know exists

Atheist One who believes that God does not exist

Atomism The materialist view of reality that perceptible material things are comprised of smallest constituents, which collectively form the first cause

Chain of being The metaphysical view in which all of reality forms a hierarchy of beings, from the most to the least perfect

Compatibilism The view that freedom of the will is compatible with determinism; contrast with *libertarianism* and *hard determinism.*

Determinism The claim that every event in nature has causes in nature that determine it as the only one possible

Double aspect theory The view that mind and body are not separate things but only two aspects of the same thing, the person

Dualism The view that persons and their bodies are distinct things that can exist without each other; named after its most famous exponent, René Descartes

First cause That from which all else comes

First cause argument The argument that there must be a first cause for the existence of anything to be fully explainable

Free will To describe the will as free is to claim that in choosing we initiate actions for which we are responsible

Free will defense An attempt to refute the argument from evil by claiming that God permits evil as a consequence of allowing there to be imperfect persons such as humans

God The perfect person (characterized by the three "omnis")

Greater goods defense An attempt to refute the argument from evil by claiming that what appears to be evil to us may be necessary for producing greater goods in other parts of the world, including the future

Hard determinism The view that the will is not free because determinism is true; contrast with *libertarianism* and *compatibilism.*

Hinduism The main religion of India; see the discussion of Shankara's monistic idealism in Chapter Six.

Idealism The view that reality is basically mental

Immanent An immanent God is not separate from nature; contrast with *transcendent*

Libertarianism The view that we have free will because our decisions are not determined by past causes; contrast with *hard determinism* and *compatibilism*

Material To be material is to be the sort of thing that is known through the senses; hence, occupying space by being composed of stuff

Materialism The view that reality is basically material; as a response specifically to the mind–body problem, that the mind is determined by (as so to be understood in terms of) the body

Metaphorical theology The project of providing for supernatural claims of traditional religion, metaphorical interpretations, consistent with naturalism, and specifically revealing them as disguised moral messages

Mind–body problem The problem of saying how the mind and body are related; the problem arises from the circumstance that there are apparently conflicting facts, leading to the conclusions that persons are and are not their bodies

Monism The view that reality forms a unified whole in which the apparently distinct things in the world are really aspects of the single reality

Mystical experience The direct experience of the world as monistic

Naturalist One who thinks that nature is all there is

Nature All that must be real for our empirical knowledge to be genuine

Omnibenevolent Perfectly good

Omnipotent Perfectly powerful

Omniscient Perfectly knowledgeable

Ontological argument The argument that God, the most perfect thing conceivable, must exist because it is more perfect to exist than to be merely imaginary

Pantheism The equation of God with nature; hence, the monistic view that reality is basically a single person, whose body is the material world and whose mind is its intelligible structure

Problem of free will and determinism The problem of how we can have free will if our decisions have prior causes

Problem of interaction The problem for Cartesian dualism of making it impossible to explain the fact that the mind and body interact

Problem of personal identity The nonempirical problem of determining the conditions under which the same person continues to exist

Problem of possible duplication The problem for a view of personal identity, like Locke's, that does not show how to determine which of two persons in the future is identical with the person who is now in question

Taoism A religion indigenous to China. Holds that reality is an undifferentiated whole known best through sensation and not through intellect

Teleological argument An argument for the existence of God based on the ground that this explains the fact that nature is orderly

Theim The view that God exists

Transcendent A transcendent God is separate from nature; contrast with *immanent*

PART THREE

Ethics

The word ethics *comes from the Greek word* ethos, *for behavior, and in particular the sort of behavior of which we humans are capable. Ethics is not the only intellectual discipline that studies human behavior. Psychology is that part of science concerned with explaining why we do what do, and so why we think and feel as we do. Psychology tries to find the causes of behavior, which explain why we actually do what we do. It is not concerned with* evaluating *this behavior, as something good or bad, right or wrong. This is how ethics differs from psychology. If successful, psychology enables us to understand how humans* are *and thus to make correct predictions about what people will do. Psychology thus treats us as objects in nature, obeying causal laws. The picture of human nature offered by psychology is that of the informed* spectator, *who understands what led someone to do something or what they are likely to do next. But in itself psychology does not tell us what we* should *do; it does not give guidance to us when we are in the thick of action, faced with decisions about what to do. At such times, it is not enough to be a spectator of our actions; we need to* create *them. For this, we need more than predictions: We need to make* evaluations *about which is the* best course of action. *Ethics attempts to discover* values, *by which to make the best choices and thus to live our lives well.*

Ethics is not concerned solely with the evaluation of actions, although this is its primary focus. We describe people *themselves as "virtuous" or "vicious" depending on how they characteristically behave, saying, for example, that someone is courageous or honest. We describe the* purposes *themselves that people have when acting as good or bad, saying, for example, that helping the poor is a worthy thing to achieve. We also evaluate different kinds of* practices or institutions, *saying, for example, that slavery is wrong or that it is good to keep promises. These are all ethical evaluations because of their fundamental link with evaluations of behavior. Courage is an ethical matter because acting courageously is; the purpose of helping the poor is an ethical matter because acts of charity are; institutions of slavery and promises are ethical matters because acts of enslavement and keeping promises are.*

In Part Three, we will accordingly concentrate on particular actions and the sorts of choices that we make. The central question of ethics is, What should I do? What should I do in general, with my life as a whole? No one has to think about this reflectively, putting the question to him- or herself in this perfectly general form and trying to come up with a satisfactory answer. But the question is still unavoidable in the sense that we must commit ourselves to an answer to it just by going through life making a series of choices. For whatever patterns there are in this series reveal the general rules by which we have lived, even if we have never examined our lives and seen these patterns. Even lower animals exhibit patterns in behavior; but lacking introspection, they have no possibility of leading what Socrates called an "examined life." We humans have the choice of living like these animals or of taking up the call to ethics.

Our first chapter in this series focuses on the nature of human happiness. How to be happy is another one of those unavoidable questions for us. Because unhappiness is dissatisfaction with the way our life is going, we cannot help but care about whether we are happy. It is not obvious, however, that pursuing happiness is the whole answer to the basic question of ethics, of how to live one's life. For, as most of us recognize, we are often required to set aside considerations of our own happiness for the sake of obligations to others. The second chapter in this part accordingly investigates the nature and source of our moral obligations in general. This paves the way for the third chapter, in which we examine the two most respected theories that not only admit the value of our own happiness but also attempt to explain our duties to others.

CHAPTER SEVEN

Happiness

HOW TO BE HAPPY? The question concerns us all, for the simple reason that we all *prefer* to be happy. This is not mysterious, since being happy is being satisfied with one's life, with the general way it is going. When we are unhappy, we want not merely to change our momentary condition, as we do when we sit on something sharp. A much greater change is called for, and often we are not able to see what that must be. This is part of what makes the problem difficult. (The other part is that even when we know what to do to be happier, we often lack the commitment to make the necessary changes.)

This chapter canvasses a number of prescriptions for happiness. We will see how various philosophers and religious traditions, studied in the last chapter, use their metaphysical outlook to ground their views on the source of human happiness. Before we look at their views, however, we clarify the nature of happiness itself. This is practically important, since, as Aristotle observed, just as an archer is more likely to hit the target if she can see it clearly, we are more likely to become happy if we know what it is.

THE NATURE OF HAPPINESS

What is happiness? Is it a *feeling*? It may be tempting to think so. After all, we often speak of being happy and being pleased as if they were the same thing. Pleasure is a feeling. This is why there is no difference between *being* pleased and *feeling* pleased (as there is no difference between being in pain and feeling pain). If happiness were a feeling, there would be no difference between being happy and feeling happy. But it is possible to feel happy while not really being happy. Someone who is unhappy may achieve momentarily the *feeling* of happiness, as some do by heavy drinking. But this feeling is a kind of illusion, creating a brief sense of happiness but not the real thing. Feelings are sensations (as discussed in Chapter Two), and as such they can be directly known in introspection. We can know directly, just by attending to ourselves, that we feel pleasure or enjoy something. It is the feeling of happiness that can be known in this way. But we can be mistaken when feeling happy, as the example of the unhappy drunk makes plain. If happiness is not a feeling, then what is it?

Aristotle gives a brief account in the following that is worth reflecting on:

> [T]he self-sufficient we now define as that which when isolated makes life desirable and lacking in nothing; and such we think happiness to be; and further we think it most desirable of all things, without being counted as one good thing among others — if it were so counted it would clearly be made more desirable by the addition of even the least of goods. . . . Happiness, then, is something final and self-sufficient.[1]

Happiness is "final" in that it is good in itself and not for anything else. Going to the dentist is good *for* healthy teeth and gums; people do not make the trip "for its own sake." But we want to be happy not for the *consequences* of being happy. Happiness is something we desire just for itself. Aristotle would *not* say that happiness is the only thing good for its own sake. Pleasure is a "final" good in that we do some things just because we enjoy them or "take pleasure" in them. What makes happiness unique among final goods is that it is "self-sufficient." When you are happy, there is nothing else you need. As Aristotle says, you are *lacking* nothing. So, happiness is the condition in which all your *needs* are met. This is why we associate happiness with *contentment*. It also explains how the unhappy drunk can feel happy without really being so. The alcohol produces this feeling by acting as an anesthetic, temporarily muting the bad feelings that would have arisen from unmet needs.

What, then, are *needs*? Are they the same as *desires*? This equation, too, may be tempting. We often talk about what we need and what we want as if these things were the same. This is especially true with children. Now we may allow that usually what we desire and what we need are the same. If you want water, this is typically because you need it, and if you need it, you are likely to be thirsty and thus want it. But there can be discrepancies. You can want something that you do not need, such as an ice cream cone when you have already eaten enough. If you are not seriously overweight, there is little problem in satisfying this desire. But you can also want something that you do *not* need to have, such as a destructive drug. There

---

1. From *Nicomachean Ethics*, trans. W. D. Ross (New York: Oxford University Press, 1980), 1097b 10–25.

is a general way in which needs are different from desires: Whenever our needs are not met, we are *harmed* thereby. You would be *disappointed* if you did not get the ice cream cone you wanted but not harmed; and if you did get the destructive drug you desire, you would get what you want but actually be harmed thereby. It is also possible to need things that you do not want. Most people agree that we need love, but the unfortunate child who is deprived of it may not know what he is missing and may not, therefore, have awakened the desire for what he needs.

The general point is important to understand. Desires for what we need are created in the first place by having those needs repeatedly satisfied, so that when we have the need in question and the opportunity to meet it, the desire is awakened in us. Children should have all of their needs met, so that they develop desires for what they need when they are on their own and doing "what they want." A good upbringing will ensure that in fact their wants will address their needs and bring genuine happiness. Without this, they can be getting everything they want and still be unhappy without even knowing what is missing.

When your needs are being regularly met, your whole life situation is appealing, and you enthusiastically look forward to living it. The obvious question then is, What *are* the needs that humans have? By answering this question, we give a view of "human nature" that shows what it takes to be happy. Each of the main positions we discuss in this chapter gives a different account of human nature, based on a different view of what we need. As we will see, these differences are associated with the sorts of differences in metaphysics that we covered in Part Two.

CRUDE MATERIALISM

Let us begin with an extreme position from which we can draw contrasts. In Chapter Five, we saw that materialism and idealism may be thought of as two poles on a single dimension. At one end is a crude form of materialism, the essence of which is to minimize the difference between ourselves and lower animals. All the claims about human nature made by dualists and idealists are denied or minimized. The fact that we are persons who can reason and reflect, and thus discover higher ideals to strive for, is ignored, denied, or downplayed. What do humans need? The answer of crude materialism is simple. We have just the same kinds of needs as other animals, for food, shelter, and sexual relief. Animals have urges, the satisfactions of which naturally lead to their own preservation and the perpetuation of their kind. Any affection for others, if it exists at all, serves either to win comrades in the struggle for life or to ensure the survival of their own offspring. Some animals—including humans—are natural predators. They must accordingly have instincts to dominate and even destroy others for the survival of themselves and their kin. The philosophical prescription for happiness is easy for crude materialists, though of course following it takes vigorous and sometimes ruthless action. You are happy when your animal needs are met, because these are your only *real* needs. Crude materialists think this point ought to be obvious, but it is not, due to the confusing effect of living in society. We are constantly pressured as we grow up to be "kind" and "fair" to others. And this is just what we should expect to happen in any society, in which the members are continually training one another to cooperate so that all members have a better chance to survive. Crude materialists do not deny the value of living in society, as this is likely to serve your (real, animal) needs. But *your* happiness depends on meeting *your* needs, and these are determined by what your material body urges you to do. As already stated, your needs are designed mainly for the welfare of you and to some extent those of your offspring. If you find yourself in conflict with people, even some others in your own society, you are basically at war with them. Your happiness depends on realizing this truth and not being duped by the effects of society in making you think you have "obligations" to others or that you would be better off by being "kind" to them. Turn the other cheek, and you will be slapped down by someone who is more in tune with his real nature.

Objection to Crude Materialism

Crude materialism is popular among many scientifically minded people who take it to be the hard-headed lesson of materialism. It is not popular among philosophers, however, even among those who are themselves materialists. The most serious problem for crude materialists is to explain how humans sometimes act differently from lower animals. Even if we grant the materialist's point that we are living bodies, how do we explain the empirical fact that humans do act for ideals other than the survival of themselves and their offspring? Humans create art and knowledge for others not related to them, including those of future generations. Many are friendly to strangers whom they can expect never to see again. Many religiously minded people direct their lives to some form of divinity far removed from their own personal existence. So, why would anyone engage in such activities if there were no human needs that prompted them?

AUGUSTINE'S DUALISM

Philosophers who deny crude materialism share the conviction that it "animalizes" us, by failing to see how we are different from lower animals. Dualism, for example, makes a clean break with crude materialism by declaring that humans have souls (or minds) that can live without the body. Other animals are simply bodies without souls. So, crude materialism makes the great mistake of failing to recognize the human soul.

One philosopher who takes this view is Saint Augustine. In the following passage, he argues against those who suppose that happiness is to be found in this life:

> If, then, we be asked what the city of God has to say upon these points, and, in the first place, what its opinion regarding the supreme good and evil is, it will reply that life eternal is the supreme good, death eternal the supreme

evil, and that to obtain the one and escape the other we must live rightly. And thus it is written, "The just lives by faith," for we do not as yet see our good, and must therefore live by faith; neither have we in ourselves the power to live rightly, but can do so only if He who has given us faith to believe in His help does help us when we believe and pray. As for those who have supposed that the sovereign good and evil are to be found in this life . . . all these have, with a marvelous shallowness, sought to find their blessedness in this life and in themselves. Contempt has been poured upon such ideas by the Truth, saying by the prophet, "The Lord knoweth the thoughts of men" (or, as the Apostle Paul cites the passage, "The Lord knoweth the thoughts of the wise . . . that they are vain").

For what flood of eloquence can suffice to detail the miseries of this life? . . . For when, where, how, in this life can these primary objects of nature be possessed so that they may not be assailed by unforeseen accidents? Is the body of the wise man exempt from any pain which may dispel pleasure, from any disquietude which may banish repose? The amputation or decay of the members of the body puts an end to its integrity, deformity blights its beauty, weakness its health, lassitude its vigor, sleepiness or sluggishness its activity—and which of these is it that may not assail the flesh of the wise man? Comely and fitting attitudes and movements of the body are numbered among the prime natural blessings; but what if some sickness makes the members tremble? What if a man suffers from curvature of the spine to such an extent that his hands reach the ground, and he goes on all fours like a quadruped? Does not this destroy all beauty and grace in the body, whether at rest or in motion? What shall I say of the fundamental blessings of the soul, sense and intellect, of which the one is given for the perception, and the other for the comprehension of truth? But what kind of sense is it that remains when a man becomes deaf and blind? Where are reason and intellect when disease makes a man delirious? We can scarcely, or not at all, refrain from tears, when we think of or see the actions and words of such frantic persons, and consider how different from and even opposed to their own sober judgement and ordinary conduct their present demeanor is. And what shall I say of those who suffer from demoniacal possession? Where is their own intelligence hidden and buried while the malignant spirit is using their body and soul according to his own will? And who is quite sure that no such thing can happen to the wise man in this life?[2]

Since the supreme good is life eternal and the supreme evil is death eternal, we must be able to live without our bodies to achieve what is most good for us. Crude materialists see us merely as bodies, which would make the supreme evil the inevitable fate of all.

Dualism is a very widespread belief. It is held by anyone who believes it possible to live independently of one's body. Those who believe in reincarnation, for

---

2. From *The City of God*, trans. Rev. Marcus Dods.

example, depict the soul in a bodiless state while making the transfer to a new life. Dualism itself does not imply the existence of God, though of course many dualists are theists. Augustine's view contains details not admitted by all dualists. It is, however, a view that is enormously influential and that highlights how dualism can be linked with theism. Many dualists want God to exist to ensure the kind of afterlife they hope for. Augustine, however, thinks we need God in this life to be worthy of it. For eternal life, we must live rightly, but we lack the power to do so on our own. We need God's help, not only to answer our prayers but to give us the faith we need to do what we know to be right. (Many Christians today say that we need God's "grace" to *want* to do good.) In other passages, Augustine says that the final reward of our good efforts is to unite with God and see him "face-to-face." Both dualism and theism must be true for us to be as happy as we can be.

STOICISM

The double aspect theory was a direct response to dualism (see Chapter Five). The latter makes such a sharp distinction between mind and body as to make their interaction mysterious. The double aspect theory brings together mind and body as two aspects of the same thing. Pantheism takes this model of mind and body and transfers it to nature as a whole (see Chapter Six). Pantheists are sincere in regarding their position as religious. They refer to the whole of nature as God and see everything else, including us, as merely parts or features of this single reality. God "creates" other things the way the ocean creates waves, just by moving itself. Since God (nature) includes all there is, there is nothing outside God exerting any influence on "him." God is *free*, in the sense of being completely *self-directed*. Pantheists have seen in the freedom of "God" an important clue about how to live. To be happy, we should model ourselves on the whole of nature by gaining complete self-control. This position was developed mainly by the Stoics (named after the *stoa*, or porch, on which they regularly met). The link between happiness and self-control is explained in the following by Epictetus, a Roman slave who lived in the first to second century A.D.:

> There are things which are within our power, and there are things which are beyond our power. Within our power are opinion, aim, desire, aversion, and in one word, whatever affairs are our own. Beyond our power are body, property, reputation, office, and, in one word, whatever are not properly our own affairs.
>
> Now the things within our power are by nature free, unrestricted, unhindered; but those beyond our power are weak, dependent, restricted, alien. Remember then, that, if you attribute freedom to things by nature dependent, and take what belongs to others for your own, you will be hindered, you will lament, you will be disturbed, you will find fault both with gods and men. But if you take for your own only that which is your own,

and view what belongs to others just as it really is, then no one will ever compel you, no one will restrict you, you will find fault with no one, you will accuse no one, you will do nothing against your will; no one will hurt you, you will not have an enemy, nor will you suffer any harm.

Aiming therefore at such great things, remember that you must not allow yourself any inclination, however slight, towards the attainment of the others; but that you must entirely quit some of them, and for the present postpone the rest. But if you have these, and possess power and wealth likewise, you may miss the latter in seeking the former; and you will certainly fail of that, by which alone happiness and freedom are procured.

Seek at once, therefore, to be able to say to every pleasing semblance, "You are but a semblance and by no means the real thing." And then examine it by those rules which you have; and first and chiefly, by this: whether it concerns the things which are within our own power, or those which are not; and if it concerns anything beyond our power, be prepared to say that it is nothing to you.

Remember that desire demands the attainment of that of which you are desirous; and aversion demands the avoidance of that to which you are averse; that he who fails of the object of his desires, is disappointed; and he who incurs the object of his aversion, is wretched. If, then, you shun only those undesirable things which you cannot control, you will never incur anything which you shun. But if you shun sickness, or death, or poverty, you will run the risk of wretchedness. Remove aversion, then, from all things that are not within your power, and transfer it to things undesirable, which are within your power. But for the present altogether restrain desire; for if you desire any of the things not within your power, you must necessarily be disappointed; and you are not yet secure of those which are within your power, and so are legitimate objects of desire. Where it is practically necessary for you to pursue or avoid anything, do even this with discretion, and gentleness, and moderation.[3]

We humans have the ability to choose what we do. The unwise go after things that may be impossible for them to attain, such as wealth and social status. They also try to escape from things that are unavoidable, such as sickness and death. This causes frustration and grief. The wise accordingly examine their real position in the world and restrict their efforts to things they are capable of achieving. In this way, they ensure that they reach their own goals.

The wise are happier in being more successful in what they do. But their happiness comes most of all from their *sense of freedom*. The Stoics were determinists (see Chapter Five). Their religious feeling came mainly from contemplating the order of nature (the mind of God for them). Natural events are determined in accordance with eternal laws that collectively form this order. But humans are unique by having within them a "spark of God." We are capable of achieving a kind

---

3. From Epictetus, *Enchiridion*, 1, 2, trans. Sanderson Beck.

of freedom analogous to God's. This comes by acting *rationally* in the sense of acting with genuinely good reasons. Suppose, for example, that you are tempted to have another drink late in a party, knowing that you will regret it tomorrow. It is *irrational* to succumb to the desire because you have no *good* reason for doing so. If you do take the drink, you "have your reason," but you can see in retrospect that this was not a good reason. You will realize that you regarded one moment of your life as intrinsically more valuable than another. Why should the morning of the hangover be regarded as any less important than the moment of the night before? When you drink "as if there is no tomorrow," you are acting *arbitrarily*. There is no good reason for valuing one moment more than another, but you do it anyway. If we ask *why* you did it, all that you can point to is the strength of the desire and your own lack of will. In this way, it was the desire and not your own knowledge of what is best that was in control. You see yourself as pushed about by external forces (such as the desire to drink). You lack *self-respect* since it was not really your *self* that originated your action. What genuinely springs from yourself is only what you do by seeing what is best. It is only by acting rationally that you free yourself from dependence on external forces. According to the Stoics, human happiness comes mainly from the consciousness of freedom, in which we recognize our affinity with God.

PLATO ON UNDERSTANDING

Idealism distances itself the most from crude materialism. In its simplest (and least credible) expression, it denies altogether the reality of the material world, including the body. In more sophisticated versions, it claims that mind is more basic in reality than matter. Thus, Plato likened material things to reflections or shadows cast from the eternal Forms. Your body is part of the material world and thus represents how you are *similar* to other things in nature. To deny or downplay the reality of matter, as idealism does, is therefore to emphasize how we are *unique*. Idealist conceptions of human nature put the greatest emphasis on the distinctively human. In the last chapter, we examined two forms of idealism, represented by Plato and Shankara. We now turn to how their views of basic reality influence their views of human need.

Beginning with Plato, let us recall how he divided reality into two basic spheres. The things we know directly in experience come and go, and they thus form the world of change. These changes, however, take place against an eternal background that makes them intelligible. Humans have intellect, by which they may contemplate the eternal world. This world consists of the Forms, or *kinds* of things. By contemplating the Forms, we come to understand what things are. We grasp the essential natures of the things we see around us, what makes them the sorts of things they are. For Plato, it is the intellect above all that is distinctively human. And human happiness comes mainly from exercising this power, coming to *understand* what is only made familiar by the senses. By consigning matter, and with it the body, to a lesser status in reality, happiness is to be found mainly in the mind, as Plato suggests in the following:

> What again shall we say of the actual acquirement of knowledge? — is the body, if invited to share in the inquiry, a hinderer or a helper? I mean to say, have sight and hearing any truth in them? Are they not, as the poets are always telling us, inaccurate witnesses? And yet, if even they are inaccurate and indistinct, what is to be said of the other senses? — for you will allow that they are the best of them? Then when does the soul attain truth? — for in attempting to consider anything in company with the body she is obviously deceived. Then must not existence be revealed to her in thought, if at all? And thought is best when the mind is gathered into herself and none of these things trouble her — neither sounds nor sights nor pain nor any pleasure — when she has as little as possible to do with the body, and has no bodily sense or feeling, but is aspiring after being? And in this the philosopher dishonors the body; his soul runs away from the body and desires to be alone and by herself?[4]

Notice that the operation of the senses actually constitutes a kind of *hindrance* for the "pure" operation of the intellect. The crude materialist will see the value of the intellect only in its ability to help us satisfy our animal needs. For Plato, the need to understand the world is basic to human nature — indeed, the most important for human happiness.

HINDUISM ON DETACHMENT

Idealistic views of human nature stress the distinctively human. Plato emphasizes the need for understanding, since he sees the intellect as what is most importantly unique in human nature. A different emphasis, which is no less idealistic, is found in Hinduism, especially as explained by Shankara. Shankara likens the entire material world to one great dream. Unlike the crude materialist who sees in himself nothing but an animal body, Shankara actually says, "I am bod*iless*."

Hinduism is known for teaching that happiness comes mainly from an attitude of *detachment* from material things. We tend to develop such an appetite for material possessions and wielding power in the material world that we become practically enslaved to material things. The crude materialist sees nothing but success in the continual hoarding of possessions. But material things are ephemeral, because the material world in essence is the world of change, the "cycle of birth and death." Since nothing material lasts, we are bound to be disappointed in life unless we recognize that our true nature is to stand above the material world, as an

---

4. Plato, *Phaedo*, trans. Benjamin Jowett, 65a–e.

unchanging spectator of it all. It is this view that Shankara expresses in the following passage:

> The highest—which is of the nature of Seeing, like the sky, evershining . . . That I am and I am forever released . . .
> I am Seeing, pure and by nature changeless . . .
> The continuous series of pains due to the body, the intellect and the senses is neither I nor of Me, for I am changeless. And this is because the continual series [of pains] is unreal; it is indeed unreal like an object seen in a dream.[5]

Whereas Plato prized the intellect, Shankara here seems to emphasize our power of *introspection*. For it is this that allows us be a spectator of "the continuous series of pains" and other mental events. The self is likened to the sky against which troubles and pains pass by like so many clouds. One detaches from them, gains liberation from them, by identifying oneself as the one who stands back from them in introspection. Our most important human need, then, is to realize our identity with Pure Consciousness. This realization is "enlightenment," and the need for it shows what is special about human nature and what we must achieve to be happy.

BUDDHISM

Before we turn to materialism, let us look at Buddhism, for this religion is closely related to Hinduism. (It is, in fact, merely a protestant reaction to it.) Like Christianity and Islam, Buddhism teaches that anyone can enter the religion and enjoys equal status therein. Traditional Hinduism declared that humans reincarnate, reentering a new body after death appropriate to the life they have lived. A bad life gathered "bad karma," consigning oneself to a lower state of life, perhaps living as a lower animal for another round in the "cycle of birth and death." Eventually, with enough good deeds, one could escape from the cycle altogether and live in eternal bliss. Unfortunately, the caste system was introduced into Hinduism (from the West, around 1500 B.C.). This divides humans by birth into classes declared to be ranked with respect to their current qualification for achieving eternal bliss. Lower castes have lower social status, supposedly appropriate for the sin of being born to a lower caste. Buddhists (like progressive Hindus today) reject the caste system entirely. But they have a prescription for happiness that is in keeping with their Hindu origin.

Buddhism is named after its founder, Siddhartha Gotama, known as "the Buddha" (the "enlightened one") and born in what is now Nepal in the sixth century B.C. The following selection is supposed to be of his own words:

---

5. From *A Thousand Teachings: The Upadesasahasri of Sankara*, trans. and ed. Sengaku Mayeda (Tokyo: University of Tokyo Press, 1992).

[T]hese two extremes ought not to be practiced by one who has gone forth from the household of life. What are the two? There is devotion to the indulgence of sense-pleasures, which is low, common, the way of ordinary people, unworthy and unprofitable; and there is devotion to self-mortification, which is painful, unworthy and unprofitable.

Avoiding both extremes, the [enlightened person] has realized the Middle Path: it gives vision, it gives knowledge, and it leads to calm, to insight, to enlightenment, to [Nirvana]. And what is that Middle Path . . . ? It is simply the Noble Eightfold Path, namely, right view, right thought, right speech, right action, right livelihood, right effort, right mindfulness, right concentration. . . .

The Noble Truth of suffering (*Dukkha*) is this: Birth is suffering; aging is suffering; sickness is suffering; death is suffering; sorrow and lamentation, pain, grief and despair are suffering; association with the unpleasant is suffering; dissociation from the pleasant is suffering; not getting what one wants is suffering—in brief, . . . [all the forms of] attachment are suffering.

The Noble Truth of the origin of suffering is this: It is this thirst (craving) which produces re-existence and re-becoming, bound up with passionate greed. It finds fresh delight now here and now there, namely, thirst for sense-pleasures; thirst for existence and becoming; and thirst for non-existence (self-annihilation).

The Noble Truth of the cessation of suffering is this: It is the complete cessation of that very thirst, giving it up, renouncing it, emancipating oneself from it, detaching oneself from it.

The Noble Truth of the Path leading to the Cessation of suffering is this: It is simply the Noble Eightfold Path, namely right view; right thought; right speech; right action; right livelihood; right effort; right mindfulness; right concentration. . . .

[W]hen my vision of true knowledge was fully clear . . . regarding the Four Noble Truths, then I claimed to have realized the perfect Enlightenment that is supreme in the world. . . . And a vision of true knowledge arose in me thus: My heart's deliverance is unassailable. This is the last birth. Now there is no more re-becoming (rebirth).[6]

Siddhartha Gotama often denied any interest in metaphysics (which is why we did not cover Buddhism in the last chapter). Nevertheless, he did emphasize the *impermanence* of things, which we have seen is that feature of the material world that leads the Hindu to detach from it by identification with Pure Consciousness. But all talk of Pure Consciousness is surely metaphysical. Buddhism looks at the world just as we experience it with our senses. What we find is that nothing lasts. Like Hinduism, Buddhism prescribes ridding yourself of the craving for material things. But unlike Hinduism, this is to be achieved not by a metaphysical insight about your real identity with the First Cause. If Buddhism has a

6. From "Setting in Motion the Wheel of Truth," in *What the Buddha Taught*, by Walpola Rahula (New York: Grove Weidenfeld, 1959).

metaphysical outlook (which is arguable), it is a negative one, which denies the reality of anything permanent "underlying" the world of change. Above all, it denies the reality of a *self*, which supposedly persists as one and the same thing throughout all the changes of one's life. (Shankara's Pure Consciousness would be such a self, as would be the mind of Cartesian dualism.) All such belief in permanent things "behind" the world of change is given by the Buddha as the chief source of the attachment to things that causes unhappiness.

There are three great evils to avoid, according to Buddhism: unenlightenment, greed, and hatred. We fail to be enlightened when we believe in permanent things, such as a "self" that goes on through change, perhaps even after the death of the body. The obsessive craving for an "afterlife" must be counted as among the ways we attach to supposedly permanent things. Such attachments are the source of the emotions of hatred and greed. For these arise from an unjustifiable concern for the self. People who are greedy are seeking to gain things for their own use. Those who harbor hatred toward others see them as enemies in the competition to hoard possessions, including social status. Once we detach from the impermanent altogether and fully accept the world of change, we are released from such emotions and develop instead compassion for all living things. We stop suffering from the pervasive, debilitating emotions of hatred and greed and attain *nirvana*—literally "extinction" of the self and, hence, the state of bliss that results. (Please note that this is a naturalistic interpretation of Buddhism that would be denied by those many religious Buddhists who believe in an afterlife through reincarnation. I give this interpretation as more in keeping with the core insights of the Buddha.)

TAOISM

The Taoists are like the Stoics in recommending that we model ourselves on the natural world. For the Stoics, this meant understanding one's place in the world, so that one could act freely. Since the Taoists have a radically different conception of the natural world, they give a very different interpretation of the prescription to act "naturally."

Taoism is extremely opposed to Platonism. Not only is it materialistic, but also the material world is not thought to have an intelligible structure. Language and thought impose distinctions on what is essentially an "uncarved block." To live "naturally" is therefore to live as much as possible in freedom of man-made rules, conventions, and all that is artificial. Such a life is described in the following, also from the *Tao Te Ching*:

> Learn to yield and be soft, if you want to survive.
> Learn to bow and you will stand in your full height.
> Learn to empty yourself and be filled with the Tao. . . .
>   the way a valley empties itself into a river.
> Use up all you are and then you can be made new.
> Learn to have nothing and you will have everything.

> Sages always act like this and are Children of the Tao.
> Never trying to impress, their being shines forth.
> Never saying "this is it," people see what the truth is.
> Never boasting, they leave the space they can be valued in.
> And never claiming to be who they are, people can see them.
> And since they never argue, no one argues with them either.[7]

It is noteworthy that Taoist thought originated with hermits. They hold that society itself is a great artifact, and like language, it causes us to lose touch with our true nature and what is really important to us. Real human needs are simple and come mainly from close contact with the Earth. Nature operates by the principle of yin and yang, the passive and active. What this means is that nature has its own rhythms and cycles, and what seems like a general trend is bound to be reversed. Day follows night; droughts are followed by rain. Humans, through language and society generally, try to deny what is natural. They are dissatisfied with nature and want to change it for their "own good." But nature takes its revenge with all efforts to change its course. Today we are seeing a population explosion made possible by technology, carrying with it global pollution and environmental destruction—all due to the foolish choice to become "civilized," to form large and powerful organizations, like nations, by which humans try to change nature instead of learning to live within it.

Taoists are like crude materialists, in distancing themselves from idealism. They do not see in this metaphysics, however, a prescription for violence and conquest. Such destructive attitudes they explain as being due to the pernicious effect of forming societies. Large organizations build up wealth, to be fought over, and concentrate power, to be used in plundering other societies. It is the artificial, the man-made, that is the main source of human unhappiness. As we will see in Part Four, Taoism is close to "anarchism" in preferring small societies over large ones.

EPICURUS'S HEDONISM

Previously we contrasted Taoism with another form of materialism. Atomism is not monistic, and it affirms the reality of the natural order. This view of basic reality was held by Epicurus, a Greek philosopher of the fourth to third centuries B.C. Epicurus's materialism is reflected in his commitment to *hedonism*, from the Greek word for *pleasure*. Hedonism in ethics identifies pleasure with the highest good and thus construes the happy life as one that maximizes enjoyment. Plato, the idealist, argued at length against hedonism, associating it with crude materialism. But although the metaphysics of Epicurus is close to crude materialism and his ethics is hedonistic, his prescription for happiness is surprisingly close to that of Plato.

---

7. From *The Illustrated Tao Te Ching*, trans. Man-Ho Kwon, Martin Palmer, and Jay Ramsey (New York: Barnes & Noble, 1993).

Prior to Epicurus, hedonists were known for recommending a life filled as much as possible with intense pleasures. Since the most intense pleasures are those of the body—food, drink, and sex—they saw little value in the life of the mind. Pleasures are empirically known, and it seems a plain fact of experience that we find them good. Given a metaphysical commitment to materialism and the basic reality of the empirical world, hedonism is a likely position in ethics to conclude.

Epicurus is especially interesting for starting with these "vulgar" assumptions but coming to a very different view of the good life. His position is clear, down-to-earth, and embodies useful wisdom, as the following passage reveals:

> Unhappiness comes either through fear or through vain and unbridled desire: but if a man curbs these, he can win for himself the blessedness of understanding . . . Of desires, all that do not lead to a sense of pain, if they are not satisfied, are not necessary, but involve a craving which is easily dispelled, when the object is hard to procure or they seem likely to produce harm . . . Wherever in the case of desires which are physical [natural], but do not lead to a sense of pain, if they are not fulfilled, the effort is intense, such pleasures are due to idle imagination, and it is not owing to their own nature that they fail to be dispelled, but owing to the empty imaginings of the man . . . .
>
> The disturbance of the soul cannot be ended nor true joy created either by the possession of the greatest wealth or by honor and respect in the eyes of the mob or by anything else that is associated with causes of unlimited desires . . . We must not violate nature, but obey her; and we shall obey her if we fulfill the necessary desires and also the physical [natural], if they bring no harm to us, but sternly reject the harmful . . . The man who follows nature and not vain opinions is independent in all things. For in reference to what is enough for nature every possession is riches, but in reference to unlimited desires even the greatest wealth is not riches but poverty . . . .
>
> When we say, then, that pleasure is the end and aim, we do not mean the pleasures of the prodigal or the pleasures of sensuality, as we are understood to do by some through ignorance, prejudice, or willful misrepresentation. By pleasure we mean the absence of pain in the body and of trouble in the soul. It is not an unbroken succession of drinking-bouts and of merry-making, not sexual love, not the enjoyment of the fish and other delicacies of a luxurious table, which produce a pleasant life; it is sober reasoning, searching out the grounds of every choice and avoidance, and banishing those beliefs through which the greatest disturbances take possession of the soul . . . .
>
> Unlimited time and limited time afford an equal amount of pleasure, if we measure the limits of that pleasure by reason.
>
> The body receives as unlimited the limits of pleasure; and to provide it requires unlimited time. But the mind, grasping in thought what the end and limit of the body is, and banishing the terrors of futurity, procures a complete and perfect life, and has no longer any need of unlimited time.[8]

---

8. From *Epicurus: The Extant Remains*, trans. Cyril Bailey (Oxford: Clarendon, 1926).

Unlike the earlier hedonists, who advocated a life of intense, bodily pleasures, Epicurus recommended and lived a "simple life," with little excitement. For he believed that happiness required two main things: health of the body and peace of mind. He agrees with Augustine that we cannot be happy while in physical pain or discomfort. But he thinks that this situation can be largely avoided by most people with a prudent regard for physical health. His main lesson, though, pertains more to peace of mind. The great majority of people, he believed, suffered from unnecessary fears. In his day, these included especially the fear of an afterlife governed by angry gods. We must admit that this fear made sense, for if we find this life to be filled with suffering, should we not expect more of the same if the afterlife is governed by the same gods who oversee this life? The main purpose of philosophy, he concluded, was to banish those fears that are unnecessary because they are based on false beliefs. He argued in particular for the *mortality* of the soul as a cure for fear of the afterlife. This is where his atomism comes in; he used it to argue that there could be no more pain after the dispersal of one's atoms. His main point is, however, easy to apply today. Many people have fears that they could eliminate by serious and sustained reflection on the sources of these fears. Do we, for example, have as much to fear as we think we do about failing to be a great success in the business world? Or about incurring the disapproval of relatives and daily acquaintances? Epicurus encourages us to see the value in frequent reflection on our inner lives, to discover the fears that destroy peace of mind and to eliminate them, either by changing our lives or by disproving the beliefs on which they are based.

When we have health of the body and peace of mind, free of pain and fear, we achieve, according to Epicurus, the highest state of human existence: *serenity*. Our true needs are fulfilled, and we feel a contentment that cannot be exceeded. And we know that this is the best that life can be, because a true philosophy of life convinces us that this is so. We realize that although continued existence would offer more of this good state of existence, it cannot offer us anything better. So, once we have attained serenity, our lives are, in an important way, complete, and we do not feel the need to live more. With this realization, we lose the fear of death, since death cannot steal what we have already attained. Those who live with fear know deep down that they are not fulfilled; that life could be better; and that if they die, they will have failed to attain the highest state. They accordingly fear death and hope desperately for immortality.

Epicurus's optimism is based on the belief that most people can secure a life with bodily health and with enough time to reflect and to enjoy the company of good friends, also devoted to living the best life. But many people fail to take this path in life, and so he diagnoses how they go wrong. One of the main problems is that "idle imagination" operates to create desires for things that we do not need. We imagine ourselves in luxury or in positions of power and work hard to achieve these. Usually our efforts are wasted, but even when successful, the pleasures they afford are like those of the drug addict or overeater, serving to distract more than to fulfill. What Epicurus is mainly concerned to point out is that such distractions only momentarily obscure and do not eliminate those fears that destroy peace of mind.

The quiet life of reflection recommended by Epicurus is remarkably similar to that advocated by the Buddha. Like Epicurus, the Buddha addresses the problem of happiness by diagnosing the cause of normal unhappiness. Also like Epicurus, he identifies the cause of normal suffering as due to desires that can be eliminated through a true philosophy of life. Epicurus's state of serenity is much like the state of nirvana promised by the Buddhist way of life. But whereas Buddha focuses on the emotions of hatred and greed, Epicurus focuses on fear. Buddha's diagnosis, as we have seen, is that the negative emotions arise from an unjustifiable concern for the self. Epicurus sees these same emotions as arising from the operation of idle imagination, causing us to want things we do not need. By striving for the mostly imaginary goods of great power and luxury, we fail to attend to our true needs of attaining health of body and peace of mind. Even if successful in these unnatural pursuits, we do not even *enjoy* life, since the distractions of our pursuits do not eliminate the underlying fears that we have not confronted and that continue to disturb our peace of mind. The hedonist commitment to a life of pleasure leads Epicurus to be wary of intense, momentary pleasures and to seek pleasure instead in a steady state of serenity, based on bodily health and inner confidence, won through patient reflection.

NATURALIZED CHRISTIANITY

When discussing Buddhism, I offered a conception of nirvana that was like Epicurus's conception of serenity, in being *naturalistic*. Buddhism—as I explained it—sees happiness as attainable in *this* life. It must be admitted, however, that most of the world's Buddhists believe in reincarnation and are staking their hopes on it. In the same way, most Christians seem to hold a view like that of Augustine, in which real happiness is only found in the *next* life. For a greater sense of completeness and fairness, I want lastly to discuss a naturalistic form of Christianity that is in fact held by many sincere Christians today.

According to what we will call "naturalized Christianity," the prescription for life offered by Jesus has nothing to do with gaining a reward for oneself in the afterlife. Naturalized Christians spurn all such interpretations of the message of Jesus as based on a purely selfish desire for one's own welfare. Like Buddhists, they think happiness comes from renunciation of selfishness and pouring one's efforts into brotherly love. We are "saved," according to this form of Christianity, not in the sense that we have a ticket to another world but in that we have in this world overcome the anxiety of separateness and loneliness through our love for others. Brotherly love is recommended, not because it is what God wants and doing his bidding will extend your own life. It is because it is truest to your own nature, which is expressed mainly through caring for others. Humans are not bound to live like animals, as the crude materialists think, in perpetual competition and warfare. They can decide to love each other and live in harmony. It is by seeing and feeling yourself to be part of humanity that we truly "join with the eternal."

When discussing metaphorical theology, I gave some evidence that Jesus' own view of heaven was really naturalistic. The twentieth-century mythologist Joseph Campbell makes a strong case in the following passage for such an interpretation by assembling a number of quotes attributed to Jesus, drawn from the recently discovered (and admittedly controversial) *Gospel According to Thomas*:

> Cleave a piece of wood, I am there; lift up the stone and you will find me there. . . .
> The Kingdom of the Father is spread upon the earth and men do not see it. . . .
> If those who lead you say to you: "See, the kingdom is in heaven," then the birds of heaven will precede you. If they say to you: "It is in the sea," then the fish will precede you. But the Kingdom is within you and it is without you. If you will know yourselves, then you will be known and you will know that you are the sons of the Living Father. But if you do not know yourselves, then you are in poverty and you are poverty.[9]

Christianity depicts the supreme being as loving. Naturalized Christianity interprets this metaphorically as a claim about human nature. We are sons of the Father in the sense that what is distinctively human is our capacity to extend our love even to strangers and the downcast. The person of Jesus demonstrates what humans can achieve in this respect. We accept Jesus into our hearts when we commit ourselves to open our hearts as he did. The self-centered hope for an eternal extension of one's own life only interferes with this kind of development of the heart. The Kingdom is not some far-off place where our selfish desires will be fully satisfied. The Kingdom is here, within you and all around you, in the sense that happiness is to be achieved in this life. We enter the Kingdom, here and now, when we renounce the self-centered orientation in life for the expansive orientation of unlimited love. The similarity of naturalized Christianity with Buddhism is striking.

CONCLUSION

One of the main lessons of this chapter is that philosophical accounts of happiness are typically based on certain metaphysical views of reality. Generally speaking, a metaphysics will give us a conception of our place in the world. It will set limits on what we can do (such as the materialists' limit on our life span), and it will open up opportunities for choice (such as the idealists' vision of a life unlike that of a lower animal). And by giving a framework in which to understand what are our basic needs, it supports a view of the happy life.

Although there are significant differences between the various prescriptions for happiness we have covered in this chapter, I hope it is clear that most of them are consistent and have important messages to incorporate into your life. Many of

---

9. From *The Outer Reaches of Inner Space: Metaphor as Myth and Religion* (New York: Harper & Row, 1986).

them can be seen as tailored to a kind of life circumstance. In tough and disappointing circumstances, for example, Stoicism offers some peace of mind. The Taoist picture is useful to remember when we feel overwhelmed by the pressures of society. Epicurus has wisdom useful for assessing our commitments to excitement, power, and prestige. Plato and Shankara help us to see generally the value of not overestimating such mundane pursuits. Buddhism and Christianity are especially useful when dealing with others. And for the faithful, Augustine clarifies the need for God's help in living rightly.

Since you cannot avoid caring about your own happiness, you do well to understand what happiness is and to see how the best recommendations for achieving it can be incorporated into your decision making. As we will see in the next chapter, however, there is a good deal more to planning your life than trying to achieve happiness.

STUDY QUESTIONS

1. Justify the claim that happiness is not a feeling.
2. Explain how needs are different from desires, and illustrate your answer with original examples.
3. What makes us happy, according to crude materialism? What is the most serious problem for crude materialism?
4. Why does Augustine think that happiness cannot be found in this life? How does his view of happiness depend on both dualism and theism?
5. According to Stoicism, how is the happy person like God?
6. How, according to Plato, does the intellect contribute to happiness? How does his view of the intellect differ from that of the crude materialists?
7. What do Hindus mean when they recommend being "detached"? How does Shankara use his metaphysics to make this recommendation?
8. What are the main obstacles to nirvana, according to Buddhists?
9. Compare Epicurus's view of serenity with the Buddha's view of nirvana. How are their prescriptions for happiness different? Are they consistent?
10. How does Epicurus use materialism to support hedonism? How is his hedonistic view of happiness different from previous expressions of hedonism?
11. Contrast Stoicism with Taoism with respect to their views about what it is to "live naturally."
12. How is the prescription for happiness of naturalized Christianity like that of Buddhism?

CHAPTER
EIGHT

Morality

WHAT TO DO? This may be considered the main question of ethics. For ethics is that branch of philosophy concerned generally with how things *ought* to be. And we wonder how things ought to be primarily to *change* them. If we did not have the power to change things by making choices, there would be little point in asking how they ought to be. We would be merely passive observers in our journey through life. All thinking could help us only to *understand* how things actually are. We would not be able to put this understanding to *use*.

The question of what to do is not the same as the question of what to do *to be happy*. It is true that we cannot avoid caring about whether we are happy. This point is so obvious that many philosophers, especially in ancient times, made it the basis of their whole ethics. For them, the basic question of ethics, "What should I do?" was not distinguished from the question "What should I do to be happy?" But even if your own happiness is bound to be a great concern of yours throughout your life, it is not obvious that it is the only thing that matters when you are faced with a decision about what to do. Many people are, in fact, outraged by the suggestion that what one ought to do is just the same as what will make one happy. Are we not, in fact, often *obligated* to take the interests of others into account? If it is time to repay money that I borrowed from you, it seems that I *ought* to pay you, even if I think this will *not* make me happy. People with impulses to cruelty *ought* to inhibit them, regardless of how satisfying it would be to indulge them. This is because, it seems, it is simply *wrong* to act in those ways. It is a common fact of human life that we have and use a sense of "right and wrong" in talking about what people do. We have a sense of **morality.**

THE NATURE OF MORALITY

Let us try to get clear about what morality is before we look at some alternative theories about it. The first thing to notice is that morality pertains to *choice*. Choosing involves awareness of alternatives. The dog who enters the room and finds two food bowls in separate corners *has* alternative courses of action. But it can *have* alternatives without *knowing* that it does. It may seem that a dog is making a choice when it looks back and forth from one food bowl to another before striking off for one. Yet the dog may not be remembering one when looking at the other, knowing that it could go for either the remembered bowl or the bowl now seen. It may be simply drawn to each in succession as it looks back and forth without realizing that it has a choice. Humans have the ability to see at once that different courses of action are open to them. This is what creates that feeling of free will (discussed in Chapter Five). But what causes them to choose one course of action over another?

To choose it is not enough just to predict what will happen if you do one thing or another. Such predictions, based on empirical knowledge of cause and effect, are necessary for choice, but something else is needed. The person making the choice must *evaluate* his options, as Aristotle says in effect in the following: "[F]or whether this or that shall be enacted is already a task requiring calculation; and there must be a single standard to measure by, for that is pursued which is *greater*. It follows that what acts in this way must be able to make a unity out of several images."[1]

Aristotle allowed that other animals have imagination. He would say that when our dog imagines a food bowl (as when expecting to see one), it has an "image" of a bowl. What we can do is to imagine what it would be like to act in either of two ways. We can bring to mind at once the images of both actions. To choose, we must *rank* the outcomes, as if putting one image above another into a single hierarchy. This is why Aristotle says that in choosing we make "a unity out of several images." The important point for us is that choosing requires more than predicting the outcomes of the alternatives that lie open for us. We must see that we have alternatives and evaluate which one is *best*.

THE PROBLEM OF MORAL MOTIVATION

Morality is a puzzling subject. On the one hand, the right thing to do often conflicts with what you would most like to do. You may be tempted not to pay a debt to someone who has forgotten it and then realize that it would be wrong to do so.

---

1. From "De Anima," in *The Basic Works of Aristotle*, ed. Richard McKeon (New York: Random House, 1968), 434a7–10.

In going against your wishes, thinking that you *ought* to pay it can seem like an unwelcome voice, coming from someone else. On the other hand, this thought about what to do is something you really accept, to guide you in making *your* choice. Sometimes we say that we know that something is "wrong" when we have no aversion to it whatsoever. If you are in a foreign country where drinking is illegal, you may acknowledge that it is "wrong" while feeling no guilt about doing it anyway. But here what you mean by saying it is wrong is that *other people think* it is wrong. If you yourself really thought it was wrong, you would sincerely disapprove of it. Now the point is that often we do really think something is wrong that we would like to do anyway. And if we ourselves really think it is wrong, we must have some aversion to it.

But how can you be averse to something you would like to do? If you are to forgo doing what is most pleasant and to do what is in some cases quite difficult, you must have a good reason. But this reason must somehow make doing the right (and less pleasant) thing *attractive*, and the wrong (but more pleasant) thing somehow *repugnant*. An important goal of ethics is to understand how this can be so. To answer the philosophical question of what to do is to say what is in common to all better choices that *makes* them better. Any satisfactory answer will explain what is the *reward* of doing what is right and what is the *penalty* for doing what is wrong. This is the **problem of moral motivation.**

All theories are attempts to explain and thus to solve problems. Moral theories are developed by attempting to answer the problems that arise in thinking generally about what to do. In our introductory survey, we will attend mostly to the two problems already presented. First there is the question of the *content* of morality: What in general is the right or best thing to do? Second there is the question of *motivation*: What motivates people to do what is right and avoid what is wrong? In our discussion of happiness, we looked to human nature to see what we need. Now we look again to human nature to see how we are motivated. As before, we will be able to classify our views of human nature with the sorts of metaphysical outlooks we canvassed in Part Two, especially those that respond to the mind–body problem. We will not, however, follow exactly the same sequence of positions as in the last two chapters. Instead, we will devote this chapter to three moral theories that are popular in the world at large but not among philosophers today. By seeing the objections to them, we will be able to appreciate the two moral theories of the next chapter, which are the most respected in modern ethics.

PSYCHOLOGICAL HEDONISM

Let us begin, as we did in the last chapter, with a view that is associated with crude materialism. To be happy, you must get what you *need*; crude materialists minimize distinctively human needs and in this way "animalize" us. To do what you *ought* to do, you must be *motivated* to do it. Since crude materialists see us as little more than animals, they will attempt to explain human motivation in terms applicable to other animals as well. **Psychological hedonism** is a good example of such a theory. It says that all of our choices are motivated by the pursuit of pleasure and the avoidance of pain. (The name comes from the Greek word *hedone*, for "pleasure.") Since other animals are motivated the same, psychological hedonists think human behavior can be understood as caused by the same sorts of desires. A **moral psychology** is a theory of how to understand moral behavior. Psychological hedonism is a moral psychology that minimizes distinctively human motives. Psychological hedonists do not say that there is no difference in the causes of human behavior. Any theory of why we do what we do must allow for the fact that we make choices. Psychological hedonists admit that we make choices but say that the *purpose* of all of our choices is either to increase our pleasure or to diminish our pain. Whenever we choose to do anything, our ultimate goal is to *feel* better.

HUMAN SELFISHNESS

Psychological hedonism may seem harmless enough, even commonsensical. But it turns out to have startling consequences. If the goal of everything you do is to make you feel better, this means that you are always *selfish*. Selfish people (called **egoists**) care only for themselves. According to psychological hedonism, the only kind of motive you *ever* have is to make *yourself* feel better. You may think, for example, that you are honorable in keeping your word. But what do you want from this, the psychological hedonist will ask? Do you not want to be trusted in the future? Is it not, then, your future comfort that motivates you to be honest? You may think that you help others in need just because you care about them. But when you think of what it will be like when you do, do you not anticipate enjoying it? Is it not, then, your own pleasure that you hope to obtain? If you doubt this, read the following selection from Plato to see what really motivates you:

> Now that those who practice justice do so involuntarily and because they have not the power to be unjust will best appear if we imagine something of this kind: having given both to the just and the unjust power to do what they will, let us watch and see whither desire will lead them; then we shall discover in the very act the just and unjust man to be proceeding along the same road, following their interest, which all natures deem to be their good, and are only diverted into the path of justice by the force of law. The liberty which we are supposing may be most completely given to them in the form of such a power as is said to have been possessed by Gyges, the ancestor of Croesus the Lydian. According to the tradition, Gyges was a shepherd in the service of the King of Lydia; there was a great storm, and an earthquake made an opening in the earth at the place where he was feeding his flock. Amazed at the sight, he descended into the opening, where, among other marvels, he beheld a hollow brazen horse, having doors, at which he, stooping and looking in, saw a dead body of stature, as appeared to him, more

than human and having nothing on but a gold ring; this he took from the finger of the dead and rescinded. Now the shepherds met together, according to custom, that they might send their monthly report about the flocks to the King; into their assembly he came having the ring on his finger, and as he was sitting among them he chanced to turn the collet of the ring inside his hand, when instantly he became invisible to the rest of the company and they began to speak of him as if he were no longer present. He was astonished at this, and again touching the ring he turned the collet outward and reappeared; he made several trials of the ring, and always with the same result—when he turned the collet inward he became invisible, when outward he reappeared. Whereupon he contrived to be chosen one of the messengers who were sent to the court; where as soon as he arrived he seduced the Queen, and with her help conspired against the King and slew him and took the kingdom. Suppose now that there were two such magic rings, and the just put on one of them and the unjust the other; no man can be imagined to be of such an iron nature that he would stand fast in justice. No man would keep his hands off what was not his own when he could safely take what he liked out of the market, or go into houses and lie with anyone at his pleasure, or kill or release from prison whom he would, and in all respects be like a god among men. Then the actions of the just would be as the actions of the unjust; they would both come at last to the same point. And this we may truly affirm to be a great proof that a man is just, not willingly or because he thinks that justice is any good to him individually, but of necessity, for wherever anyone thinks that he can safely be unjust, there he is unjust. For all men believe in their hearts that injustice is far more profitable to the individual than justice, and he who argues as I have been supposing, will say that they are right. If you could imagine anyone obtaining this power of becoming invisible, and never doing any wrong or touching what was another's, he would be thought by the lookers-on to be a most wretched idiot, although they would praise him to one another's faces, and keep up appearances with one another from a fear that they too might suffer injustice.[2]

The ring of Gyges in Plato's story is supposed to represent the power to *get away with* selfish behavior. Socrates' opponent in this passage, Thrasymachus, asks us to consider honestly and in our own heart whether we would ever refrain from doing what we most felt like doing if no one (even God) would ever find out, so that we would completely escape any punishment. If we agree with him, that we would not, then we are supposed to see that in real life people are always selfishly motivated. According to common morality, we are "supposed" to respect the rights of others, and in real life we usually have the selfishly good reason that if we do not we will be punished somehow. But this means that we are acting not really out of a "sense of honor" but rather out of a simple sense of self-protection. Thrasymachus

---

2. Plato, *Republic*, trans. Benjamin Jowett, 359b–360d.

therefore concludes that the just and the unjust person each follow the same path, the one of self-interest. There is no difference in *character* between, say, Jesus or Buddha, on the one hand, and Hitler or Charles Manson, on the other. They are simply choosing different *means* for promoting their own happiness.

ETHICAL HEDONISM

Psychological hedonism says what we *actually* do. What, if anything, can it tell us about what we *ought* to do? The answer is supplied by a commonly accepted principle, that *"ought implies can."* If it really is true that you *ought* to do something, it must be *possible* for you to do it. What you ought to do is what you have most reason *for doing*. You can have no good reason for doing something that is literally impossible for you to do. We wonder what we ought to do when we are faced with a *choice*. What you ought to do is one of the alternatives that lies open to you. Now, psychological hedonism says that it is impossible to do anything but seek your own pleasure and avoid your own pain. This being so, it cannot be true that you ought to do otherwise. This would be like telling you that you ought not to be human or that you ought not to be an animal. So, psychological hedonism *does* tell us something about what we ought to do, by *restricting* what we ought to do to choosing courses of action that lead to our naturally determined goal of feeling better.

Ethical hedonism says that what we ought to do is to pursue most effectively the existence of our own pleasure and the absence of our own pain. Pleasure and the absence of pain are the only things of *value* to us when we make choices. Ethical hedonism makes the apparently outrageous claim that every one of us *ought* to be selfish in everything we do. How could any serious philosopher—or any real person, for that matter—believe such a thing? In the history of ethics, there have been a remarkable number of ethical hedonists. This is because they have been convinced of *psychological* hedonism. For as we have seen, if nature restricts our purposes to how we ourselves feel, the only thing left to deliberate about when deciding what to do is what *means* to adopt to this end. If you are deciding what route to take on a journey when the destination is already set, the only thing to think about is what is the best way to get there. According to psychological hedonism, the goal of all our choices is already set, so that all that we have left to choose is the best way to reach it. It is *nature* that determines what we care about by giving us our ultimate concern to feel better. Everyone will allow that what we "ought" to do is to make the choice supported by the best reasons. According to psychological hedonism, good reasons can favor one choice only as the most effective way of feeling better.

PRUDENCE

Psychological hedonism does not say that we are always moved to do what we most feel like doing at the moment of choice. This would deny that we ever act from choice at all. For when we decide to *pursue* some goal, we adopt a plan to follow until we reach that goal. Following a plan requires self-control. To follow a plan, you must monitor your behavior and inhibit impulses to do things that take you off course. If your plan is to go to work, you must inhibit any impulse to lie down and go to sleep or wander off to watch television. The power of choice comes with the power of self-control. It allows us to pursue what we value, what we think is best, in spite of how we feel at the moment. The ethical hedonist says that your highest value is to be pleased and not pained. But humans have futures and know that they do. When you act best to increase your pleasure and reduce your pain, you must, therefore, take the future into account. When you do, you see that the present moment is no more important than any future moment. It would be *foolish*, therefore, to cause much future pain for a small amount of present pleasure or to miss out on much future pleasure to avoid a small amount of present pain. It is foolish to drink too much now for a momentary thrill if this means suffering a painful hangover tomorrow; it is foolish to miss the pleasures of a prosperous future life by avoiding the minor discomforts of disciplining yourself now to acquire the skills that will allow that to happen. The ethical hedonist says, therefore, that you should be *prudent*. The **prudent** person does not value the present moment more than future moments but acts in his own *long-term* best interests. An ethics of prudence is endorsed in the following excerpt from the twentieth-century Russian American writer Ayn Rand:

> Accept the fact that the achievement of your happiness is the only *moral* purpose of your life, and that happiness — not pain or mindless self-indulgence — is the proof of your moral integrity, since it is the proof and the result of your loyalty to the achievement of your values. Happiness was the responsibility you dreaded, it required the kind of rational discipline you did not value yourself enough to assume — and the anxious staleness of your days is the monument to your evasion of the knowledge that there is no moral substitute for happiness, that there is no more despicable coward that the man, who deserted the battle for his joy, fearing to assert his right to existence, lacking the courage and the loyalty to life of a bird or flower reaching for the sun. Discard the protective rags of that vice which you called a virtue: humility — learn to value yourself, which means: to fight for your happiness — and when you learn that *pride* is the sum of all virtues, you will learn to live like a man.
>
> As a basic step of self-esteem, learn to treat as the mark of a cannibal any man's *demand* for your help. To demand it is to claim that your life is his property — and loathsome as such a claim might be, there's something still more loathsome: your agreement. Do you ask if it's ever proper to help another man? No — if he claims it as his right or as a moral duty that you owe him. Yes — if such is your own desire based on your own selfish pleasure in the value of his person and his struggle.[3]

---

3. From *Atlas Shrugged* (New York: Random House, 1957).

Of course, it must be admitted that often, perhaps very often, others make demands on us that we have no obligation to comply with. But is *every* demand the "mark of a cannibal"? If you have stolen from someone who now demands back what is hers, is she being a cannibal? Is a child complaining of parental neglect a cannibal? It is the logic of ethical hedonism that leads to such extreme conclusions. And ethical hedonism is based on psychological hedonism. Why, then, would anyone think psychological hedonism is *true*?

AN ARGUMENT FOR PSYCHOLOGICAL HEDONISM

A very popular argument for this moral psychology goes as follows. Whenever we choose, it is to get something we want; and when we get what we want, we are pleased thereby; so, whenever we choose, it is really to promote our own pleasure. First, it is pointed out that if you help someone in need, you know it will make you feel better; or, if you fulfill your obligation, you know you will avoid feeling guilty. Then it is concluded that this is *why* you are doing it. Whenever you help someone you "love," you know that you yourself will be satisfied; so *this* is really why you do it: to gain that internal sense of satisfaction. People do not really perform their "obligations" to others out of some mysterious "sense of duty"; they do so to avoid deprivations of their own needs.

This commonly accepted argument is based on confusion. For even if you know that something will happen as a *result* of your doing something, it does not follow that this is *why* you did it. To conclude this is to ignore the possibility that the result, though foreseen, is *unintended*. People who regularly stutter when they talk or stumble when they walk may well *foresee* that they will stutter or stumble, but they do not *intend* to do so. So it can happen that altruistic people foresee that they will be pleased by helping others without this being their *motive*, their *reason why* they did it. If they are altruistic, helping other people pleases them, but they do not do it *for* the pleasure. The pleasure is simply a *by-product* of their action. Aristotle pointed out that we judge the character of a person by what pleases and displeases him. When we see that people are pleased by helping others, this is *evidence* that they are altruistic, not a sign that they are somehow doing it *for* their own pleasure. So also, the person who acts out of a sense of obligation may well foresee that were he to avoid his obligations, he would feel guilty. But this does not mean that he refrains from this *in order to* avoid the guilt. He just realizes that *because* he is responsible, acting irresponsibly would make him feel guilty: The guilt would occur as a by-product of the wrong action.

What is the difference between those consequences of our action that are merely by-products and those that are intended? We have said that only the latter are our motives, our reasons why we acted. But how can we *tell* which is which? The answer lies in the fact that our motives are *causes* of our behavior, the sort of thing that *explains* why we behave as we do. Suppose, for example, that you want to reach a water fountain but must cross a hot surface on bare feet to do so. If you want the water badly enough, you will suffer the heat. But you do not cross the surface *in order to* get your feet hot. Your belief that your feet will get hot is not a cause of your acting, not the sort of thing to mention in explaining why you walk to the water fountain. Causes are the sort of thing that produce effects, so that when we "take them away," we "take away" the effect. But if you were to learn that the surface were not really hot, your belief that your feet would get hot would be "taken away"—but this would not stop you from walking. If, on the other hand, you were to learn that the water fountain was dry, you would not walk. This is because your belief that you would get water there was a genuine motive and not just a thought you happened to have in mind.

DISPROVING PSYCHOLOGICAL HEDONISM

By applying what we know from Part One about empirical causes, we can now see clearly how to *tell* whether a thought about a foreseen consequence of an action is a motive or only a by-product. Suppose, for example, that someone pays back a debt, and we want to know her motive. She could be doing it from a sense of obligation or to keep her reputation. Now, it may be impossible to tell in a single instance, but this is what we should expect. For once again we are in that familiar situation of having different hypotheses for the same observed fact, and we must look to other circumstances to test them (see Chapter Three). Each hypothesis is attempting to explain the same fact (that the debt was repaid) by pointing to a trait of character. One says that the person is honest, the other that she acts from self-interest. The important thing to realize is that each hypothesis is genuinely testable, by making predictions about how she will behave in other circumstances. If the person is honest, she will regularly pay debts, even when there is no evident benefit to herself. If she is an egoist, she will not pay debts when (as with the ring of Gyges) she can get away with avoiding it. Whether or not people are unselfish is thus an *empirical, testable* matter.

If we are capable of acting for reasons that make no reference to how we feel, such as "This will please her" or "I owe him the money," then psychological hedonism is false. To disprove it, we only need empirical data for a hypothesis that the person in question acted with such a nonselfish reason. I can only say that while there is a great deal of selfishness and that often we are selfish when we think we are not, there seems to be abundant evidence for many nonselfish acts. You will become convinced of this only by considering for yourself what are the best explanations for the actions of people you know.

SELFISHNESS IS SELF-DEFEATING

Many people will, unfortunately, continue to be selfish even if convinced that they can be otherwise. All four of the moral theories we will study next say that sometimes we ought to be unselfish. Before we get to them, it is worth meeting egoists on their own terms, by making a case that selfishness itself is *self-defeating*. It is a familiar thought in the history of ethics that trying to be happy is not what makes you happy. (In the last chapter, we saw that this was emphasized especially by the Buddha.) According to this view, our own happiness comes more as a by-product than through making it what we are always intending to produce. One consideration that supports this view concerns the importance that egoists must attach to their own deaths. According to ethical hedonism, the only thing that is important to you is your own pleasure; if this is so, with your death must come the end of all that is important to you. There is no way for you to look beyond your death with hopes for good things to come, since after your death, nothing matters. The approach of your impending death is increasingly depressing, and the final moments are met with utter despair. Actually, the problem exists to some extent throughout your life. You are "imprisoned" in your self. You cannot take an interest in the things and persons around you unless you somehow see that this will benefit you. Many egoists desperately hope for an "afterlife" in which their own individual life goes on, for this is all that matters to them. Atheists who have struggled with the question of how to cope with the fact of death have sought a different resolution. What has been offered from some of the best of them is the idea that "salvation" from the fear of death comes by cultivating unselfish interests. This idea is expressed eloquently by the twentieth-century English philosopher Bertrand Russell:

> [W]e should desire the happiness of others, but not as an alternative to our own. In fact the whole antithesis between self and the rest of the world . . . disappears as soon as we have any genuine interest in persons and things outside of ourselves. Through such interests a man comes to feel himself part of the stream of life, not a hard separate entity like a billiard ball, which can have no relation to the other entities except that of collision. All unhappiness depends upon some kind of disintegration, or lack of integration; there is disintegration within the self through lack of coordination between the conscious and unconscious mind; there is lack of integration between self and society, where the two are not knit together by the force of objective interests and affections. The happy man is the man who does not suffer from either of these failures of unity, whose personality is neither divided against itself nor pitted against the world. Such a man feels himself a citizen of the universe, enjoying freely the spectacle that it offers and the joys that it affords, untroubled by the thought of death because he feels himself not really separate from those who come after him. It is in such profound instinctive union with the stream of life that the greatest joy is to be found.[4]

The atheist's prescription for how the enlightened person copes with the fact of death offers in effect a metaphorical interpretation of the "afterlife" that is taken

---

4. Bertrand Russell, *The Conquest of Happiness* (New York: Liveright, 1971), 248–249.

seriously by some students of religion. According to them, life truly goes on in the plain and empirically observable sense that we are succeeded by other people and other living beings generally. We are "saved" when we realize that our own individual existence is not uniquely important, for it is only a moment within a much longer history of life on earth. Much in philosophy and in religions around the world encourages us to see our "true self" as being much greater than that of the individual person, tied to a particular perishable body. The atheist offers in effect an interpretation of what this amounts to that requires no belief in the supernatural.

THE DIVINE COMMAND THEORY

Dualism distances itself from crude materialism by declaring the existence of an immaterial soul or mind, capable of existing without the body altogether. In the last chapter, we saw in Augustine's account of human nature a dualistic theory of happiness. The needs of the body are simply to maintain its physical integrity and to produce others of the same species. The needs of the soul are radically different and are satisfied only in the knowledge of and union with God. A dualistic theory of morality will find in human nature motives to do good that do not belong to the body. Our second moral theory breaks cleanly from crude materialism by saying that humans are capable of acting with a purpose nowhere found in other animals. We are capable of looking above the motives urged on us by our animal bodies to do God's will. The knowledge of other animals is limited, as Plato said, to the ever-changing material world. *They* cannot be expected to know of God or his plans. But *we* can know God and what he wants. This gives us a choice. We can turn from God and live like animals (the way the psychological hedonist says falsely that we *must!*), or we can lift ourselves above animal life and live as children of God. What we *ought* to do is obey God. Our second theory is called accordingly the **divine command theory.** It is also called **voluntarism** to indicate that right and wrong is ultimately due to God's volition, or *will*.

The divine command theory is very influential historically, and it continues to be embraced by many people today. Some people equate a morally good person with one who is "God fearing." Some consult religious authorities for guidance in life on the ground that they must know best what God wants. Some think that disputes about what is right are decisively settled by what is written in a holy text, such as the Bible or the Koran. Some have claimed that people who do not know of God cannot go to heaven, since no matter what they have done in life, they have not obeyed God.

Voluntarists have squarely addressed the problem of moral motivation. Some have pointed to the fact that the world, including ourselves, was created by God. Since we owe our very existence and continued sustenance to God, we are obliged to do what he wants. This appeals to our sense of gratitude. Some remind us of our future destiny to explain moral motivation. As Augustine said, the reward of obeying

God is eternal life, and the penalty of disobedience is eternal death. With stakes of this magnitude, it is not difficult to understand what would motivate someone to do the right thing.

Voluntarists use a view of human nature that is relatively controversial. Of course, they are theists. If they try to provide moral motivation with a future reward, they must say that we can survive the deaths of our bodies, in which case they are dualists as well. These commitments do not, of course, disprove the divine command theory, but they make defending it rather difficult.

Plato's Objection

Despite the common acceptance of the divine command theory, it is widely thought by philosophers to have been decisively refuted by Plato. In his dialogue *Euthyphro*, Socrates is walking with a young man by this name, who is on his way to court to charge his father with the legal crime of "impiety." (Note that this was one of the main charges that led in real life to Socrates being condemned to death.) Since *impiety* means not honoring your moral obligations, the father is being charged in effect with doing what is morally wrong. Read now the actual passage:

Socrates: The point which I should first wish to understand is whether the pious or holy is beloved by the gods because it is holy, or holy because it is beloved of the gods. . . .

And what do you say of piety, Euthyphro: is not piety, according to your definition, loved by all the gods?

Euthyphro: Yes.

Socrates: Because it is pious or holy, or for some other reason?

Euthyphro: No, that is the reason.

Socrates: It is loved because it is holy, not holy because it is loved?

Euthyphro: Yes.

Socrates: And that which is dear to the gods is loved by them, and is in a state to be loved of them because it is loved of them?

Euthyphro: Certainly.

Socrates: Then that which is dear to the gods, Euthyphro, is not [the same as being] holy, nor is that which is holy [the same as being] loved of God, as you affirm; but they are two different things.

Euthyphro: How do you mean, Socrates?

Socrates: I mean to say that the holy has been acknowledge by us to be loved of God because it is holy, not to be holy because it is loved.

Euthyphro: Yes.

Socrates: But that which is dear to the gods is dear to them because it is loved by them, not loved by them because it is dear to them.

Euthyphro: True.

Socrates: But, friend Euthyphro, if that which is holy is the same with that which is dear to God, and is loved because it is holy, then that which is dear to God would have been loved as being dear to God; but if that which is dear to God is dear to him because loved by him, then that which is holy would have been holy because loved by him. But now you see that the reverse is the case, and that they are quite different from one another.[5]

Socrates asks Euthyphro to choose between saying that the gods love what is right because it is right and saying that it is right because the gods love it. These are not only different things to say, but they are actually *inconsistent*. For if the gods love an action because it is right, they must *first* see what it is about it that makes it right, and then, as a *result* of seeing this, they are pleased. Their pleasure is not the *cause* of its being right, as the voluntarists say: It is an *effect* of it. Once we realize that we cannot have it both ways, Plato expects us to opt for the first choice, saying that the gods love what is right because it is right. And we can see why especially in light of Aristotle's observation that we judge the character of people by what gives them pleasure and pain. An honest person is pleased by seeing acts of honesty and is displeased when seeing acts of dishonesty. So, in general, a truly moral person is pleased as a result of seeing the right thing done. If voluntarism were true, God would not himself be a moral person, which seems absurd, since he is omnibenevolent. For he would not love what is right because it is right: Whatever he loved would automatically be right. The same point can be put in terms of his commands. God would not command us to do what he sees is right: *His* reason for commanding us would have nothing to do with morality! This is because if voluntarism were true, *whatever* he commanded would automatically come out right. This means that God himself would not choose as a moral person does, by *first* seeing what choice would be right and what wrong, and then choosing to do what he sees to be right. God could not choose this way since he would see that any choice of his could not be wrong. Voluntarism thus has the startling consequence that any kind of action would be right if only God commanded it. If God had commanded us to be cruel and dishonest, then it would have been right to do so. Of course, no one thinks that God would do that, but this is because we think of God as good and thus as not being willing to command us to do what is wrong. But this means that he *first* sees what is wrong and then forbids us to do this instead of the opposite: His command is an effect of his seeing what is wrong, not the cause of it, as voluntarism says.

Some people object even to the idea that it is possible for God to command what is wrong, so that Plato is mistaken in supposing that he has a choice of doing

---

5. Plato, *Euthyphro*, trans. Benjamin Jowett, 10a–d.

what is wrong in the first place. They think this because God is omnibenevolent *by definition*: Any being making a wrong choice would be less than omnibenevolent and thus not God. Plato claims that for God to be good, God must choose the right over the wrong and thus to have a choice of doing wrong. But for God to have a choice of doing wrong, they claim, would be to have a choice of not being God, which is absurd. It is not obvious, however, that an omnibenevolent being could not do wrong. The German philosopher and theist Gottfried Leibniz claimed that God's omnipotence guaranteed him the *power* to do what is wrong, as his omniscience guaranteed his wisdom in discerning this; his omnibenevolence ensured that he *wanted* to do what is right, not that he lacked the power to do otherwise. And if we deny him this power, we seem to deny him the status of being a person. God's "commands" no longer seem like real commands, made by a reasoned choice. But then we have given up the divine *command* theory.

Consequences of Plato's Objection

Plato's criticism of voluntarism has important consequences. First, even if God does not exist, this has nothing to do with whether there is a difference between right and wrong. Perhaps the world would be better if he exists, but his nonexistence would not imply the downfall of morality. This means that morality is a *secular* matter. Religious texts may be rich with ethical wisdom (and many surely are), but the moral truths themselves can be stated and discussed without any religious commitment. This has the beneficial result that being of different religious faiths is no reason for having different moral opinions. Because right and wrong are not a matter of what God says, it does not matter whether different texts appear to give contradictory reports of what he wants.

It is worth emphasizing, however, that a theist can fully accept Plato's criticism of voluntarism and still claim that the highest experience in life is that of "loving God" or that the best way to live is to "follow God" or do "God's will." This will be possible for theists if they are careful to interpret these phrases so that they do not imply that we first come to know what God wants before we know what to do. In the following passage, the sixteenth-century Catholic nun Saint Teresa presents the view that we love and follow God *by* doing what we know to be right: "Let everyone understand that real love of God does not consist in tear-shedding, nor in that sweetness and tenderness for which usually we long, just because they console us, but in serving God in justice, fortitude of soul and humility."[6]

RECOGNIZING GOD'S WORD

Plato's objection is directed to voluntarism's account of the *content* of morality. It denies that what *makes* an action right is that God wants it. This does not show, however, that voluntarism is wrong in how we *discover* what to do. After all, if a holy

---

6. From *The Perennial Philosophy*, ed. Aldous Huxley (New York: Harper & Row, 1945).

text *does* contain God's word, then its ethical teachings are *correct*, even if they are not correct because he orders them. Why cannot we simply take advantage of the fact that we have God's word and not bother to think for ourselves? Why rely on our own imperfect reason when we have the word of God already before us?

The problem with this hopeful suggestion is revealed in an ancient Jewish story of a rabbi who, while walking along, suddenly hears God giving him a command. Now, being a devout man of God, he is willing, of course, to follow God. But *how does he know* that the voice he hears is really the voice of God? He reasons that he can be sure that this is the voice of God only if he knows that what he is being instructed to do is right; if the command is to do something wrong, then it could not be the word of God, but only of a malevolent imitator. To be sure, he must *first* determine for himself whether the instructions are morally right. But then, it occurs to him, he will not be *using* the instructions themselves to learn what to do. In fact, the problem applies generally to any voice or written text purporting to be the word of God. Unless you *already know* that the instructions are morally correct, you do not know they are the word of God. People think they are reading or hearing the word of God only when they are already convinced it is right. This means that their moral convictions do not come from the words themselves.

SOCIAL RELATIVISM

Voluntarism expresses the commonly held belief that morality is "based on religion." We will call the last moral theory of this chapter **social relativism,** since it says that what you ought to do depends on the *society* in which you live. According to this theory, standards of right and wrong are set by one's society, so that what you ought to do is what is demanded by your own society. This idea is attractive to many who are *scientifically* minded, the most extreme of whom have thought that all knowledge is empirical. It has seemed to them that morality, too, can be discovered empirically, by studying the society in which one lives. For do we not learn what is right and wrong in a society by seeing what people condemn and condone? And where do individuals get their moral beliefs but from their elders, who school them in what society approves and disapproves. As the twentieth-century anthropologist Ruth Benedict observes:

> We do not any longer make the mistake of deriving the morality of our locality and decade directly from the inevitable constitution of human nature. We do not elevate it to the dignity of a first principle. We recognize that morality differs in every society, and is a convenient term for socially approved habits. Mankind has always preferred to say, "It is morally good," rather than, "It is habitual," and the fact of this preference is matter enough for a critical science of ethics. But historically the two phrases are synonymous.[7]

---

7. From "Anthropology and the Abnormal," *Journal of Psychology* 10 (1934): 59–82.

According to social relativism, our moral opinions all result from what psychologists call *conditioning:* People around us react to our actions by making some kinds of them pleasant and others unpleasant. We find that when we steal or lie and are found out, there is social punishment, in the form of spankings, fines, or at least disapproval and the consequent threat of isolation. When we keep our hands off of others' property, tell the truth, and so on, we avoid their sanctions and are welcomed into their company. The theory is based on the plain fact that we are social animals, who need and want the company of others and who find that there are certain rules, certain restrictions on behavior, that we must accept to live in society. The internal sense that certain actions are "wrong" is, according to this theory, ultimately just the fear of "banishment from the herd" that we have learned through conditioning to expect if we perform these.

This theory, if true, shows us exactly what the *content* of morality is. To know what to do, you need to know the rules of your society. And this, as we have seen, is an *empirical* matter. For it is by observing how people behave that we find out what they approve and disapprove, and the rules of society are simply summarizations of these attitudes. Ethical disputes, such as whether abortion is wrong or whether great differences in wealth should avoided, can be resolved by empirical studies of what most people want. As in democratic societies, the majority rules.

Second, it provides a straightforward explanation of moral motivation. When we learn from others in society what we "ought" to do, it is clear that if we fail to do it, society itself will impose *penalties* on us. The *reward* of doing the right thing is acceptance into society.

Although this theory *could* be accepted by one who took any position on the mind–body problem, it is, like ethical hedonism, especially appealing to crude materialists. For it asks us to admit only that we are animals, no different in kind from all other animals whose behavior can be conditioned by rewards and penalties.

MORAL RELATIVISM

Now one consequence of this theory, which Benedict makes clear, is that the content of morality is not the same for all people but differs from one society to another. The name for this position is **moral relativism.** According to this view, the fact that you were raised as you were, in a society that condemns stealing, makes it wrong *for you* to steal, even if it would be right *for* those who were raised with approval for stealing. According to moral relativists, there are no "absolute" standards of right and wrong that apply to all societies. Different societies make their own rules of conduct, so that what is right for some might be wrong for others.

Despite its appearance of wholesome modesty, moral relativism is not obviously true. Notice first that it makes criticism of any society impossible. If what *makes* an action right is just that it is what a society approves, then a whole society *cannot* be wrong. To condemn a practice, such as slavery, which is approved by all the members of that society, one would have to be assuming the moral standard of *another* society. This would just mean, however, only that it is wrong for *that* society, and not for the original. But does this seem true? If enough people get together and decide to approve of slavery, does that somehow *make* it right? If so, there could be nothing to persuade these people through reasoned argument to become a "better" society. This would be like asking them to accept the standards of *another* society that, according to moral relativism, could not be (absolutely) "better." There could be, therefore, no such thing as moral *progress*, in which a whole society changes their moral opinions for the better (say, by giving up slavery or acknowledging the right of women to vote), for this would again be like changing from one kind of society to another, and moral relativism tells us that we can never say that one society has a *truer* view of right and wrong.

MORALITY AND THE EMPIRICAL

What can we make, then, of the claim that we already know empirically that social relativism is true? Let us ask what *can* be learned about morality empirically and thus scientifically. What a social scientist like Benedict finds empirically when studying a society is that certain practices are condoned in some societies and condemned in others. The ancient Greek historian Herodotus, for example, found that while the Greeks burned the dead, in India they were eaten. (Both societies, when told of the practice of the other, were shocked.) Now, it is important to realize that in itself this does not mean that they differ in their moral *principles*. The basic question of ethics, "What should I do?" is fully answered only with a principle that explains what *makes* an action right or wrong. Also, two societies could adhere to the same moral *principles* while condemning and condoning quite different *practices*. In Herodotus's example, it seems that both the Greeks and Indians shared a common commitment to honor the dead and that this belief was merely expressed in different ways. When we ask *why* a society condemns or condones a practice, what they believe *makes* the practice wrong or right, we are seeking the underlying moral principles that they accept. And great differences in practices can hide shared commitments to the same moral principles.

Finding out what are the underlying moral principles of a society is indeed an empirical issue; it just requires a good deal more investigation and theorizing. We need to look at all the different practices that are condemned and condoned in that society to see what they have in common. But even when we do our best, what will we have discovered? To say that these are "their" moral principles is just to report what they *believe* about right and wrong. Why should anything follow from this about what *is* right and wrong? What people *believe* is in general empirically discoverable: the people themselves have (fallible) access to their beliefs in introspection, and observers can watch how they behave (see Chapters Two and Three). When it comes to moral beliefs, we look in particular to what they approve of and disapprove of. But again, this shows only what they *think* is right or wrong, and nothing obviously follows from this about what *is* right or wrong. The problem has to do with the nature of empirical knowledge. As we saw in Chapter Four, Kant summarized it by saying that "experience tells us how things are but not how they ought to be." It just does not seem to be the business of the senses to inform us of how things ought to be or what we ought to do. The senses give us a picture of the world in which we must act, but they do not themselves give us the basic *guidance* that we need to make our choices. While we look to social scientists to teach us about moral *beliefs*, we should not expect from empirical science a view of moral *content*.

Objection to Social Relativism

Social relativism is a claim about morality, about what is right and wrong, and as such it is supposed to help us guide our behavior. If we want to do what is right, we are supposed to look to the standards of our own society and follow these. There is a serious problem with this advice, and that is that each of us belongs to more than one society.

Suppose I belong to a nation in which stealing is forbidden. But I might also join and thus belong to a gang in which stealing is permitted. Because social relativism denies the existence of any standard by which a "whole society" can be judged wrong, neither the standard of my nation nor that of my gang can be judged absolutely wrong. If I am tempted to steal, all that I have to do to get moral permission is to think of myself as a gang member. But now it seems, with a little ingenuity, I can excuse any action to which I am tempted. For I can also create in my mind a little society of those who condone that action, even if this is only the society of myself. Since my choice of society is arbitrary, any choice of moral standard is arbitrary. This is a very serious problem for social relativism, since (as we saw in Chapter One) we cannot regard any of our opinions, including moral opinions, as arbitrary. This is what explains why social relativism is widely rejected by philosophers today.

EXTERNAL COMMANDS

It is instructive to see that social relativism is also subject to Plato's criticism of the divine command theory. For either God or society to have the *authority* to issue commands, they must be *good*. For if either is not good, how could it be their commands that define what we ought to do? Once we know that a certain command has been issued by someone, all that we know is a certain fact about reality, about how things actually are. There is always the separate question of what to do about it. We must evaluate the command for ourselves before we can see whether we ought to follow it. Usually this requires little thought. If you decide to comply with the commands of the police, this may be because you see them as supporting the security of your community or simply because you want to stay out of jail. Either way, you follow the command to achieve something that *you* value.

This is an essential fact about choice. To see an action as right you must see it as leading to something you see as good. Following a command, issued by anyone, will appear right only if it appears to promote some value of yours. This is why if you contemplate God or society commanding you to be cruel to innocent children, you (presumably) simply cannot see this as something you ought to do. What *good* would it do? This is a question you must always ask yourself whenever faced with any choice at all. People who obey God to get into heaven see this as a necessary means for achieving a blissful afterlife. If they thought that to get to heaven they had to *disobey* God, his command would no longer appear right. People who obey God out of a sense of gratitude do so to serve the moral purpose of respecting those who have given their help to them. If God created the world to make people miserable, gratitude would be out of place, and his commands would again no longer appear good. The same goes for the commands of society. If you comply with them for social acceptance, it is this that makes them compelling and not the fact that society commands them. If social acceptance required disobeying society, social relativism would seem absurd. The same problem would arise if commands to do things somehow burst into your own consciousness. Unless you see what purpose of yours following them would serve, they might as well have come from a stranger. It is true that when we do decide what to do we issue a command to ourselves to do it. But as always, what *justifies* a command is what purpose it serves. Commands do not make anything right. It is what is right or good that justifies any command.

CONCLUSION

Theories of morality tell us what to do. But what we ought to do must be appealing to us. A satisfactory theory will accordingly include a moral psychology that explains what motivates us. Moral psychologies, like accounts of what we need, are influenced by more general metaphysical outlooks. We have found that ethical hedonism and social relativism appeal to crude materialism in offering relatively animalistic accounts of human motivation. By contrast, voluntarism is held by theists who typically offer dualistic accounts of moral motivation. Voluntarism and social relativism are both subject to Plato's criticism of any moral theory that explains morality as blind obedience to a supposed authority. Social relativism suffers also from its commitment to moral relativism that itself makes choosing arbitrary. Ethical hedonism suffers from neither of these problems. It gives a definite prescription for life that does not rest on blind obedience. Instead, it appeals to the obvious fact that we prefer pleasure and abhor pain. But the moral psychology on which it is based errs crucially in its account of human purpose. Many find its exultation of selfishness repugnant and even deeply unwise.

The three theories of this chapter are nevertheless important to understand. They have been held by many philosophers in the past and continue to be held by many people today. Our discussion of morality continues through the next chapter and thus to the end of Part Three. The two theories of the next chapter should avoid the problems we have encountered so far.

STUDY QUESTIONS

1. How does choosing require distinguishing between good and bad?
2. What is the problem of moral motivation? Why should a moral theory have a solution to it?
3. Why does ethical hedonism follow from psychological hedonism?
4. Why does prudence require self-control?
5. Explain the argument for psychological hedonism given in the text. How is it based on confusion? How is it possible to refute psychological hedonism?
6. Why does Russell say that selfishness makes you unhappy?
7. How do voluntarists try to solve the problem of moral motivation?
8. What is Plato's objection to voluntarism? How does it have the implication that morality is a "secular" matter?
9. What is the problem of finding out what to do by recognizing the word of God?
10. How has social relativism appealed to the scientifically minded?
11. How does social relativism attempt to solve the problem of moral motivation?
12. What is objectionable about moral relativism?
13. How is social relativism subject to Plato's objection to voluntarism?

CHAPTER
NINE

Benevolence and Justice

WHAT TO DO? In the last couple of centuries, philosophical discussions of morality have been influenced mainly by the ethical theories of David Hume and Immanuel Kant. Neither philosopher confuses the question of what to do with the question of how to be happy. Both believe that we have obligations to help others in need and to respect their moral rights. Hume lived in a time when it was dangerous to be an atheist publicly, but he probably was one. Kant began as a theist and became an agnostic, but he remained sympathetic to theism throughout his life. Neither, though, was a voluntarist. And both rejected moral relativism, believing that the content of morality is the same for all. Hume was an idealist, so at some point we will consider his moral theory in this light. Kant argued extensively against idealism on behalf of our material nature, but he was no crude materialist. As we will see, he was deeply influenced by the Stoics and thus the double aspect theory.

One more point is worth emphasizing from the start, which will be of great importance in our discussions in social philosophy in Part Four. Both philosophers subscribe to what I will call **humanism,** in that they believe that every human has the same moral value. Neither believes that moral obligations extend only to one's family and friends or only to the members of one's tribe or nation or sex or race. They differ in how they *explain* what obligations to others we have, and they differ somewhat (though not very much) in what they say is the *content* of morality. But both were strongly opposed to the idea that we have no moral obligations to "those" people.

ALTRUISM

Modern ethics has struggled a great deal with the issue of selfishness. Most philosophers have felt that it is wrong to be an egoist, a completely selfish person who cares for nothing but his own welfare. But they have found it difficult to say what is wrong with egoism. This preoccupation is evident in the moral theories of Hume and Kant. Let us begin, therefore, by clarifying the nature of selfishness.

Two ways of being nonselfish appear to be prevalent in human life and happen to figure largely in the two theories of this chapter. One is **altruism.** In being *altruistic*, a person helps another (as is suggested by the Latin root of the word, *alter,* for "other"). But not all helping is altruistic. If you help someone for a purely selfish gain, expecting a "return" on your "investment," then you are not altruistic. Helping is altruistic only when your *motive* is the unselfish one of contributing to the *other* person's welfare. In being altruistic, you may *foresee* that by helping others you will be pleased, but as we saw in the last chapter, that does not mean you are doing it *in order to* be pleased. So long as the pleasure of helping others occurs as an unintended by-product, your action can still have the unselfish motive of being aimed at the happiness of the other person. In this case, the pleasure of helping is not the motive but only the evidence that you really were altruistic. If psychological hedonism were true, altruism would be literally *impossible*, since its very nature involves an unselfish motive.

One of the greatest critics of psychological hedonism was in fact David Hume. Our discussion of the last chapter benefited by his insights, since he saw that there is an abundance of *empirical* evidence of altruism. He pointed out, for example, that most people, when they read of the suffering of people in distant lands and times long ago, are moved by a feeling of sympathy for these people, regardless of any possible benefit they see for themselves. As we will see, Hume used the empirical fact that humans are moved by sympathy for others to give a powerful theory of the content and motivation of morality.

JUSTICE

Justice consists in respecting the moral rights of others. If you keep a promise because you owe it to the other person, you act justly. If you keep it for a selfish reason, such as preserving your ability to borrow in the future, you act *as* justice *requires*, but not *for the sake of* justice. If psychological hedonism were true, no one would genuinely *respect* the rights of others: They would avoid violating their rights for selfish reasons such as avoiding punishment and retaining social membership. Someone is a *just person* only if he or she really cares about whether things are fair and that people fulfill their responsibilities to one another. As an altruistic person is moved by sympathy, a just person is moved by respect for the rights of others. These appear to be quite different motives. It seems possible to have no obligation to help someone in need and still to help that person out of compassion and not because you owe it to her. On the other hand, it seems possible to have no sympathy for someone, perhaps because she has angered you, but still to honor a promise made to them simply because of your obligation to that person. It is the respect for justice that takes center stage in the ethical theory of Kant.

SOCIAL VIRTUES

Let us call **benevolence** the virtue of acting altruistically and **justice** the virtue of respecting the rights of others. To call each of these *virtues* is to commend them, as *good* traits of character. A *character trait* is an established way of making choices, reflecting certain *values*. To say that benevolence is a virtue is thus to commend people who value the *happiness* of others; to say that justice is a virtue is to commend those who value the *rights* of others. Both are *social virtues* in that they pertain to how we should treat others. (Courage and self-control, by contrast, would normally be counted as virtues that are *not* social.) If benevolence and justice really are virtues, as we normally think, then we ought both to take an interest in the happiness of others and to respect their moral rights.

Hume and Kant count both character traits as virtues, but they differ in which one they give *priority*. Are we to understand the moral person *basically* as one who is benevolent or as one who is just? This is the main issue that divides them. But why, we may ask, must we choose? Why not say that a *good person* is both benevolent and just and leave it at that? The reason is that ethicists want to arrive at a *single* moral principle, explaining in "one fell swoop" the difference between moral right and wrong or good and bad, to avoid conflicting advice. So long as we remain at the level of character traits, of generally good ways of behaving, and we allow that there are several of these virtues, the possibility remains that we will be faced with a choice that we cannot resolve. Do we, for example, give a criminal the punishment he deserves, which justice requires, or do we act out of compassion and be merciful? Do we honor a debt to someone financially well-off or let ourselves be moved by sympathy to renege on the debt to help a needy person? If all that we say is that benevolence and justice are both virtues, we have no way of resolving these problems. Maybe this is just the way it is. But we can at least understand why an ethicist would want to avoid this conclusion. We need to establish what makes an *action* right — *any* action right — to have an ethical view that tells us what to do even when presented with such conflicts.

REASON OR SENTIMENT?

Hume did not try to say what, in general, made an action right. As we will see, however, he came close, and others drew the obvious conclusion from his theory. Hume was concerned, though, with some of the deepest issues in ethics, as we can see from the following passage:

There has been a controversy started of late, much better worth examination, concerning the general foundation of *morals;* whether they be derived from reason or from sentiment; whether we attain the knowledge of them by a chain of argument and induction or by an immediate feeling and finer internal sense; whether like all sound judgment of truth and falsehood, they should be the same to every rational, intelligent being, or whether, like the perception of beauty and deformity, they be founded entirely on the particular fabric and constitution of the human species....

It must be acknowledged that both sides of the question are susceptible of specious arguments. Moral distinctions, it may be said, are discernible by pure *reason:* else, whence the many disputes that reign in common life, as well as in philosophy, with regard to this subject; the long chain of proofs often produced on both sides, the examples cited, the authorities appealed to, the analogies employed, the fallacies detected, the inferences drawn, and the several conclusions adjusted to their proper principles? Truth is disputable, not taste: what exists in the nature of things is the standard of our judgment; what each man feels within himself is the standard of sentiment. Propositions in geometry may be proved, systems in physics may be controverted, but the harmony of verse, the tenderness of passion, the brilliancy of wit must give an immediate pleasure. No man reasons concerning another's beauty, but frequently concerning the justice of his actions....

On the other hand, those who would resolve all moral determinations into *sentiments* may endeavor to show that it is impossible for reason ever to draw conclusions of this nature. To virtue, say they, it belongs to be *amiable,* and vice *odious.* This forms their very nature and essence. But can reason or argumentation distribute these different epithets to any subjects and pronounce beforehand that this must produce love, and that hatred? Or what other reason can we ever assign for these affections but the original fabric and formation of the human mind, which is naturally adapted to receive them?

The end of all moral speculations is to teach us our duty, and, by proper representations of the deformity of vice and beauty of virtue, beget corresponding habits, and engage us to avoid the one, and embrace the other. But is this ever to be expected from inferences and conclusions of the understanding, which themselves have no hold of the affections or set in motion the active powers of men? They discover truths. But where the truths which they discover are indifferent and beget no desire or aversion, they can have no influence on conduct and behavior. What is honorable, what is fair, what is becoming, what is noble, what is generous takes possession of the heart and animates us to embrace and maintain it. What is intelligible, what is evident, what is probable, what is true procures only the cool assent of the understanding, and, gratifying a speculative curiosity, puts an end to our researches.

Extinguish all the warm feelings and prepossessions in favor of virtue, and all disgust or aversion to vice; render men totally indifferent to these distinctions; and morality is no longer a practical study, nor has any tendency to regulate our lives and actions.

These arguments on each side (and many more might be produced) are so plausible that I am apt to suspect they may, the one as well as the other, be solid and satisfactory, and that *reason* and *sentiment* concur in almost all moral determinations and conclusions. The final sentence, it is probable, which pronounces characters and actions amiable or odious, praiseworthy or blamable; that which stamps on them the mark of honor or infamy, approbation or censure; that which renders morality an active principle and constitutes virtue our happiness, and vice our misery — it is probable, I say, that this final sentence depends on some internal sense of feeling which nature has made universal in the whole species. But in order to pave the way for such a sentiment and give a proper discernment of its object, it is often necessary, we find, that much reasoning should precede, that nice distinctions be made, just conclusions drawn, distinct comparisons formed, complicated relations examined, and general facts fixed and ascertained.[1]

MORALITY AND PRACTICE

Hume appreciated that morality is a "practical study," in that moral opinions must be attended by appropriate dispositions to *act*. If you really think that it is wrong to steal, you must feel an *aversion* to stealing; if you think you ought to be honest, you must feel some *desire* to tell the truth. The point of reasoning about what is right and wrong is, after all, to decide what to *do*, not merely to decide what is *true*. A successful moral argument must conclude not merely in a *belief* about what is right but also in a *disposition* to do that sort of thing when the circumstance arises. According to Hume, there is no such belief without the corresponding disposition. Anyone who says that stealing is wrong but shows no respect for the property of others will *automatically* be accused of insincerity.

PRACTICE AND SENTIMENT

In the prior passage, Hume uses this point to argue for the essential role of "sentiment" (feeling) in moral opinion. As we will see, it is *feeling* that plays the crucial role in his moral psychology. To understand this, we must see how sentiment is contrasted by him with *reason*. This is not really a new issue for us, for many times in this text we have been concerned with the mental difference between us and "lower" animals. Hume is following a tradition that goes back to the Greeks in calling "reason" that special ability that separates our minds from those of other animals (see especially Chapter One). Plato and Aristotle assigned to this mental power the

---

1. David Hume, *An Enquiry Concerning the Principles of Morals* (1777).

special function of discerning right from wrong, true from false—generally, making distinctions of *value*.

Hume disagrees with them about the nature of reason. In another passage, he brashly declares that reason is a "slave of the passions," knowing full well that this opinion *reverses* the position of the greatest Greek philosophers. For Plato and Aristotle, the main function of reason was to discover what is right (true, good, and so forth) to *correct* such "lower" influences as those of the passions. The virtuous person was accordingly one who listened to and followed reason, whereas the contemptible person was (as they said) a "slave to his passions" (overeating, getting drunk, being carried away by anger, acting greedy, and the like). Hume breaks with this tradition because he has a quite different view of what, in general, we *do* discover when we use our power of reason.

PRACTICAL REASON

Reason, according to Hume, is really just the power to make *inferences* (see Chapter Two). We can see what implications this has for *practical* reasons if we recall (from the last chapter) what is involved whenever we make a choice. First, we must *predict* what will happen as a result of performing each action we are considering. This, according to Hume, is the *only* place where reason is involved. Second, we must *evaluate* the various outcomes, deciding which is best. But whereas the Greeks saw this as the business of reason, Hume has denied any role to reason here; so he turns instead to "sentiment" to explain what leads us to evaluate as we do. When we make our evaluation, what causes us to think one outcome is the "best"? Remember that when we come to this conclusion, we must automatically be *disposed* to do that. But where does that desire come from? By reasoning, we just see what will *happen*, according to Hume; but by thinking one choice is best, we must *want* that. Because this desire does not come from our reasoning, it would seem to be based on some desire we already have. If, for example, you are already thirsty and use your reason to predict that by walking around the corner will you get to water, then it is the combination of this reasoning with the desire for water—that you already have—that leads you to think you *ought* to do this. When Hume says that "sentiment" is needed for moral opinion, his main point is that we must have desires that do *not* come from reasoning to have a reason to do anything: a *practical* reason. Reason has an influence on what we do, but only by getting us to see the *means* we must take for *ends* that we *already have*.

This leads Hume to make the startling remark that it would not be *contrary to reason* to prefer the destruction of the whole world over scratching one's finger. He expects all of us to react with horror at such a preference, and he himself would agree that it would be definitely *wrong* to act on such a monstrous preference. His point is that it is not by reasoning alone that we come to the conclusion that this is wrong: If we did not already have a certain "sentiment"—sympathy for mankind—

we would have no *aversion* to acts of widespread violence and *could* not see them as wrong.

Some readers have supposed that Hume must, therefore, be a moral relativist. For do we not *differ* between ourselves in how we feel about things, in what we like and dislike? If to think something is right, I must want it; and if you do not want it, you cannot think it is right. There is no possible way in which you and I can agree. Hume is adamant that he is not a moral relativist, however, and goes to great length insisting that there is a difference between saying, "I like it," and saying, "It is good." It is true, he admits, that to think something is good it is *necessary* to like it, but merely liking something is not the same as its being good; moreover, he points out, we know how to tell the difference.

DISCOVERING WHAT IS RIGHT

Here is his explanation of how we know what is morally right in our dealings with others. First, reason plays the essential role of enabling us to achieve an *objective* view of things. Let us see what this means. Suppose two animals are in a fight. Each animal knows what is going on, but only from its own point of view. We humans are able to think about how things are for other creatures, even ones at other times and places. This takes reason, since it involves making inferences to other minds (recall the discussion of this in Chapters Two and Three). Animals suffer, but those who lack reason cannot realize that others suffer, too. (Animals who instinctively aid others of their kin who are suffering are not thereby *thinking* of their suffering.) When we do discover, through reasoning, that others are suffering, our natural human "sentiment" of sympathy causes us to feel sorry for them. When, therefore, we contemplate doing something, we can see whether it is wrong by using our reason to gain an objective view, especially one that takes into account the suffering of others, and by allowing ourselves to be moved by our natural sense of sympathy. This willingness to look at things objectively and to allow ourselves be moved by sympathy is, according to him, *exactly what it takes* to be a morally good person.

MORAL AGREEMENT

How does this explain the difference between saying that you like something and saying that it is good? Hume's answer is that when you say only that you like something, you are *not* taking the objective point of view but are speaking only for yourself and how you are affected by that thing. If I say that I like chocolate, this is a remark about how chocolate affects me alone. But if I say that cruelty is *wrong* or that kindness is *good*, I am speaking in effect for *everyone*. The reason is that if I have successfully achieved an objective view of things, I am seeing things the way that anyone would who used their reason to look at the same facts. The *objective* view is that which all thinkers can *share*. Remember, however, that Hume is known for denying that we can arrive at moral opinions by reasoning alone; so, just achieving an objective view of the facts is not enough to see whether something is good or bad. For this, Hume tells us, we must "look within our breasts" to see how we *feel* about it. And it is a fundamental fact about human nature, he argues, that we *share* the feeling of sympathy. This is his explanation for why we *agree* so much about what is good and bad. Reason is still a "slave of the passions," but, fortunately, reason enables different people to have the same facts in mind, and the feeling of sympathy that we naturally share leads us to approve and disapprove of the same acts when we do.

MORAL DISAGREEMENT

Moral disagreement is still possible for Hume. Some people do not have all the facts, and some people refuse to look at the facts. The latter can happen in fits of anger or credulity (when a selfish interest is at stake). There is also the extreme case in which someone entirely lacks sympathy for his fellow man. Hume cites as an example the Roman emperor Nero, who was "hardened from flattery and a long perseverance in the most enormous crimes." His point is that Nero is *naturally* like us, in being human: He has an innate *capacity* to be moved by the suffering of others. But due to the way he was treated and chose to act himself, this capacity no longer *operates*, as it does in normal, healthy individuals. For this explanation to be plausible, such insensitivity must be fairly rare and explainable by unusual circumstances. Hume accordingly spends a good deal of time trying to show that this is so.

HUME ON MORAL MOTIVATION

About the *content* of morality, Hume is clearly no egoist. Although he does not say what makes any action right, he does say that the right thing to do in our dealings with others is an expression of benevolence for humans in general. This shows clearly that he is a humanist. But *why* should we so care for others? Why do we have a *good reason* for caring for all humans? First, Hume will say that when we do act benevolently, we are merely giving expression to our own natural desires. Sympathy is part of "the particular fabric and constitution of the human species." Someone like Nero is a stunted individual who cannot be really happy.

There is a second part to his solution to the problem of moral motivation. Humans, as we have seen, are capable of using their power of reason to see things objectively. We are capable of thinking of how it is for others. One way we do this is to see how others react to our own behavior. On Hume's own account of morality, the morally good person is everyone's friend. Everyone approves of such a person and finds her company agreeable. By looking through the eyes of others, good people find themselves agreeable. The bad person is no friend of others and may well be an enemy. When morally bad (selfish) people see themselves the way others do, they find themselves disagreeable. This is part of the penalty of immorality.

What if they avoid this negative judgment of themselves by avoiding seeing things from the perspective of others? People called *sociopaths*, who lack a sense of conscience, seem to do this as a matter of course. For normal humans, this is virtually impossible. And even the effort to hide from the facts is itself a kind of penalty.

HUME'S MORAL THEORY

Hume constructed a *moral theory*, which explains a variety of facts about morality. He explains how morality is a "practical study" by requiring that the feeling of sympathy plays an essential role in moral opinion. He explains how arguing for moral opinions is still possible since we need to reason to bring to mind the relevant facts and achieve an objective view. He explains how agreement about what is right and wrong is possible by requiring that our moral opinions spring from a common view of the facts and the common sentiment of sympathy. This same explanation is also used to show how moral disagreement is still possible. He offers a solution to the problem of moral motivation by explaining the rewards of moral behavior and the penalty for immoral behavior. Finally, he explains how we discover for ourselves what we ought morally to do, without blind obedience to an outside authority such as God or society. We look at facts objectively and allow ourselves to be moved by sympathy. Human nature includes both reason and sympathy. The cooperation of these two capacities allows us to discern the difference between right and wrong.

BENEVOLENCE AS FUNDAMENTAL

Now, the whole theory clearly puts forth *benevolence* as the chief moral virtue, at least insofar as morality is concerned with our relation to others. This is because benevolence is the virtue in which we are motivated by sympathy, and sympathy, according to Hume, is what underlies *all* moral opinions (about how we should treat others). We began our discussion with the observation that benevolence is widely thought to be only one of two main "social" virtues, along with justice. If Hume's account is correct, our moral opinions about what justice requires must also be explained as being due to sympathy. The virtue of justice must be shown somehow to be a *manifestation* of the virtue of benevolence. But as we saw, this *looks* mistaken. It seems that treating people sympathetically and respecting their rights are quite different attitudes.

It may seem that Hume can patch things up easily by simply admitting that in addition to sympathy, we humans have a passion for justice, and that both sentiments can move us when we look at things objectively. We saw that this will create the problem of resolving conflicts in certain difficult cases. But for Hume there is a another problem that prevents him from taking this way out. That problem is due to the limited role that he allows to reason. It is not that he cannot allow that there is such a sentiment (the passion for justice), and it seems a plain empirical fact that there is. Most people are angry when hearing of injustices and satisfied when hearing that justice prevails. The problem for Hume is that the passion for justice arises only *after* coming to the conclusion that a situation is just or unjust. We must *first* see that rights have been respected or violated before our passion for justice is aroused. Since the moral opinion must come first and then cause the passion for justice, we cannot be "looking within our breast" for the passion to use this discovery about how we feel to see whether rights have been respected. This is how the passion for justice is crucially different from sympathy. We feel sympathy just by realizing that others are suffering; no prior opinion about what is good or bad is required. This is why Hume can use the feeling of sympathy, but not the feeling for justice, to explain what produces our moral opinions in the first place.

EXPLAINING JUSTICE

Hume takes up the problem of explaining how, despite appearances to the contrary, our moral convictions about justice are really due to our benevolence. In the passage we will read shortly, he begins by pointing out that no one would dispute the fact that justice has **utility,** by which he means that it is *useful* to society to make "a partition of goods" into things that are *mine* and *yours.* If we did not allow that certain precious goods, such as land or stores of food, *belonged* to someone, then there would often be fighting over them, as there is with animals. Recognizing individual rights has "utility" mainly because it *prevents war;* in particular, it prevents people *fighting over scarce goods.* (This fact will be especially important to remember for our discussions in social philosophy in Part Four.) Now, if this were the *only* reason why we approve of respecting rights — to prevent war — it would be easy for Hume to explain how the virtue of justice is really just based on benevolence. For surely war is one of the greatest causes of suffering, and sympathy alone leads us to abhor it. The main purpose of the passage quoted later is to convince us that, in fact, we do approve of justice *only* for its utility. If successful, Hume defends his theory of morality in which benevolence is the fundamental social virtue.

SUPERSTITION AND MISERY

Before we read this passage, it will be helpful to see what is really motivating Hume. The greatest philosophers win our admiration not only for their intelligence but for their goals in writing in the first place. Hume is, of course, writing with the goal of explaining the nature of morality, but why does he think his account is a good thing to know? Who, especially, does he think it is important to refute? What moral opinions are not only mistaken but *pernicious*? Well, given his account, it would be any moral outlook that is *unsympathetic,* one that *contributed* to suffering in the world rather than helping to alleviate it. More than anything, Hume was an opponent of *superstition*; he saw, in particular, that it was superstitious belief that most perverted our sense of morality. He was especially opposed to those who believed in an angry and vengeful God, creating (as the divine command theory depicts) justice through his decree. To find out what justice requires, we look to holy texts, with no regard for human welfare. The "deal" is that if we do what God says, no matter how unpleasant this may be, we win the reward of heaven. But Hume was a naturalist, and so he thought that sacrifices to "the gods" simply lead to an unnecessary increase in human suffering. Let us now read the passage in which he tries to show that *true* justice is just a manifestation of benevolence.

Hume on Justice

That justice is useful to society, and consequently that *part* of its merit, at least, must arise from that consideration, it would be a superfluous undertaking to prove. That public utility is the sole origin of Justice, and that reflections on the beneficial consequences of this virtue are the sole foundation of its merit, this proposition, being more curious and important, will better deserve our examination and inquiry.

Let us suppose that nature has bestowed on the human race such profuse *abundance* of all *external* conveniences that, without any uncertainty in the event, without any care or industry on our part, every individual finds himself fully provided with whatever his most voracious appetites can want or luxurious imagination wish or desire. His natural beauty, we shall suppose, surpasses all acquired ornaments: the perpetual clemency of the seasons renders useless all clothes or covering; the raw herbage affords him the most delicious fare; the clear fountain the richest beverage. No laborious occupation required; no tillage, no navigation. Music, poetry, and contemplation form his sole business; conversation, mirth, and friendship, his sole amusement.

It seems evident that in such a happy state every other social virtue would flourish and receive tenfold increase; but the cautious, jealous virtue of justice would never once have been dreamed of. For what purpose make a partition of goods where everyone has already more than enough? Why give rise to property where there cannot possibly be any injury? Why call this object mine when, upon seizing of it by another, I need but stretch out my hand to possess myself of what is equally valuable? Justice, in that case, being totally useless, would be an idle ceremonial and could never possibly have place in the catalog of virtues. . . .

Again, suppose that, though the necessities of the human race continue the same as at present, yet the mind is enlarged and so replete with friendship and generosity that every man has the utmost tenderness for every other man, and feels no more concern for his own interest than for that of his fellows: It seems evident that the *use* of Justice would, in this case, be suspended by such an extended benevolence, nor would the divisions and barriers of property and obligation have ever been thought of. Why should I bind another, by a deed or promise, to do me any good office when I know that he is already prompted by the strongest inclination to seek my happiness and would of himself perform the desired service, except the hurt he thereby receives be greater than the benefit accruing to me; in which case he knows that, from my innate humanity and friendship, I should be the first to oppose myself to his imprudent generosity? . . .

To make this truth more evident, let us reverse the foregoing suppositions and carrying everything to the opposite extreme, consider what would be the effect of these new situations. Suppose a society to fall into such want of all common necessaries that the utmost frugality and industry cannot preserve the greater number from perishing and the whole from extreme misery: it will readily, I believe, be admitted that the strict laws of justice are suspended in such a pressing emergency and give place to the stronger motives of necessity and self-preservation. Is it any crime, after a shipwreck, to seize whatever means or instrument of safety one can lay hold of, without regard to former limitations of property? . . .

Suppose, likewise, that it should be a virtuous man's fate to fall into the society of ruffians, remote from the protection of laws and government, what conduct must he embrace in that melancholy situation? He sees such a desperate rapaciousness prevail, such a disregard to equity, such contempt of order, such stupid blindness to future consequences. . . . He . . . can have no other expedient than to arm himself, to whomever the sword he seizes, or the buckler, may belong; to make provision of all means of defense and security. And his particular regard to justice being no longer of *use* to his own safety and that of others, he must consult the dictates of self-preservation alone, without concern for those who no longer merit his care and attention. . . .

Thus the rules of equity or justice depend entirely on the particular state and condition in which men are placed, and owe their origin and existence to that *utility* which results from their strict and regular observance. Reverse, in any considerable circumstance, the condition of men: produce extreme abundance or extreme necessity, implant in the human breast perfect moderation and humanity or perfect rapaciousness and malice; by rendering justice totally *useless*, you thereby totally destroy its essence and suspend its obligation upon mankind.[2]

Hume's strategy is to imagine a variety of circumstances in which justice would *not* have utility and to get us to see that whenever justice loses its utility we no longer approve of it. Remember that the "utility" of justice, of making a distinction between which things are "mine" and "yours," is to prevent fighting over scare goods. If this is the *only* thing divisions of property are good for, then whenever no goods are scarce or when dividing them into property does not stop the fighting, justice loses its utility, and, if Hume is right, we no longer think justice is good. This is exactly what he tries to show in the quoted passage. When there is no scarcity of goods, no one would even think to divide them into "mine" and "yours"; when people are such perfect friends that they are completely unwilling to fight, they would not demand property rights even if the goods were scarce; when there is such extreme scarcity that people must fight to survive, they forget talk of property rights; and, finally, when others are such rogues that they would not respect

---

2. David Hume, *An Enquiry Concerning the Principles of Morals* (1777).

such rights anyway and would always be willing to take things by force, people are reduced to thinking about survival, and again they cease to think in terms of who owns what. Property rights do have utility in most circumstances, but only because there is typically a *moderate* scarcity of goods and people are *moderately* friendly. Go to either extreme, with regard to scarcity or friendliness, and justice loses its utility; since we cease to think justice is good in these circumstances, we see that we value justice only for its utility. This means that the virtue of justice is really just a manifestation of benevolence. So Hume argues.

UTILITARIANISM

When we consider how Hume explained the goodness of the character trait of justice in terms of its utility, it is a short step to applying the idea to individual actions. This view, called **utilitarianism,** says quite generally that what makes an action right is that it has the most utility. Since utility is just usefulness in creating happiness, this means that the right action is supposed to be the one, among the alternatives, that produces the most happiness. Although the original utilitarians understood happiness in sensate terms, as the "greatest balance of pleasure over pain," one could adopt a different account of happiness, such as the Aristotelian notion of satisfying needs, and still retain the original idea. (Having already discussed the topic in Chapter Seven, we will talk simply of "happiness" and leave those discussions aside.) The morally good person, according to utilitarianism, is concerned above all with happiness. Unlike ethical hedonism, which tells us to maximize our *own* happiness, the utilitarian tells that we should try to maximize happiness *in general*. It is clear that utilitarianism retains some of the most important aspects of Hume's ethics. For Hume, morally good people are basically benevolent in their dealings with others, seeing value in the happiness of others as well as in their own. Utilitarians say in effect that it is just this attitude of benevolence that should guide us in all of our actions.

Utilitarianism gives a plausible account of many moral judgments and has been accepted by many philosophers. Consider, for example, the straightforward way that it explains how to make the following decisions. Suppose you are passing through a door and have an opportunity to hold the door open to someone following you with packages in her hands. Most people would think you should hold the door open, but why? What *makes* it the right thing to do? The utilitarian says simply that the other person's happiness is as important as yours, and the little bit of inconvenience involved in holding the door is offset by the greater convenience to the other person by your doing so.

Remember that utilitarianism is offering a moral *principle*, which explains what all right actions have in common. As such, it should explain what this example has to do with apparently different examples, such as rape and stealing. But this is not difficult. Take a violent crime such as rape. Surely, the little bit of intense pleasure afforded the perpetrator is greatly offset by the enormous unhappiness caused the victim. It is important to realize that utilitarianism insists that we measure happiness "in the long run." We must take into account, for example, the psychological trauma caused by violent crime. What about stealing? What if you steal from someone who is richer than you? Would the greater happiness you will get from the possession justify the act? Again, we must take into account the long run. Will you change your character so that you will steal often in the future? Will this cause others to follow your example and become thieves as well? Will the theft cause the person you stole from to be more insecure and bitter from now on? Will this make him a less benevolent person? And so on.

Utilitarianism not only provides plausible explanations in uncontroversial cases; it also provides clear guidance for solving all ethical problems. Take the issue of whether homosexuality is wrong. The voluntarist is apt to search through a holy text, and some today have claimed to find divine prohibitions against it. The utilitarian asks instead whether it contributes to the happiness of the people involved; and if it does, without harming others, then it is all to the good. In general, utilitarianism provides a moral framework in which all questions of right and wrong are reduced to *empirical* issues about what leads to the most happiness. In finding out what to do, we must use our best knowledge of the empirical world, including the best results of science, to predict what will reduce suffering and generally make people happy. There is *nothing* more to right and wrong than this.

Objections to Utilitarianism

Critics of utilitarianism have been mainly concerned to deny that utilitarians give a proper account of justice. They are dissatisfied with attempts to explain our concern with justice, as Hume does, as merely due to benevolence. They point out that if this is so, we might as well solve questions of justice by appealing straight through to the "greatest happiness" principle of utilitarianism itself. But doing this, they maintain, gives outrageous results in a variety of cases. Let us review some of these:

1. *The scapegoat.* Suppose that a town is outraged by some crime and will be happy only by seeing someone hang. You are the sheriff and believe the real criminal will not be found. Yet you can convict an innocent traveler and thus please the crowd by hanging him. If more total happiness results, should you do it?
2. *The happy slave.* You live in a society that condones slavery and have the opportunity to buy a slave you can afford, who would save you much drudgery. Suppose that the slave would be happier with you than in his old, harsh surroundings, even though he does not consent to being a slave. Both of you are made happier, and we may suppose, more happiness in general results. Is slavery okay in this case?
3. *The forgotten debt.* You borrow money from someone who is financially well-off and who has forgotten the loan. You or someone else you know

would get more pleasure from the money than this person. Should you renege on the debt to increase total happiness?
4. *The happy criminal.* A vicious, unrepentant criminal is sentenced to punishment. Consider two possible outcomes. In one, he is really punished. In the other, extraterrestrials secretly replace him by an insensate but otherwise indistinguishable android, while spiriting the criminal to another planet where he harmlessly lives out his life in great (unrepentant) enjoyment. Is the second outcome better by having more total happiness?
5. *The paternalist.* Someone believes she knows more about your welfare than you do or at least sees that you are not willing to act as well as you might on your own behalf. Say you want to quit smoking but take a pack of cigarettes on a camping trip anyway. She sees that you would be better off without them and secretly takes them and throws them away. Suppose your resentment is offset by the increased pleasure felt with greater health, so that total happiness is increased. Would that make her paternalistic action okay?
6. *Draconian laws.* The ancient Greek leader Draco gave extremely harsh punishments for relatively minor crimes on the ground that they were effective. If you really want people to stop littering, give them the death penalty. Suppose that one person was executed for this, thus stopping all littering, and the increased visual pleasure outweighed the person's lost happiness. Would this justify the punishment?

The Pattern in the Objections

There is a pattern in all of these examples that critics think show what is wrong with utilitarianism. In each case, someone's rights are violated in the effort to increase total happiness. Happiness is bought at the price of injustice. The scapegoat has a right not to be used just to make others happy. The slave has a right to freedom, even if denying this would make him happier. In this respect, the happy slave case is like that of **paternalism.** Doing something to make someone happy is not okay if it infringes on that person's own right to choose. People have a right to have their debts paid back; they do not lose this right by forgetting or by happening to be in a situation where their money would make someone else happy. The case of the criminal who escapes punishment also denies rights: the right of others in society to see that justice is done, and even the right of the criminal to be treated with respect by getting what he deserves.

It might seem funny to mention this last right, for who would ever insist on it? But consider the following. Suppose that you are found guilty of murder and sentenced to death. The prosecutors then suggest that your life could be made valuable by giving you a frontal lobotomy and using your living body for research for the next decade. Might you not insist on getting what you deserve? The idea that punishment must "fit" the crime is also used to object to draconian laws. The person who is made an "example" is used for a good social purpose, but this is unjust and wrong if the punishment denies her right to get *only* what she deserves.

DEONTOLOGY

If you believe that these examples show that the "greatest happiness principle" of utilitarianism has exceptions, then you are not a utilitarian, even if you were initially attracted to it. This has important consequences for how you ought to argue for your moral opinions. Utilitarian arguments are really common in life, but you should *never* give them. This may seem an excessive conclusion, but the point is this. A utilitarian argument is one that tries to justify a course of action on the *sole* ground that it will lead to more happiness. But you (we are supposing) do not believe that this is enough; for you subscribe to the view that insists that *first* we must see whether an injustice would be committed. The slogan for people who insist that we first check for injustices before proceeding with the happier outcome is "the end does not justify the means": The end (of greater happiness) does not justify the means (when this involves injustice).

These critics of utilitarianism subscribe to **deontology** (from the Greek *deon*, for "duty"), in that they hold that we must study the duties required by justice before we can say whether an outcome is good. But how can we *justify* our view that an act commits an injustice? Hume argued that our passion for justice was due ultimately to our sympathy. But the earlier examples suggest to many philosophers that this is not so. His most powerful critic was Kant, who thought that our opinions about justice could be established with no appeal to sympathy or any other sentiment. He accordingly rejected Hume's view about the limitations of reason and defended a view of reason like that of Plato and Aristotle. Let us see how he went about this.

DUTIES TO ONESELF

Hume's moral theory is only about how to treat others. Kant's moral theory includes a view about how we are obligated to treat ourselves as well. It may seem funny to say that you have moral duties to yourself. If you choose to violate a duty to yourself, who would there be to complain? There is, however, a response to this question. You may think of a moral duty to yourself as a duty to your "future self." When you violate a duty to yourself, as we will see, it is you, in the future, who will find fault with yourself, in the present. So, we may understand duties to ourselves on the model of duties to others, treating our future selves as if they were different people. It will prove helpful to understand first how we ought to treat ourselves, before seeing how we ought to treat others. Here is Kant's own explanation:

> The most serious offense against the duty one owes to oneself is suicide. . . . Suicide is an abomination because it implies the abuse of man's freedom of action: he uses his freedom to destroy himself. . . . Man is free to dispose of his condition but not of his person: he himself is an end and not a means; all else in the world is of value only as a means, but man is a person and not a thing and therefore not a means. . . .

Freedom is, on the one hand, that faculty which gives unlimited usefulness to all other faculties. It is the highest order of life, which serves as the foundation of all perfections and is their necessary condition. All animals have the faculty of using their powers according to will. But this will is not free. It is necessitated through the incitement of stimuli, and the actions of animals involve a *bruta necessitas*. If the will of all beings were so bound to sensuous impulse, the world would possess no value. The inherent value of the world, the *summum bonus* [highest good], is freedom in accordance with a will that is not necessitated to action. Freedom is thus the inner value of the world. . . .

The supreme rule is that in all the actions which affect himself a man should so conduct himself that every exercise of his power is compatible with the fullest employment of them. . . .

Not self-favor but self-esteem should be the principle of our duties to ourselves. This means that our actions must be in keeping with the worth of man. . . . Just as law restricts our freedom in our relations with other men, so do our duties to ourselves restrict our freedom in dealing with ourselves. All such duties are grounded in a certain love of honor consisting of self-esteem; man must not appear unworthy in his own eyes; his actions must be in keeping with humanity itself if he is to appear in his own eyes worthy of respect. To value approbation is the essential ingredient of our duties to ourselves.[3]

THE NATURE OF FREEDOM

Your duties to yourself, according to Kant, can be summed up as the duty to respect your own freedom. Freedom is a power that humans, but not other animals, have. It is the power to choose. As we saw in the last chapter, choosing is a relatively sophisticated affair, requiring the ability to contemplate alternative courses of action in order to adopt the one that appears best. To respect your own freedom you must, at a minimum, refrain from actions that would diminish your own long-range freedom. Going to sleep results in a temporary loss of one's ability to choose, but it does not of course diminish long-range freedom, because it is required for recuperation, the return of one's freedom. But there are many things we do for the momentary reward that do result in a net loss of our own freedom. Here are some of Kant's own illustrations:

> A drunkard does no harm to another, and if he has a strong constitution he does no harm to himself, yet he is an object of contempt. We are not indifferent to cringing servility; man should not cringe and fawn; by doing so he degrades his person and loses his manhood. If a man for gain or profit submits to indignities and makes himself the plaything of another, he casts away the worth of his manhood. Again, a lie is more a violation of one's duty

---

3. Immanuel Kant, *Lectures on Ethics*, trans. Louis Infield (Indianapolis: Hackett, 1963).

to oneself than of one's duty to others. A liar, even though by his lies he does no harm to anyone, yet becomes an object of contempt, he throws away his personality.[4]

To understand Kant's point about the drunkard, we must admit that getting drunk is not like going to sleep. Maybe there are rare occasions in which it is recuperative (and maybe there are not), but Kant is thinking of the typical case in which a person chooses to get drunk just for the momentary pleasure, despite the fact that this diminishes his freedom. As we all know, an essential part of being drunk is having poorer judgment. One is not as good at pondering alternative courses of action or at deciding which is best. This is why in such a state we often do things we regret. But even if we slip by without serious mishap, Kant thinks we should feel remorse. He would surely say this is much more so if it becomes a habit. For then we are choosing to live like an animal. But what is wrong with that, you might ask, if you are having fun?

THE VALUE OF FREEDOM

Kant thinks it is only *rational* to value your own freedom. This means that those who do *not* value it display a failure of *understanding*. He thinks that all of us, all of us who can reason and use this power to choose, *ought* to value our own freedom. Now, if even this much can be shown, it will be an important response to Hume. For recall that Hume held that we could not discern anything about what we ought to do without looking "within our breasts" to see how we feel. Kant's argument involves no appeal whatsoever to "sentiment." So, if he is correct, Hume is wrong on a most fundamental principle of his moral theory (that "reason is a slave of the passions"). What Kant says of *any* person is that "as a rational being he necessarily wills that all his faculties be developed, inasmuch as they are given to him for all possible purposes." Let us try to see what this means.

There is something that we can assume about everybody, regardless of how they feel (what are their "sentiments"). It is that they have *values*, that some things *matter* to them. Freedom is important to you because it is a capacity to promote what you think is important, to make decisions on the basis of what matters to you. Freedom is *not* merely a capacity to pursue certain *kinds* of goals. Developing your golf stroke increases your ability to play golf, but it does not increase your ability to pursue your purposes, whatever they are. The one thing that you can count on to be true about you throughout your life is that *something* will matter to you. You do not know what this will be in the distant future. If, therefore, you pursue a present pleasure at the expense of your long-range freedom, you have diminished your power to get what you want — not on this particular occasion but in general. Think of all the goals you have now and ever will have. The greater your freedom, the

---

4. Kant, *Lectures on Ethics*.

more likely you will achieve these. To pursue a present pleasure at the expense of freedom is, therefore, to value one goal above the totality of all the goals you ever will have. This is irrational, because it amounts to not really caring about what is (supposed to be) what you most care about.

Our discussion of credulity in Chapter One provides a perfect example. In acting credulously, a person does what she *feels* like doing. It is unpleasant in an inquiry to look at facts that support what you want not to be true. But if you seek the "present pleasure" of looking only at welcome facts, the (unintended) result will very likely be false beliefs. Your map of the world will be damaged; it will be less useful to you in getting what you want, regardless of "where you want to go." Knowledge itself is a large component of freedom. The more you know, the more you know how to pursue your purposes effectively. (The more detailed and accurate a map you have, the better it serves you in planning your trips.) Even if no one ever *wants* to diminish her freedom (and who would?), she sometimes wants to do things that would have the unintended result of diminishing it. By foreseeing this unintended consequence, she should recognize that she has a duty to herself to refrain.

This same kind of reasoning should apply to all the examples Kant gives of duties to oneself. The servile person, for example, is one who allows others to make his decisions. In slavishly doing what someone else wants him to do, he makes himself in effect the tool of the other person. This amounts to using *his* freedom to promote the *other* person's goals. Why would anyone do that? Perhaps to avoid the burden of thinking for himself. The "present pleasure" of shirking that burden is what would appeal to such a person. The fact that he is throwing away his freedom does not occur to him, or, if it does, he tries not to think about it. Even if freedom is in fact important to everyone, it is possible to understand why someone would use their freedom (would choose) in such a way as to diminish it.

KANT ON MORAL MOTIVATION

Even though we have looked at only a small part of Kant's account of morality, what he says about your duties to yourself holds the key to his own solution to the problem of moral motivation. When an immoral person comes to understand what she has done, she is an "object of contempt" in her own eyes. Whenever you choose, it *appears* that you are free to act one way or another and that you act to promote your own values. But this appearance can be a delusion. When you act against what is really important to you by submitting to an urge, the urge makes something appear good that, on reflection, you can see was not really good. It looks in retrospect that it was the urge and not really yourself that was in control. You see that you were a "slave of passion."

As we saw in Chapter Seven, the Stoics taught that happiness comes mainly from acting with good reason, since this is how we become conscious of our own freedom. Kant denies that this is enough for happiness, but he does insist that it provides a unique and important satisfaction. It is the consciousness of freedom that gives us a sense of *dignity*. And this, for Kant, is the reward of morality.

YOUR OWN RIGHT TO FREEDOM

From the fact that your freedom is necessarily important to you, it is a short step to the conclusion that you ought to regard yourself as having a *right* to freedom. To have a right to something, according to Kant, is to be the only person who is morally permitted to use it without the consent of another. You have a right to use your bicycle, for example, if you can use it whenever you please, but it is wrong for anyone else to use it without your permission. You have a right to freedom if it is morally permissible for you to make your own choices without the consent of others. Now, if you have good reason to respect your own freedom, you ought to object as well to the actions of others that have the same effect as violating your duty to yourself.

This happens in two main ways: *coercion* and *deceit*. You are coerced when someone else uses force against your own will. In light of the above, it is clear why you ought to oppose this. Your will is your freedom, your power to choose so as to get what you think is best. Coercion diverts you from your path, making it unlikely that you will get what you want. It is like being on a trip and having your car break down or having it blown from the road by a storm. Deceit also diminishes your freedom. It is like credulity in damaging your map of the world. In Kant's ethics, coercion and deceit are the two main ways in which others violate your rights. If you fail to acknowledge the right not to be coerced or deceived, you implicitly consent to having your freedom taken from you. And this, we have seen, is irrational.

OTHERS' RIGHT TO FREEDOM

So far we have been making points that could be accepted by an egoist. One who cares only for herself might admit that this care should take the form of protecting her own freedom, both by refraining from self-destructive acts and by preventing the coercion and deceit of others. Kant maintains, however, that others have the same right to freedom that you do. If we can see what justifies this claim, we will have his own explanation of what is wrong with egoism. Here is his argument:

> [R]ational nature exists as an end in itself. Man necessarily thinks of his own existence in this way; thus far it is a subjective principle of human actions. Also every other rational being thinks of his existence by means of the same rational ground which holds for myself; thus it is at the same time an objective principle from which, as a supreme practical ground, it must be possible to derive all the laws of the will. The practical impera-

tive, therefore, is the following: Act so that you treat humanity, whether in your own person or in that of another, always as an end and never as a means only.[5]

We encountered this talk of ends in themselves and means in a previous quotation of Kant's. A means is like a tool, something that has value only in what it can be used for. If someone coerces or deceives you, they are using you like a tool, with no regard to your own purposes; thus, they are failing to treat you as an end in itself. Kant says that humans necessarily think of themselves as ends in themselves. This should probably not be interpreted as a remark about human psychology. As his own example of servility clearly shows, people can shirk the burden of thinking for themselves and thus allow themselves to be tools of others. His point seems to be instead the one made before, that you *ought* to regard yourself as an end in itself.

However, Kant then goes on to say that all other rational beings think of their own existence the same way. This means that *they* have just as much reason as *you* do for thinking that *they* are ends in themselves. And you see this. In doing so, it should strike you as *arbitrary* to respect your own rights but not the rights of others. You see that you ought to respect your rights because you are *a rational being*, capable of reasoning in particular about what to do. But then what *explains* why you have a right to freedom is something very general about you, something that applies to everyone else. If it is the fact that you are a rational being that explains why you have this right—and not, for example, that you are male, or American, or just you—then it explains why *every* rational being has the very same right. Sheer *consistency* is what should lead you to see what is wrong with egoism. (See Chapter One for a discussion of consistency.)

This explains how egoists are "slaves of passion." As the Stoics taught, you are the true author of your actions only if you can justify them to yourself (see Chapter Seven). To maintain your dignity, you must act with good reasons, which means that you avoid arbitrariness in what you think is right. If you are an egoist, you are arbitrary in respecting your freedom but not that of others. There is no good reason for drawing the line where you do. Why, then, do you act? To serve some purpose of your own. But because your action is not justified, it is the desire that prompts it and not yourself that is your authority.

THE FORMULA OF HUMANITY

Utilitarianism gives us the "greatest happiness" principle to explain what in general we ought to do. Kant gives us several principles but claims they are different ways

---

5. Immanuel Kant, *Fundamental Principles of the Metaphysics of Morals*, trans. Thomas Kingsmill Abbott (1785).

of saying the same thing. The "practical imperative" in the earlier quote is one of these formulations. It is called the **formula of humanity,** since it says that we should treat all humans, including ourselves, as ends in themselves and never merely as means. The "merely" here is important. We often *serve* others, as, for example, when we act as parents or friends. Although we are "used" by the people we help, we are not treated *merely* as means. This is because we have *consented* to serve—we do so willingly, for some purpose of our own (which may be altruistic). This is the crucial difference between being a servant and being a slave. Slaves are simply coerced into doing what others want and are therefore treated merely as means. (In fact, all wrongdoing, for Kant, can be understood on the model of slavery.)

JUSTICE

We are now in a position to understand Kant's view on what justice requires. Hume tells us that justice comes into existence when we make a "partition of goods" into mine and yours. Kant would agree, adding that what is most fundamentally *yours* is your own freedom. This does *not* mean that you are free to do whatever you want. After all, others have the same right to freedom. If your right to freedom were not *restricted* in some way, you would be free to do anything, including coercing and deceiving others to serve your own purposes. Your right to freedom is therefore restricted by the fact that you are not free to treat others as mere means. This does *not* mean, as we will soon see, that it is *always* wrong to coerce or deceive others. But it does mean that there must be a strong presumption against these ways of diminishing another's freedom. The rule of thumb is to avoid forcing people to do things against their will or to lie to them. To really see what this means, you must reflect on the spiraling effects of your decisions. You probably do not literally push people around. But do you vote for candidates to Congress or the presidency who will support oppressive governments overseas? Do you purchase products from corporations that drive people from their land so that these corporations can make their products for a higher profit? The more humanity becomes interrelated, the greater the possibility of creating distant effects that you would not condone if you knew about them.

JUSTIFIED FORCE

Under what circumstances, then, is it *not* wrong to coerce or deceive? The general answer is given by the formula of humanity itself. After all, like the utilitarian's principle of greatest happiness, this is supposed to apply to *all* choices. So the question becomes, When does the obligation to respect everyone's freedom permit or even require that we use force or fraud? Since coercion and deceit diminish freedom, these cases are no doubt relatively rare. But recall that everyone should have the *same* right to freedom. We have seen that if your right to freedom is not restricted, no one else would have any right to freedom. For then you would be free to treat them as mere means.

Now, force *can* be used to prevent people from overstepping their bounds. So, *this* use of force is justified by the formula of humanity itself. This sort of case is familiar. We feel that it is right to stop a bully from doing violence to a weaker person. Or to mount an army to protect a nation from foreign invasion. Or even to kill a would-be murderer if necessary for self-defense. The prevention of injustice, then, is one special reason that entitles us to use force. As these examples show, there is no limit on the amount of force that may be necessary.

What if someone has already committed an injustice, a violation of the rights of another? If we do not respond appropriately, we in effect consent to the injustice. There cannot be rules without sanctions for disobeying them. If you say, "Respect the freedom of others, but if you do not, nothing will happen," how can the command to respect their rights be taken seriously? Deontology has been used to support the **retributive theory of punishment,** which says that the main point of punishment is to give the perpetrator what he *deserves*. It is fine if the punishment has other beneficial effects, such as protecting society, acting as a deterrent, and reforming the character of the criminal. But these are secondary to the main purpose of doing what justice requires. The retributive theory of justice says that the main purpose of punishment is to *restore* the equality of rights that was disturbed by the injustice. This means that the appropriate response to injustice is to restrict the freedom of the perpetrator just enough to establish that his right to freedom is no greater than that of other people. This is why the punishment must "fit" the crime. The *harm* that is done by injustice is the loss of another's freedom. To restore the balance, the criminal should have his own freedom restricted to the same degree. This is why cold-blooded murder can only be fully addressed by the death of the perpetrator. (Whether this should be administered by an imperfect government is another question.) The punishment must also not restrict the freedom of the criminal *more* than was committed by his injustice. This is the problem with draconian laws, which we saw could be justified by utilitarianism. Making an example of someone by giving him more than he deserves treats the criminal as a mere means. Such a person is used as a tool for a social purpose, and "the end does not justify the means."

It is significant that in explaining how coercion or deceit can be justified, we concentrated on the use of force. Kant once argued that it is always wrong to lie, but many Kant scholars today think his own theory can sometimes condone it. Cases of justified deceit, however, seem to be harder to find. Perhaps the clearest cases in which you have a right to deceive are those in war, where deceit is a valuable tool for making an aggressor less effective in denying your freedom. But, of course, this assumes that *you* are not on the side of the aggressor.

FREEDOM AS FUNDAMENTAL

Let us return to the idea that what is *fundamentally* yours is your own freedom. What this means is that among all your moral rights, it is the right to freedom that *explains* why you have the others. Why do you have a right to *life*? Because to be free, you have to be alive. It would be absurd to acknowledge a person's right to freedom but not her right to life. The same reasoning explains why you have a right to your *body*. It would be absurd to say that I respect your freedom but reserve the right to tie up your body and use it as doorstop.

It is very common for people to appeal to their rights to justify what they want. If we do have such rights, as deontology affirms, this must be sometimes legitimate. What is very often missed, however, is that there must be *restrictions* on the right to freedom and so on the other rights based on it. A bad argument against abortion (or the death penalty) is based on the simplistic idea that killing is wrong because it denies the right to life. Another bad argument, now for the permissibility of abortion, is based on the simplistic idea that it is wrong to restrict what a person does with her own body because it violates her right to her own body. But the right to life must be restricted, for otherwise you could not defend your own right to life by killing a would-be murderer in self-defense. And the right to one's own body must be restricted, for otherwise you could use it to pull the trigger of a gun that kills an innocent person.

You do have a right to life and a right to your body. But these rights do not cover those special cases in which life may be taken or a body may be controlled in order to prevent injustice. Especially in the difficult cases, in which people disagree, it is not enough to wave your rights over what you want. You must consider whether they really do apply to the case at hand.

THE PRIORITY OF JUSTICE

The main objection to utilitarianism was that in certain, perhaps rare, cases, it is possible to create greater happiness by ignoring someone's moral rights. We can now see how Kant would explain the sorts of examples that seem to deontologists to show what is wrong with the greatest happiness principle. He would say, for example, that it is wrong to deny the right to freedom and life of an innocent person, even if many people would derive pleasure by seeing him hang while believing that he is guilty. This is another case of using a person as a tool for a social purpose. It is wrong to force someone against her will into slavery, even if she would derive pleasure in her new life. Until the person consents to be there and becomes a servant instead, her right to freedom has been denied. It is not even permissible to force a fellow adult to do something for her own good. We do condone this action in the case of children, but only because they are not yet competent to decide for themselves. But even here, the rule to follow is to use only force that they would agree was proper when they reach the age of reason.

Even though these are rather peculiar examples, they reflect a profound difference in attitude toward the value of happiness. In the cases in which "happiness is bought at the price of injustice," Kant would say that the happiness that results is not even *good*. Take the case of slavery. The utilitarian *weighs* the happiness of the slaveholder against the unhappiness of the slave. Of course, in real life, this will result in slavery being wrong in virtually all cases. But the deontologist will not even allow the happiness of the slaveholder to be put on the scales in the first place. If the slaveholder's happiness comes from slavery, it is simply not good at all. If you adopt this view, it changes radically how you look at the world. When you see people prospering in a world in which many suffer, you wonder how they got their advantage.

THE DUTY OF SELF-DEVELOPMENT

Your chief duty to yourself is to respect your own freedom. Kant held that this includes not only *avoiding* actions that diminish your long-range freedom but also taking an interest in *developing* your freedom, such as becoming educated or improving your health. You have a duty to yourself to make yourself generally more competent and effective as a decision maker. It is up to you when and how you fulfill this duty. What is wrong is never to take advantage of opportunities to develop your freedom. If you always choose watching a game show instead of the news or, for that matter, watching television instead of reading or exercising, you do not take as seriously as you should the value of your own freedom. Although your actions are not diminishing your freedom, they result in something similar—a lower level of freedom than you might have had.

This means that if you respect your freedom only by avoiding actions that diminish your freedom without taking opportunities to develop it, you are in a way *inconsistent*. Your freedom is important to you because it is a power for realizing what matters to you. This is the reason for not diminishing your freedom, and this same reason shows that you ought to care about increasing it. So if you admit the first duty and not the second, you are inconsistent in the application of this reason.

It is important to see that Kant argues for the duty to develop your freedom by pointing out the inconsistency in not recognizing it. Remember how the duty to respect the rights of others was argued? It was that it would be inconsistent to respect your own rights but not those of other persons. This is how he differs from Hume. Reason is not a slave of the passions for Kant, since all that it takes to see our moral duties is to see what consistency requires, and this does not require the presence of a feeling like sympathy.

THE DUTY TO HELP OTHERS

Our duties of justice pertain to how we treat others. We ought to respect the rights of others, most fundamentally, by not diminishing their freedom. Kant thought, however, that we also have a duty to help others in need, as he explains in the following by applying his formula of humanity:

> It is not enough that the action does not violate humanity in our own person as an end in itself, it must also harmonize with it. Now there are in humanity capacities of greater perfection, which belong to the end that nature has in view in regard to humanity in ourselves as the subject: to neglect these might perhaps be consistent with the maintenance of humanity as an end in itself, but not with the advancement of this end.[6]

Just as you should take an interest in developing your own freedom, you should take an interest in the happiness of others. Once again we may understand this duty in terms of what consistency requires. You value your own happiness just because you are a person, with purposes you want to achieve. Everyone else has the same reason to value their happiness. Sheer consistency requires you to admit that their happiness is just as important as yours.

How is this different from utilitarianism? Kant does not say that it is your constant duty in every choice to do your bit to increase the world's happiness. This is the claim of utilitarianism, and it has led to the charge (correct or not) that utilitarianism is too demanding. In a world in which many suffer, this could require that you work full-time just to contribute to charity, regardless of what happens to you in the process. But for Kant, your duty to help others is limited by your duty to yourself not to diminish your own freedom. You are not required to drive yourself into the ground in the effort to help others even if this would produce more happiness in the world. This would be to make yourself a tool for a good social purpose.

The clearest cases in which you do have a duty to help others, for Kant, are those in which there is a real need for help and you are able to provide this assistance without diminishing your own freedom. If a child falls into a pond and you can save her by throwing a rope, you should. Many philosophers today would say that those who spend their resources on trivial luxuries are not throwing the rope.

RESPONSIBILITY

One of the most striking differences between utilitarianism and deontology pertains to their attitudes to the past. Utilitarianism is called "forward looking" because it says that to determine what to do, all that counts is what will produce the most happiness in the future. Deontology is called "backward looking" because it says

---

6. Kant, *Fundamental Principles of the Metaphysics of Morals.*

that to tell whether the future consequences are good, we must first see that we are respecting justice. And often what justice requires is determined by what happened in the past.

As we saw when discussing punishment, many deontologists say that punishment should be based on what people deserve, as a result of what they did in the past. By contrast, utilitarians have argued for penal institutions on such "forward-looking" considerations as protecting society and deterring future crime. A similar point can be made about compensation. Should people be compensated for how they were wronged in the past, or should all dispensations of resources be based on their future effects? What is strikingly different about the two theories is that utilitarianism does not base its recommendations on what people *deserve*, since this is always a backward-looking consideration.

Recall from Chapter Five that whether we really deserve anything at all is denied by hard determinists. They think the whole practice of holding people responsible for their actions is based on a false metaphysics. We are not really free to choose since everything that happens, even what decisions we make, is determined by a chain of events coming from the distant past. This attitude toward freedom and responsibility is consistent with utilitarianism but not with deontology.

KANT AND THE STOICS

In the last chapter, we examined moral theories that were associated with (crude) materialism and dualism. The other two main positions on the mind–body problem were idealism and the double aspect theory. We may now see how the two theories of this chapter are associated with these.

Recall that it was the Stoics especially who used the double aspect theory when developing their view of happiness (see Chapter Seven). Happiness comes from a harmony between mind and body. In the happy person, the body responds fully to the mind, doing what the mind understands to be best. Much the same picture of mind and body can be discerned in Kant's ethics. The body is the source of the "passions," and when you are a slave to them, there is a kind of split between your mind and body. Your mind tells you (in its best moments) to do one thing, but (acting on passion) your body enacts another. You bring mind and body together, as if they were two aspects of a single whole, when your body responds to what your mind sees to be right. Just through thinking, you can see that everyone has the same right to freedom. When you adopt this morality, what your mind discovers in thought is put into action by your body.

Kant's ethics differs from that of the Stoics in being a theory of morality and not of happiness. Kant explicitly denies the Stoics' claim that morality (doing what is right) is enough for happiness. Morality is a matter of respecting equal freedom. Happiness is a matter of getting what you want. The world of nature provides no guarantee that the former will be rewarded with the latter. As mentioned before (in

Chapter Five), nature is unjust. Morally good people often do not get the happiness they deserve. Kant feels that it is therefore reasonable to hope that nature is not all there is. We may hope that there is an afterlife, overseen by God, who will ensure that justice is done.

HUME'S IDEALISM

Hume was an idealist. His ethics is *consistent* with idealism, in that doing the right thing is explained in purely *mental* terms (and not, as in Kant, as the domination of body by mind). In the moral person, it is reason and feeling that are in harmony. What you ought to do is to be moved by sympathy when viewing things objectively.

There are, however, deeper ways in which Hume's idealism affects his ethics, which we can only touch on now. Berkeley, you may recall (from Chapter Eight), said that only minds and their contents are real. For Hume, there is nothing more to a mind than its contents. There is nothing more to your mind than the various thoughts, feelings, desires, and so forth, that you know in introspection. This diminishes the difference between one mind and another. An analogy might help. If you put similar items of clothing in different boxes, no matter how much the contents look alike, you can still see clearly how they are different by seeing that they are in two different boxes. For Hume, it is as if you take away the boxes leaving only two piles of clothes. Now, even though they are lying in two different places (as your mental contents and mine are separated by our two bodies), the difference between the two piles seems less real. It is not difficult to see the two piles as more like one pile that is spread out a bit. How could such an abstruse difference in their metaphysical views make a difference in their moral theory?

Justice exists when people respect each other's rights. To have a right to something is to be unique among all people in a certain way. Your right to your own body, for example, means that no one but you is permitted to use it, unless you (and no one else) gives consent. As Hume described justice, we "make a partition of goods" into mine and yours. To take justice most seriously, as deontologists do, you must take seriously the difference between the possessors of rights, the individual persons. But for Hume, we take the moral point of view when we use reason to *ignore* our differences so that we can be moved by the feeling of sympathy that we *share*. People are most moral when they are most benevolent, and on Hume's account, this means that they cease to compete and begin functioning as one. The deontologist's preoccupation with justice makes more of the fact that we are different people than Hume's metaphysics would admit.

CONCLUSION

Hume did not affirm utilitarianism, but he laid the groundwork for it. Utilitarianism became very popular in philosophy during a long time in which Kant's ethics was widely misinterpreted. My impression is that deontology is dominant today, but both philosophies are still well represented. Neither suffers from the sorts of objections leveled against the three moral theories of the last chapter. Both are powerful theories in the sense that they give plausible explanations of facts about morality that call for explanation. Since social philosophy, as we will see, is mainly an extension of ethics, we will consult these two theories regularly throughout Part Four.

We can now see how both are humanistic. For utilitarianism, the happiness of everyone is equally important. This does not mean that everyone has an equal *right* to happiness. It means that when you are trying to increase the world's happiness, the happiness of people of all kinds counts the same. For deontologists, everyone has the same right to freedom, regardless of race, country, sex, or age. The main difference between the two theories lies in their attitudes toward justice. Must justice be preserved for happiness to be good? Or can enough happiness offset a certain degree of injustice? This is a question on which reasonable people have disagreed. In consulting our two main moral theories in social philosophy, the question of what justice requires will loom large.

STUDY QUESTIONS

1. How are both Hume and Kant "humanists"?
2. How is acting *altruistically* different from acting from a *sense of justice*?
3. What does Hume mean by saying that "reason is a slave of the passions"?
4. What, according to Hume, are the respective contributions of reason and sentiment in producing our moral judgments?
5. How does this account, with its reliance on the role of sympathy, lead to utilitarianism?
6. Who did Hume and the utilitarians see as their main opponents? Illustrate the kind of morality they were most concerned to deny.
7. How does Hume explain our concern for justice as due to our sympathy?
8. Give some examples of injustices that seem to be counterexamples to the greatest happiness principle.
9. What is Hume's solution to the problem of moral motivation?
10. What duties do we have to ourselves, according to Kant? Give several examples. How is Kant's argument for these duties supposed to disprove Hume's view that reason is a "slave of the passions"?
11. How does the person who violates these duties lack freedom?
12. What is Kant's solution to the problem of moral motivation?
13. What is the argument, addressed to *you*, that you have a *right* to freedom?
14. Given this argument, how is it that sheer consistency is supposed to lead you to see that others have the same right to freedom?
15. What are the two main social vices, according to Kant? Explain how there can be exceptions.

16. What is the difference in viewpoint between Hume and Kant on the goodness of happiness?
17. According to Kant, why do we have a duty sometimes to help others in need? How is his view different from utilitarianism?
18. How is deontology but not utilitarianism inconsistent with hard determinism?
19. How does Kant's moral theory show the influence of Stoicism?
20. In what way is Hume's theory idealistic?

Glossary for Part Three

Altruism A kind of action in which it is one's ultimate purpose to help another person

Benevolence The character trait of being altruistic

Deontology The position that what we have a right to do must be determined first in order to assess whether the consequences of our actions are good

Divine command theory Same as *voluntarism*

Egoist Someone who cares only for himself

Ethical hedonism The position that accepts the moral principle that what makes an action right is that it produces the most pleasure, in the long run, for oneself

Formula of humanity Kant's deontological principle of the content of morality, which enjoins us to treat everyone as an end in itself and not as a mere means

Humanism The thesis that all humans have the same moral value

Justice The situation in which people have what is morally theirs; the virtue of respecting the rights of others

Moral psychology A philosophical theory meant to explain moral motivation

Morality The phenomenon that there are commands about what to do that claim the highest authority

Paternalism The phenomenon of acting against a person's will for her own good

Problem of moral motivation The problem of how to understand the attraction of doing the right thing, or the repulsion of doing the wrong thing, when you feel like acting immorally

Prudence Enlightened self-interest, valuing the future as much as the present

Psychological hedonism The thesis in psychology that everyone is always motivated ultimately just to feel better

Retributive theory of punishment The thesis that punishment should be determined primarily by what the criminal deserves

Social relativism The empirical thesis that there are differences in moral opinion

Utilitarianism The thesis that what makes an action right is just that it leads to more happiness than the alternative choices the person has; traditionally understands happiness as the greatest balance of pleasure over pain

Utility The characteristic of causing happiness

Voluntarism The position that accepts the moral principle that what makes an action right (or wrong) is that it is what God wants (or forbids); same as the divine command theory

PART
FOUR

Social Philosophy

Social philosophy and social science involve different kinds of inquiry. Social scientists use empirical methods (such as those we discussed in Part One) to study how real societies actually are. It is possible in philosophy to study how societies actually are by engaging in a metaphysical inquiry into the nature of society, and we will do a bit of this in our first chapter of Part Four. But social philosophy has in fact been almost entirely an extension of ethics. Philosophers have been mainly interested in how societies ought *to be. Their conclusions have, therefore, been based mostly on their ethical views.*

Chapter Ten begins with a discussion of what societies are as a preparation for considering how they ought to be. After this general reflection on method, the chapter deals in turn with three especially familiar and important kinds of social organizations: friendships, families, and schools (or educational institutions in general). The rest of Part Four carries on the same kind of inquiry with discussions of economies (in Chapter Eleven) and political organizations (in Chapter Twelve). Separate chapters have been devoted to the last two areas owing to the enormous attention that they have received from social philosophy.

CHAPTER
   TEN

Good Society

WHAT MAKES A SOCIETY good? To answer this question, we will examine a variety of ways that people typically live together. We form friendships, we belong to families, we create institutions such as schools for education, and we form economic and political systems. We will study each of these separately. Before we do so, however, we will attempt to get clear about the general nature of human social organizations. This will provide clues as to how we may ethically evaluate them.

THE NATURE OF SOCIETY

What *is* a society? Many kinds of animals form societies. What do all these have in common? We address this question first before seeing what is special about human societies.

All societies are organizations. The members do not simply live near each other, but they cooperate to achieve common purposes. This does not mean that the members must be conscious of the purposes of their society. Ants and termites may not be conscious at all, yet the natural outcome of their cooperation is to sustain both individual members and their society itself. The formation of societies is an extension of the same process that led to multicelled organisms. The cells of these complex organisms had ancestors that were single organisms that acted separately and much the same. In multicelled organisms, the cells perform different functions. But they cooperate since their various activities combine to achieve common purposes. Human societies are similar in that they are formed when different people adopt different social roles, such as that of a friend, a parent, a teacher, a producer or a consumer, or a citizen. By adopting such roles, they work together for such purposes as enjoying companionship, nurturing the young, educating, providing food and other material needs, and securing protection.

Human societies differ in that they are organized (to some extent) by *choice*. Our families, for example, are much like those of other animals, but we can think about how and why to form them. This allows us to alter them (for better or worse) in accordance with our conceptions of how things ought to be. Social roles are created when people accept the rules that define them, and humans are able to decide even what rules to follow. We may, for example, decide against patriarchy, in which the father rules, in favor of an arrangement in which the decision-making power is more evenly spread. Like all decisions, this would be based on what is thought to be best. Human societies reflect ethical values. (This explains the much greater diversity we find among them.) They are (to some extent) *artifacts*, created by humans to serve purposes of their own.

Human societies are *composed* of people, but are the societies themselves *like* people? Some philosophers have called societies "artificial persons." They are artificial in that we make them for some purpose. But how are they like *us*? We often talk of the *values* espoused by a society or of the *spirit* that animates it. This encourages us to see societies as artificial persons. Many philosophers, however, think the comparison is dangerous. If we say that a whole society is *happy*, for example, this may obscure the fact that what is really going on is that many people within it are happy at the expense of others. If we say that a society with slaves is happy, we ignore the misery of the slaves. If we say that a society is *alive*, this may encourage us to see its members as being like cells of an organism. And then we might come to think that the whole point of human life is to give oneself to society. The extent to which a society is like a person is, however, one of the issues philosophers debate.

HAPPINESS IN SOCIETY

Our study of ethics in Part Three suggests two main ways in which societies or social organizations within them may be evaluated. Chapter Seven focused on happiness and thus what is good *for* someone. We use this part of ethics when we single out a particular person (perhaps oneself) or a particular group (such as the members of a minority or the poor) and ask how a certain organization helps or hurts them. Why do we need friends? What kind of family is best for the children? What kind of school best serves those who need education? In what kind of economy will you prosper the most? What kind of government should you support to protect your own interests? These are just some of the questions that call for a theory of happiness.

MORAL BEHAVIOR IN SOCIETIES

Chapters Eight and Nine both explored the question of what to do. Only an egoist would equate this question with the question of how to be happy. A theory of morality will say how the various members within a certain kind of organization should behave. Is it appropriate to insist on your rights with a friend? What are the responsibilities of parents? What do children owe their parents? Should educators be more like friends or parents? Should students be considered customers? Is it OK to sell a product you know to be worthless or to manipulate people into wanting it? If you are poor, do you have a right to insist on being helped even if you do not work? Do you have a right to have a say in what laws will be enforced in your society? Each of these is a practical question for anyone who has a certain social role. The correct answers to them tell you what you are obligated to do when performing that role or what rights you are permitted to insist upon.

SOCIETIES IN THE BEST WORLD

There is another way in which a correct theory of morality helps to evaluate social organizations of various kinds. A moral theory will yield a vision of how the *world* should be. More precisely, it will say how *we* should act, not merely as individuals but *together*. Many people think it is morally OK to spend much of your time taking care of yourself, doing what is good *for you*. But there is also the question of what is "just plain" *good*. This is what all of us ought to work together to create and sustain. Should we all try as much as possible to be like friends to one another or to be more like business associates, leaving friendship for more intimate relationships? Is it a good thing to have so many children raised by a single parent or by people other than their biological parents? Is it good if most people get their news from media controlled by the government or by large corporations? Who should decide what to produce, and who should get it? Are great differences in wealth unfair or the natural result of freedom? What good is it to have governments that pass laws that are enforced whether you like them or not? These questions are not about how individuals fulfilling certain social roles should behave. They are about the *purposes* that we ought to have when organizing in the first place.

THE BEST WORLD

How should the world be? Egoists want the world to be good for them. Voluntarists want the world to be in accordance with God's will. We will not pay much attention in Part Four to such discredited views of morality. Since utilitarianism and deontology have been the most respected moral theories in modern ethics, it is these that we will consult when considering how a particular social organization makes the world better or worse. As I have emphasized before, they have much in common. Most of all, they are both humanistic. They agree that everyone has the same moral rights and that the happiness of everyone is equally important. This must be interpreted with some care. Kant thought that people *deserve* happiness only by being moral. But he also thought that we have a duty to help others in need, and "others" here means *everyone*. Utilitarians allow cases in which the happiness of some can be sacrificed for a net gain in happiness. But individual sacrifice is based only on one's circumstance and not because of one's race, sex, nationality, age, or wealth.

Despite their common commitment to a humanistic outlook, utilitarianism and deontology are still inconsistent. Their main point of disagreement pertains to how happiness should be *distributed*. The essence of utilitarianism is to evaluate the world in terms of the sheer *amount* of happiness in it. One world is better than another if it is happier, even if some people are happier than others. Deontologists do not say that everyone has the same right to be happy. Their position is a good deal more complicated. Everyone has the same right to freedom, and how we use our freedom determines what we deserve. The demand for equal freedom marks a significant difference between the two moral theories. Consider the deontological language (highlighted by me) that pervades the following passage, written by the contemporary feminist philosopher Virginia Held:

> The *liberation* of women requires an end to *oppressive* state *interferences* with women's reproductive *choices* and to *oppressive* domestic situations where women are subject to abuse; and it requires economic *independence* for women through employment or some equivalent such as family allowances. It also requires the psychological *empowerment* of women to overcome traditional practices of *disregarding* and *trivializing* women and their views and of seeing women as sexual *objects* and *exploitable* care givers.[1]

Although utilitarians would agree that it is generally wrong to think of women (or other people) as objects, to be exploited, disregarded, or trivialized, or to interfere with their choices and that it is generally good for women (or other people) to be empowered, liberated, and independent, this is only because these are generally good *means* for promoting happiness. For deontologists, these are conditions that *must* be met in *any* society of which we can approve. For the deontologist, Held's demands for women ring with a sense of the highest moral authority, which is why those most concerned with oppression and liberation typically look to deontology to inform their moral outlook.

This does not mean that deontologists always occupy the higher moral ground. Consider this statement by the contemporary philosopher and self-described utilitarian, Peter Singer, who is explaining here what his attachment to the political left basically means:

---

1. From "Feminist Social and Political Philosophy," in *The Encyclopedia of Philosophy Supplement*, ed. Donald M. Borchert (New York: Simon & Schuster, 1996).

If we shrug our shoulders at the avoidable suffering of the weak and poor, of those who are getting exploited and ripped off, or who simply do not have enough to sustain life at a decent level, we are not of the left. If we say that that is just the way the world is, and always will be, and there is nothing we can do about it, we are not part of the left. The left wants to do something about this situation.[2]

Notice the difference in emphasis. What matters most for a utilitarian like Singer is that there is avoidable suffering. Suffering is usually bad, according to deontologists, but their condemnation of it is more qualified. They are typically willing to allow suffering when it is deserved, as in just punishment or when the individual has simply brought about their own trouble. Utilitarians, such as Singer, tend to brush aside such considerations and respond to suffering regardless of the cause. We will keep in mind these differences in emphasis when we examine how societies affect the world for better or for worse.

THE DANGER OF SOCIETY

Although the various social organizations that we will study are generally thought to be good, philosophers have differed greatly on the importance that they attach to society in general. The Chinese Taoists, as we have seen, were wary of all things artificial, including human society. This is indicated explicitly in the following passage from the *Tao Te Ching*:

> The more taboos and restrictions there are in the world, the poorer the people will be.
> The more sharp weapons the people have, the more troubled the state will be.
> The more cunning and skill man possesses, the more vicious things will appear.
> The more laws and orders are made prominent, the more thieves and robbers there will be.[3]

Now, the Taoists were not really opposed to all society. But they thought it should be minimized. Human societies are formed by adopting rules of interaction. But all rules are *restrictions* on choice and thus threaten freedom. Human societies also develop technology, such as sophisticated weapons, that can be used against individuals, thus depriving them of safety and the choice of living in solitude. Wealth is amassed, which leads to a struggle for its possession. Finally, although not indicated in the quoted passage, large societies tend to create hier-

---

2. From *A Darwinian Left: Politics, Evolution and Cooperation* (London: Weidenfeld & Nicholson, 1999).
3. From *A Source Book in Chinese Philosophy*, trans. and comp. Wing-tsit Chan (Princeton, NJ: Princeton University Press, 1963).

archies of domination among their members. The leaders of large organizations — whether of governments, corporations, unions, or churches — have more control over the power that that organization creates and channels. This can too easily be used against weaker people within and without the organization in question.

THE NEED FOR SOCIETY

What, then, is there to say in favor of society in general? From our humanistic perspective, we will favor those that promote human happiness and justice. As we saw in Chapter Seven, what it takes to be happy is to satisfy our needs. The Taoists were materialists, and, as we also saw, materialists tend to emphasize those needs that we share more widely with other animals. Idealistic views of happiness, by contrast, tend to emphasize distinctively human needs. Plato offers in the following passage a vision of human nature that will provide a useful general classification of our needs:

> The soul of the thirsty, then, in so far as it thirsts, wishes nothing else than to drink, and yearns for this and its impulse is toward this. . . .
> If anything draws it back when thirsty, there must be something different in it from that which thirsts and drives it like a beast to drink. . . .
> [S]ome men sometimes though thirsty refuse to drink. . . .
> What, then, should one affirm about them? Is it not that there is a something in the soul that bids them to drink and a something that forbids, a different something that masters that which bids? . . .
> [T]hey are two and different from one another, naming that in the soul whereby it reckons and reasons the rational, and that with which it loves, hungers, thirsts, and feels the flutter and titillation of other desires, the irrational and appetitive. . . .
> But now the *thumos*, or principle of high spirit, that with which we feel anger, is it a third? . . .
> [T]he principle of anger sometimes fights against desires as an alien thing.[4]

The human "soul" has three parts. Like other animals, we have desires for material goods. But unlike other animals, we have the power of reason by which we discover what laws or rules to follow. Unfortunately, reason is not always in control of the passions, and we are slaves to them. In the healthy soul, reason rules. This reveals the presence of a good will. The will is the power to enforce the rules that define how to live rightly.

Now, corresponding to these three parts of the soul, we can distinguish three kinds of needs: material, intellectual, and what we will call spiritual needs. Material needs are those of the body; intellectual needs are those of the mind. We need

---

4. Plato, *Republic*, trans. Benjamin Jowett, 436a–440d.

food, clothing, shelter, and the like, for bodily health. We need knowledge and understanding for the mind. Our principal **spiritual need** is to have the will to do what we know to be right. We are "inspired" in our sense when we come to desire what is good. Theories of happiness differ in which of these kinds of needs they emphasize. The crudest forms of materialism recognize only material needs. Idealism emphasizes our intellectual and spiritual needs. Idealists, of course, recognize the importance of society for meeting our material needs. But they have seen society as crucially important for meeting our "higher" needs. Society is necessary for lifting us from the animal level of existence so that we may live like human beings.

THE ETHICS OF CONFUCIUS

Some of the ways in which society "humanizes" us are fairly obvious. It is only in the society of others that we learn a language, and many philosophers would say that unless we can understand a language we cannot even think (in the special sense of thinking described in Chapter One). With either no language or no thought, we would be just like lower animals. It is very plausible that we need society not only for our intellectual needs but for our spiritual ones as well. We learn to care about what is good by being rewarded for moral behavior, and this comes mainly from the approval of others.

The Taoists were materialists who did not place much value in understanding the world. (The wise move with an intuitive sense of what is natural.) The other major philosophical movement of China differed sharply from Taoism by describing the best life in terms of fulfilling social roles. It was how to live in society that characterized the ethics of Confucius, of the sixth to fifth century B.C. The following gives the flavor of what he prescribed:

> Few of those who are filial sons and respectful brothers will show disrespect to superiors, and there has never been a man who is not disrespectful to superiors and yet creates disorder. . . .
>
> Filial piety nowadays means to be able to support one's parents. But we support even dogs and horses. If there is no feeling of reverence, wherein lies the difference? . . .
>
> In serving his parents, a son may gently remonstrate with them. When he sees that they are not inclined to listen to him, he should resume an attitude of reverence and not abandon his effort to serve them. He may be worried, but does not complain. . . .
>
> Let the ruler *be* a ruler, the minister *be* a minister, the father *be* a father, and the son *be* a son. . . .
>
> There are three kinds of friendship which are beneficial and three kinds which are harmful. Friendship with the upright, with the truthful, and with the well-informed is beneficial. Friendship with those who flatter,

with those who are meek and who compromise with principles, and with those who talk cleverly is harmful.[5]

HEGEL ON SOCIETY

Confucius was concerned mainly with morality, with what we ought to do. But he thought that we were better off when we did fulfill our social duties. How might this be explained? A direct reply to the Taoists would explain how it is good for us to perform social roles. Recall that a main complaint of theirs about society is that it is the very essence of society that *rules* be imposed. But rules are restrictions on behavior and thus seem to diminish our freedom. The nineteenth-century German philosopher Georg Hegel argued that we must accept the rules of society to *increase* our freedom. His point was not that we must accept this sort of restriction of our freedom as a necessary evil for achieving good results. This would mean that we would be even better off if we could get these goods without the burden of the rules. If children could get the nurturing they need without their parents having to accept the responsibility of raising them, by rejecting this responsibility, the parents would have greater freedom. Hegel argues instead for the unobvious point that we are most free and happy only if we have taken on the responsibilities of such social roles. How can this be?

Hegel's point is that it is only by taking on social roles that we gain that consciousness of our own freedom that the Stoics thought was the key to human happiness (see Chapter Seven). As a successor of Kant, Hegel thought that we are truly free only when we respect the moral rights of others (see Chapter Nine). This means that we are *conscious* of our own freedom only when we see ourselves as moral people who demonstrate a commitment to justice. But we need others' approval to be assured of our own moral goodness. People tend to regard themselves as others see them. How we think of our own moral character and the value of our works depends largely on how they are mirrored in the reactions of others. Notice that the need in question is not merely to know that good things are done but to know that it is *oneself* that is the source of the goodness. Humans are capable of reflective thought, and especially of reflecting on their life as a whole. When you do think about your life, you want to see that it is *good*, that the efforts you make in your life are to good effect, so that *your* life *matters*.

Hegel claims that we can see ourselves as moral agents only if there are social roles for us to fulfill. It is the *customs* of a society that supply these roles. There are, for example, customary ways, within a given society, for being a good father or husband or for performing a certain job in the economy. Moral duties, such as keeping your promises or telling the truth, are the same for everyone. What Hegel calls "customary" duties pertain to the unique situation in life of a given individual. By

---

5. From *A Source Book in Chinese Philosophy*, trans. and comp. Wing-tsit Chan.

taking on the duties of being the husband of this *particular* woman, the father of *these* children, the carpenter who performs *those* jobs, you see your efforts not only as morally good but as *unique*. No one else does or can fulfill the particular set of responsibilities that largely define *who you are*. By taking on these responsibilities, you get a sense of how your particular life makes the world better. As Hegel himself says of "customary" duties:

> [T]hey are not something alien to the subject. On the contrary, his spirit bears witness to them as to its own essence, the essence in which he has a feeling of his selfhood. . . . In an ethical community, it is easy to say what man must do, what are the duties he has to fulfill . . . he has simply to follow the well-known and explicit rules of his own situation. Rectitude [morality] is the general character which may be demanded of him by law or custom. But . . . rectitude often seems to be something comparatively inferior . . . because the craving to be something special is not satisfied with what is absolute and universal; it finds consciousness of peculiarity only in what is exceptional. . . . The various facets of rectitude . . . are also properties of the individual, although not specifically of him in contrast with others.[6]

To be really satisfied by participating in the life of a community, however, one must be able to approve of its collective goals and how they are met. A society with slaves could be highly "organic," with each person having specific roles that give everyone a sense of who they are within the larger scheme of things. But because it denies the moral rights of some of its members, participation in it does not provide the satisfaction of knowing that your contribution to it is *good*. The operations of the community must be moral, and be known as such, before its various roles can provide the context for meaningful participation.

The best communities express widespread appreciation and recognition for the performance of one's particular "customary" duties. Because everyone is working together, they approve of each other for doing their part within the whole. By helping others and respecting their rights, you exhibit to others your freedom, which is reflected back to you in their approval. By experiencing this approval, you gain consciousness of your own freedom.

As we saw in Chapter Six, Hegel held a monistic form of idealism that has been compared with the Hindu metaphysics of Shankara. He was an idealist by thinking that the ultimate purpose of the world is to produce minds such as ours. He was a monist by encouraging the view that our many minds are merely facets of common mind, which may be identified with the mind of God. This common mind is actually created *by us* when we create morally good societies. The development of civilization is the gradual development of a common, morally good consciousness. By forming the best societies, we fulfill the purpose of the world to bring

---

6. From *The Philosophy of Right*, trans. T. M. Knox (Chicago: Encyclopaedia Britannica, 1952).

God into existence! One cannot find a view of society more extremely opposed to the pessimism of the Taoists.

FRIENDSHIP

We have considered the nature of human societies and how to evaluate them ethically. We also have seen how philosophers differ in their estimation of society in general. For the rest of Part Four, we will examine separately several different kinds of social organization. In each case, we will not attempt to cover all the questions that have been raised about it. For each our purpose is to sample a few issues that are especially interesting and important. Different questions will pertain to the different kinds of ethical evaluations we have classified.

We first examine friendship. (Philosophers understand the term broadly enough to include lovers.) Why do we need friends? By knowing how the best friends contribute to happiness, we know what kind to seek. What is peculiar about how friends should treat each other? Is it, for example, appropriate for friends to insist on what the other owes them, or should genuine friends be above that kind of self-oriented concern? These are the main questions we will discuss.

Aristotle on Friendship

One of the first theories of friendship was created by Aristotle. Aristotle claimed that humans are "social animals." He meant not simply that we actually live in societies but that we must live with others to develop as human beings. Like Plato, Aristotle gives the highest priority to the importance for happiness of understanding the world. But he emphasizes almost as much the importance of society for what we are calling our spiritual development. In the following set of remarks, he explains why we need friendship for meeting our "higher" needs:

> [T]he solitary person's life is hard, since it is not easy for him to be continuously active all by himself; but in relation to others and in their company it is easier, and hence this activity will be more continuous. It is also pleasant in itself, as it must be in the blessedly happy person. For the excellent person, in so far as he is excellent, enjoys actions expressing virtue, and objects to actions caused by vice, just as the musician enjoys fine melodies and is pained by bad ones. . . .
>
> [L]oving is like production, while being loved is like being acted upon; and [the benefactor's] love and friendliness is the result of his greater activity. . . .
>
> Further, good people's life together allows the cultivation of virtue. . . .
>
> [I]n the case of humans beings what seems to count as living together is this sharing of conversation and thought. . . .
>
> [Good friends] seem to become still better from their activities and their mutual correction. For each molds the other in what they approve of, so that "[you will learn] what is noble from noble people." . . .

[M]an alone is the only animal whom [nature] has endowed with the gift of speech ... whereas mere voice is ... found in other animals ... the power of speech is intended to set forth the expedient and the inexpedient, and therefore likewise the just and the unjust. And it is characteristic of man that he alone has any sense of good and evil, of just and unjust, and the like.[7]

[M]an, when perfected, is the best of animals, but, when separated from law and justice, he is the worst of all; since armed injustice is more dangerous, and he is equipped at birth with arms, meant to be used by intelligence and virtue, which he may use for the worst ends ... but justice is the bond of men in [societies].[8]

The solitary life is not the best life, because we need others, especially friends, to satisfy our distinctively human needs to understand and act rightly. Friends are those with whom we live, who know us as individuals and care for our well-being. They help us, in fact, in the development of both understanding and will. By living with them, we are able to develop our understanding, mainly in speech. Friends help us to understand the world better, by correcting our mistakes and supplying new information. Good friends also help us to develop spiritually. By approving our good actions and discouraging our bad ones, we gradually develop the desire to do what is right. Without friends, we could (in favorable circumstances) satisfy our merely animal needs, but we would not fully develop or live as human beings.

To benefit the most from friendship, we must have the best kind of friend. Aristotle distinguished three types according to three "objects of choice." Our purpose in choosing anything, he held, depends on whether we choose it as a means for achieving something else, as something pleasurable or as something good. The "useful" friend was the lowest type and would include people who are merely business associates. We care for them only because they help us to get something else that we want, such as money or positions of power. If we could get this more easily without their help, friendship with them would be of no value. Friendships "of pleasure" are the next highest type. We value the company of such friends for its own sake because they are fun to be with. The last and highest type for Aristotle was the friendship "of virtue." Such friends enjoy each other's company, but the basis of their friendship is their mutual admiration of each other's moral and intellectual excellence. They are people of good character, inquisitive, kind, and just. These qualities are what they admire in each other. They see each other not merely as sources of pleasure but as good people. It is only such friends who help each other in their intellectual and spiritual development.

Aristotle also argued that friendships of virtue last the longest. This is because good people tend to retain the good character they have developed, whereas what

---

7. From *Nicomachean Ethics*, trans. Terence Irwin (Indianapolis: Hackett, 1985).
8. From "Politics," in *The Basic Works of Aristotle*, ed. Richard McKeon (New York: Random House, 1941).

makes them useful or fun to be with is less likely to last. (If he is right, marriages are more likely to last if they are between morally good people who admire each other's character.)

Hume on Friendship

Utilitarians are bound to place the highest value on friendship. Their whole moral outlook encourages us to spread the attitude of friendship as widely as possible. Utilitarianism is contrasted with deontology mainly by the lesser importance that it attaches to justice. We might expect this difference to be reflected in their conception of friendship. Utilitarianism, as we saw in the last chapter, developed from the moral theory of David Hume. In the following passage, Hume argues that considerations of justice would not exist at all between perfect friends:

> [S]uppose that, though the necessities of the human race continue the same as at present, yet the mind is enlarged and so replete with friendship and generosity that every man has the utmost tenderness for every other man, and feels no more concern for his own interest than for that of his fellows: It seems evident that the *use* of Justice would, in this case, be suspended by such an extended benevolence, nor would the divisions and barriers of property and obligation have ever been thought of. Why should I bind another, by a deed or promise, to do me any good office when I know that he is already prompted by the strongest inclination to seek my happiness and would of himself perform the desired service, except the hurt he thereby receives be greater than the benefit accruing to me; in which case he knows that, from my innate humanity and friendship, I should be the first to oppose myself to his imprudent generosity?[9]

Perfect friends care for each other just as much as they care for themselves. Justice exists when people respect the moral rights of each other. But what would be the point of insisting that you have a right to something you want with someone who already cares that you have it?

We can see a difference here with deontology by recalling (from the last chapter) their different attitude toward paternalism. Utilitarianism is relatively lenient about doing things for the good of another even if this requires acting against that person's will. Since Hume's perfect friends are motivated purely by benevolence, they would seem to be unconcerned about being paternalistic toward one another. Of course, people do not like having their will ignored or thwarted, but a utilitarian will be obliged to take that sort of annoyance into account. When another's happiness is promoted by deceit or even by force, the perfect friends of that person will presumably feel free to resort to such means. But the deontologist will insist that "the end does not justify the means" even between perfect friends. Even perfect friends are obliged to respect each other's right to equal freedom.

---

9. From *An Enquiry Concerning the Principles of Morals* (1777).

Kant on Friendship

Kant himself offered his own theory of the best form of friendship in the following passage:

> In ordinary social intercourse and association we do not enter completely into the social relation. The greater part of our disposition is withheld; there is no immediate outpouring of all our feelings, dispositions and judgments. We voice only the judgments that seem advisable in the circumstances. A constraint, a mistrust of others, rests upon all of us, so that we withhold something, concealing our weaknesses to escape contempt, or even withholding our opinions. But if we can free ourselves of this constraint, if we can unburden our heart to another, we achieve complete communion. That this release may be achieved, each of us needs a friend, one in whom we can confide unreservedly, to whom we can disclose completely all our dispositions and judgments, from whom we can and need hide nothing, to whom we can communicate our whole self. . . . We all have a strong impulse to disclose ourselves, and enter wholly into fellowship.[10]

We need to fully *disclose* ourselves to another, to be heard and recognized. Kant goes on to say that this helps us to "correct our judgment," but it is clear from what he says here that in addition to this, we need the communion and fellowship that only come from actual communication with a trusted friend. Is this because we need to discover fully who we are, what we feel and want and think, and our own powers of introspection are relatively imperfect? Or is it that we need to see in our friend someone who accepts us and acknowledges our right to have feelings and opinions of our own, so that we come to believe, as we need to believe, that we are deserving of existing as a person? Since Kant does not explain his view, we can only speculate on why he attaches such importance to the need to reveal ourselves to a trusted friend.

FAMILY

What good are families? I take it to be obvious that the main purpose of families is to provide the nurturing that children need. But how to nurture, what should be its main direction, is a question worthy of clarification. This is the first question we will discuss. Second, who should govern in a family? In many families the father has made the rules that others, including the mother, must follow. But is the patriarchal family just? Finally, even if we think that our own families should not be patriarchal, what gives us the right to tell people of different cultures how their families should be? Among the many questions about the family that philosophers have discussed, these are the ones we will address.

---

10. From *Lectures on Ethics*, trans. Louis Infield (Indianapolis: Hackett, 1963).

The Goal of Independence

How to nurture children depends on what children need. For the specifics about nutrition, medical care, and the like, we should consult experts in the relevant scientific fields. Philosophers offer instead general visions of human need, and we have canvassed a number of these in our chapter on happiness. Without showing preference for any of these, we can still agree that children should have all of their needs met, including not only material ones but intellectual and spiritual ones as well. This point is worth mentioning since their material needs are so obvious and obviously important that it is easy to lose sight of the "higher" needs. Nevertheless, practically all parents agree that children should be educated. But does this just mean that they should acquire marketable skills? Or does it mean that children actually need a broad understanding of the world and are harmed without it? Again, it will be widely agreed that children must learn the right way to behave. But does this just mean that they should act like the people around them or that they come to care about such ideals as justice, freedom, and compassion for all? In the following excerpt, the nineteenth- to twentieth-century English philosopher Bertrand Russell summarizes his view on how parents (or other caregivers) should meet children's needs:

> The primitive root of the pleasure of parenthood is twofold. On the one hand there is the feeling of part of one's own body externalized, prolonging its life beyond the death of the rest of the body, and possibly in its turn externalizing part of itself in the same fashion, and so securing the immortality of the germ-plasm. On the other hand, there is an intimate bond of power and tenderness. The new creature is helpless and there is an impulse to supply its needs, an impulse which gratifies not only the parent's love toward the child, but also the parent's desire for power. So long as the infant is felt to be helpless, the affection which is bestowed upon it does not feel selfish, since it is in the nature of protection to a vulnerable portion of oneself. But from a very early age there comes to be a conflict between love of parental power and desire for the child's good, for, while power over the child is to a certain extent decreed by the nature of things, it is nevertheless desirable that the child should as soon as possible learn to be independent in as many ways as possible, which is unpleasant to the power impulse in a parent. . . . If you feed an infant who is already capable of feeding himself, you are putting love of power before the child's welfare, although it seems that you are only being kind in saving him the trouble. If you make him too vividly aware of dangers, you are probably actuated by a desire to keep him dependent upon you. If you give him demonstrative affection to which you expect a response, you are probably endeavoring to grapple him to you by means of his emotions. In a thousand ways, the possessive impulse of parents will lead them astray, unless they are very pure in heart. . . . But this demands on the part of the parent from the first a respect for the personality of the child—a respect which must be not merely a matter of principle, whether moral or intellectual, but

something deeply felt with almost mystical conviction to such a degree that possessiveness and oppression become utterly impossible.[11]

The main direction that nurturing should take, according to Russell, is toward the eventual *independence* of the children. Ideally, this would mean not only that they can earn a living for themselves (and thus secure their material needs) but that they can think for themselves and make their own plans. It would be difficult to find a philosopher who would disagree. For it is widely thought among them that humans differ from other animals in their ability to reason. We develop this ability by being able to form our own opinions and make our own plans. To make children dependent is to stunt their development as human beings. On the assumption that we need to become independent, dependency diminishes human happiness. It is not good *for* the individual children, and it will reduce the happiness in the world. For utilitarians, this point is enough to condemn it. And because the reduced happiness of children is certainly not deserved, it will be equally condemned by deontologists. There is something even more sinister about it according to deontologists, for domination is a clear-cut example of the injustice of denying equal freedom. This does not mean that parents do not have authority over children. But the deontologist will insist that the purpose of exercising this authority is always to promote the eventual freedom of the child. The ultimate purpose of nurturing children is to aid their development into independent adults. If Russell is right, this view will require a "respect for the personality" of the child that will check the parent's natural desire to exercise power.

Patriarchy

Who should govern the family? Organizations are democratic when everyone governs. Even if democracy is good for many other organizations, it is not practical for families, since children lack the competence to direct their lives. This leaves the parents (or other caregivers) to make the rules within the family. As we have already noted, patriarchy is traditional in many cultures and continues to exist in some today. Yet it is vehemently criticized by feminists. Why? Let us again see whether we can get some insight into an explanation from the ethical material we have at hand.

The case for patriarchy has often been based on the assumption that women are like children in lacking the competence necessary to make wise decisions within the family. This view was prevalent even in Western societies not long ago. We can get a sense of what this was like from the eighteenth-century English philosopher Mary Wollstonecraft:

> To account for, and excuse the tyranny of man, many ingenious arguments have been brought forward to prove, that the two sexes, in the acquirement of virtue, ought to aim at attaining a very different character. . . .

---

11. From *The Conquest of Happiness* (New York: Liveright, 1971).

> Women are told from their infancy, and taught by the example of their mothers, that a little knowledge of human weakness, justly termed cunning, softness of temper, outward obedience, and a scrupulous attention to a puerile kind of propriety, will obtain for them the protection of man; and should they be beautiful, every thing else is needless, for, at least, twenty years of their lives.
> How grossly do they insult us who thus advise us only to render ourselves gentle, domestic brutes! . . .
> Children, I grant, should be innocent; but when the epithet is applied to men, or women, it is but a civil term for weakness. . . .
> [A]ll the writers who have written on the subject of female education and manners . . . have contributed to render women more artificial, weak characters, than they would otherwise have been; and, consequently, more useless members of society. . . .
> Rousseau declares that a woman should never, for a moment, feel herself independent, that she should be governed by fear to exercise her natural cunning, and made a coquettish slave in order to render her a more alluring object of desire, a sweeter companion to man, whenever he chooses to relax himself. He carries the arguments, which he pretends to draw from the indications of nature, still further, and insinuates that truth and fortitude, the corner stones of all human virtue, should be cultivated with certain restrictions, because, with respect to the female character, obedience is the grand lesson which ought to be impressed with unrelenting rigour.
> What nonsense![12]

Wollstonecraft admitted that in her own day women appeared more frivolous than men, but she attributed this to their education. She hoped for a day when, with the same education, their equal capacity would be evident. That day has obviously arrived. Wollstonecraft claimed that the education of women in her day was due to the simple "tyranny of man." The domination of women is no better than the domination of children, and in some ways arguably worse. At least children with dominating parents can usually escape them in adulthood. Moreover, the injustice with women is compounded by the fact that the wife is another adult whom the husband claims to love.

Patriarchy in Other Societies. It is widely assumed among educated people today that patriarchy is wrong. If so, many societies even today stand condemned. But to make these cross-cultural moral judgments is something that itself arouses complaints. Who are we to say how others should live? Why should one society (such as our own) dictate how another should conduct its business?

This line of questioning will be found compelling to the social relativists discussed in Chapter Eight. If what is morally required is just to accept the ways of

---

12. From *A Vindication of the Rights of Woman*, ed. Carol H. Poston (New York: Norton, 1988).

your own society, then patriarchy would not be wrong *for* societies already patriarchal. Having discredited social relativism, we must be prepared to criticize how whole societies operate (including our own). A patriarchal society might be morally justified if *all* the individuals of the society in question were informed adults who *agreed* to a particular living arrangement. But very often what we find is that certain men within the society rely on local scriptures or traditions to justify patriarchy, and then they complain that outsiders have no right to meddle. In the following passage, the contemporary American philosopher Martha C. Nussbaum challenges the idea that a history of sexual discrimination within a whole group exempts them from moral criticism:

> [W]hat is to happen . . . with women who are not only suffering what ought to be called gross and systematic rights violations, but precisely on account of those deprivations (of political voice, mobility, assembly, education, often equal nutrition and health care) are unable to move their own community in the direction of change? If they are not able to work outside the home, they are not able to assemble, etc., it is much harder to move their own community, much less any other group. Should this subgroup within the nation even be thought of as "their" community, just because they are in it and are unable to leave? We think that the family is a type of community. Nonetheless, if a husband beats a wife, or tries to prevent her from voting or going out of the house, we do not hesitate to intervene — or if we do hesitate, we shouldn't. I see no reason why a tribal or religious group should have any more latitude legally than a family should in abridging the fundamental rights of adult citizens.[13]

Nussbaum is relying on the point, especially emphasized by the deontologists, that every *individual* has equal moral rights. It is not *groups* of people as such who have moral rights. (This is another example illustrating the danger of taking too literally the idea that societies are "artificial persons.") If a majority or powerful minority within a group claims that in "their group" it is sanctioned by tradition to deny women equal moral rights, then the deontologist condemns this claim as *unjust*. It is simply another example of some individuals denying the equal freedom of others.

SCHOOLS, CHURCHES, AND THE MEDIA

The last kind of organization we examine in this chapter has education itself as its sole or main purpose. Schools are clear examples. But churches also count since there is not only intellectual education but spiritual education as well. In our technologically advanced society, the media (newspapers, magazines, radio, and television) have become extremely influential in conveying information, so they should be examined in assessing how well our society is being educated.

13. From "Religion and Women's Human Rights," *Criterion* 36 (Winter 1997).

We will ask three questions. First, what should be the purpose of schools? We say, "To educate," but what should this goal mean? By getting clear about this point, you are better able to evaluate whether a particular school is good, and you make a better educator if you take on the role. Second, churches have come to serve many different purposes. But is there some important purpose they serve best, so that churches should exist even in scientifically advanced societies? Reflecting on this question should help in choosing which church to attend or whether to attend at all. Finally, do media news programs serve genuinely to educate or to propagandize? Getting this issue right can help you to avoid being manipulated.

School Education

All schools will say their purpose is to educate. But are different schools really doing different things by "educating"? Do some schools in fact have aims that are harmful even if they do not admit it or see this themselves? As we saw in discussing families, Bertrand Russell gave a diagnosis of how parents can unwittingly go astray in nurturing their children. In the following passage, he gives a similar diagnosis of how schools may serve the wrong end:

> The prevention of free inquiry is unavoidable so long as the purpose of education is to produce belief rather than thought, to compel the young to hold positive opinions on doubtful matters rather than to let them see the doubtfulness and be encouraged to independence of mind. Education ought to foster the wish for truth, not the conviction that some particular creed is the truth. But it is creeds that hold men together in fighting organizations: Churches, States, political parties. It is intensity of belief in a creed that produces efficacy in fighting: victory comes to those who feel the strongest certainty about matters on which doubt is the only rational attitude. To produce this intensity of belief and efficiency in fighting, the child's nature is warped, and its free outlook is cramped, by cultivating inhibitions as a check to the growth of new ideas. In those whose minds are not very active the result is the omnipotence of prejudice; while the few whose thought cannot be wholly killed become cynical, intellectually hopeless, destructively critical, able to make all that is living seem foolish, unable themselves to supply the creative impulses which they destroy in others. . . .
>
> Certain mental habits are commonly instilled by those who are engaged in educating: obedience and discipline, ruthlessness in the struggle for worldly success, contempt toward opposing groups, and an unquestioning credulity, a passive acceptance of the teacher's wisdom. All these habits are against life. Instead of obedience and discipline, we ought to aim at preserving independence and impulse. Instead of ruthlessness, education should try to develop justice in thought. Instead of contempt, it ought to instill reverence, and the attempt at understanding; towards the opinions of others it ought to produce, not necessarily acquiescence, but only such opposition as is combined with imaginative apprehension and a clear realization of the grounds for opposition. Instead of credulity, the object should be to stimulate constructive doubt, the love of mental adventure, the sense

of worlds to conquer by enterprise and boldness in thought. Contentment with the status quo, and subordination of the individual pupil to political aims, owning to indifference to the things of the mind, are the immediate causes of these evils; but beneath these causes there is one more fundamental, the fact that education is treated as a means of acquiring power over the pupil, not as a means of nourishing his own growth. It is in this that lack of reverence shows itself; and it is only by more reverence that a fundamental reform can be effected.[14]

Russell is wary of saying that true education aims at knowledge and understanding, since he fears that this is too easily interpreted by educators as an excuse for indoctrinating children with certain beliefs. So instead he urges that the aim be more for developing children's ability to think for themselves. Recall that this ability is a main part of the independence that he thought parents should aim for in their nurturing. In the case of parents, this is threatened by a prolonged desire to exercise power. Now the concern is that educators use children as tools for their own political ends. Notice that the "educators" he has in mind are not simply schoolteachers, since those he cites represent churches, states, and political parties. Many people influence the teaching of the young, and many of these see this as an opportunity to inculcate certain creeds they regard as important.

What is wrong with that? Russell claims "the child's nature is warped," since he believes that humans flourish only when they think freely, without fear of arriving at forbidden beliefs. It is in this way that the wrong kind of "education" is bad *for* them. Because utilitarians are concerned above all to maximize happiness, they will lodge *moral* criticism against such indoctrination. Deontologists would complain especially of the injustice of *using* children as tools to serve one's own political agenda. Russell's view of human nature is one we associated with idealism, because it emphasizes the importance of satisfying "higher" needs. From this perspective, it becomes especially clear how education can be misdirected to the detriment of both the individuals who receive it and the world at large.

Churches and Spiritual Education

Let us turn now to the question of how churches should be. What valuable purpose or purposes do churches serve? What we find in fact is that many different purposes are served by different churches. Some people organize to learn the teachings of a certain religion and renew their commitment to the way of life it recommends. Others meet to explore their own religious beliefs and ways of developing them, even by assimilating the teachings of other religions. Some churches exist mainly for creating and sustaining a community of friends, who share a commitment to help each other in times of need. Of course, one church can serve several such purposes. There is, however, no reason in advance to suppose that the activities of a church are above criticism. Some churches convey the message that those not

---

14. From *Principles of Social Reconstruction* (London: Unwin, 1916).

of the faith are lesser in the eyes of the Lord. Some demand agreement with a definite set of beliefs at the expense of genuine concern with truth and free thinking. Some promote a fearful outlook on the world that diminishes joy and makes people bitter and mean. Some claim to have an understanding of the world and its sources of good fortune that is utterly devoid of justification. To such observations, it may be said that *any* kind of organization has its share of bad examples.

So let us ask about the ideal. Is there any purpose that is served by the best churches and best served by them? When we envisage the best society, now that we have vast scientific knowledge, will we find a place for churches?

There is one form of education that churches especially claim to offer, and that is spiritual education. In keeping with Plato's tripartite division of the soul, I defined this type of education as developing the desire to do what is right, or we might say, the love of what is good. This may seem a bad definition for the "spirituality" that we associate with religion. But is it? It would be if ethical hedonism were true. For if what is good is what is good for oneself, who needs "inspiration" to be selfish? From our humanistic perspective, however, we acknowledge that what is "just plain" good is not the same as what is good for oneself (though it need not conflict with it, either). It is possible, however, to acknowledge *intellectually* what is good without really having a *passion* for it. Inspiration, as we have defined it, is whatever creates this passion. Since we are assuming that ethical hedonism is false, this means that inspiration creates a passion that transcends concern for oneself. And it is arguable that this *is* the essence of religious spirituality. (Spiritual people are surely not simply those who are interested in getting themselves into heaven, for this is merely a selfish concern.)

As we saw in the last chapter, Hume believed that morality arose from such a passion. The moral person looks at things objectively and is aroused by a feeling of sympathy for the suffering of humanity. Deontologists will admit no less the value of an impersonal moral passion, as the passion for justice would be. Russell (who was much influenced by Hume's ethics) eloquently describes this sort of passion as follows:

> It is possible to feel the same interest in the joys and sorrows of others as in our own, to love and hate independently of all relation to ourselves, to care about the destiny of man and the development of the universe without a thought that we are personally involved. Reverence and worship, the sense of an obligation to mankind, the feeling of imperativeness and acting under orders which traditional religion has interpreted as Divine inspiration, all belong to the life of the spirit. And deeper than all of these lies the sense of a mystery half-revealed, of a hidden wisdom and glory, of a transfiguring vision in which common things lose their solid importance and become a thin veil behind which the ultimate truth of the world is dimly seen. It is such feelings that are the source of religion, and if they were to die most of what is best would vanish out of life.[15]

---

15. From *Principles of Social Reconstruction*.

Here the connection is made between moral passion and religious feeling, and with it, the suggestion of how churches might best offer something vitally important. There is certainly no hope that science can offer spiritual education. As we saw in Part One, science offers understanding of the world as we actually find it. While philosophy aims for a different kind of understanding, it appears that one can fully understand what is good and not yet care about it (though this view was famously challenged by Socrates). Many churches in the past (and some still today) have claimed to have exclusive knowledge of the supernatural. But that any really does is doubtful, in light of the disagreement among them and the difficulty of establishing nonempirical claims about reality that we witnessed in Part Two. Perhaps, then, what the best churches are best at offering is *spiritual* education. Churches that do play a vital role in the society at large.

THE MEDIA

In our technologically developed society, intellectual and spiritual development have become increasingly influenced by the media. American children, for example, watch an astonishing amount of television (around twenty-five hours per week by some estimates) in which their views of the world are being formed and their tastes are being influenced, especially by carefully designed advertising. Is this influence good for them? What the actual effects are is a matter for social scientists to determine. But the sorts of worries that are expressed can be understood in ethical terms. Does that much passive enjoyment make children relatively passive, less likely to think for themselves or to be creative in shaping their own lives? Are certain topics silently screened out under the influence of owners and advertisers so that their view of the world becomes incomplete and skewed? Are appetites for excessive consumption created at the expense of other needs, so that they become what the German sociologist Max Weber called "bred consumers"?

Similar questions can be raised about other media, such as newspapers and radio. If the answers to any or all of these questions is yes, then an effect of the medium in question is to *reduce freedom*. Making people passive sets them up for manipulation. And because freedom is the general capacity to choose effectively, an incomplete or skewed "map of the world" also diminishes one's freedom. Finally, to have your appetites created for things you do not really need is to influence you to act against your own, best interests.

In countries in which the media are directly controlled by the government, there is little hope in getting the sort of information citizens need to avoid being manipulated by government propaganda. To get a view of how the media *can* operate against our interests with a supposedly "free press," consider these observations by Noam Chomsky, a contemporary American linguist:

> In capitalist democracies there is a certain tension with regard to the locus of power. In a democracy the people rule, in principle. But decision-making

power over central issues of life resides in private hands, with large-scale effects throughout the social order. One way to resolve the tension would be to extend the democratic system to investment, the organization of work, and so on. That would constitute a major social revolution, which, in my view at least, would consummate the political revolutions of an earlier era and realize some of the libertarian principles on which they were partly based. Or the tension could be resolved, and sometimes is, by forcefully eliminating public interference with state and private power. In the advanced industrial societies the problem is typically approached by a variety of measures to deprive democratic political structures of substantive content, while leaving them formally intact. A large part of this task is assumed by ideological institutions that channel thought and attitudes within acceptable bounds, deflecting any potential challenge to established privilege and authority before it can take form and gather strength. The enterprise has many facets and agents . . . [including] . . . thought control, as conducted through the agency of national media and related elements of the elite intellectual culture.

There is, in my opinion, much too little inquiry into these matters. My personal feeling is that citizens of the democratic societies should undertake a course of intellectual self-defense to protect themselves from manipulation and control, and to lay a basis for more meaningful democracy.[16]

Chomsky has an extremely cynical view of our media (too cynical, in many people's opinion). But his thesis is worth considering, and you are not likely to hear it from the media themselves! Democratic countries have the *potential* for being guided by all the citizens together. But suppose that *in fact* the course is really being set mainly by a powerful few, such as the heads of government and large corporations. Suppose further that those who hold the reins of power do not wish to share it. (Whether and to what extent these suppositions are true are empirical questions investigated especially by social scientists.) Then the problem arises for them as to how to continue to hoard the power when democracy provides the rest of the population the means for demanding their share. Chomsky's thesis is that they use thought control, exerted mainly through the media. He does not suppose that this occurs with deliberation behind closed doors. Rather, he believes, those in power use their influence in subtle ways to ensure that only the views they like get heard. He points out, for example, that since media are corporations selling audiences to other corporations, they are not likely to air criticism of corporate power or consumer culture. In this way, they function much like media in countries where governments blatantly control the news. The general point is simply that it makes sense to question the source. And because *every* source is likely to represent *some* bias, we should deliberately seek information from a variety of sources, including especially those not being promoted by the people already in power.

---

16. From *Necessary Illusions: Thought Control in Democratic Societies* (Boston: South End Press, 1989).

CONCLUSION

Societies are formed when the members adopt special functions by which they cooperate for common purposes. Human societies are formed partly by choice and can thus be changed by conceptions of how things ought be. Philosophers have differed in their enthusiasm for society in general. Our treatment of ethics in Part Three centered on two main questions: how to be happy and what to do. Theories in responses to these can be used to evaluate human societies. Theories of happiness tell us whether a particular society is good *for* certain individuals. Moral theories tell us how people within a society ought to *behave*. They also tell us how the *world* should be, what we should be trying to achieve in forming societies in the first place. In keeping with the history of modern ethics, we favor the moral theories of utilitarianism and deontology in making moral assessments. Though similar in their humanistic outlook, they differ still in their attitude toward justice.

Many ethical questions can be raised about what makes a friendship, a family, or an educational institution good. The few we raised for each of these were picked mainly for their evident interest and importance. Our discussions were also meant to illustrate how ethics is applicable to social philosophy. It is not surprising that ethics has so much to say about society, since so much of our lives are spent in the company of others. By studying different social organizations, we appreciate how society serves different human needs. This chapter has focused especially on the need for seeking out companionship and for developing into independent adults, who think for themselves and care for what is good. We have thus focused so far mainly on how society serves our "higher" needs. The next two chapters examine social organizations that serve our more basic needs of subsistence and protection.

STUDY QUESTIONS

1. How are human societies like and unlike those of other animals?
2. Why do Taoists want society to be minimized?
3. How, according to Hegel, can the restrictions of society make you free?
4. What kind of friends do we need and why do we need them? Explain the answers of both Aristotle and Kant.
5. Is there a concern for justice in perfect friendships? Contrast the answers of utilitarians and deontologists.
6. What, according to Russell, does it take for a parent not to become possessive and oppressive?
7. According to Russell, why should education of the young aim more for *thought* than *belief*? Why has it often not done so?
8. How can churches offer spiritual guidance?
9. How does Nussbaum defend criticizing groups that traditionally deny women's rights?
10. How, according to Chomsky, are the major media not really "free"?

CHAPTER
ELEVEN
Economic Justice and Prosperity

WHAT MAKES AN ECONOMY good? We will need to clarify what an economy is before we address this question. But we are all familiar with economic activities, including farming and ranching; manufacturing goods such as clothes, buildings, vehicles and other tools; and providing services such as physical protection, medical care, education, and entertainment. When we stand back and compare the economic activities of whole societies, we find certain differences. Some societies are far more productive than others. Some produce a greater variety of goods and services. There are also differences in what is produced. Societies differ, for example, in whether they devote their resources mainly to waging war or to alleviating poverty. There are also differences in who decides what to produce and who will get it. In the Soviet Union, for example, approximately twenty people made such decisions for a nation of 350 million. Differences persist, too, in how wealth is distributed. In many countries, the rich and poor are clearly defined, while in others the differences in wealth are not so great.

The *science* of economics is the empirical study of the actual conditions of economies and the causes and effects of these conditions. Economic *philosophy*, a branch of social philosophy, has been mainly an extension of ethics, concerned with ethically *evaluating* economies.

THE NATURE OF ECONOMIES

Before we turn to our ethical questions, let us examine the nature of economies in general. What *is* an **economy**? As a social organization, an economy consists of people somehow working together by adopting different roles. Any economy involves both producers and consumers. The produce of an economy consists of both goods and services. In a developed economy, the producers will occupy many different roles depending on what they produce. Thus, for example, farmers, clothiers, and builders produce goods, while police officers, teachers, and medical personnel provide services. The *purpose* of any economy is to produce goods and services and distribute these to consumers.

Besides the people who produce and consume, economies also contain a stock of **capital**. Not all goods are consumed. When our human ancestors began fashioning tools hundreds of thousands of years ago, they produced goods that were not to be consumed but to be used in future production. When an edge was put on a stone, labor was spent in producing a good that would not be consumed. It would instead increase the productivity of the human who used it. With a sharp stone in hand, a human could cut through hide instead of laboriously chewing through it. Capital is property used to enhance the productivity of human labor. Not all property is capital; a shirt or house is (typically) not used as a tool of production. But factories, trucks, and computers are.

Not all capital is artificially produced. When land, minerals, oil, and water are used in production, they count as **natural capital**. Together the capital of an economy (both natural and artificial) comprises its "capital stock," and generally an increase in capital stock means an increase in worker productivity.

THE VALUE OF ECONOMIES

What good are economies? Economies are social organizations and so do not exist when individuals forage for themselves. If nature gave us what we wanted with no effort on our part, there would be no need for economic organization. As it happens, however, we must transform nature to get what we want.

The members of a society can greatly increase their collective productivity by dividing their efforts into specialized tasks. In the earliest agricultural societies, for example, some members (typically the priests) specialized in retaining the knowledge of agricultural technique and in directing the various farming activities in light of this knowledge. Others planted and harvested. Others moved earth to irrigate the fields. Others fashioned the tools. By working together, they satisfied their material need for food. Eventually they improved their techniques so that a smaller portion of the population was required to produce food, allowing others to create new kinds of goods and services. Economic growth meant an increase in the satisfaction of human needs and thus of human happiness.

Yet even in many of these earliest economies, economic production led to disaster. Soil was depleted of nutrients; the available wood was used up; the game disappeared through hunting. Today the extent of environmental destruction is far greater, owing to a much larger human population equipped with far more powerful technology. Hilary French of the Worldwatch Institute gives an indication of the purely economic value of preserving the environment:

Human beings remain fundamentally dependent on the natural world. One shortcoming of conventional economics is its failure to account for the critical services provided by natural ecosystems such as forests, wetlands, coral reefs, rivers, and seas. In 1997, a team of 13 ecologists, economists, and geographers published a path-breaking article that puts a price tag on the value of a range of functions provided by these ecosystems. The study covered a broad array of services, including genetic resources, flood control, pollination, water supply, and erosion control. The authors arrived at the stunning conclusion that the economic value of "nature's services" adds up to some $33 trillion each year—almost as much as the entire gross world product.

Despite their value to humankind, ecosystems are being degraded at an unparalleled rate as a result of human activity. One benchmark of the losses is the rapid rate at which species are being extinguished. Biologists warn that as many as one fifth of all plant and animal species could disappear within the next 30 years. Another measure of ecological health is the extent to which humans have transformed ecosystems from their natural state into crop land, pasture, plantations, human settlements, and other uses. Many countries have already seen more than half their land area undergo this conversion, including Argentina, Australia, India, Mexico, South Africa, and Spain.[1]

Not many centuries ago, so much less economic activity was taking place that it seemed impossible to exhaust a natural resource. Today we see the rainforests rapidly diminishing, the fish of the sea dwindling, desert area increasing, and aquifers and topsoil gradually becoming depleted. Then there is the problem of waste. In the past, nature consumed our waste and eventually converted it to useful materials. Today we burden nature beyond what it can handle. The atmosphere now contains 25 percent more carbon dioxide, raising the Earth's temperature and threatening to swamp vast areas of coastal land in the near future. Enormous amounts of harmful chemicals are dumped into the air, ground, and waters, eventually finding their way into our food, drinking water, and lungs. Other forms of pollution include increased noise and decreased visual beauty.

Economic activity sometimes has disastrous social effects. Countries that prepare for war tend to start them. Even when the product is benign, the process may be vicious. Beef and fancy fruits are not guns and bombs, but their production often requires the forceful expulsion of native people from their land. In the twentieth century, such displaced people often destroyed forest to grow food, and some starved while a few in their country became rich exporting "cash crops."

Our material needs, for food, clothing, shelter, and protection, are the most basic. Nothing else appears important while these needs go unmet. To secure these most fully and reliably, we form economies. But we also need the resources of nature for meeting these same material needs. And we need the freedom of not being invaded by others. The best economies are productive in supplying the goods and

---

1. From *Vanishing Borders: Protecting the Planet in the Age of Globalization* (New York: Norton, 2000).

services we need and want. But they are also not destructive of the resources and conditions that must exist to satisfy these same needs and desires.

THE VALUE OF ECONOMIC GROWTH

How much of our lives should be spent on economic production? In many of the earliest agricultural societies, people had little choice but to work most of the day to avoid starvation. But the development of technology has made it possible for societies today to grow all the food they can use by employing only a very small portion of the population. Of course, there are other things we want that require further economic production. But at what point have we gone far enough? At what point is economic activity yielding products less important than what we are losing by reducing our free time? This question is addressed in the following passage by the nineteenth-century English philosopher John Stuart Mill:

> I am not charmed with the ideal of life held out by those who think that the normal state of human beings is that of struggling to get on; that the trampling, crushing, elbowing, and treading on each other's heels, which form the existing type of social life, are the most desirable lot of human kind . . . the best state for human nature is that in which, while no one is poor, no one desires to be richer, nor has any fear of being thrust back, by the efforts of others to push themselves forward. . . . It is only in the backward countries of the world that increased production is still an important object: in those most advanced, what is economically needed is a better distribution, of which one indispensable means is a stricter restraint on population. . . . It is scarcely necessary to remark that a stationary condition of capital and population implies no stationary state of human improvement. There would be as much scope as ever for all kinds of mental culture, and moral and social progress; as much room for improving the Art of Living, and much more likelihood of its being improved, when minds ceased to be engrossed by the art of getting on. Even the industrial arts might be as earnestly and successfully cultivated, with this sole difference, that instead of serving no purpose but the increase in wealth, industrial improvements would produce their legitimate effect, that of abridging labor. Hitherto it is questionable if all the mechanical inventions yet made have lightened the day's toil of any human being. They have enabled the greater population to live the same life of drudgery and imprisonment, and an increased number of manufacturers and others to make fortunes.[2]

Mill was a utilitarian. (In fact, he gave the position its name.) He held what we have called an "idealistic" conception of happiness, which emphasizes the importance of satisfying our "higher" needs. The ultimate purpose of an economy, ac-

---

2. From *Principles of Political Economy* (New York: Appleton, 1984).

cording to him, is to secure our material needs to release time for mental cultivation and the improvement of society. The ideal economy would secure these needs with the minimum of human time and labor. This would maximize the time we could spend on nurturing our children, on enjoying art, on developing our understanding of the world, and on deepening our relationships with family and friends.

The idea that we should bend our efforts toward ever greater economic production is widely espoused in our society today. Mill argued against it on utilitarian grounds. In the happiest world, economic production is necessary but limited so that time for mental and social activities can be maximized. This is why we should abandon the goal of continual economic growth. As we will see later, however, some people today benefit very much by a social commitment to continual growth. Even if such growth is not good, it is still good *for them*.

CAPITALISM AND SOCIALISM

Who owns the capital? In economic philosophy, this is a *moral*, not a legal, question. The question of who has *legal* rights to capital is an empirical question about what protections are actually guaranteed by a particular government. Legal rights may conflict with moral rights. In a slave economy, the slaves are capital, and if the government permits slavery, the slaveowners have a legal right to their slaves. But since the slaves presumably have a moral right to their own bodies and lives, the legal right denies their moral rights. When we ask, "Who owns the capital?" we want to know how the capital *ought* to be possessed.

Capitalism and **socialism** are kinds of economies that differ in how the capital is owned. An economy is *capitalistic* when its capital is *privately* owned. In a *socialist* economy, the capital is *collectively* owned. A "capitalist," in economic philosophy, is someone who *advocates* the private ownership of capital. In answer to the question of who owns the capital, the capitalist will say that one portion belongs to this person or group, and another portion is owned by another person or group. A socialist will say that the capital is commonly owned: It is "ours." In real life, the law typically provides for a mixture of both. The public school system, the park system, and the military all have capital (buildings, land, equipment) that are commonly owned. The capital possessed by small business people and large corporations is privately owned. In real life, few people would advocate either a purely capitalistic or a purely socialistic economy. But as we will see, there are a variety of reasons why many philosophers have leaned in one direction or the other.

DISTRIBUTIVE JUSTICE

Economic power is the power to influence the economy, which means the power to decide what will be produced or how the product will be distributed. Economic power is, therefore, a good *for* the individual who has it. But it is not obvious that such goods should be shared equally, especially from a deontological perspective, which emphasizes the importance of what people deserve. Aristotle argues for inequalities of such goods in the following:

> For if the people involved are not equal, they will not [justly] receive equal shares; indeed, whenever equals receive unequal shares, or unequals equal shares, in a distribution, that is the source of quarrels and accusations.
> This is also clear from considering what fits a person's worth. For everyone agrees that what is just in distributions must fit some sort of worth, but what they call worth is not the same.[3]

Distributive justice is what justice requires in the distribution of benefits and burdens within a society. Distributive injustices occur when people receive benefits (such as money) without deserving them or when they bear more than their share of the burden (such as doing all the work). What Aristotle claims is that people can differ in such a way that an equal distribution of burdens or benefits is *unjust*. To deontologists, there are two ways in which people differ on that matter. Some people *deserve* more goods than others, perhaps by working more, producing more, or producing something of great value. Some people are *entitled* to more, because of what they have received in trades and from gifts.

DEONTOLOGICAL CAPITALISM

Capitalism allows for large inequalities in the distribution of economic power. In capitalism, the capital is privately owned, and some people can have much more than others. This means that they have more say in what will be produced in the economy, because they decide how their capital will be used. Those with more capital also receive a larger share of the goods and services produced in the economy. This is because the owners of capital essentially rent it to workers whose productivity is thereby increased. If you have spent your own labor putting an edge on a stone, you might lend it to someone who has not. You *rent* it if you get something in return. The person who uses it to skin an animal he has killed might agree to giving you some of the meat in exchange for saving himself the effort of using his teeth. If you have fashioned many such stones, you can rent them to many hunters, in which case you get a large amount of meat.

A crucial question for capitalists to answer is how individuals can come to acquire rights to capital. According to humanism, since all people are moral equals, they start off with equal rights, whatever these are. Capitalism allows that they may become unequal in their rights to control and reap the rewards of the capital stock. So, how do they get these rights?

---

3. From *Nicomachean Ethics*, trans. Terence Irwin (Indianapolis, IN: Hackett, 1985).

LOCKE'S THEORY OF PROPERTY

The obvious answer is that people come to own capital that they themselves have created. If you are the one who has gone to the effort to put the edge on the stone, why in the world should what you have produced all by yourself suddenly become common property? Of course, if you decide to give it to your community, then it becomes common property. But this, the capitalist argues, is just because it was yours alone to give in the first place. This position was developed most thoroughly by John Locke. Because capitalists have relied heavily on his theory, I quote it at some length:

> [I]t is very clear, that God, as king David says, Psalm. cxv. 16. has given the earth to the children of men; given it to mankind in common. But this being supposed, it seems to some a very great difficulty, how any one should ever come to have a property in any thing. . . . I shall endeavour to shew, how men might come to have a property in several parts of that which God gave to mankind in common, and that without any express compact of all the commoners.
>
> . . . The earth, and all that is therein, is given to men for the support and comfort of their being. And tho' all the fruits it naturally produces, and beasts it feeds, belong to mankind in common, as they are produced by the spontaneous hand of nature; and no body has originally a private dominion, exclusive of the rest of mankind, in any of them, as they are thus in their natural state: yet being given for the use of men, there must of necessity be a means to appropriate them some way or other, before they can be of any use, or at all beneficial to any particular man. The fruit, or venison, which nourishes the wild Indian, who knows no enclosure, and is still a tenant in common, must be his, and so his, i.e. a part of him, that another can no longer have any right to it, before it can do him any good for the support of his life.
>
> Though the earth, and all inferior creatures, be common to all men, yet every man has a property in his own person: this no body has any right to but himself. The labour of his body, and the work of his hands, we may say, are properly his. Whatsoever then he removes out of the state that nature hath provided, and left it in, he hath mixed his labour with, and joined to it something that is his own, and thereby makes it his property. It being by him removed from the common state nature hath placed it in, it hath by this labour something annexed to it, that excludes the common right of other men: for this labour being the unquestionable property of the labourer, no man but he can have a right to what that is once joined to, at least where there is enough, and as good, left in common for others. . . .
>
> It will perhaps be objected to this, that if gathering the acorns, or other fruits of the earth, &c. makes a right to them, then any one may ingross as much as he will. To which I answer, Not so. The same law of nature, that does by this means give us property, does also bound that property

too. God has given us all things richly, 1 Tim. vi. 12. is the voice of reason confirmed by inspiration. But how far has he given it us? To enjoy. As much as any one can make use of to any advantage of life before it spoils, so much he may by his Labour fix a property in: whatever is beyond this, is more than his share, and belongs to others. Nothing was made by God for man to spoil or destroy. And thus, considering the plenty of natural provisions there was a long time in the world, and the few spenders; and to how small a part of that provision the industry of one man could extend itself, and ingross it to the prejudice of others; especially keeping within the bounds, set by reason, of what might serve for his use; there could be then little room for quarrels or contentions about property so established.

But the chief matter of property being now not the fruits of the earth, and the beasts that subsist on it, but the earth itself; as that which takes in and carries with it all the rest; I think it is plain, that property in that too is acquired as the former. As much land as a man tills, plants, improves, cultivates, and can use the product of, so much is his property. . . .

Nor was this appropriation of any parcel of land, by improving it, any prejudice to any other man, since there was still enough, and as good left; and more than the yet unprovided could use. So that, in effect, there was never the less left for others because of his enclosure for himself: for he that leaves as much as another can make use of, does as good as take nothing at all. No body could think himself injured by the drinking of another man, though he took a good draught, who had a whole river of the same water left him to quench his thirst: and the case of land and water, where there is enough of both, is perfectly the same.[4]

Locke says repeatedly that natural things, including portions of land, are *originally* common property. But property is useful only if individuals have exclusive control of it. For land to be useful to anyone, a person must have her own portion of it. How do individuals gain a right to a certain portion of land or other natural object, when originally it is common property? Locke's answer is that they "mix their labor" with it. If you are the one who put the edge on the stone, the tool that results is a "mixture" of the natural stone and your own labor. Locke says that each person owns his own labor. Since the labor that the tool embodies is yours, the tool itself is yours. Since the tool consists in part of the stone, which is a natural object, you have come to own by yourself a portion of nature. By tilling the soil to make a vegetable garden, you come to own the land. By building a house from trees and mud, you come to own these natural materials themselves.

A Deontological Defense of Locke's Theory

Locke's theory of property can be defended by deontology. More than utilitarianism, deontology emphasizes individual rights. Your most fundamental right is to your own freedom. So long as you do not interfere with others' equal rights to be

---

4. From *The Second Treatise of Civil Government* (1690), Chapter 5.

free, you have a right to direct your energy as you please. This means that you *morally* own your own energy. If anyone else, including God or society, owned your labor, you would be their slave.

Locke's theory allows great differences in property ownership to develop. First, some people work harder than others and so mix more of their labor with more of nature. Thus, they come to have more of nature despite the fact that nature was at first commonly owned. Second, once they own a portion of nature they can give it away or trade it for something else they want. Through such exchanges, a person can come to own more of nature than the part with which he mixed his own labor. The contemporary American philosopher Robert Nozick defends inequalities in wealth that result in these various ways:

> In a free society, diverse persons control different resources, and new holdings arise out of the voluntary exchanges and actions of persons. . . . The total result is the product of many individual decisions which the different individuals involved are entitled to make. . . .
> Whatever arises from a just situation by just steps is itself just.[5]

Most important for the defense of capitalism is that the theory provides for private ownership of capital. The "wild Indian" in Locke's example comes to own the deer he kills because it was his effort alone that made the meat available. The deer, however, is not capital since it is consumed. But if you make a vegetable garden by yourself, the land itself that you thereby acquire is capital, since it is productive property. Also, because you own the land that you made into a garden, you own its product, the vegetables themselves. Since these are yours, you may consume them or trade them for things you want more. Or you may rent your land to someone else, in which case you temporarily give up your right to use it in exchange for something they give you.

Locke's Proviso

If individuals can acquire parts of nature and increase what they own through more work and through voluntary exchanges and gifts, is there no limit to how much of nature a person can own? Locke makes it crystal clear that there is a limit. He holds that portions of nature can be acquired by individuals where there "was still enough, and as good left," for others. We will call this important qualification "**the proviso.**" You can acquire land, for example, only if you leave enough for others to do the same and what you leave is as good as what you acquire. Not only can you not acquire so much that others cannot acquire the same amount, but you cannot acquire a uniquely valuable portion of land, such as the land that has the only spring of water or the most beautiful mountain.

---

5. From *Anarchy, State, and Utopia* (New York: Basic Books and Blackwell, 1974).

When Locke says that you cannot acquire portions of nature when the proviso is violated, he means that to do so is an *injustice*. It is no better than simply *stealing* from others what is *theirs*. In fact, it really *is* stealing. This becomes clear when you see how crucial the proviso is to the defense of his theory. To defend his theory, Locke wants to eliminate "room for quarrels or contentions about property so established." He argues that "he that leaves as much as another can make use of, does as good as take nothing at all." When the proviso is respected, the acquisition of natural property reduces no one else's freedom. If you leave "enough, and as good" for others, as far as they are concerned, it is as if you did not acquire property at all. Your acquisition of property does not diminish their opportunity to acquire natural property themselves. But if you violate the proviso, your acquisition of property diminishes the opportunity of others to do the same. The others have "room for quarrels or contentions" because you have used your freedom (exercised choice) in such a way that prevents others doing the same. For deontologists, this is the essence of injustice.

The upshot is that Locke's theory of property disallows the continual accumulation of limited natural resources. The world's human population is now about six billion, and it is expected to increase another 50 percent this century. In Locke's day, it was about 10 percent of what it is now. One could look to the vast frontiers and see virtually unlimited land and other natural resources that could not be monopolized by any number of people who acquired only that with which they had actually mixed their labor. As Locke said, "considering the plenty of natural provisions there was a long time in the world, and the few spenders; and to how small a part of that provision the industry of one man could extend itself," natural resources such as land seemed practically inexhaustible. That land is no longer unlimited and free for the taking is plain to anyone today who pays a mortgage.

Locke's proviso condemns the ownership of natural resources when this diminishes the opportunity of others to acquire them. This means that when enough of the land, water, minerals, and oil have been claimed, individual ownership becomes unjust. And this outcome means that differences in wealth that are created by such ownership are also unjust. Nozick, a distinguished capitalist, admits that if this reasoning is right, certain inequalities in wealth would have to be eliminated, including those based on "untransformed raw materials," including especially rental income "representing the unimproved value of the land, and the price of raw material in situ." This concession may be very great in practice. As Bertrand Russell notes, "Much that appears as the power of [artificial] capital is really the power of the landowner."[6] If this is right, much of the enormous differences in wealth that exist today are due to injustice.

Locke's proviso does not, however, show that capitalism as such is wrong. It shows only that there are limitations in what capital can be privately owned.

---

6. Bertrand Russell, *Principles of Social Reconstruction* (London: Unwin, 1916).

Locke's theory still allows the private accumulation of property, including capital, so long as this does not interfere with the equal freedom of others to do the same.

UTILITARIAN CAPITALISM

Capitalists also seek support from utilitarianism. They claim that capitalism helps to make the world a happier place. The main utilitarian argument in favor of capitalism comes from the eighteenth-century Scottish philosopher Adam Smith. What Smith argued for was the virtue of a **market economy.** In such an economy, individuals (or groups of them) own what they produce. The person who kills the deer produces an available supply of meat, and in a market economy that person alone owns this product. If individuals produce more than they consume, they own goods that they may "take to market" to trade for goods that others have produced. In the following passage, Smith describes how market economies naturally arise in human societies:

> In almost every other race of animals each individual, when it is grown up to maturity, is entirely independent, and in its natural state has occasion for the assistance of no other living creature. But man has almost constant occasion for the help of his brethren, and it is in vain for him to expect it from their benevolence only. He will be more likely to prevail if he can interest their self-love in his favor, and shew him that it is for their own advantage to do for him what he requires of them. Whoever offers to another a bargain of any kind, proposes to do this: Give me that which I want, and you shall have this which you want, is the meaning of every such offer; and it is in this manner that we obtain from one another the far greater part of those goods which we stand in need of.
> It is not from the benevolence of the butcher, the brewer, or the baker, that we expect our dinner, but from their regard to their own interest. . . .
> As it is by treaty, by barter, and by purchase, that we obtain from one another the greater part of those mutual good offices which we stand in need of, so it is this same trucking disposition which originally gives occasion to the division of labor. In a tribe of hunters or shepherds a particular person makes bows and arrows, for example, with more readiness and dexterity than any other. He frequently exchanges them for cattle or for venison with his companions; and he finds at last that he can in this manner get more cattle and venison, than if he himself went to the field to catch them. From a regard to his own interest, therefore, the making of bows and arrows grows to be his chief business, and he becomes a sort of armourer. Another excels in making the frames and covers of their little huts or movable houses. He is accustomed to be of use in this way to his neighbors, who reward him in the same manner with cattle and with venison, till at last he finds it in his interest to dedicate himself entirely to this employment, and to become a sort of house-carpenter. In the same manner a third becomes a smith or

a brazer; a fourth a tanner or dresser of hides and skins, the principal part of the clothing of savages. And thus the certainty of being able to exchange all that surplus part of the produce of his own labour, which is over and above his own consumption, for such parts of the produce of other men's labour, as he may have occasion for, encourages every man to apply himself to a particular occupation and to cultivate and bring to perfection whatever talent or genius he may possess for that particular species of business.[7]

The people in Smith's example own what they produce. This gives them an *incentive* to produce goods (or services) of good quality and in large amounts. If they produce more than they consume, they will be able to trade their products for other things they want. The better the quality of their product, and the more of it, the more goods (or services) they will receive for themselves in trade. But suppose instead that someone else owns what you produce. Suppose, for example, that what you produce is owned collectively by your whole society. What incentive do you have for working hard to produce many things of good quality? One answer would be that you will do so if you care about the members of your society. Smith, who was a friend of David Hume, believed that humans were naturally sympathetic and developed a theory of how societies were formed largely as a result of this impulse to care for others. He held, however, that in our *economic* activities we are nevertheless motivated only by self-interest. People may work altruistically within small and intimate organizations such as families and friendships, but in the larger societies it is only self-interest that really moves them to be productive. Now the beauty of markets is that they provide self-interested incentives for individuals to be most productive, in both quality and quantity. This is just because they own the products of their labor and wish to get the most from them in trade.

Markets thus contribute to the happiness of a society. The individuals of the society are most productive, doing their best to transform nature to give humans what they need and want. Notice that this argument is utilitarian. Previously we considered the deontological argument that people have a right to what they produce, including capital. Now we have a utilitarian argument, that when people are granted this right, the society as a whole is more prosperous and thus more happy.

Capitalist economies are market economies. In capitalism, individual people (or groups of them) own capital and thus own the product of putting their capital to use. The person who owns the vegetable garden owns the vegetables it produces. By owning the garden, she has an incentive to make it most productive. Capitalism is thus said to make the world a happier place mainly because it stimulates individuals to produce what the members of society need and want.

It should be noticed, however, that Smith's argument applies only to *artificial* capital. A demand for arrows will stimulate the maker of them to make more of them. But a demand for land will not stimulate those who own and sell it to make

---

7. From *An Inquiry into the Nature and Causes of the Wealth of Nations*, ed. C. J. Bullock (New York: Collier, 1909).

more of it. As land becomes more scarce, those who own it can demand more for it than what they paid. They make a profit but without producing anything of value. As Smith himself remarks, "they reap where they do not sow." A common feature of modern capitalism is private ownership of natural resources such as land, minerals, and oil. Smith's argument does not explain why this is a good thing.

MARKET SOCIALISM

Capitalist economies are market economies, but are market economies necessarily capitalistic? It is very common to argue for capitalism, as we have, by arguing for market economies. This is because it is common not to distinguish them. But we can see how they are distinct by seeing how it is possible to have **market socialism**: a market economy that is socialistic.

Recall that what is essential to socialism is that the *capital stock* is collectively owned: the land, the buildings, the equipment are all "ours." Does it follow that we collectively own all the *products* of such an economy? Not necessarily. Suppose that we do collectively own all the capital but realize that markets are, as Smith argued, good at stimulating production. We might conclude that it is in our mutual interest to allow individuals to own the products that they create. This could be achieved by collectively *renting* to individuals the capital in question under a contractual agreement between us and them that grants them ownership of the product in return for the rent we receive. Suppose, for example, that we collectively own land with rich supplies of oil. Individuals could form business enterprises that use this land to produce oil that becomes theirs to trade. The land itself would still be common property that the businesses rent from the society as a whole. In addition, the individuals who have contracted with the whole society would have a self-interested incentive to make the land productive, because the oil they produce will be theirs.

To see how similar market socialism is to capitalism, notice that it is common in capitalism for the owners of capital to rent their capital to workers. You may rent your garden to other people, on the understanding that they will own the vegetables they work to produce on your land in exchange for the rent you receive. From the perspective of the person who rents the land, it does not matter whether she rents it from individuals or from society as a whole. In either case, the renter has the same incentive to work productively.

Capitalists will find market socialism a poor substitute for capitalism. First, they make the deontological point that the capital *belongs* to those individuals who have created it or who have received it in trade or as a gift. If so, socialism represents the theft by society of what belongs to individuals. Second, capitalists may question whether markets will function as well in market socialism. In capitalism, the individual owners of capital have an incentive to make sure that the capital is *rented* wisely. If it is your capital, you will have a keen interest in making sure the rent will be paid, and you will want it to be very productive, since then you can collect more rent. How would these incentives to invest capital wisely be preserved in market socialism? This is at least a question that market socialists have to address.

Another problem with market socialism pertains to development of the capital stock. In capitalism, individual owners of capital want the capital itself to increase in value because they own it. This gives them an incentive to make their capital more productive. Factory owners, for example, want to improve the efficiency of their factories. How would this incentive be preserved if the capital in question were commonly owned?

Even though market socialism is possible, capitalism has the very great advantage over socialism of having dramatically proven its effectiveness to all the world. It goes without saying that capitalist economies are highly productive. Even if capitalists admit that their system has some flaws, they can remind us that the *point* of an economy is to *produce*, and no one can deny that capitalism *works*. Market socialism is not unknown (it is, for example, espoused in China today). But until it is really up and running, we do not know how productive it will be. Until this time, capitalists will say, it is reasonable to prefer the tried and true.

GOOD MARKETS

What makes markets good? Smith gave a utilitarian argument in favor of them. But he was also aware that certain conditions must exist in market economies for them to have the good effects he described. Many people today are convinced that the best economy is a market economy. If so, we should be clear about what a market economy should be like. Capitalism and socialism, as we have seen, are about who owns the capital. Market economies are about who owns the economic product. It remains a debatable question whether market economies are really the best overall, and we will take up the question again near the end of this chapter. Owing to their present popularity, however, we do well to consider the conditions under which markets do what they are supposed to do.

First, it must be possible for producers of the same product to exist and *compete* with one another in selling their goods or services to consumers. As a producer, you want to trade your product for the most you can get. If you were the sole producer of something of great value, such as food or clothing, you could demand a great deal for it, because others would have no real choice but to give you what you demand. This would be condemned by both utilitarians and deontologists. Many people would suffer to benefit a few, and "trade" in this commodity would amount to extortion. To avoid monopolies, it must be possible for others to enter into competition with you in supplying the same product. Then consumers have a choice of trading with you *or* your competitors, and to win this competition, you must either lower your price or offer a better product at the same price. In this way, competition rewards those who are the most productive. If you can make more arrows than your competitor, you can meet your own needs by trading them at a lower price. And if you make better arrows at the same price, consumers will of course prefer to buy them from you. In both cases, the consumer benefits. Moreover, the whole economy improves, because only the better producers are rewarded; after a while, the only ones left in any occupation are the ones who are best in delivering the good or service in question. (The similarity here with Darwin's theory of natural selection is striking and illuminating; it is known that Darwin read Smith.)

The second condition of good markets is that producers *internalize their costs*. Becoming more efficient is, unfortunately, not the only way producers can lower their costs. Producers can often get third parties to bear some of the costs of their production. Factories that belch large amounts of pollution into the air are externalizing their costs. They avoid the costs of installing devices that harmlessly eliminate pollutants. These costs are replaced by the costs that everyone around them pays by the unwelcome presence of their pollution. The air they have fouled is ugly and smelly and causes health problems. These costs are born by innocent bystanders and not by the people who are responsible for them. Examples of **cost externalization** are depressingly common. Logging companies get access to national forests at prices much lower than they would pay in an open market. This gift from government is made at the taxpayers' expense. Companies drive native people from their traditional land to extract minerals from it, without compensating the natives for the extreme harm done to them (and, of course, without their consent). Other companies export their factories to countries that offer workers no rights. Injured workers are simply fired, so that the costs of incurring injuries are externalized. The automobile industry externalizes its costs by having taxpayers build the roads on which their cars are driven. These costs would be internalized if the costs of roads were built into the price of cars with a special tax.

Cost externalization is condemned by both utilitarians and deontologists. Utilitarians condemn it because it spoils the effect of markets. Unfortunately, markets reward the externalization of costs and thus encourage harm to be done, typically to the society as a whole. To direct production to beneficial activities, societies must have laws against cost externalization. Cost externalization also gives an advantage to products that might not be purchased if their true costs were absorbed by the producers. If the price of building the road system were built into the vehicles that travel on them, people would have a greater incentive to take public transportation instead of buying the more expensive cars. Fewer vehicles would be purchased, fewer roads built, and people would pay far less for transportation. (The automobile industry accounts for a full fifth of the entire U.S. economy today.) People would have more resources to spend on other things more important to them, or they would be able to work less to provide more time for "mental cultivation" and other activities of choice. By requiring that producers internalize their own costs, consumers make more enlightened choices and get more of what they want and need.

Deontologists condemn cost externalization for its injustice. What gives the owners of a factory the right to pollute the common air supply? Why should taxpayers subsidize the logging industry? Why should all of us be burdened with very high taxes for building the road system so that those of us who want to drive cars can do so at reduced rates? Why should natives have to leave their land so that some company can come in and plunder its natural resources?

It is completely uncontroversial that markets should have competition among producers and that costs should be internalized. The reasons are plain to see from both of our humanistic perspectives. If the best economy is a market economy, in which individuals own what they produce, producers must compete with one another and be responsible for the costs of their own production.

CORPORATIONS

Before we turn to socialism, let us examine a modern development of capitalism, the emergence and growth of corporations. Corporations are so much a part of modern capitalism that it can seem that they naturally belong to a capitalist economy or a market economy. But corporations came into existence about five hundred years ago, whereas both capitalism and market economies are ancient, arising with the private ownership of tools and the trade of surplus goods. This proves that not only markets but capitalism itself can exist without them. Corporations are important to understand and evaluate, since they have become enormous powers in the modern world. Their influence today is described by the contemporary economist David Korten:

> Corporations have emerged as the dominant governance institutions on the planet, with the largest among them reaching into virtually every country in the world and exceeding most governments in size and power. Increasingly, it is the corporate interest more than the human interest that defines the policy agendas of states and international bodies, although this reality and its implications have gone largely unnoticed and unaddressed.[8]

Although capitalism can exist without corporations, corporations exist only within capitalism. **Corporations** are investment enterprises, formed by owners of capital pooling their resources and hiring managers to invest their combined capital. The individual owners, or "stockholders," hope to increase their wealth. This result can come about either by receiving their portion of the rent on the capital or by trading their portion for more than it was originally worth. The managers of the capital are hired, therefore, to invest the capital as effectively as possible, bringing in the highest possible rent and increasing the value in trade of shares of the stock.

Corporations are, however, not merely investment enterprises. They enjoy legal protections by government grant of the **corporate charter.** Originally, the corporate charter was granted to limit liability on investments. At that time, there were

---

8. From *When Corporations Rule the World* (West Hartford, CT: Kumarian Press, and San Francisco: Berrett-Koehler, 1995).

debtor prisons for those who could not pay their debts, and the debts of parents would be passed on to their children. With the corporate charter, the financial responsibilities of individuals were limited to their investments. If you invested in a project, the most you could lose was your original investment. If your project failed and in doing so caused others to lose, they could not get from you more than what you invested. Suppose, for example, that your corporation contracted to transport a cargo of jewelry by ship and the ship sank. The corporate charter would deny the legal right of those who lost their jewelry to sue you personally. They could only sue the corporation itself, which in the worst case (to you) would go bankrupt and cease to exist.

The corporate charter is certainly good *for* owners of capital. But is it a good thing? Is it good to protect investors by granting them a corporate charter? Advocates of the corporate charter can mount a utilitarian argument in favor of it. The corporate charter encourages investment. By protecting investors, capital is more vigorously put to use and productivity rises. Human needs are met and happiness is increased. The withdrawal of the corporate charter would have a chilling effect on investment that would be felt by all of us.

Critics of corporations say that they spoil the effects of markets. Corporations diminish competition among producers by consolidating capital. Their greater power allows them to drive smaller competitors out of business. (The big fish eat the little fish.) When only a few exist, they silently cooperate by fixing prices at a higher level and thus function in effect as monopolies.

Critics also claim that the greater power of corporations makes them more effective in externalizing costs. As economist Neva Goodwin says:

> [P]ower is largely what externalities are all about. What's the point of having power, if you can't use it to externalize your costs—to make them fall on someone else?[9]

One of the greatest ways in which corporations use their power to externalize costs is by influencing government. Money talks, and when corporations use their great wealth to talk to lawmakers, laws are shaped to benefit owners of capital rather than the members of society equally. Laws and regulations that would protect the environment and innocent bystanders are not passed or simply ignored.

If capitalism really is the best economic system, it remains an open question whether the individual owners of capital should be legally protected by the corporate charter. This is important for us to see. Arguments for capitalism do not necessarily support the corporate chapter or all the entitlements it has come to confer. An opponent of corporations could still be in favor of capitalism, as a market enthusiast could still be a socialist. By clarifying our terms, we see what is possible.

---

9. Quoted in Korten, *When Corporations Rule the World*.

DEONTOLOGICAL SOCIALISM

Socialists claim that the capital stock of an economy is commonly owned. If governments extend legal rights to individuals to own some it by themselves, this represents the theft of communal property by individuals and the use of government power to make the theft possible. Capitalist economies thus embody massive injustice. For socialists who appeal to deontology, this is their greatest vice. How, then, do deontological socialists justify their claim that the capital stock is "ours"?

First, socialists point to the massive violation of Locke's proviso in today's world. It is obvious that by Locke's own theory, the land of the earth is commonly owned. Even if during Locke's day land could be justly acquired by individuals, the world of today is not one of practically unlimited frontiers. Once individuals gobble up so much land that those who got there first crowd out those who get there later, Locke's own theory demands that all claims to individual ownership of land be given up (perhaps with compensation). The land returns to its original state of common ownership, and the question of how to use it becomes a communal decision. The members of society may decide, for example, that everyone is entitled to a certain amount of land as a natural birthright. No one would come into the world facing the necessity of a large mortgage payment, because everyone would already have their share of land. It is doubtful, however, that this would work unless the size of the population were stable. Another solution would be to have individuals rent the land from the society as a whole. There could still be a market on land, as today, but individuals could not increase their wealth by renting land to others.

The ownership of land is of the greatest importance, for, as Locke himself says, land is "that which takes in and carries with it all the rest." If you own land, you own many other natural resources that are "carried with" the land. So, the fact that the land of the earth is common property means that practically all of nature's goods cannot be owned individually today except by injustice. But even if we break out other natural resources such as the ocean, rainforests, and water supplies, it is clear that Locke's proviso is violated today by individual ownership of them. The fish of the sea, the rainforests, and the supply of uncontaminated water have in fact been diminishing while the human population increases. Clearly, those who have been taking from these resources have not been leaving "enough, and as good, for others," especially when we take into account all the innocent people of the future who will have less as a result of present consumption.

Locke's proviso, however, pertains only to natural capital and not to artificial capital. Even if the natural capital is common property, this leaves open the question of why the *artificial* capital should be also commonly owned. This question was addressed by the nineteenth-century English sociologist and philosopher L. T. Hobhouse, who argued that it is not really individuals so much as the whole society that creates the capital stock. As societies become more complex, it becomes increasingly impossible to distinguish the contribution made by the labor of any one individual from that of others. The physician who is handsomely paid could not work at all without nurses and other staff. For that matter, a modern hospital could not function without roads, telecommunication systems, schools that educate the people who build and operate them, police protection, and so on and so on. In more developed economies, the goods and services are produced more by whole communities than by various individual efforts. Capitalists rely on the principle that capital belongs to those who create it. If Hobhouse is right, this principle argues for socialism. If the creators of capital are really the members of society combined, then the capital *belongs* to the whole society as such.

UTILITARIAN SOCIALISM

What is most fundamental to socialism is a vision of the best society. As much as possible, the members of the best society are *friends* of one another and not enemies. They work *together* instead of against one another. They are *equals* in the sense that no one is master of another. Socialists share a conception of human nature. Humans are most happy and fulfilled when they give their labor freely, neither taking nor giving orders, and living in community with others. Bertrand Russell gives a penetrating account of this conception in the following:

> We may distinguish two sorts of goods, and two corresponding sorts of impulses. There are goods in regard to which individual possession is possible, and there are goods in which all can share alike. The food and clothing of one man is not the food and clothing of another; if the supply is insufficient, what one man has is obtained at the expense of some other man. This applies to material goods, generally, and therefore to the greater part of the present economic life of the world. On the other hand, mental and spiritual goods do not belong to one man to the exclusion of another. If one man knows a science, that does not prevent others from knowing it; on the contrary, it helps them to acquire this knowledge. If one man is a great artist or poet, that does not prevent others from painting pictures or writing poems, but helps to create the atmosphere in which such things are possible. If one man is full of good-will toward others, that does not mean that there is less good-will to be shared among the rest; the more good-will one man has, the more he is likely to create among others. In such matters there is no possession, because there is not a definite amount to be shared; any increase anywhere tends to produce an increase everywhere.
>
> There are two kinds of impulses, corresponding to the two kinds of goods. There are *possessive* impulses, which aim at acquiring or retaining private goods that cannot be shared; these center in the impulse of property. And there are *creative* or constructive impulses, which aim at bringing into the world or making available for use the kind of goods in which there is no privacy and no possession.
>
> The best life is the one in which the creative impulses play the largest part and the possessive impulses play the smallest. This is no new discovery. The Gospel says: "Take no thought, saying, What shall we eat? or, What shall we drink? or, Wherewithal shall we be clothed?" The thought we give

to these things is taken away from matters of more importance. And what is worse, the habit of mind engendered by thinking of these things is a bad one; it leads to competition, envy, domination, cruelty, and almost all the moral evils that infest the world. In particular, it leads to the predatory use of force. Material possessions can be taken by force and enjoyed by the robber. Spiritual possessions cannot be taken in this way. You may kill an artist or a thinker, but you cannot acquire his art or his thought. You may put a man to death because he loves his fellow-men, but you will not by so doing acquire the love which made his happiness. Force is impotent in such matters; it is only as regards material goods that it is effective. For this reason the men who believe in force are the men whose thoughts and desires are preoccupied with material goods.[10]

Socialists hold what we have called an "idealistic" conception of human happiness. Happy people act largely on distinctively human motives. Russell identifies these as motives to create goods, such as knowledge, goodwill, and art, that can be shared by all and not possessed by some to the exclusion of others. The happiest people are preoccupied with giving and not with taking. They are "friends of humanity" since what they give is good for all. They naturally regard others as equals. Because they have no wish to force others to act against their will, they have no desire to dominate.

Socialists believe that capitalism is responsible for much human misery. This sentiment is expressed by the eighteenth-century French philosopher Jean-Jacques Rousseau:

> The first man who, having enclosed a piece of ground, bethought himself of saying, "This is mine," and found people simple enough to believe him, was the real founder of civil society. From how many crimes, wars, and murders, from how many horrors and misfortunes might not any one have saved mankind, by pulling up the stakes, or filling up the ditch, and crying to his fellows: "Beware of listening to this impostor; you are undone if you once forget that the fruits of earth belong to us all, and the earth itself to nobody."[11]

History shows repeatedly that very many evils stem from the struggle for material possessions. From the beginnings of civilization some five thousand years ago, the accumulation of wealth has attracted people who would take it by force, often with violence. Those who have greater wealth have greater power, which they often use to force others to act against their will. Capitalism greatly increases the amount of material that can be possessed by individuals, for it differs from socialism precisely in the fact that it allows individuals to acquire portions of the capital

---

10. From *Political Ideals* (1917).
11. From *Discourse on the Origin of Inequality* (London: Dent, 1958).

stock. It thus puts the members of society into competition with one other to get their piece of the pie. Moreover, the competition is serious, since the pie consists of nothing less than the means of subsistence. The members of a capitalist society are forced into adversarial relationships with one another. They are more enemies than friends. They work against one another in the struggle for survival or for riches. And those who win come to dominate those who lose. The rich live where they wish and do what they will, while the poor take orders from them and hope to survive.

Socialists claim that capitalism deeply divides society by creating a conflict of interest between those who live off of rent and those who earn wages by working for others. Recent studies have shown that close to 50 percent of U.S. adults own some capital stock. This was trumpeted as showing how large a portion of the population are owners of capital. But the distribution of ownership tells another story. The wealthiest 5 percent of the population owns three-quarters of the stock. For that matter, the wealthiest 1 percent of the U.S. population owns almost *half* of the nation's wealth. The richest individual in the United States has as much wealth as the poorest 120 million *combined*. The rich have a very keen interest not shared with the common wage earner. It is they who have a selfish interest in continued economic growth. When the economy does not grow in productivity, the value of stock does not increase, and those who own it do not become wealthier. This is why the wealthy in a capitalist society urge the value of continual economic growth instead of realizing Mill's ideal of developing a sufficient stock for all to have their basic needs met with a minimum of work. In the last half century, the productivity of the U.S. worker has doubled. This could have been used to cut the work day in half. Instead, we had the growth of the "two-paycheck family," which means that both parents have been forced to work for others to the neglect of their children and community and the detriment of the environment. This lunacy, socialists say, is the predictable result of the conflict of interests that emerges in capitalism.

CONCLUSION

Economic philosophy ethically evaluates economies. It must accordingly evaluate not only the productivity of an economy but also its effects on the environment and social life. It will pass judgment on the ideal size of an economy because it will assess the role of economic production within the whole of human life.

In this chapter, we focused on two kinds of economy, capitalism and socialism, that differ with respect to ownership of the capital, natural and artificial. We assessed each from the perspectives of both of our humanistic moral theories, utilitarianism and deontology. Capitalists claim that capitalism most respects the freedom of individuals to acquire and trade property and that this freedom in fact serves to stimulate economic productivity to the benefit of all. Socialists claim that the artificial capital of a developed economy is commonly owned because it is produced by the combined effort of the members of society. They believe, too, that the natural capital is commonly owned according to Locke's theory of property, the very theory used to justify capitalistic ownership. They also claim that they can accept the benefits of a market economy, but capitalists raise doubts about the productivity of market socialism. Besides, markets are not in keeping with the socialist vision of the best society. In market economies, socialists say, people are still motivated by greed and fear, even if market socialism can reduce these motives.

Socialists long for the day in which economic activity forms a minimal part of social life and people develop their natural desire for friendship and community. Many capitalists believe that this desire, however understandable, is based on an unrealistic view of human nature. We are, after all, animals, born to the struggle for existence. That it is possible to transcend this condition of perpetual competition and live harmoniously is the hope of those who remain truest to the socialist literature.

STUDY QUESTIONS

1. Give a succinct but complete statement of what is an economy.
2. Explain how natural resources such as land and water can count as natural capital.
3. What are possible bad effects of an economy?
4. Why, according to Mill, should economic activity be limited?
5. What is the principal difference between socialist and capitalist economies?
6. How do (some) deontologists attempt to justify great differences in economic power?
7. How is it possible, according to Locke, for individuals to acquire parts of nature?
8. What is "the proviso"? How is it crucial for Locke's theory?
9. What is good about market economies, according to Adam Smith? What two conditions must be preserved for market economies to be good?
10. How is market socialism possible?
11. How can there be capitalism without corporations?
12. How do deontological socialists argue that the capital stock is *ours*?
13. How do socialists and capitalists differ in their view of human nature?

CHAPTER
TWELVE
Political Authority and Responsibility

WHAT MAKES A POLITICAL organization good? We are all familiar with political activities. In some countries, people vote to see who will comprise the government; in others, the members of government are chosen by the clergy or the military. In some, the government is actively involved in many aspects of life; in others, government is barely noticeable. There are differences in what governments do, too. Some are so corrupt that the members of government plunder the resources of their country to enhance their own wealth. Others do a better job in using government power for the common good. But even among these there are differences in what the government is trying to achieve. Some governments pass laws only to keep people from hurting or stealing from one another. Others use the law to come to the assistance of those in need—for example, by distributing food stamps or medical care regardless of ability to pay.

Political *science* is the empirical study of the causes and effects of such differences. Political *philosophy* has been for the most part engaged in ethically evaluating them.

THE NATURE OF POLITIES

Polities, as they are simply called, come into existence with the creation of laws. All societies, large and small, are governed by rules that say how the members ought to interact. But not all societies have laws. **Laws** are rules of interaction that are publicly announced and enforced. All rules carry sanctions, or penalties, for disobeying them, since they all say how we *ought* to be — "or else." With laws, the sanctions are imposed by force under the command of government. To be effective, the force of government must be superior to any that would challenge it. This is because the laws spell out behavior that the government has declared simply unacceptable.

Polities differ in their distribution of **political power,** the power to make the laws that all must follow. Many of the names familiar in political discussions refer to such differences. In a *monarchy* (in the strict sense of the term), only one person, such as a king or emperor, has political power. In a **democracy,** *every* citizen has this power. In a **theocracy,** political power is held by a priestly class; in a **plutocracy,** it is only the wealthy who have this power.

As we have seen, polities also differ in the *purpose* for which the laws are made. Some governments work to preserve traditional institutions, such as the church to which the people have belonged or the language they have spoken. Others try to alleviate the suffering of the poor by redistributing the wealth of the society to achieve more equality in economic power. Others try to direct the lives of individuals — for instance, by forbidding recreational drugs or prostitution. For some social organizations, the purpose is clear and uncontroversial. As these examples show, however, for polities the question arises as to what is the point of having government and laws in the first place.

POLITICAL AUTHORITY AND RESPONSIBILITY

Political authority is the right to have political power. In political philosophy, we are concerned with *moral* authority. Most governments will *claim* to have the moral right to rule, but whether they do is a question of ethics. Whether a government has a *legal* right to rule is of no interest to us, since governments cannot make themselves morally legitimate just by saying they are. Whether a government has moral authority is a serious matter. A government that lacks this authority is simply a body of people forcing others to do what it says under the threat of punishment for disobedience. Such a government is no different in kind from slaveholders who use whips and guns to secure obedience. The people themselves have no moral obligation to do what it says and have the right to rebel against it. Other governments also have no obligation to respect its existence.

A government may have moral authority and still be morally constrained in how it uses this authority. The positions we will cover claim that governments have certain responsibilities in passing laws. These may be responsibilities not to interfere with citizens, for example, in what religion they profess, what they say in public, or whom they associate with. Or they may be responsibilities to take care of the citizens — for example, by preventing violence or ensuring a decent standard of living. Our main questions of this chapter will be to determine what (if anything) gives a government political authority and what are the responsibilities of governments that have it.

THE JUSTIFICATION OF FORCE

Since polities rule only by force, or at least the threat of it, what authority and responsibility they have depends in large part on when the use of force is justified. From our humanistic perspective, there is surely a strong presumption against it. Yet there is a significant difference between utilitarianism and deontology on their attitude toward coercion. For utilitarians anything, including force, is justified by its utility or tendency to contribute to happiness. Laws are tools for making society happier. But deontologists acknowledge the use of force mainly for preventing and punishing injustice. For them, laws are tools for protecting the moral rights of individuals within society.

VISIONS OF THE BEST SOCIETY

Political philosophers have differed in their vision of the best society. We will be especially concerned with three of these, which differ in instructive ways and are each historically important.

Theocracy is the view that societies exist to serve God. The members of society share a common religious commitment, and they live together to honor this commitment. Their rulers are accordingly their religious leaders. Many of the earliest governments were theocracies, and some exist even today.

Aristocracy advocates that societies be ruled by experts in legislation (the word comes from the Greek word for "the best"). This means not those who merely claim to be experts but those who really excel in possessing all the qualities of a good legislator, including intelligence, a broad education, and sound moral character. Aristocratic societies are like theocratic ones in that the people share a common purpose. This purpose is not, however, divinely prescribed. It is simply to do what is good, to live the good life. Aristocrats believe that the good life is the same for all because it depends on our common human nature. It is an objective matter that can be studied like any other natural phenomenon. The rulers of a society should be, therefore, those who have the best understanding of this natural phenomenon.

Liberalism differs from both theocracy and aristocracy in denying that the members of society ought to share a common conception of how to live. The members of the best society are "free and equal" citizens. They are free to choose how to live, provided that they respect the right of others to do the same. They are equal in that no one is master of another. The laws of a liberal government exist mainly to prevent what is bad, especially the injustice of interfering with equal freedom. Also, they are created not by religious or moral experts but by the members of society themselves.

Theocratic Authority and Responsibility

Few philosophers today would defend theocracy. This is in large part due to the widespread rejection of the divine command theory (see Chapter Eight). Theocrats, or advocates of theocracy, claim that political authority comes ultimately from God, since all of morality is a matter of what God wants. As we have seen, even many theists deny this (to see God as good). But despite the rejection of this theory by philosophers, many people in the world, of course, still equate being moral with being obedient to God. How natural, then, to accept as legitimate only laws that seem to come from God.

Today this simple form of religious commitment is known as **fundamentalism,** and it is found in different religions today, including Judaism, Christianity, and Islam. Fundamentalism deserves to be understood, since it continues to be a powerful force in the world. Fundamentalists can be tightly organized to achieve a goal, because the leaders are given unquestioned obedience.

It is instructive to compare fundamentalism in this respect with **fascism.** Fascist societies, such as Nazi Germany, imperial Japan, and Italy and Spain in the early twentieth century, are modeled on military organizations. There is rank and hierarchy so that the whole society can respond quickly and effectively to orders from the highest government. In both fundamentalism and fascism, the leaders are invested with a special power to discern the proper destiny of their society, which is the basis of the blind obedience of the masses that gives these leaders the power of the whole society.

Confucius's Moral Leader. Theocracy and fascism suffer from a great problem. A bad ruler can lead the whole society to disaster. The problem is partly due to the obedient attitude of the people. But it is also due to the fact that it is difficult to show that a leader *is* bad. If your leader is the closest thing to God on Earth and your ultimate allegiance is to God, who are *you* to question what your leader says?

From ancient times, in both the West and the East, a response to this problem developed. Progressive thinkers urged that political leaders should be *morally* virtuous. This was, for example, a main theme of Confucius in China, and it has had a great influence in the history of China for the last two and a half millennia. It was a radical doctrine in its time, since it implied (as theocracy does not) that leaders had responsibilities toward the people that, if not fulfilled, would disqualify them and justify their replacement. Here are some representative comments attributed to Confucius:

> A ruler who governs his state by virtue is like the north polar star, which remains in place while all the other stars revolve around it. . . .
> Lead the people with governmental measures and regulate them by law and punishment, and they will avoid wrong-doing but will have no sense of honor or shame. Lead them with virtue and regulate them by rules of propriety, and they will have a sense of shame and, moreover, set themselves right. . . .
> In your government what is the need of killing? If you desire what is good, the people will be good. The character of a ruler is like wind and

that of the people like grass. In whatever direction the wind blows, the grass always bends.[1]

Aristocratic Authority

It is one thing to say (however progressively) that those with political power should be virtuous; it is more radical still to say that they should be picked in the first place because of their virtue. Aristocrats claim that political authority comes from the competence to rule. Aristocrats think, however, that the competence to make laws is not widely shared. So they recommend giving political power to those few who have the knowledge and moral character to use it wisely and beneficently. The classic defense of aristocracy comes from Plato, in the following dialogue supposedly conducted by Socrates:

> Are not the rulers in a State those to whom you would entrust the office of determining suits at law?
> Certainly.
> And are suits decided on any other ground but that a man may neither take what is another's, nor be deprived of what is his own?
> Yes; that is their principle.
> Which is a just principle?
> Yes.
> Then on this view also justice will be admitted to be the having and doing what is a man's own, and belongs to him?
> Very true.
> Think, now, and say whether you agree with me or not. Suppose a carpenter to be doing the business of a cobbler, or a cobbler of a carpenter; and suppose them to exchange their implements or their duties, or the same person to be doing the work of both, or whatever be the change; do you think that any great harm would result to the State?
> Not much.
> But when the cobbler or any other man whom nature designed to be a trader, having his heart lifted up by wealth or strength or the number of his followers, or any like advantage, attempts to force his way into the class of warriors, or a warrior into that of legislators and guardians, for which he is unfitted, and either to take the implements or the duties of the other; or when one man is trader, legislator, and warrior all in one, then I think you will agree with me in saying that this interchange and meddling of one another is the ruin of the State.
> Most true.
> Seeing then, I said, that there are three distinct classes, any meddling of one with another, or the change of one into another, is the greatest harm to the State, and may be most justly termed evil-doing?

---

1. From "The Analects," in *A Source Book in Chinese Philosophy*, trans. and comp. Wing-tsit Chan (Princeton, NJ: Princeton University Press, 1963).

Precisely.

And the greatest degree of evil-doing to one's own city would be termed by you injustice?

Certainly.

This then is injustice; and on the other hand when the traders, the auxiliary [law enforcement], and the guardian [legislator] each do their own business, that is justice, and will make the city just.[2]

Plato's argument involves an application of the principle of specialized labor. Societies are more productive, in both quality and quantity, when labor is divided into special kinds and performed by those who are best at each kind. Making laws is one kind of job to be done in society and a very important one to have done well. Because the competence to make the laws is not widely shared, Plato concludes that political power should be concentrated in the hands of the relatively few people in society who are good at making laws.

Aristocratic Responsibility

It is a short step to conclude that aristocratic leaders should make laws not merely to prevent what is bad but also to promote what is good. The argument, simply put, is, Why not? If you know what is good and you have the power to bring it about, why stop with just preventing what is bad? This sentiment is expressed by Aristotle in the following passage (Aristotle uses the Greek word *polis*—from which we get our word *political*—to refer to the best polity):

> [A]ny polis which is truly so called, and is not merely in name, must devote itself to the end of encouraging goodness. Otherwise a political association sinks into a mere alliance . . . a polis is not an association for residence on a common site, or for the sake of preventing mutual injustice and easing exchange. These are indeed conditions which must be present before a polis can exist; but the presence of all these conditions is not enough, in itself, to constitute a polis. What constitutes a polis is an association of households and clans in a good life, for the sake of attaining a perfect and self-sustaining existence. . . . It is therefore for the sake of good actions, and not for the sake of social life, that political associations must be considered to exist.[3]

Aristocracies and theocracies have a certain vision of the good life. Because their governments have the responsibility of promoting this with law, they feel entitled to enter intimately into the lives of the citizens. They will in particular address issues about how to develop the moral character that will inspire the people to live the best life. Theocracies, for example, typically demand as a matter of law performing rituals, accepting sexual restrictions, avoiding intoxicants, and of course

---

2. Plato, *Republic*, trans. Benjamin Jowett, 433e–434d.
3. Aristotle, "Politics" 3, trans. Ernest Barker, in *The Politics of Aristotle* (Oxford: Clarendon, 1946), 1280b.

practicing only the "true" religion. Both see nothing wrong with censorship or preventing troublemakers from getting together. Many people today, especially in Western societies, would object to such government intrusion into their "private" lives. To support this demand to restrict government, they reject the view that it is the responsibility of government to mold character for a certain way of life.

Liberal Authority

For liberals, political authority comes from the moral right of individuals to govern their own lives. A liberal government must somehow get its authority from the individual members of society. Liberal philosophers have disagreed about how this may happen. But some form of *consent* is evidently required. No adult has the right to tell another how to live. Liberals are opposed to all relationships of domination and obedience, of which master and slave is merely the most extreme example. No matter how good the intentions of those who rule, if they pass laws without the consent of those required to obey them, they violate their moral right to govern their own lives. It is possible, however, for people to give their consent to a government and thus become obligated to accept its laws. Even if they are punished for breaking one of these, in giving their consent in advance, they implicitly accept this punishment.

Liberal polities are, therefore, *democratic*. In democracies, every citizen has political power and indeed the same amount. This is because in a true democracy, you get political power just by being a citizen, and no one is more of a citizen than another. Large democracies typically have a certain body of legislators who actually make the laws. But they are democracies if these legislators are genuinely representatives, merely "re-presenting" the preferences of the people.

Countries today are often classified as democratic or not, as if democracy were an all-or-nothing phenomenon. This approach is seriously misleading, since democracy is an ideal toward which a society may get closer or farther away. Democrats say that political power should be shared equally by all citizens. When some citizens have more than others, there is a departure from true democracy that democrats wish to oppose. If, for example, wealthy citizens have more influence over what the law will say by making large contributions to political campaigns, then to that extent the society is plutocratic and not democratic.

This illustrates an important point about how to classify a society with respect to political power. The same society may be both democratic and plutocratic, for example, to certain *degrees*. If politicians in a nominally democratic society represent everyone to some extent but also favor their wealthy contributors by designing laws in their favor, then to certain degrees the society is *both* democratic *and* plutocratic. If you really favor democracy, you want political power to be possessed *equally* by all citizens, and you will oppose unequal distributions of this power. Socialists, for example (see the last chapter), say that great differences in economic power go hand in hand with differences in political power, so that if you really care about democracy, you ought to be a socialist. Capitalists who profess to be democrats ought, therefore, to support laws that prevent wealth from having political influence.

UTILITARIAN LIBERALISM

Liberalism has been supported by humanism in both utilitarian and deontological forms. But utilitarians and deontologists give different explanations of why everyone has the right to decide how to live. For utilitarians, the justification is (as always) that this arrangement has the greatest utility. The nineteenth- to twentieth-century American philosopher John Dewey justifies democracy on this ground:

> The very fact of exclusion from participation is a subtle form of suppression. It gives individuals no opportunity to reflect and decide what is good for them. Others who are supposed to be wiser and who in any case have more power to decide the question for them and also decide the methods and means by which subjects may arrive at the enjoyment of what is good for them. This form of coercion and suppression is more subtle and more effective than is overt intimidation and restraint. When it is habitual and embodied in social institutions, it seems the normal and natural state of affairs. The mass usually become unaware that they have a claim to a development of their own powers. Their experience is so restricted that they are not conscious of the restriction. It is part of the democratic conception that they as individuals are not the only sufferers, but that the whole social body is deprived of the potential resources that should be at its service. The individuals of the submerged mass may not be very wise. But there is one thing they are wiser about than anybody else can be, and that is where the shoe pinches, the troubles they suffer from.[4]

Dewey is arguing for democracy over aristocracy. Because individuals know better than any group of wise leaders what bothers them, they are better at making laws that reduce their suffering. Moreover, by excluding them from government, their growth is stunted, and society loses the benefit of their talents. Societies are happier when all their members have the right to participate in making law.

The Slide to Tyranny

Dewey is in effect responding to Plato's argument for aristocracy, as every serious defender of democracy since Plato has had to do. It is interesting that Plato himself later offered a powerful argument for not choosing aristocracy over democracy. While still maintaining that aristocracy is the best form of government, Plato thought that such a government would degenerate into the worst form of government. In a **tyranny,** power is still concentrated in the hands of a few people, but

---

[4]. From "Democracy and Educational Administration," *School and Society* 45, no. 1162 (April 3, 1937).

now these people use their political power for selfish ends. Plato realized that even if political power could be given to those who were truly best, both intellectually and morally, nothing would stop the power from eventually passing into the hands of those who would abuse it. The leaders themselves might become corrupt, or their successors might be. In a democracy, the people have the power to replace tyrannical leaders and avoid the worst form of government. So, even if aristocracy is the best form of government, it is better to have democracy to avoid the "worst-case scenario"—which history has shown to be disastrous.

Political Competence and Liberal Education

What of the crucial assumption that the competence to rule is not widely shared? If the people are ignorant or apathetic, how will they succeed in avoiding tyranny? Plato's second argument (the one in favor of democracy) can be defended by pointing out that competence comes in degrees, and the worst forms of tyranny do not require sophisticated education to discern. Nevertheless, it can also be admitted that tyranny and democracy, like other forms of government, also exist only in degree. *To the extent that* people are well informed and willing to participate in government, they will use their political power in a society in which they have democratic rights to prevent tyranny.

Democracy is an ideal that can be approached by having widespread education and political involvement. The reason for approaching this ideal, revealed in Plato's second argument, is that it is just what is needed to diminish tyranny. **Liberal education** is meant to be education that liberates the individual from intellectual dependence. In aristocratic societies, only those selected to rule would be provided such a broad education in science and the humanities. The case for liberal education being available to all is that such education is necessary for a truly democratic society.

DEONTOLOGICAL LIBERALISM

Utilitarians *can* support other forms of government, since utilitarianism can be used to support *anything* so long as it happens to lead to greater happiness. But deontology is made for liberalism. Its basic principle of justice is that equal freedom be maximized. Restrictions on freedom are justified only to preserve equal freedom. So long as you are not reducing the freedom of others, you have a right to live as you wish without interference. Liberalism is basically a view of the best society, in which all the members are free and equal. Deontology says in effect that liberal society is what justice requires.

This does not mean that deontologists must be in favor of democratic polities. For a deontologist may be opposed to the whole idea of polities and laws. Deontologists are liberals, but some liberals believe that equal freedom is maximized only when the yoke of government and law is thrown off altogether.

ANARCHISM

Anarchism, as philosophers understand the term, denies the moral authority of laws and thus of political societies altogether. The name may seem to suggest that anarchists want disorder and perhaps even violence. But in fact their main goal is justice and the maximization of freedom that this implies. Anarchists believe that government and laws have no place in a truly liberal society. To be free and equal, it is vital that power be equally distributed in a society. Regardless of their stated intentions, governments concentrate power and eventually use this against their own citizens and against innocent people in foreign lands. Polities by their very nature institutionalize oppression.

Anarchists are thus highly suspicious of claims to special authority, and sometimes the term is used just to indicate this attitude. This general distrust of authority may itself be due to complaints about the harmful effects of large organizations in general or even about the restricting effects of social rules themselves. Anarchists have accordingly even sought roots for their position among thinkers like the Taoists, who generally prefer the natural over the artificial, including the rules of society. The Taoists felt that "that government is best which governs least." We see this sentiment expressed in the following story by the ancient Taoist philosopher Chuang Tzu:

> Horses have hoofs to carry them over frost and snow; hair, to protect them from wind and cold. They eat grass and drink water, and fling up their heels over the champaign [open field]. Such is the real nature of horses. Palatial dwellings are of no use to them.
>
> One day Po Lo appeared, saying: "I understand the management of horses."
>
> So he branded them, and clipped them, and pared their hoofs, and put halters on them, tying them up by the head and shackling them by the feet, and disposing them in stables, with the result that two or three in every ten died. Then he kept them hungry and thirsty, trotting them and galloping them, and grooming and trimming, with the misery of the tasseled bridle before and the fear of the knotted whip behind, until more than half of them were dead.
>
> The potter says: "I can do what I will with wood. If I want it curved, I use an arc; if straight, a line."
>
> But on what grounds can we think that the natures of clay and wood desire this application of compasses and square, of arc and line? Nevertheless, every age extols Po Lo for his skill in managing horses, and potters and carpenters for their skill with clay and wood. Those who *govern* the empire make the same mistake.
>
> Now I regard government of the empire from a different point of view.
>
> The people have certain natural instincts: to weave and clothe themselves, to till and feed themselves. These are common to all humanity, and all are agreed thereon. Such instincts are called "Heaven-sent."
>
> And so in the days when natural instincts prevailed, men moved quietly and gazed steadily. At that time, there were no roads over mountains,

nor boats, nor bridge over water. All things were produced, each for its own proper sphere. Birds and beasts multiplied; trees and shrubs grew up. The former might be led by the hand; you could climb up and peep into the raven's nest. For then man dwelt with birds and beasts, and all creation was one. There were no distinctions of good and bad men. Being all equally without knowledge, their virtue could not go astray. Being all equally without evil desires, they were in a state of natural integrity, the perfection of human existence.

But when Sages appeared, tripping up people over charity and fettering them with duty to their neighbor, doubt found its way into the world. And then, with their gushing over music and fussing over ceremony, the empire became divided against itself.[5]

As a political doctrine specially concerned with justice, however, anarchism has its roots in nineteenth-century criticism of both the **state** (the largest polity) and the great disparities in wealth created by capitalism. In fact, modern anarchists see the state in sinister terms, as serving mainly to protect the accumulated wealth of the rich. John Locke had said that the function of the law was to protect property. The French anarchist Pierre Joseph Proudon declared that "property is theft," meaning that the great wealth accumulated by owners of capital was in effect stolen from the workers who created it. The laws of the state, in protecting this property, were an unjust tool of coercion.

HOBBES'S DEFENSE OF THE STATE

Anarchism poses a serious challenge for anyone defending the state and the existence and enforcement of laws generally. Even to say that the state and its laws have a legitimate purpose at all requires somehow trying to justify the use of force against unwilling members of society.

Perhaps the strongest case against anarchism was made by the seventeenth-century English philosopher Thomas Hobbes. Aristotle had anticipated Hobbes somewhat in saying that laws are necessary since most men never achieve moral virtue. The implication was that if the moral character of humans *could* be sufficiently developed, no one would willingly steal from or hurt others because he would see this to be wrong, and that recognition itself would dissuade him.

Aristotle was, however, pessimistic about the possibility of developing moral character so extensively that laws would be unnecessary. Like socialists, the anarchists view human nature as essentially good, thus holding out the promise that society could exist without laws. By contrast, Hobbes is thought by many (though not all) to have been a psychological hedonist (see Chapter Nine). In the following, his case for the need for law is clearly based on a more pessimistic view of human nature:

5. From *Selections from the Philosophy of Chuang Tzu*, Wisdom of the East Series (London: J. Murray, 1911).

> [I]n the nature of man we find three principle causes of quarrel. First, competition; second, diffidence; thirdly, glory.
>
> The first maketh men invade for gain; the second, for safety; and the third, for reputation. The first use violence to make themselves masters of other men's persons, wives, children, and cattle; the second, to defend them; the third, for trifles, as a word, a smile, a different opinion, and any other sign of undervalue, either direct in their persons, or by reflection in their kindred, their friends, their nation, their profession, or their name.
>
> Hereby it is manifest that during the time men live without a common power to keep them all in awe, they are in condition which is called war; and such a war as is every man against every man. For *war* consisteth not in battle only, or the act of fighting, but in a tract of time wherein the will to contend by battle is sufficiently known. . . . All other time is peace.
>
> Whatsoever therefore is consequent to a time of war, where every man is enemy to every man; the same is consequent to the time, wherein men live without other security than what their own strength and their own invention shall furnish them withal. In such condition there is no place for industry, because the fruit thereof is uncertain: and consequently no culture of the earth; no navigation, nor use of the commodities that may be imported by sea; no commodious building; no instruments of moving, and removing, such things as require force; no knowledge of the face of the earth; no account of time; no arts; no letters; no society; and which is worst of all, continual fear, and danger of violent death; and the life of man, solitary, poor, nasty, brutish, and short.[6]

It is difficult to imagine a more extreme difference of opinion than that of Hobbes and Chuang Tzu on the "natural" state of man, when the state, with its laws, does not exist. Rather than living in harmony with both nature and one's fellow man, Hobbes says we are in a state of *war* with one another. He defines the condition of war as existing not merely when there is no actual fighting but also when people are *willing* to resort to force to take what they want. War is disadvantageous for everyone, for when everyone is willing to forcibly take from others, no one's possessions or life are secure. Hobbes thinks it is only human nature to take from others when you can get away with it, because (as he says in another passage) the basic drive of human life is "a perpetual and restless desire of power after power, that ceaseth only in death."

Anarchists hold that the use of government power is an infringement of individual freedom. Hobbes argues in effect that it is a necessary *guarantee* of individual freedom. Without the power of government a state of war exists, and people do not even *try* to carry through on long-range plans, such as plowing fields or building boats and bridges. "There is no place for industry," he tells us, "because the fruit thereof is uncertain." Freedom is the general capacity to make plans and act on

---

6. From "Leviathan," in *Social and Political Philosophy*, ed. John Somerville and Ronald E. Santoni (New York: Doubleday, 1963).

them. Freedom is diminished when we are unsure that we can reap the fruits of our industry because of the threat from invasion. Laws that eliminate this threat, including those that prohibit violence, theft, and broken contracts, secure our freedom. Of course, such laws would be condoned by utilitarians, because misery is reduced and happiness promoted when people can plan for their future without fear of interference by others. But deontologists may also argue that such laws are necessary to preserve the equal right to freedom.

WORLD GOVERNMENT

Hobbes's argument eventually leads to the conclusion that it would be best to have a completely inclusive, world state, with laws that apply to all humanity. He realized that the various nations of the world were like individual people who did not belong to a common political society. By his own argument, the nations of the world are in a state of war with one another so long as there is even a willingness to fight over scarce goods such as land and other treasures. The only way to end this condition of insecurity and danger is to create a state with the power to prevent war. Because war is the source of some of the greatest injustices, the eventual creation of a single world state is required by justice. If you accept Hobbes's argument that smaller groups of people should form a state to avoid war, it is difficult not to extend the argument to having these groups form ever larger political organizations until the largest is reached and all war is made illegal.

This does not mean that smaller political organizations would no longer exist. One of the great advantages of small societies is that they have a greater chance of being democratic. In very large organizations, whether governmental or corporate, authority and power are concentrated at the top. Even if the leaders are democratically elected, after the election individuals tend to feel small and powerless when the leaders are so far removed from them. Many democrats accordingly endorse the principle of **devolution:** As much as possible authority and responsibility should be passed down to smaller organizations, leaving only the necessary minimum at the higher levels. If a world state is necessary to prevent war, this role could be its only function. The various nations of the world could still have their own laws, with their special functions, but they would contribute the material and human resources to a world government with a world military charged only with keeping the peace.

It might be, however, that the function of the world state should not be restricted to keeping the peace. The prevention of war is a concern of all humanity as a fundamental requirement of justice. But so is the preservation of the Earth. Any nation that destroys parts of nature is making an assault on the most fundamental resources for all of humanity, including all who will live in the future. The prevention of such assaults is just as necessary as the prevention of war. Maybe more so. If the Earth's environment needs legal protection, only a political organization with global reach could guarantee it.

LIBERAL RESPONSIBILITY

Now that we have seen how it might be justifiable for a liberal society to have a government with laws, let us turn to the question of what such a government should do. What should be the purpose of laws in a liberal society of free and equal citizens? Anarchists are liberals and want no laws at all. Although we have by no means refuted anarchism, most liberals think that government is necessary. To examine their views, let us suppose that the best liberal society will be a polity. Where will the best liberal society draw the line between what is and what is not the "business of government" to pass laws over?

Before we examine differences in views of liberal government, let us look at their similarities. Liberalism got its name from the idea that citizens should have "liberties" that protect them against government. Liberals agree that these include freedom of speech, religion, and association. Theocrats and aristocrats see such guarantees as impediments to effective government. But liberals in general regard them as necessary for individuals to live together as free and equal members of the same society. Liberals deny that government can assume that we share a conception of the good life. Accordingly, governments have no business in passing laws to shape character for a certain life. Liberals are therefore more tolerant of different sexual practices or marriage arrangements or the use of intoxicants.

The very essence of liberalism is to impose limits on government. Its main purpose is simply to secure the conditions for people to live as free and equal citizens. But what does this include? Does it mean that government should prevent only such wrongs as stealing and violence? Or does it include taking active steps to make sure that everyone has the conditions for a decent life?

LIBERTARIANISM

Although Hobbes himself thought it was legitimate to pass laws for purposes other than establishing the state of peace, some philosophers have been attracted to the idea that this alone should be the purpose of laws and the state. They call their position **libertarianism** (not to be confused with libertarianism with respect to the problem of free will), because they believe that their position most respects individual freedom. They agree with anarchists that we should be suspicious of claims to authority, and they think that actual governments often overstep their bounds and legislate on matters that should be left to individual decision. This includes not only government efforts to mold character for the "right" life but also taxation of the wealthy to help the poor. However well meaning these efforts might seem, they violate the true purpose of the law, which is simply to keep the peace by preventing people from interfering with one another. They agree with anarchists in wanting to see a society in which individual freedom is maximized, but they believe that a *"minimal state"* will be necessary, as Hobbes explained, to prevent the threat of invasion.

REFORM LIBERALISM

Libertarianism is contrasted especially with **reform liberalism,** which advocates the *"supportive state."* Reform liberals are like libertarians in their most general view of the proper function of laws and the state. Like libertarians, they tend to be deontologists, because they describe this function in terms of respecting the equal right to freedom among all individuals. Where they differ is in their understanding of what this right encompasses. Libertarians see this right "negatively," as guaranteeing the absence of interference by other people. Reform liberals claim that real freedom requires more: We must have access to vital *resources* for freedom, including land, food, medical care, and education. Without this access, people have "**false freedom**": Maybe no one is actually standing in their way, but they still lack freedom in the basic sense of the general capacity to make plans and act on them. The proper purpose of the government, therefore, is not merely to prevent people from interfering with each other but also to take active steps to give people the support they need for true and full freedom. Reform liberals accordingly defend taxation for such support as food stamps, government-funded medical care, and public education.

Despite appearances, there is a great difference between libertarians and anarchists in their view of the state. It is not merely that libertarians tolerate a small role for government, whereas anarchists tolerate none. The role they do allow is just the sort of thing that anarchists oppose. Recall that anarchists have seen the Hobbesian "defense of property" as having the effect in modern life of protecting the unjust advantages of the rich. They disagree with Hobbes in thinking that humans are automatically in the state of war whenever there is no state to prevent them from stealing from one another. The state of war and the propensity to greedy behavior behind it really come about because the state makes possible the accumulation of wealth. This situation then creates a distinction between the rich and poor, in which both know the poor are not getting a fair share, and the rich want to keep it that way. It is the rich, not the poor, who need laws and the state. They need the state to protect their wealth and to make possible its continual accumulation.

This discussion shows that reform liberals have something important in common with anarchists that separate both from the libertarians. Libertarians do not have a commitment to equalize economic power; among the measures they most oppose are the redistribution of wealth. By contrast, anarchists think that the protection of accumulated wealth is the main (sinister) function of the state. Reform liberals permit differences in wealth, but not when the least well-off are driven into the state of "false freedom." Hence, even though they (unlike the anarchists) want a substantial role for the state, what they want is for the state to ameliorate the effects of capitalism that give rise to the anarchist objection to the state in the first place.

ECONOMIC JUSTICE

Liberals in general agree that government exists mainly to protect the moral rights of its citizens. They disagree in what government must do to protect these rights. Because libertarians want government to play a minimal role, it is worth seeing what kinds of government action can be justified on libertarian grounds. This will show what any liberal other than an anarchist ought to agree to.

Libertarianism is sometimes thought to justify the present economic system pretty much as it stands. But whether this is so depends on what has happened in the past and what economic theory is right. What if, for example, there has been a history of much economic injustice, so that the present distribution of wealth is highly unjust as a result? The libertarian Robert Nozick admits that in such a case, measures of *rectification* are in order. You may recall (from the last chapter) his principle that if you start off with a just distribution of wealth and allow a history of just transfers, the end result is just regardless of how great the difference in wealth. But when the origin is not just (perhaps by the use of slaves) or when there has been a history of injustice (perhaps by buying legislation and thus defeating democracy), libertarian principles call for a redistribution of wealth. Because it is impossible to single out individuals and determine compensation, an alternative is to tax the rich to provide the poor with social services such as public education, medical care, and child care. This approach will be unfair to many people but arguably fairer than doing nothing. The present point is that whether these social services should be provided according to libertarian principles is not just a question of the proper function of government. Given the right empirical facts, they can be justified on such uncontroversial grounds as returning to people what has been stolen from them.

We should also expect libertarians to oppose the formation of monopolies and thus to be wary of corporate mergers. To monopolize a vital resource such as land is to prevent people from accessing their own property (see Locke's theory in the last chapter). We should also expect them to be vigilant over commercial activities that externalize costs (also discussed in the last chapter). Governments that allow companies to pollute common supplies of air, water, and ground, for example, are permitting them to attack and degrade common property, an offense analogous to stealing. For that matter, governments have an obligation to deny the possession of individual property when Locke's proviso to leave "enough and as good for others" is violated. Governments that grant legal rights to own property when doing so crowds out others to do the same are simply contributing to the injustice instead of eliminating it.

Finally, the issue between capitalism and socialism is a serious one in determining what a liberal government should do. Capitalists think that government should protect property rights, including individual rights to capital. Socialists think that government should protect the communal property right to the capital stock. It is doubtful that libertarians are entitled to assume (as many do) the capitalist view of property. If libertarianism is a view about the function of government that says that there should be laws against such interferences as theft, whether government should allow capitalist ownership depends on what counts as theft.

COMMUNITARIANISM

The last position we will look at on the proper function of government is **communitarianism.** Although reform liberals allow greater scope to government than libertarians, they still advocate the limitation of government to securing individual liberty. The communitarians are opposed to liberalism in general. They have a view of the best society that derives from Aristotle and Hegel (see Chapter Ten). Their favored communities are relatively small and composed of people who are bonded together by a shared vision of the good life. To this end, they condone the use of the law for purposes other than the liberal goal of guaranteeing the equal right to freedom. They claim that even when we add the sort of support that reform liberals allow, liberalism in general guarantees liberties that may be destructive of the sort of community a group of people may wish to create and live in. The contemporary American philosopher Michael Sandel indicates the difference with some examples:

> Communitarians would be more likely than liberals to allow a town to ban pornographic bookstores, on the grounds that pornography offends its way of life and the values that sustain it. But a politics of civil virtue does not always part company with liberalism in favor of conservative policies. For example, communitarians would be more willing than some rights-oriented liberals to see states enact laws regulating plant closings, to protect their communities from the disruptive effects of capital mobility and sudden industrial change. More generally, where the liberal regards the expansion of individual rights and entitlements as unqualified moral political progress, the communitarian is troubled by the tendency of liberal programs to displace politics from smaller forms of association to more comprehensive ones. Where libertarian liberals defend the private economy and egalitarian [reform] liberals defend the welfare state, communitarians worry about the concentration of power in both the corporate economy and the bureaucratic state, and the erosion of those intermediate forms of community that have at times sustained a more vital public life.[7]

It should not be supposed that communitarians have given up altogether the ideal of a society in which freedom is maximized. Like Hegel, they think that true freedom exists only when one is a contributing member of a community. But

---

7. From *Justice and Economic Distribution*, 2d ed., John Arthur and William H. Shaw (Englewood Cliffs, NJ: Prentice-Hall, 1991).

particular communities have their own purposes. If a group of people chooses, for example, to form a religious community, there will have to be laws that support this common purpose but are not required by every person everywhere to be free. If the purpose of the law is only to guarantee the sort of very general freedom that every person needs, then the law cannot be used to promote the individual goals of a particular community. Liberals worry that to condone the use of the law to promote the self-proclaimed "common purpose" of some people is an invitation to oppression. Out the window go such hard-fought rights as those guaranteeing freedom of religion, expression, and association. Sandel claims instead that "intolerance flourishes most where forms of life are dislocated, roots unsettled, traditions undone."

The communitarian conception of the purpose of law seems to apply only to those small societies that can count as genuine communities. Even if small communities have a right to impose legal restrictions in pursuit of their common goal (which may require full unanimity to avoid oppression), the communitarian conception of the function of law would not seem to apply to larger societies, such as nations. For at such a scale, no such assumptions may be made about what everyone wants beyond the liberal goal of securing the conditions of equal freedom so that various individuals can pursue the lifestyle of their choice. We may also observe that Hegel himself thought that the best society required diversity among its members, and he was particularly critical of societies composed of a particular "people" or ethnic group. In the best society, it is clear to its members that they are bound together, not by natural ties such as blood relations but by "spiritual" ties of allegiance to universal ideals, such as the concern for truth and justice, which all persons ought to share. Ethnic diversity within a society helps people to see that the cement of their society is spiritual in this sense and not merely ethnic. Because persons reach their full development only by seeing themselves as spiritual beings (guided by such universal ideals), being a member of an ethnically diverse society is, for Hegel, a condition of full personal development.

CONCLUSION

Polities are formed when rules of interaction become laws, publicly announced and enforced. They differ in how political power is distributed and in the purpose for which the laws are made. Theocrats, aristocrats, and liberals differ in their vision of the best society and in their theories of the origin of political authority and the content of political responsibility. Plato argued for aristocracy but saw the danger of tyranny. Liberalism has been supported by both utilitarians and deontologists. Anarchists appeal to deontology, but Hobbes gave a deontological defense of the state. Liberals who accept the state have differed in their view of political responsibility, owing to different conceptions of freedom. Communitarians think the law may be used to promote a shared vision of the good life.

STUDY QUESTIONS

1. How can a society exist without laws?
2. Explain how a particular government can be both democratic and plutocratic to certain degrees.
3. Where does political authority come from? Contrast the answers of theocrats, aristocrats, and liberals.
4. Contrast their views on the best society.
5. How is fundamentalism like fascism?
6. What is good about aristocracy, according to Plato? Why is there a danger of an aristocracy becoming a tyranny?
7. How does democracy avoid or diminish tyranny?
8. Why is liberal education especially important in democratic societies?
9. Explain the anarchists' position that they are truest to the *liberal* view of society.
10. What is wrong with anarchism, according to Hobbes? How does his argument support a world government?
11. What is the difference between libertarianism and reform liberalism? Explain the charge of the latter that the former would ensure for many only false freedom.
12. How can a libertarian be a socialist?
13. How is communitarianism opposed to liberalism?

Glossary for Part Four

Anarchism The position that denies the political authority of polities

Aristocracy The view that the best society cooperates to create the best life, determined by human nature, and that only experts in legislation should make the laws, since political authority comes from legislative competence

Capital Productive property; **natural** capital includes land, minerals, oil, fish, and forests; **artificial** capital includes factories, tools, and patented ideas

Capitalism The economic system in which capital is privately owned; compare and contrast with *market economies*; and contrast with *socialism*

Communitarianism The position that it is proper for the law to be designed to protect communities by promoting a certain conception of the good life

Corporate charter The government grant of legal rights that protect investors

Corporations Investment enterprises protected by the corporate charter, granted by government and creating legal rights that protect investors

Cost externalization The phenomenon of getting innocent third parties to bear a cost of production

Devolution The tendency to assign political functions to smaller organizations, leaving larger political organizations with minimal functions

Distributive justice What justice requires in the distribution of burdens and benefits within a society

Economic power The power to influence the economy, deciding what to produce and who will get it

Economy A social organization in which goods and services are produced and distributed

False freedom The condition in which people lack the resources for action while not being forcibly prevented from acting by other people

Fascism The kind of society that is highly unified, on the model of a military organization, with political power possessed by a leader who is thought to have special knowledge of the welfare and destiny of the society, itself thought of as a superperson to whom is owed extreme allegiance and possible sacrifice

Fundamentalism Religious commitment to be guided primarily by a literal interpretation of a particular holy text

Laws Rules of society that are publicly announced and enforced

Liberal education That kind of education that is liberating in the sense of making one intellectually independent; arguably necessary for competence to participate effectively in democratic society

Liberalism The view that the best society respects the freedom of all individuals to live as they choose (includes anarchism, libertarianism, and reform liberalism)

Libertarianism The political position that says that the proper function of the state is only to establish peace by keeping people from interfering with one another; contrast with *reform liberalism*

Market economy One in which decisions about what to produce and how to distribute it are made by individuals who own what they produce

Market socialism A market economy in which the capital is collectively owned but rented to individuals who privately make decisions of production and distribution and profit thereby
Plutocracy The condition in which political power is possessed only by the wealthy, or to the extent to which people are wealthy
Political authority The moral right to exercise political power
Political power The power to determine what the law says
Polity A political organization, unified by laws
Reform liberalism The political position that says that the proper function of the law is not only to keep people from interfering with one another but also to ensure that everyone has access to the necessary resources for true freedom; contrast with *libertarianism*
Socialism Most generally, a view of the best society that favors cooperation over competition; as an economic system, declares the common ownership of capital
Spiritual need The need to want what (reason tells you) you ought to want, so that your impulses are not in conflict with what you believe is right
State A political institution whose laws are supreme (such as those of nations today)
Theocracy The view that the best society exists to do what God wants; as a political position, says that only religious leaders should make the law since they know best what God wants
The proviso In Locke's theory of property, the condition on just acquisition of a portion of nature to leave as much and as good for others
Tyranny The misuse of political power for selfish ends

EPILOGUE

The Value of Philosophy

WHAT GOOD IS PHILOSOPHY? What is it good *for*? And how is it good *for you*? These are three distinct questions, and we will address all of them in this chapter. First is the question of whether philosophy is a good thing, something we should care about. Second is the question of what philosophical knowledge is good *for*. Philosophy is a kind of inquiry, meant to yield knowledge. What can you *do* with the special kind of knowledge provided by successful philosophical inquiry? The third question concerns how this knowledge is good *for you*. How are you better off with it? What needs of yours does it meet? How can it contribute to your happiness? Because an answer to any of these three questions requires an understanding of the nature of philosophy, we begin with a review of what philosophy *is*. To complement this review, we also take an overview of the material we have covered in this text to see how our understanding of philosophy has been illustrated in the various areas we have covered.

THE NATURE OF PHILOSOPHY

The introduction gave a general view of philosophy that should now be easier to understand. Philosophy may be summarized as the study of *how to be*. There are various ways each of us ought to be. There are ways we ought to *believe*, given the evidence before us. There are things we ought to *do*, given the choices we face. There are things we ought to *want*. And there are ways we ought to *feel*.

What we should believe or do or want or feel typically depends on the circumstance. If you see a tree, you have good reason for believing a tree stands before you. Those who lack such experiences may have no reason to believe in it. If you are thirsty and see a water fountain, you have good reason to walk to it. Those who are not thirsty or who do not see the fountain may have no reason to do the same. Nevertheless, there are *norms* that we use that do not depend on our particular circumstance. A *norm* is a guide, a rule that we follow whenever a kind of situation arises. In the example of the tree, you might be using the norm that says that it is right to believe in material objects that appear to your senses unless you have special reason to doubt them. In the example of the water fountain, the norm might say that it is right to do what will result in getting what you want unless you have a special reason not to do that.

Norms are *general* in that they apply to any number of circumstances. These two norms, for example, apply *whenever* it appears a certain way to you or *whenever* you want something and see how to get it. They tell you something about the right way to form beliefs about reality or the right way to act. Because norms are general, they can apply to fresh circumstances in which you are unsure what is the right or most reasonable way to be. Take the norm that you ought to feel guilty if you have violated the moral rights of others. This norm applies *whenever* you commit injustices. If you have acted unjustly and are unsure how to feel about it, the norm would tell you how you *ought* to feel.

In fact, we *need* norms to decide how we ought to be. If you are unsure how you ought to feel or what you should do, you need a rule or norm to decide the issue. (Analogously, if you want to know what is legal, you need to know a law that shows what to do.) But although you must use norms whenever deciding what is right, it is not necessary to be *conscious* of the norm you are following. You may never have thought of the very general norm of belief that says that if it appears that a certain material object is before you, you may believe it is there unless you have a special reason to doubt it. But this is in fact a norm you follow throughout the day as you negotiate your way through the material world. Even if you are not conscious of the norm, you *show* that you are using it by what you believe when using your senses.

We apply norms to decide how to be *by* making judgments. A judgment is a mental act of coming to think something is true (see Chapter One). You decide to do something, for example, by judging that that action is the best one among your options. You decide how to feel by judging a certain reaction to be the most appropriate one in your circumstance. Judgments are made in light of reasons that make a certain decision appear right or justified. Norms are what guide us in seeing which decisions are right. All judgments involve the application of norms, just as all legal verdicts involve the application of laws. You cannot be a thinker without using norms that say how you ought to be.

Norms are themselves thoughts, which are either true or false. The norm that you should never be angry, for example, is something that can be asserted and debated. To accept and use a norm is therefore to have a certain *opinion* that may be correct or incorrect. Because all thinkers use norms that say what to believe or do or want or feel, all thinkers *have* opinions on these very general issues, even if they have never thought about them.

These are the issues that are central to philosophical inquiry. Philosophy is different from other intellectual disciplines in that it questions the norms that are used in making judgments about what to do, what to believe, and so forth. In all other disciplines, as in daily life, we *use* norms of which we may not even be aware. Philosophy calls attention to these norms and investigates whether they are in fact correct. It is not enough to say that philosophy is "the study" of such norms. Psychologists can study the norms we *actually* follow through empirical observation of human behavior. But to say that *in fact* this is how we decide what to do or what to believe is not to say that this is how we *should* make these decisions. Philosophy aims to discover what are the *correct* norms to follow when we make the kinds of decisions that all thinkers face.

All of us, all thinkers, use such norms and thus have opinions about what is right to believe or do or feel or want. As thinkers, we cannot avoid having opinions on just the sorts of issues that philosophy critically examines. This is how philosophical issues are "unavoidable," as suggested by the title of this text. Philosophy examines and debates issues to which we all commit ourselves just by being thinkers. This is how philosophy "confronts" the unavoidable.

Philosophy can be divided into areas that correspond to different kinds of norms for making judgments. In metaphysics, we want to find the correct norms for making judgments about how things actually are. In ethics, we want to find the correct norms for making judgments about how things could be better. Logic is the most general area of philosophy, since it seeks the norms for making true judgments in general, regardless of subject matter.

Philosophy is thus all about *how to think*. We may say, if we wish, that the main questions of philosophy are questions such as, "What is there?" "What should I do?" or "How is it appropriate to feel?" But this response can be misleading. In philosophy, we are not in the real-life situation of asking these questions. We are discussing the kinds of questions themselves and asking how such questions should be answered. We are asking how to *think* about these kinds of situations. We are asking how to *distinguish* between true and false, right and wrong, good and bad, real and imaginary, and so on.

Answers to such questions may nevertheless carry implications about what is real or what is good. If we learned in metaphysics that we ought to acknowledge as real only what appears to the senses, then we could say that only material objects are real. We would have a comprehensive view of reality and not just a prescription for how to think about it. Again, suppose that we learn in ethics that all decisions about what to do should be settled by determining what produces the most happiness. Then we could say that happiness itself is what is basically good, and we would have a comprehensive view of goodness or of how the world ought to be. In philosophy, we achieve such comprehensive views *by* shifting to the question of how in general to make a certain kind of judgment.

A PHILOSOPHY

The study of philosophy is meant to help you develop *your philosophy*. Your philosophy is a body of opinions about the right way to feel or act or desire or believe. Together they give a picture of *how to be*. A *developed* philosophy will include opinions in all the main areas of philosophy. It will say what your beliefs, desires, intentions, and feelings should be like. It will give a picture of your *ideal self*. Let us now take an overview of what we have covered in this text to see how it can help you develop such a picture.

AN OVERVIEW

We began with logic, which is the study of how our judgments should be, regardless of subject matter. Chapter One mentioned two norms for judgments in general: Your judgments should be mutually consistent and individually supported with adequate reasons. We added that it is good to have judgments about a particular subject made coherent with explanations. This began the depiction of your ideal self. Ideally, you will have adequate reasons for what you think, and together what you think will be consistent and coherent. In real life, we all fall short of this ideal, but we can recognize it as something to strive for. To elaborate further this part of the picture of your ideal self, we pondered what it is like to have adequate reasons for your judgments. We found, for example, that you can have good reasons without being able to give them and without ruling out all possibility of error. These are important details to add to your picture of your ideal self, insofar as your judgments go.

We continued to explore how to get adequate reasons in Chapter Two. We found that we need sources of direct knowledge and canvassed some different kinds, both uncontroversial and controversial. Delving into the question of what are sensation and introspection helped to clarify what it is to get knowledge directly by these sources. This added more detail to the picture of your ideal self. Ideally, your beliefs will originally spring only from reliable sources. On the assumption that sensation and introspection are reliable, understanding what these are helps to understand how your beliefs ought to be.

Chapter Three began the discussion of what we are entitled to infer from these basic beliefs. We saw that in fact we use our conviction in cause and effect when making inferences from sensation and introspection. We made the choice not to question this assumption so that we could turn to the question of how to use it. This led to an examination of how to choose between competing hypotheses. The principle that we are entitled to infer the hypothesis that explains more of what we know is itself a norm for belief. It is a norm that adds to your picture of your ideal self. Ideally, you will be inferring those hypotheses that explain the most. (A main purpose of exploring this kind of judgment was to get a view of the nature of science. This was used in Part Two to contrast science with religion.)

The material of Part Two was more controversial. Metaphysics studies reality by exploring how to distinguish what is real from what is not. To make this kind of distinction, we need norms for belief, beliefs specifically about how things actually are. We saw in retrospect that we have already discussed some of these, since sensation, introspection, and inferences from these are all about how things actually are and not about how they ought to be. The principle that we are entitled to trust our senses unless there is a special reason for questioning them is, for example, a norm for what to believe about reality. If correct, it tells us one way to recognize what is real. But it does not explain how we can know about the existence of God, or heaven, or freedom and responsibility. What would entitle us to make such claims about reality? How could it ever be right to think such things are real? This is how philosophers discuss whether "there are" such things.

When discussing personal freedom, for example, the question was whether the fact that we make choices is enough to conclude that we are responsible for them. Of course, we all know that we do in fact make choices, and so, we asked simply whether "we are" responsible for our choices. But the philosophical question can be put by saying, "Suppose we make choices. Would that make us responsible for them?" It is a question of what to say or what to think in a hypothetical situation. Philosophers discuss whether making choices provides evidence for judging that we are morally responsible for what we do.

This "shift to thinking" is even more obvious in the issue of personal identity. Imaginary situations are described, involving a person at one time and a person at another time, and the question is what to say or think about it. If the body of a person is exactly copied in the future, would the same person reappear with the copied body? The question is really how to interpret the situation. If the situation were as described, should we think it is the same person or a different one? It is a question of how to count persons, which is a question of how to think about them.

It is obvious to all that something is real. But does this *show* that there is a first cause, something from which everything else comes? Again, we may put the question by asking, "*Is* there a first cause?" But the philosophical question is really about what counts as a good reason for thinking a first cause is real. Suppose there is something real. Would that show that there is a basic reality that creates everything else? Or, suppose only that God is the most perfect thing conceivable. Would this show all by itself that God exists? This is how philosophers discuss "the existence" of God. As with freedom and personal identity, the question is how your beliefs about reality should be. Answers to these questions develop your picture of your ideal self, insofar as you have beliefs about reality.

Part Three turned to a different kind of judgment. In ethics, we are not concerned with how to say what is real but how to distinguish between what is good and bad, just and unjust, good for you and bad for you, and so forth. We sought norms for marking such distinctions. We all use such norms when deciding what to do or what to want. Ethics aims to discover which of these norms are correct. It develops your picture of your ideal self. It tells you how your desires and intentions ought to be.

Part Four was mainly an extension of ethics. Here we were concerned about how to apply the same sorts of distinctions, between what is good and what is bad for you, what is "just plain" good and bad, just and unjust, and so forth. But our philosophy was "social" because we asked how to make such ethical evaluations about societies or social organizations within them. Work in this area still helps to develop your picture of your ideal self. You see how you ought to be when occupying a social role, such as parent or friend or citizen. The norms of social philosophy are (mainly) ethical norms. They might include the principle to respect everyone's right to be free or always do what produces the most happiness. Social philosophy is the exploration of how to apply these norms in social situations. It is because human life is so much a social life that social philosophy occupies such a large part of ethics. Your picture of your ideal self will be incomplete if it does not include how you ought to be in relation to others.

THE UNITY OF PHILOSOPHY

Our overview was meant to show how our understanding of philosophy has been reflected throughout the text. Another way of viewing what we have done brings out an important fact about philosophy. Different areas of philosophy are connected with one another. Consider, for example, the transition we made from logic to metaphysics. In Part One, we distinguished among different sources of knowledge, including sensation and introspection. In Part Two, we classified reality in terms of them. Material objects are what we know by the senses; minds are what we know in introspection. We then talked about how these kinds of reality are related to one another. Is mind a feature of matter or something existing separate from it? Is mind basic to reality, as idealists and theists think, or is matter the source of everything else? The questions of metaphysics are very largely couched in terms borrowed from logic.

In ethics, we found that views of happiness and morality often depend on metaphysical positions. The Taoists' form of materialism, for example, leads them to favor a life close to the earth, with a minimum of artificiality. This in turn leads them to anarchism in their view of the best society. By contrast, an idealist will naturally favor views of happiness that encourage the development of what is distinctively human, such as understanding and moral virtue. Since these develop mainly in society, in social philosophy idealists will tend to favor more complex societies, despite their artificiality. Because materialism and idealism come from a kind of bias for sensation or for introspection and intellect, we can see even in social philosophy an influence from logic.

Ethical views of morality depend on metaphysics no less than views of happiness. The divine command theory is plainly based on theism. Those who espouse social relativism or ethical hedonism typically do so from a materialist perspective. Deontology depends on a metaphysical conviction in freedom and responsibility.

Social philosophy consists mainly of applying ethical views to society. So, when evaluating families, friendships, schools, economies, and polities, we used terms that ultimately came from metaphysics and logic.

The interconnectedness of philosophical issues does much to explain how philosophers can continue to disagree about particular issues. The disagreement between utilitarianism and deontology, for example, which figured throughout Part Four, persists so long as there is disagreement about whether we are truly responsible for our actions. And this disagreement persists so long as philosophers do not agree about how mind is related to matter.

This means that a developed philosophy will not be a hodgepodge of different opinions. It will form a kind of whole, in which one's views in logic, metaphysics, and ethics somehow hang together. As you develop your own philosophy, you gradually come to see connections in your views of how to form beliefs about reality, what to care about, what to do in life, and how to feel in your reactions to things.

THE GOOD OF PHILOSOPHY

How is philosophy a good thing? Philosophical knowledge, as we have just seen, tells us in the most general terms how we ought to be. But what is good about being that sort of person? There is something funny about this question. The way we ought to be *just is* how it is good for us to be. The question therefore amounts to asking what is good about being good. It makes sense to ask what *makes* you a good person (not just in what you do but in what you care about, how you form beliefs about reality, and what you want). The answers to this sort of question are given by a whole philosophy. But philosophy is the search for the norms to follow to make you a good person, *whatever* this takes. It is good that we become this kind of person since being this kind of person just is what it is good for us to be.

PHILOSOPHICAL KNOWLEDGE

I have spoken freely of philosophical "knowledge," resulting from "successful" philosophical inquiry. Many students, however, finish their first course in philosophy feeling that the only thing they really learned is what certain people have *said* in response to certain questions, rather than the correct answers to these questions themselves. Did you really learn, for example, how to live your life? Or did you just learn certain *views* about how to live, such as utilitarianism or deontology?

To address this worry, let us remind ourselves of what is distinctive about philosophy. Philosophy is mainly about the *right* way to be. This is a kind of question that cannot be answered for you by experts. You come to have philosophical knowledge about such matters only when you see for yourself why something is right or wrong. This recognition requires a certain kind of emotional response. If you really think something is wrong, you have an aversion to it. Take, for example, the norm of logic that you ought not to believe a contradiction, such as the thought that George Washington was the first U.S. president and he was not. This norm seems to *me* to be correct, since when I imagine my thinking a contradiction, I recoil. What about you? It is only if you put the question to yourself whether any such judgment could be true and, in doing so, sense your own aversion that you really think it is *wrong* to believe contradictions.

Of course, however, a reaction of yours can be mistaken. To correct it or confirm it, the only thing possible is to listen to reasons. This is why we study alternative opinions. If you do not take seriously your responsibility to put the question at hand to yourself, all you *can* learn is just the opinions themselves. But this misses the whole point. In philosophy, listening to alternative opinions is what corresponds to examining observational data in empirical inquiries.

But why suppose that philosophical *knowledge* is even possible in the first place? First, we cannot avoid having philosophical opinions, as we saw earlier. To have an opinion is to accept a certain thought as true. This is why philosophy cannot be dismissed as being about matters on which there are no true answers. Second, we must regard our own opinions as justified (see Chapters One and Two). It is absurd to give your opinion on any matter and then add that you have no good reason for thinking that way. Because we cannot avoid having philosophical opinions, we must admit that it is possible to justify them. On the assumption, defended in Chapter One, that knowledge is justified true belief, we must admit that philosophical knowledge is possible.

PHILOSOPHICAL DISAGREEMENT

If philosophical knowledge is possible, why do philosophers continue to disagree about many of the same issues? It is true that there are some issues, known for a long time, on which philosophers have persistently disagreed. The problem of free will and determinism is a good example. Nevertheless, the extent to which philosophers disagree can be easily exaggerated. As explained earlier, no experts in philosophy can just tell you what to accept. To think for yourself, you have to hear opposing sides. Philosophy classes tend, therefore, to concentrate on issues on which reasonable people have disagreed. Too much of this approach, however, creates the impression that there is "no right or wrong," or at least no way of knowing what is right.

I tried to avoid creating this impression by calling attention to many issues on which modern philosophers have reached a remarkable degree of consensus. It is, for example, "common knowledge" among them how inferences to hypotheses are justified through testing. Very few philosophers today subscribe to either voluntarism or moral relativism. Materialism seems to be the predominant response to the mind–body problem. And it would be difficult to find a philosopher today who is not a humanist or who does not support democracy.

One source of disagreement pertains to the fact that philosophical positions often have serious consequences. Many philosophers, for example, would say that very much economic injustice exists in the world today. A consequence of their view is that the rich should fork over much of their wealth. The rich are not likely to find their reasons persuasive, therefore, no matter how good they are. As the English philosopher Thomas Hobbes said, "If the fact that two plus two had political consequences, a faction would rise up to deny it."

There is one more fact to bear in mind to understand the appearance of persistent philosophical disagreement. Real philosophers *very* often do not subscribe wholeheartedly to any one position on a controversial matter. When explaining *positions* like utilitarianism or deontology, it is natural to talk about what "utilitarians" or "deontologists" think. But in real life, relatively few philosophers will say unequivocally that such labels apply to them. I find myself, for example, drawn to deontology but not entirely confident about the metaphysical commitment to free will on which it is based. The positions themselves (which are just thoughts) are set in stark contrast with one another. But real philosophers often agree a good deal in wavering between them.

THE PRACTICALITY OF PHILOSOPHY

After their first exposure to philosophy, some students complain that it is not "practical." For many other kinds of knowledge, it is easy to see how to put them to use. Knowledge of nutrition can be used to improve your diet. Knowledge of finances can be used to manage your money. Knowledge of mechanics can be used to repair your car and other pieces of machinery. But what can you do with what you learn in philosophy?

If all that you have learned is what certain people have said, there is little you can do with this knowledge besides dropping names. But this is not the kind of knowledge philosophers seek. They want to know such things as how to act, what to believe, and how it is appropriate to feel. If we keep this point in mind, it ought to be fairly obvious how philosophy is practical.

Whether a certain kind of knowledge is practical depends on what you want. If you do not want to do your own taxes or fix your own car, knowledge of tax law or auto mechanics will not be practical *to you*. For you do not have the kind of purpose that would be served by having it. Philosophy is practical *for* those who want to make true judgments, to have beliefs that correspond to reality, to care about what is genuinely good, or to do what is right. If you are the kind of person who has these values, philosophy helps you by clarifying how to realize them. If you really care about the *quality* of your beliefs, your intentions, your desires and feelings, you will see the value in knowing the norms to follow to make them as they ought to be.

Plato's Upward Path

In our last reading, Plato gives an account of how people come to have these values that indicates his own answer to how philosophy can be good for us. As we will see, the passage bears important similarities with the Allegory of the Cave, which we read in the introduction. In this dialogue, Socrates is receiving a lesson on love by a wise, old woman, Diotima. (It helps to see the connection with the Allegory of the Cave to realize that the Greek for "beauty" could also be translated as "goodness.")

> For he who would proceed aright in this matter should begin in youth to visit beautiful forms; and first, if he be guided by his instructor aright, to love one such [physical] form only—out of that he should create fair thoughts; and soon he will of himself perceive that the beauty of one form is akin to the beauty of another; and then if beauty of form in general is his pursuit, how foolish would he be not to recognize that the beauty in every form is one and the same! And when he perceives this he will abate his violent love of the one, which he will despise and deem a small thing, and will become a lover of all beautiful forms; in the next stage he will consider that the beauty of the mind is more honorable than the beauty of the outward form. So that if a virtuous soul have but a little comeliness, he will be content to love and tend him, and will search out and bring to the birth thoughts which may improve the young, until he is compelled to contemplate and see the beauty of institutions and laws, and to understand that the beauty of them all is of one family, and that personal beauty is a trifle; and after laws and institutions he will go on to the sciences, that he may see their beauty, being not like a servant in love with the beauty of one youth or man or institution, himself a slave mean and narrow-minded, but drawing towards and contemplating the vast sea of beauty, he will create many fair and noble thoughts and notions in boundless love of wisdom; until on that shore he grows and waxes strong, and at last the vision is revealed to him of a single science, which is the science of beauty everywhere. To this I will proceed; please give me your very best attention:
>
> "He who has been instructed thus far in the things of love, and who has learned to see the beautiful in due order and succession, when he comes toward the end will suddenly perceive a nature of wondrous beauty (and this, Socrates, is the final cause [the ultimate purpose] of all our former toils)—a nature which in the first place is everlasting, not growing and decaying, or waxing and waning; secondly, not fair in one point of view and foul in another, or at one time or in one relation or at one place fair, at another time or in another relation or at another place foul, as if fair to some and foul to others, or in the likeness of a face or hands or any other part of the bodily frame, or in any form of speech or knowledge, or existing in any other being, as for example, in an animal, or in heaven or in earth, or in any other place; but beauty absolute, separate, simple, and everlasting, which without diminution and without increase, or any change, is imparted to the ever-growing and perishing beauties of all other things. He who from these

ascending under the influence of true love, begins to perceive that beauty is not far from the end. And the true order of going, or being led by another, to the things of love, is to begin from the beauties of earth and mount upwards for the sake of that other beauty, using these as steps only, and from one going on to two, and from two to all fair forms, and from fair forms to fair practices, and from fair practices to fair notions, until from fair notions he arrives at the notion of absolute beauty, and at last knows what the essence of beauty is. This, my dear Socrates," said the stranger of Mantineia, "is that life above all others which man should live, in the contemplation of beauty absolute; a beauty which if you once beheld, you would see not to be after the measure of gold, and garments, and fair boys and youths, whose presence now entrances you; and you and many a one would be content to live seeing them only and conversing with them without meat or drink, if that were possible—you only want to look at them and to be with them. But what if man had eyes to see the true beauty—the divine beauty, I mean, pure and dear and unalloyed, not clogged with the pollutions of mortality and all the colors and vanities of human life—thither looking, and holding converse with the true beauty simple and divine? Remember how in that communion only, beholding beauty with the eye of the mind, he will be enabled to bring forth, not images of beauty, but realities (for he has hold not of an image but of a reality), and bringing forth and nourishing true virtue to become the friend of God and be immortal, if mortal man may. Would that be an ignoble life?"[1]

The speech of Diotima represents the development of *spirit*. You may remember from Chapter Ten that Plato distinguished three parts of the "soul." Like other animals, we have desires. But humans also have intellect, which gives them the capacity to know what is good. Intellect and desire may not, however, be in harmony. If you know what is good to do but do not want to do it, intellect and desire conflict with one another. Spirit is the third part of the soul, responsible for bringing them together. To be "inspired" is to come to want what you know through thinking to be good. Now, Plato describes stages that it is good for us eventually to pass through. Each stage represents the discovery of new kinds of good things. This is an achievement of intellect. The stage is not fully reached, however, until one comes to desire or love good things of that kind. The whole development is, therefore, the development of spirit.

The details of his account do not concern us much, but even they are not implausible. We are naturally attracted at first to particular, sensible things, such as a particular toy or a particular friend. At this first stage, our desires are no different in kind from those of other animals. But then, if we do develop—and there is no guarantee that we will—we come to see that what makes them attractive is something general, something that is shared by certain other things. If you love a particular song because it is rhythmic and passionate, it "stands to reason" that other songs

---

1. Plato, *Symposium*, trans. Benjamin Jowett, 210a–211e.

with these same characteristics are just as lovable, even if you do not yet love them. Spirit operates if your love extends to what you now see to be just as good as what you originally loved.

One of the most important examples of this kind of development is the transition from egoism to morality. It is natural to care for yourself. But through thinking you can see that what makes you worthy of this care is not unique to yourself. Everyone else is just as worthy of care as you are. This point, however, is a purely intellectual realization. The egoist is one who never advances beyond self-love. But the egoist has intellect and is capable of seeing the arbitrariness of her love. If she realizes that she *should* care about other humans but does not *in fact* care for them, there is split within her between intellect and desire.

In Plato's story, love for material things advances to love for souls. You are more advanced if you can love someone for the kind of person he is and not just because you find him physically attractive. The story continues by depicting love for abstract things like institutions and bodies of knowledge. You advance further by coming to see the value of institutions such as marriage or rule by law. The more advanced person also appreciates the understanding offered by scientific theories, even if these have no obvious "practical" application. Eventually you come to love good things of all kinds. Now that you have the full range of them in view, you are able to see what *makes* them good. At the highest stage of development, you are guided by this knowledge of "the essence" of goodness.

The Allegory of the Cave

The Allegory of the Cave (our reading in the introduction) sheds light on this special kind of knowledge. Whereas the speech of Diotima represents the development of *desire*, the Allegory of the Cave represents the development of *belief*. At first we believe only in sensible things, just like other animals. We become "enlightened" when we see that these are manifestations of the "Forms" (see Chapter Six). Plato's favorite examples are *ideals* such as truth, understanding, justice, happiness, and freedom. It is *these* that make good things good. What makes beliefs good, for example, are things like truth, justification, and explanation (see Chapter One). What makes actions good are things like respect for equal freedom and benevolence. To "know the essence of goodness" is to know these ideals. The fullest knowledge of them will be an understanding of *what they are*. Plato would say that only if you understand what, for example, truth or justice *is* can you truly *care* about truth or justice *itself*. Locke said that although everyone will *say* they care for the truth, there are "very few lovers of truth for truth's sake" (see Chapter One). The story of Diotima's speech would *explain* why such people are rare.

PLATO ON PHILOSOPHY

No one has influenced our conception of philosophy more than Plato. Philosophy has traditionally been regarded as inquiry conducted by the intellect alone. Plato gives an account of what kind of knowledge we get from such inquiry.

Above all, we come to understand the ideals that make things good. This squares nicely with the conception of philosophy we have followed. We have regarded philosophy as primarily the search for the correct norms for making decisions of all kinds. Above all, philosophy, like other disciplines, seeks *principles*. Principles are fundamental in our thinking. They are the thoughts we give for our deepest explanations. Not all norms are principles. Many of the norms we follow in deciding what to do, for example, are more like rules of thumb. The norm that says not to bump into people while walking is a good one to follow, but it does not say what *makes* it wrong to do so. This is the business of principles like the greatest happiness principle of utilitarianism or the formula of humanity in deontology. To know which of these is correct is to have knowledge of "the essence" of right action. It is knowledge of such principles that comprises Plato's knowledge of "the essence of goodness." Because this knowledge is practical only for those who genuinely care about ideals for their own sake, Plato's story would also explain why many people do not *see* the practical value of philosophical knowledge.

PHILOSOPHY AND HAPPINESS

Whether such knowledge can contribute to happiness depends on what we need. If our needs are just like those of other animals, as crude materialists think, it is doubtful that such knowledge will be useful in meeting them. Plato, however, has an idealistic conception of human need. What we need most of all is to become the kind of person depicted in his story. Of course, we need food, air, water, and the like. But the ultimate purpose of satisfying these needs, according to Plato, is to provide the conditions for intellectual and spiritual development. Human happiness comes from a harmony between the parts of the soul. Just as the body is healthy when the organs function harmoniously, our souls are healthy when desire harmonizes with intellect through the influence of spirit.

DIGNITY

I suggested in the introduction that people are drawn to philosophy largely from a sense of dignity (another of our ideals). I want to end by explaining this with the materials at hand. For the Stoics, especially, the sense of dignity is central to human happiness (see Chapter Seven). They explain this with a conception of dignity that comes largely from Plato. The Stoics agree with Plato that happiness comes mainly from being guided by intellect and not by brute desire. What the Stoics emphasize is that it is by intellect that we become *independent*.

What separates us from the brutes is our ability to make judgments. And the judgments we make can be attributed to nothing but *ourselves*. This is why we are held *responsible* ultimately for the judgments we make. External forces create desires, impressions, and feelings, and these are what move other animals and us when we are like them. When we allow ourselves to be dominated by their influence, we are dependent on them, "slaves" to them. But we can gain independence from them by judging for ourselves what to do, what to believe, what to want, and how to feel. Now, the sense of dignity, according to the Stoics, is the *consciousness* of this independence. It is this consciousness which, they say, is most important for human happiness.

When we become independent, we become like "God" (the whole of nature), the most independent being of all. In Plato's story, the most advanced person is described as a "friend of God" and "immortal." The Stoics would explain human "immortality" as the achievement of intellect and spirit. When we are moved by external forces, what we believe, want, and so forth, are determined by our particular circumstances in space and time. But when we are moved by judgment and reason, we occupy a timeless perspective that all thinkers can share.

PHILOSOPHY AND DIGNITY

How does this conception allow us to understand being drawn to philosophy from a sense of dignity? Recall that in philosophy we become aware of the norms that we use unconsciously in making judgments. So long as we are unconscious of them they come from our external circumstances. The Nazis taught their children not to feel compassion for the suffering of the weak. Slaveholders taught their children not to respect their slaves' right to freedom. The children who learned unconsciously such norms for how to feel or what to do got them only because they happened to be born to Nazis or slaveholders.

Because the norms we use in making judgments of all kinds define the *kind of person* we are, so long as we are unconscious of our norms, we have not *chosen* what kind of person to be. Once we become conscious of them, however, we can see alternatives, and we can listen to reasons for accepting some and rejecting others. It is only then that we can *justify* our norms and *choose* what kind of person to be. To know that your norms have been handed to you by others is to suffer humiliation. To know that you have chosen them yourself is to experience dignity. This is possible only by the study of philosophy.

STUDY QUESTIONS

1. What is a *norm*? Give an original example of a norm for belief about reality, for what to do, for how to feel, and for what to want that all belong to *your* philosophy. (These do not have to be principles.)
2. Why are philosophical opinions unavoidable?
3. What is good about successful philosophical inquiry?
4. Why must we admit that philosophical *knowledge* is possible?
5. For whom is philosophy practical? (Be as clear as you can in describing what is different about such people.)

6. What is the development of spirit? Illustrate your answer with an example from Diotima's speech.
7. How would Diotima's story explain Locke's remark that "there are very few lovers of truth for truth's sake"?
8. What kinds of norms are principles? Give an example that illustrates your answer.
9. What kind of harmony is necessary, according to Plato, for human happiness?
10. How do Stoics explain what is the sense of dignity?
11. In what way is philosophy necessary to choose what kind of person to be?

BIOGRAPHIES

The following are the most famous philosophers from the past mentioned in the text.

Anselm, Saint (1033/4–1109 A.D.) Italian monk, most famous for discovering the ontological argument for the existence of God (see Chapter 6).

Aquinas, Saint Thomas (1225–1274 A.D.) Italian monk who developed Christian philosophy by interpreting it in terms of Aristotle's philosophy. "Thomism" became and still is official Catholic doctrine. Aquinas sets out all the major arguments for the existence of God, except the ontological, which he did not accept (see Chapter 6).

Aristotle (384–322 B.C.) Both Greek, Plato and Aristotle are the most influential philosophers in the West. Aristotle entered Plato's academy at seventeen and was his colleague until Plato's death. He developed an extraordinarily comprehensive, subtle, and deep system of philosophy, many of the positions of which are still live today. Reality is nature, a dynamic whole consisting of things with individual natures they are striving to fulfill. Humans fulfill theirs and achieve happiness by understanding nature, and nature fulfills its purpose by being understood. He was the first biologist and the first to present a logical system. The rediscovery in Europe during the Middle Ages of Aristotle's philosophy was a major cause of the intellectual development that marks recent Western history.

Augustine, Saint (354–430) The first great Christian philosopher, born in North Africa, extremely influential in the formation of Christian doctrine. All the main theistic defenses against the argument from evil come originally from Augustine (see Chapter 6). Augustine borrowed heavily from Plato, interpreting his form of the good (see the introduction) as God.

Berkeley, George (1685–1753) Irish, Christian bishop. Against Locke, he defended an extreme form of idealism, according to which only minds (ours and the mind of God) exist. Although apparently absurd, idealism proved attractive to many philosophers for over two centuries, some of whom developed more sophisticated and credible versions of it.

Buddha (563–483 B.C.) Born Siddhartha Gotama to a royal family in what is now Nepal (called by his followers "the Buddha," meaning "the one who is awake"). He taught a theory of happiness, according to which suffering can be ended by eliminating the cravings that lead to greed and anger, which themselves arise from a mistaken belief in the permanence of things, including a continuing self (see Chapter 7). Today one out of seven people in the world are counted as "Buddhists," though their doctrines are largely derived from local traditional religions.

Chuang Tzu (369–? B.C.) With Lao-Tzu, one of the greatest Taoist Chinese philosophers. He taught that all things are in perpetual change, eventually turning into their opposites (living to dead, bad to good, beautiful to ugly, and so forth). The wise shun worldly success and fame and seek instead a global perspective of reality, from which they can know and cultivate their individual natures and thereby live harmoniously with the Tao.

Confucius (551–479 B.C.) The name *Confucius* is a Westernization of "Kung Fu-Tzu," meaning "great master." Born poor, he became a government official and then a traveling teacher. He was a humanist who defined responsibilities for various social roles and taught that political leaders should be morally virtuous, radically implying that morally corrupt leaders can be deposed. Confucius became the most influential thinker in Chinese history, largely because desirable positions in government could be won only by knowing his philosophy.

Descartes, René (1596–1650) French philosopher and mathematician, often called the "father of modern philosophy." Descartes rigorously developed mind–body dualism (see Chapter 5) in an attempt to separate two realms of reality for religion and science, thus showing that they do not conflict. Minds, free and rational, are the subjects of religion; causally determined bodies and material things generally are for science. He also attempted to demonstrate much knowledge with certainty, a project continued for centuries and eventually abandoned entirely by fallibilists today (see Chapter 2).

Dewey, John (1859–1952) American philosopher, known especially for his defense of democracy and his belief that education should foster independence.

Epictetus (55–135 A.D.) A Roman slave who eventually won his freedom and became a teacher, he is one of the most important Stoic philosophers (see Chapter 7), teaching that independence through living rationally is the key to happiness.

Epicurus (341–270 B.C.) Greek philosopher, atomistic materialist, and hedonist. He taught that the happiest, most pleasant life comes not from intense sensual pleasures but from health of body and peace of mind. Epicurus's "Garden" was a secluded community of friends devoted to a quiet life of reflection.

Feuerbach, Ludwig (1804–1872) German philosopher, humanist, and naturalist. Feuerbach influenced the development of metaphorical theology (see Chapter 6), teaching (provocatively) that religion was only an imaginative creation, reflecting emotional needs.

Hegel, Georg (1770–1831) German philosopher who criticized and developed Kant's philosophy. Defended a monistic form of idealism, in which the consciousness of individual human minds participate in a world "Spirit," which is gradually achieving self-awareness throughout history as societies recognize individual freedom and provide contexts for mutually recognized moral behavior.

Hobbes, Thomas (1588–1679) English philosopher, materialist, atheist. Against anarchism, he argued strictly from self-interest that governments are necessary to keep the peace and are justified just when they do (thus providing grounds for political revolution).

Hume, David (1711–1776) Scottish philosopher, best known for his ingenious insights into the limitations of empirical knowledge, including especially the exclusion of knowledge of causality, which stimulated Kant, by his own account, to become a philosopher. Hume was a naturalist who saw himself as the first empirical psychologist, teaching that humans were less rational than previously supposed. His ethics opposed superstition and led to utilitarianism (see Chapter 9). Although now regarded as one of the greatest philosophers, Hume was not understood by philosophers of his time and became a historian.

James, William (1842–1910) American philosopher and psychologist, he was respected for his knowledge of religions and his defense of nonrational religious belief.

Kant, Immanuel (1724–1804) German and widely thought to be the greatest of modern philosophers, he was originally a physicist and began philosophy late in life, largely in response to Hume. He agreed with Hume that reality is known by us mainly through sensation, but he argued for a larger role for reason in human knowledge. Reason supplies principles for knowing about empirical reality and morality in the first place. Restricting the use of reason to the natural world also set him in opposition to those (such as Leibniz) who thought that supernatural reality could be known by reason alone. In ethics he is the chief exponent of deontology (see Chapter 9); like the Stoics, he teaches rational independence, but as an end in itself and not as the key to happiness.

Lao Tzu (sixth century B.C.?) Although it is uncertain whether he really existed, Lao Tzu (literally "Old Master") is supposedly the founder of Taoism and author of the *Tao Te Ching* (*The Way and Its Power*; see Chapters 6 and 7). Originally a philosophy of hermits, Taoism is naturalistic and holds that basic reality (the Tao) cannot be linguistically comprehended. Nature has rhythms, which the wise intuitively sense and follow, living close to the earth and avoiding the artificialities of social life. Stories say that he debated with Confucius, who advocated an orderly social life, opposed by Taoists as unnatural.

Leibniz, Gottfried (1646–1716) German philosopher and mathematician. Leibniz rigorously defended a strange idealistic system, in which much about reality is argued just by thinking about the implications of God's existence, including the fact that this must be "the best of all possible worlds."

Locke, John (1632–1704) English philosopher who responded to Descartes. Although a theist who believed in moral knowledge, he emphasized how little can be known with certainty and how much knowledge is empirical. He advanced influential positions in all areas of philosophy; his well-developed democratic theory was used by Thomas Jefferson in crafting the original documents of the United States.

Mill, John Stuart (1806–1873) English philosopher and (socialist) economist, Mill was extreme in his reliance on empirical knowledge. Mill coined the term *utilitarianism* (see Chapter 9), defended liberalism (see Chap. 12), and condemned the oppression of women.

Plato (429–347 B.C.) Greek philosopher who, with Aristotle, is most influential in Western philosophy. Though preceded by a series of great thinkers, Plato developed a whole philosophical system (see the epilogue) that emerges in dialogues in which his mentor, Socrates, expresses the favored positions. Plato opposed various forms of relativism and skepticism by arguing that ideals like justice, knowledge, and friendship have objective natures ("Forms"), which make possible genuine knowledge of them. The Forms are unchanging and eternal, and known solely through the intellect. Human happiness is a harmony within the "soul" in which the intellect rules desire. Moved to philosophy after Socrates was put to death by Athens, Plato hoped that corrupt government could be avoided through the moral and intellectual education of political leaders.

Rousseau, Jean-Jacques (1712–1778) French philosopher. Rousseau questioned the practical value of learning and romanticized the "noble savage," arguing that society is the main cause of human trouble. He was a socialist and democrat, arguing that true democracy exists only in small communities in which a general consensus can be reached.

Russell, Bertrand (1872–1970) English philosopher. The grandson of a prime minister, Russell wrote extensively both within and without philosophy, frequently changing positions. Awarded the Nobel Prize for literature, Russell enjoyed fame and influence in his time. He did important work in the foundations of mathematics and logic, and he was politically a liberal socialist and feminist.

Shankara (788–820) Indian philosopher who provided an interpretation of the holy texts of ancient Hinduism that is now orthodox among Hindu scholars. Shankara taught a monistic idealism (see Chapter 6) in which reality is known basically through introspection (see Chapter 2), by which one sees oneself as "identical" with (merely a portion or aspect of) the basic reality, Pure Consciousness. This "enlightenment" promotes happiness by freeing oneself from attachment to material things (see Chapter 7).

Smith, Adam (1723–1790) Scottish philosopher and economist. By explaining an "economy" as a self-regulating mechanism, Smith was a founder of the modern science of economics. He gave a utilitarian argument in favor of market economies that has made him popular with capitalists and libertarians (see Chapters 11 and 12), although he himself argued for government corrections of market failures.

Socrates (470–399 B.C.) The views of Socrates are difficult to distinguish from Plato's, since he did not write and most of what is known comes from Plato's dialogues, in which Socrates expresses Plato's views. Socrates was put to death for impiety and for stimulating the young to think independently (a threat to traditions on which those in power depend). He is most known and admired for his relentless, reflective critiques of reasoning, the most distinctive characteristic of Western philosophy. Whereas previous philosophical speculation in Greece was mainly metaphysical, Socrates turned the method of pure thinking to ethical matters as well. In ethics he held that moral virtue would necessarily result from ethical knowledge, so that "no one knowingly errs." Philosophy is thus the key to improving society.

Spinoza, Benedict (or Baruch) (1632–1677) Dutch philosopher, originally an orthodox Jew, but eventually expelled for his unorthodox views. In response to Descartes, Spinoza laid out a rigorously defended philosophical system on the model of mathematics, in which he defended the double aspect theory of mind and body. Spinozism is in the Stoic tradition (see Chapter 6), pantheistic and deterministic, and teaches that happiness comes mainly from liberation through rationality (see Chapter 7).

Wollstonecraft, Mary (1759–1797) English philosopher, liberal feminist. She took an interest in the education of women and taught (against Rousseau) that women were naturally equal to men in their power to reason.

Emulate Immolate Emaculate

①